CUBASE SX POWER!

Robert Guérin

Cubase SX Power!

Copyright ©2002 Muska & Lipman Publishing, a division of Course Technology

Credits: Senior Editor, Mark Garvey; Development Editor, Ben Milstead; Production Editor, Rodney A. Wilson; Copyeditor, Karen Annett; Technical Editors, Laurence Payne, Greg Ondo, and Mike Uwins; Proofreader, Don Prues; Cover Design and Interior Design and Layout, Chad Planner, *Pop Design Works;* Indexer, Kevin Broccoli, *Broccoli Information Management.*

Publisher: Andy Shafran

Library of Congress Catalog Number: 2002113692

ISBN 1-929685-85-8

5 4 3 2 1

Muska & Lipman Publishing
2645 Erie Avenue, Suite 41
Cincinnati, Ohio 45208
www.muskalipman.com
publisher@muskalipman.com

About the Author

Robert Guerin

Web sites: zerodb.ca or www.wavedesigners.com, e-mail: rguerin@zerodb.ca

A composer for the past fourteen years and a music enthusiast since 1976, Robert has worked on various personal and commercial projects, such as feature and short films, television themes, and educational and corporate videos. Composing, arranging, playing, recording, and mixing most of his material, he has developed working habits that allow him to be creative without losing the sense of efficiency.

As a professor, Robert has put together five courses covering a wide range of topics, such as computer software for musicians, digital audio technologies, sound on the Web, sound in multimedia productions, how musicians can get job interviews, hard disk recording, and many more topics. He has been a program coordinator at Trebas Institute in Montreal and a part-time professor at Vanier College also in Montreal. Robert has developed online courses on sound integration in Web pages and has written articles for audio- and music-related online magazines.

As an entrepreneur, he has developed many skills necessary in today's culture. Robert has expanded his knowledge and expertise to ensure his business survival by adopting new multimedia and Web-related technologies.

Robert is also the author of two other books with Muska & Lipman: *Cubase VST Power!* and *MIDI Power!*

Acknowledgments

I would like to give thanks to the following people for their help and support throughout the writing process, and for putting up with my caffeine-induced personality at times: Andy Shafran and his team at Muska & Lipman: Mark Garvey, Ben Milstead, Don Prues, and Jim Boyatt. Christopher Hawkins at www.streamworksaudio.com for his input, Stefane "the Mac guy" Richard for his Mac tips and screenshots, and all the technical editors that worked really hard to make this book what it is. Everyone I've contacted throughout the writing process—including Steinberg's staff (Lars Baumann, Georg Bruns, and Greg Ondo) and the Cubase.net forum users who have provided some valuable tips when everyone else was busy doing other things (a special thank you goes out to Alex a.k.a. "AlexDJ" Bellinger for his Step Designer tip)—your help is appreciated and this book would not have been possible without your support.

Merci à tous!

Contents

7 MIDI Track Recording and Editing 141

8 MIDI Editing Windows 167

9 Audio Recording and Project Editing 193

10 Browsing and Processing Options .213

11 Audio Editing Windows 235

12 Mixer and Channel Settings 261

13 Working With Automation 291

14 Working In Sync 313

Introduction

Cubase has been around for a while now. I remember using its ancestor, the Pro 24 software on my Atari ST, in 1987 to create musical arrangements for composition assignments during my University training years. Since then, many things have changed and Cubase has made the transition from a MIDI sequencer to a Virtual Studio Technology (VST) software. This new version (Cubase SX and SL) grows on the knowledge Steinberg has acquired from years of user comments like yours. If you are new to Cubase, you can expect this software to help you through your entire musical creation process. If you are a veteran Cubase user, you will find much of the things you loved and a few new features that are worth the upgrade. Hopefully, in both cases, this book will help you to get the most out of this great tool.

Like any software, as it allows you to do more things and do them in a more intuitive way, the learning curve becomes more and more abrupt. You will find very extensive documentation on all available features found in Cubase on the CD-ROM provided with the software, but you have to sift through over 1400 pages of electronic format documentation. For most users, this might seem like an overwhelming task. This book covers the most important features as well as some lesser-known features in step-by-step examples and online tutorial files to practice what you have learned in many of the chapters.

Beyond describing the features of the program and how they work, I address "why" to use certain features and "when" they can become useful to you. All of the Cubase SL features are included in Cubase SX, so for those of you who have this version of the software, the book should address your questions as well. Because Cubase is also available in both Macintosh and PC versions in quite similar environments, it doesn't really matter which platform you are using: how to use the features and functions is the same. At the time this book was released, the Macintosh version was still in the Beta testing stage, so there might be slight differences due to OS specific issues. Because we have been working closely with Steinberg during the writing period, these differences should probably not affect the level of help you can get from reading this book.

I offer you my fifteen years of experience working with the software as well as my insight into some tips and tricks that have been very useful in getting the job done throughout these years. As a professor and program coordinator in sound design vocational schools in Canada, I have answered questions from many students who have wanted to work with this tool to create music. I have drawn from their most frequently asked question list and answered them in a way that I hope you will find enlightening.

Enjoy.

About the Exercise Files

At the ends of Chapters 4 through 13 and Chapter 16, you will find sections called "Now You Try It." These sections point you toward tutorials located on the Muska & Lipman website. You'll find those files by navigating to www.muskalipman.com and clicking on the "Downloads" link. These tutorials give you the opportunity to practice what you have learned during the chapter. Most of the steps needed to perform the tasks in the tutorials are described in this book, so you may want to keep your book close by if you are not familiar with these procedures at the beginning. Feel free to visit the link provided to view the content of these tutorial lessons and download the necessary content files needed to complete them.

You need to use a file decompression utility to access the content found inside the downloadable documents. Here's where you can find such tools:

▶ For PC users: You can download a copy of WinZip at www.winzip.com.

▶ For Mac users: You can download StuffIt at www.stuffit.com.

After you have downloaded one of these utilities, you can decompress the files to a folder on your computer. Each file contains a Cubase project file that you may open in Cubase SX or SL and may also contain media files. In this case, make sure the media files (such as audio files) are located inside an audio folder under your project's folder. If Cubase can't find the audio files, use the Find Missing Files option in the Pool menu to locate these files on your hard disk.

How This Book Is Organized

Let's take a look at what you will find in these pages through a short description of each chapter. At the end of this book, you will also find seven appendixes that will surely come in handy after you understand what MIDI is all about.

▶ Chapter 1, Introducing Cubase: This chapter contains an overview of MIDI and digital audio to make sure you understand the underlying concepts related to Cubase as a digital audio multitrack recorder and MIDI sequencer.

▶ Chapter 2, Setting Up Your Environment: Here, we look at how your computer needs to be configured to ensure the best possible results when using Cubase.

▶ Chapter 3, A Guided Tour of Cubase SX/SL: This chapter shows you most of the panels, windows, and dialog boxes you will encounter in your Cubase projects. We look at how to access each one of these windows and give a short description of their purpose in Cubase.

▶ Chapter 4, Navigating the Project Window: Finding your way around a project means that you can get to a part of your project easily, without having to rely on scroll bars all the time. We look at how you can achieve this through the use of Markers and Transport panel functions. This chapter also gives you an overview of the different context menus available in most of the Cubase windows and panels.

▶ Chapter 5, Working With Tracks: When working on a project, you will use the Project window, which is your main workspace. It is important to define each area of this window and understand why, when, and how to use them. We also discuss the use of VST Instruments and external MIDI device configurations so that Cubase can understand which tools you use outside the computer. After your external devices are configured in Cubase, you can control them directly from Cubase.

▶ Chapter 6, Track Classes: Unlike an audio multitrack recorder, Cubase allows you to record not only digital audio, but also MIDI events and automation. It does so through several track classes. Each track class allows you to perform different tasks. This chapter discusses each one of these track classes so that you will know when to use them in your project. This chapter also includes information on effects available in each track class.

▶ Chapter 7, MIDI Track Recording and Editing: This chapter looks at the setup process involved in recording MIDI events as well as the concept of quantizing these events. Furthermore, we look at functions that can be applied to MIDI events directly in the Project window inside Cubase.

▶ Chapter 8, MIDI Editing Windows: Growing on the knowledge you acquired in Chapter 7, this chapter focuses its attention on the different MIDI editing environments found inside Cubase.

▶ Chapter 9, Audio Recording and Project Editing: Here, you will find the audio version of what was discussed in Chapter 7, that is, the setup process involved in recording digital audio inside Cubase and several editing options relating to audio events in the Project window. We also discuss how Cubase handles audio on your hard disk.

▶ Chapter 10, Browsing and Processing Options: In this chapter, we take a look at a few new editing environments, such as the Project Browser and the Offline Process History panel. We also explain how to use and why you should use offline audio processes rather than adding audio effects that are processed in real time as you play the project.

▶ Chapter 11, Audio Editing Windows: This chapter is devoted entirely to audio editing windows, discussing the Pool, Sample Editor, and Audio Part Editor. These three editing environments allow you to do pretty much anything you want to audio events that have been either recorded or imported into your Cubase project.

▶ Chapter 12, Mixer and Channel Settings: After you have recorded or edited audio and MIDI events, the next most important task is to start thinking about mixing it. In this chapter, you will find information on how to use the mixer and most importantly, what you can expect the mixer to do for you. This implies a look at the different channel types represented in the mixer as well as different mixer routings available when using groups and effects.

▶ Chapter 13, Working With Automation: Cubase not only offers you a recording and editing environment for your musical projects, it also allows you to automate a mix. It does so by creating automation subtracks to tracks containing audio or MIDI events. We look at how to use these automation subtracks and how to create and edit automation to make sure your musical mix sounds as good as you hear it.

► Chapter 14, Working In Sync: Synchronization today implies many things. In this chapter, we try to define how it relates to Cubase and how you can get Cubase to work in sync with other devices, both inside and outside the computer. We also discuss how to use the VST System Link to get different computers running a compatible application to work together as one big studio system that stays in perfect synchronization without using network connections.

► Chapter 15, Distributing Your Work: Once all is done, you need to print your final mix to a format that you can distribute to people who don't have Cubase. Getting your music out there is almost as important as making it. With this in mind, this chapter looks at how you can create a mixdown of your project so that it can be mastered, converted, and distributed on a CD or on the Web through simple examples.

► Chapter 16, Score Editing: Creating musical scores with MIDI tracks in your project can produce high-quality results. We take a look at how the score functions work inside Cubase and what you need to do to convert your music into printable notes on a piece of paper.

► Appendix A, The How To Do It Reference Guide: This appendix gives you a quick reference to all the How To sections discussed inside the chapters of this book, organizing them into simple-to-use and musician-oriented categories so that you can quickly find what you are looking for.

► Appendix B, Using MIDI Effects: In this appendix, you will find a description of the MIDI effects and how they can be used on MIDI tracks for both technical and creative purposes.

► Appendix C, Logical Editing: For the logical musician that lies inside of you, here is the Logical Editor found in Cubase. This appendix describes how you can use this tool to edit MIDI events in a way that may take much longer in other editing windows.

► Appendix D, Optimizing Through Customizing: Sometimes, it's easier when you can configure Cubase to respond the way you want it to. This appendix offers you a few solutions on how you can customize certain parameters so that they do exactly that.

► Appendix E, About Surround Sound Mixing: If you are a Cubase SX user, you will come across surround sound capabilities. This appendix describes how you can create surround sound mixes and output your mixes to a suitable surround encoder.

► Appendix F, Cubase Resources On The Web: For those of you who want to find out more on Cubase or have practical questions, you will find additional resources related to Cubase in this appendix.

► Appendix G, Key Commands Reference Guide: This appendix is a quick guide to one of the most useful tool Cubase offers: key commands (in other words, keyboard shortcuts). Using them will save you lots of time!

1

Introducing Cubase

Before starting your work in Cubase, it is important to understand what Cubase is all about, what it can do, and how different MIDI and digital audio really are. In this chapter, you are introduced to Cubase and gain a better understanding of some basic MIDI and digital audio principles. In this chapter, you will:

▶ Find out how Cubase evolved throughout the years

▶ Discover Cubase's basic key concepts

▶ Be introduced to MIDI fundamentals

▶ Be introduced to digital audio fundamentals

▶ Discover how sound is digitized and what the parameters are that affect the quality of your digital audio recording

▶ Learn how MIDI and digital audio are handled inside Cubase

▶ Understand MIDI tracks, ports, channels, inputs, and outputs

▶ Understand audio tracks, channels, inputs, and outputs

▶ Discover the basic concept behind 32-bit, floating-point digital audio recording

▶ Find out why the sound card you use affects the quality of your digital audio recording

What is Cubase?

Cubase is a toolbox for musicians. In this toolbox, you'll find tools to record, edit, mix, and publish MIDI and audio information as well as tools to convert MIDI into printable music sheets.

In 1984, Steinberg created its first MIDI sequencer, which eventually became known in 1989 as Cubase. With the advent of MIDI, the computer could talk to musical instruments and vice versa, and Cubase was designed to help musicians capture their MIDI sequences and performances. At that time, the processing power of computers was insufficient to properly record digital audio. Therefore, musicians had to wait almost ten years before they could record audio digitally using a computer. Steinberg was one of the first companies to develop an integrated system that could record to both MIDI and digital audio.

In 1996, Cubase became not only a MIDI sequencer, but also a full audio production tool, contributing in many ways to the development and democratization of the creative process that lies inside every musician. Cubase VST (Virtual Studio Technology), the predecessor to Cubase

SX, provided you the necessary software tools to replace many hardware components with software equivalents. Finally, Cubase SX integrates features that were developed in earlier versions, adds new features that were developed, and streamlines them in a new, easier-than-ever interface. Here is an overview of the tools included with Cubase SX:

▶ **MIDI recording environment**. Cubase allows you to record and play back MIDI information.

▶ **MIDI editing environment**. After your MIDI information is recorded, you can edit it using one of many views available in Cubase.

▶ **Virtual Instruments**. If you do not own external sound modules, Cubase provides you with a way to generate sounds using a format called VST Instruments. A Virtual Instrument is the software version of a synthesizer, residing inside your computer and using your sound card to generate the sounds it produces. You no longer need to purchase expensive synthesizer modules, because they are part of your virtual studio environment.

▶ **Audio recording environment**. Cubase is a very powerful multitrack recorder that uses a sophisticated recording system, which supports up to 32-bit audio file formats. Combined with a good sound card, microphone, and preamplifier, this can only lead to high-quality recordings. Obviously, the result depends on your creativity and musical "chops" as well, but at least the tools are within your reach.

▶ **Audio editing environment**. After your sound is captured on disk, Cubase offers you all the tools necessary to cut, copy, paste, punch in, punch out, enhance, and manipulate your audio signals in an intuitive working environment.

▶ **Mixing environment**. After you have recorded, edited, and manipulated your MIDI and audio information, you can mix every track using a virtual mixing board not unlike its hardware counterpart. This virtual mixer can accommodate multiple busses, multiple effects, MIDI tracks, Virtual Instrument tracks, and audio tracks. Finally, you can automate your mix easily and create complex mixes without leaving your computer.

▶ **Effects galore**. Using the built-in audio and MIDI effects, adding third-party effects, or using effects already present on your system (such as the DirectX effects available in Windows), you can color your sound in a wide variety of ways. The Macintosh version supports only VST effects. Your imagination is your only barrier here.

▶ **Multimedia production environment**. Along with audio production, Cubase offers many synchronization tools useful in multimedia productions and video productions, making it a great postproduction environment for today's producers. You can even interact with other musicians around the world using Cubase and the Internet.

A Brief Overview of MIDI

The acronym MIDI stands for "Musical Instrument Digital Interface." It represents two things: First, MIDI is a communication system used to transmit information from one MIDI-compatible device to another. These devices include musical instruments (samplers, synthesizers, sound modules, drum machines) and computers (this could be managed by software inside your computer or could be hardware-based such as a synchronization device). Second, it represents the hardware—the ports and jacks found on all MIDI instruments and the MIDI cables connecting them to allow the transmission of musical data. Every time a key is pressed or a wheel is moved, one or more bytes are sent out from a device's MIDI Out port. Other devices connected to that sending device are looking for those bytes to come over the wire, which are then interpreted back into commands for the device to obey.

MIDI sends information at a rate of 31,250 bps (or bits per second). Because MIDI is transferred through a serial port, it sends information one bit at a time. Every MIDI message uses ten bits of data (eight for the information and two for error correction). This means that MIDI sends about 3,906 bytes of data every second (31,250 bps divided by 8 bits to convert into bytes). If you compare this with the 176,400 bytes (or 172.3 kilobytes) transfer rate that digital audio requires when recording or playing back CD-quality sound without compression, MIDI may seem very slow. But in reality, it's fast enough for what it needs to transfer. At this speed, you could play approximately 500 MIDI notes per second.

What Does MIDI Really Transmit?

MIDI sends or receives the following information:

▶ Events related to your performance, such as a note played or released.

▶ Parameters for these actions, such as the channel setting. Each MIDI cable or port can support up to sixteen channels of information, much like having up to sixteen separate instruments playing at once.

▶ Wheels and pedal controls (pitch bend wheels, modulation wheels, sustain pedals, and switch pedals).

▶ Key pressures of pressed keys, also known as *Aftertouch* information sent by the controller keyboard or by the sequencer to a sound module. Note that not all keyboards support this function, but when they do, the information is sent as MIDI data.

▶ Program changes (or patch changes) as well as sound bank selections.

▶ Synchronization for MIDI devices that have built-in timing clocks that let you set them to a desired tempo, like a drum machine, then follow or trigger another sequencer or drum machine to play in beat-to-beat synchronization.

▶ Special information, also called System Exclusive messages, used to alter synthesizer parameters and control the transport of System Exclusive-compatible multitrack recorders.

▶ MIDI Time Code or MTC, which is a way for MIDI-compatible devices to lock to a SMPTE device—a translation of SMPTE into something MIDI devices can understand.

You can think of MIDI as an old mechanical piano using a paper roll. The holes in the paper roll contained the moments where the musician played the notes but not the sound of the piano itself. MIDI information is transmitted in much the same way, capturing the performance of the musician but not the sound of the instrument he or she played on. You will always need some kind of sound module that can reproduce the sounds recorded in MIDI. This sound module could be an external synthesizer module, a sampler, a virtual synthesizer inside your SX software, or even the synthesizer chip on your sound card. This is precisely what Cubase allows you to do: record a musical performance from a MIDI instrument into your computer, thus creating a virtual paper roll.

MIDI Connectors

There are two or three sockets on MIDI devices: In and Out, or In, Out, and Thru. These are located on the backs of every hardware-based MIDI instrument or device. Usually, two-port configurations are reserved for computer-related hardware (see the left side of). As you will see with virtual synthesizers, you still have MIDI Ins and MIDI Outs, but you won't have physical sockets in which to plug cables (see the right side of Figure 1.1).

Figure 1.1
On the left side is an example of a two-connector configuration typical of computer MIDI interfaces; on the right side is a three-connector configuration typical of keyboards and sound modules

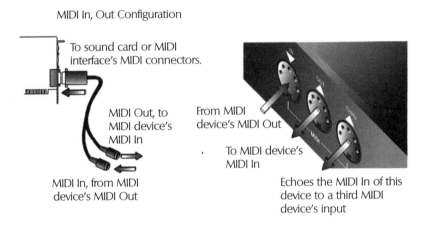

MIDI In, Out Configuration

To sound card or MIDI interface's MIDI connectors.

MIDI Out, to MIDI device's MIDI In

MIDI In, from MIDI device's MIDI Out

From MIDI device's MIDI Out

To MIDI device's MIDI In

Echoes the MIDI In of this device to a third MIDI device's input

NOTE
Because most software can control what goes to the MIDI Out port and can switch between Out and Thru inside the application, there is no need for a third port. This is the case in Cubase.

MIDI Out

The most important concept to understand is that MIDI does not transmit sound over wires the way audio components in a sound system do. Instead, it sends a digital code that represents what and how an event is being played on the instrument. As you play on a MIDI keyboard, the computer in the instrument examines your performance. The instrument's computer then converts it into a stream of MIDI codes that translates your actions. That information is sent out over an instrument's MIDI output to other synthesizers that reproduce the performance, but they use their own sounds to reproduce this performance.

A MIDI output does not echo (retransmit) any MIDI events your device receives from its MIDI input. If you want to do so, you need to use the MIDI Thru connector, which is described in the "MIDI Thru" section.

MIDI In

MIDI keyboards can be viewed as being two machines in one (see Figure 1.2):

▶ **A MIDI interface.** The computer processor that monitors the keyboard, program memory, front panel displays, and MIDI ports.

▶ **A sound module.** The part under the control of the onboard computer, the electronics that actually make the sounds.

Figure 1.2
Configuring your
keyboard's MIDI input

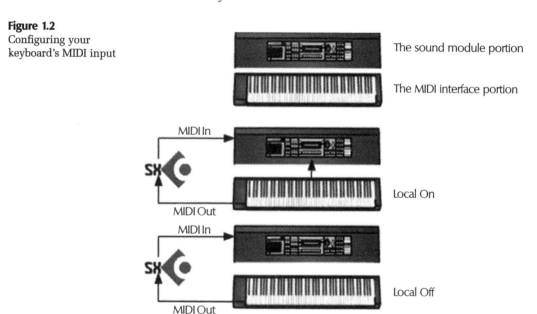

The sound module portion

The MIDI interface portion

MIDI In

MIDI Out

Local On

MIDI In

MIDI Out

Local Off

The MIDI input receives incoming MIDI information and sends it to the instrument's computer. The computer analyzes and acts upon the information in much the same way as a performance on the original instrument, such as pressing a key to play a note. There is no difference to the sound-making parts of a synthesizer, whether the command to play notes comes from a key press on the instrument itself or as a command from other MIDI devices.

This said, when you are working with a sequencer such as Cubase SX, it is recommended that you set your keyboard's Local properties to Off. The local setting on a keyboard tells this keyboard to play the sounds directly when you press the keys when it is set to On and does not play the sounds locally when it is set to Off. In other words, setting the local MIDI control parameter to Off disconnects the bridge that exists inside your keyboard between the actual MIDI input (the keyboard) and the sound module part, which allows you to hear the keyboard's sounds as you play the keys.

When using Cubase, you send MIDI from the keyboard to Cubase using the MIDI Out. Cubase then records the information you play and sends back the information using the keyboard's MIDI In connector. If your keyboard's MIDI setting is not set to Local Off, the sound module portion of your keyboard plays the sounds twice: once when you play the notes on your keyboard and once when Cubase sends the MIDI information back to it.

MIDI Thru

To send MIDI data on to other instruments in a chain, a third MIDI connector called Thru duplicates any MIDI messages that come through the MIDI input of an instrument. This repeats (or echoes) the MIDI information, sending it to another device. An important concept to understand when putting together a MIDI-based music system is that anything played on a keyboard goes only to the MIDI Out and not to the MIDI Thru. This third port is very useful when you want to avoid MIDI loops when hooking your MIDI devices together.

A MIDI loop occurs when MIDI information is sent from one instrument to another and then back to the initial instrument. This causes the instrument to play each note twice and, in some cases, causes a feedback of MIDI data that could potentially cause your sequencer to crash.

If you have a MIDI patch bay or a multiport MIDI interface—MIDI devices with multiple MIDI inputs and outputs called MIDI ports—you are better off using a separate MIDI output for each connected device, thus reducing the amount of information flowing in a single MIDI wire. Each MIDI port in a MIDI setup allows you to send or receive up to sixteen MIDI channels. For example, if you are using a MIDI interface with four MIDI ports, you will have four MIDI inputs and four MIDI outputs and will have control over sixty-four MIDI channels. If you do not own a multiport or MIDI patch bay, daisy-chaining MIDI devices using the MIDI Thru socket is your best bet (see Figure 1.3).

Figure 1.3
Using the MIDI Thru connector to hook multiple MIDI devices together

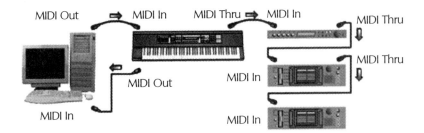

A Brief Overview of Digital Audio

Digital audio is quite different from analog audio. Let us take a moment to see what the differences are and how this can affect your result. Digital audio recordings, like analog audio recordings, are not all created equal. Recording with higher digital resolutions and superior equipment (analog-to-digital converters) in conjunction with the technology available in Cubase SX or SL allows you to create a better-sounding result. How this works and why digital recordings are different from analog recordings is important to understand.

What Is Analog Sound?

We hear sound when our eardrums vibrate, moving back and forth anywhere between twenty and twenty thousand times every second. This is called frequency and is measured in Hertz. A human's ear at its peak (when we are young and our ear has not been subjected to countless hours of noise) can perceive sounds between 20 Hz and 20 kHz (kilohertz). When a musical instrument is played, it vibrates. Examples of this include the string of a violin, the skin of a drum, and even the cone of a loudspeaker. This vibration is transferred to the molecules of the air, which carry the sound to our ears. If the frequency of the vibration is slow, we hear a low note; if the frequency is fast, we hear a high note. If the vibration is gentle, making the air move back and forth only a little, we hear a soft sound. This movement is known as amplitude. If the amplitude is high, making the windows rattle, we hear a loud sound!

If you were to graph air movement against time, you could draw a picture of the sound. This is called a waveform. You can see a very simple waveform at low amplitude on the left side of Figure 1.4. The middle waveform is the same sound, but much louder (higher amplitude). Finally, the waveform on the right is a musical instrument, which contains harmonics—a wider range of simultaneous frequencies. In all of these waveforms, there is one constant: The horizontal axis always represents time and the vertical axis always represents amplitude.

Figure 1.4
The vertical axis represents the amplitude of a waveform and the horizontal axis represents the time.

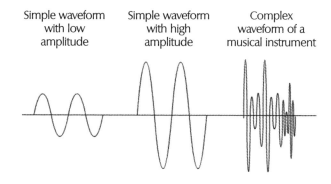

Simple waveform with low amplitude   Simple waveform with high amplitude   Complex waveform of a musical instrument

Real-life sounds don't consist of just one frequency but of many frequencies mixed together at different levels of amplitude (loudness). This is what makes a musical piece sound interesting. Despite its complexity, a waveform can be represented by a graph. At any given time, the waveform has measurable amplitude. If we can capture this "picture" and then reproduce it, we've succeeded in our goal of recording sound.

A gramophone record does this in an easily visible way. Set up a mechanism that transfers air vibration (sound) into the mechanical vibration of a steel needle. Let the needle draw the waveform onto a groove in tinfoil or wax. "Read" the wiggles in this groove with a similar needle. Amplify the vibration as best you can. Well done, Mr. Edison!

Instead of wiggles in a groove, you might decide to store the waveform as patterns of magnetism on recording tape. But either way, you're trying to draw an exact picture of the waveform. You're making an analog recording using a continuous stream of information. This is different from digital audio recordings, as you will see later in this chapter.

The second dimension of sound is amplitude, or the intensity of molecule displacement. When many molecules are moved, the sound is louder. Inversely, if few molecules are moved in space, the sound is softer. Amplitude is measured in decibels (recorded in analog as a change of voltage and in digital as a numeric representation of this voltage value saved in bits), because this displacement of molecules creates energy. When the energy is positive, it pushes molecules forward, making the line in Figure 1.4 move upward. When the energy is negative, it pushes the molecules backwards, making the line go downward. When the line is near the center, it means that fewer molecules are being moved around. That's why the sound appears to be softer in volume.

Space is a third dimension to sound. This dimension does not have its own axis because it is usually the result of amplitude variations through time, but the space affects the waveform itself. In other words, the space affects the amplitude of a sound through time. This will be important when we talk about effects and microphone placement when recording or mixing digital audio. But for now, know that the environment in which sound occurs has a great influence on how we perceive the sound.

What Is Digital Sound?

To understand digital audio, we have to compare it to its analog counterpart.

Analog sound is represented in time by a continuous wave of energy. It is the variation of this energy that moves a speaker forward and backward in its place, creating the air molecule displacement once again. As we mentioned earlier, sound is the continuous change of amplitude (or energy) through time. In digital audio, there is no such thing as continuous—only the illusion of a continuum.

In 1928, mathematician Harry Nyquist developed a theory based on his finding that he could reproduce a waveform if he could sample the variation of sound at least twice in every period of that waveform. A period is a full cycle of the sound (see Figure 1.5), measured in Hertz (this name was given in honor of Heinrich Hertz, who developed another theory regarding the relation between sound cycles and their frequency in 1888). So, if you have a sound that has 20 Hz, you need at least 40 samples to reproduce it. The value that he kept in the sample is the voltage of that sound at a specific point in time. Obviously, in the '20s, computers were not around to keep the large number of values needed to reproduce this theory adequately, but as you probably guessed, we do have this technology available now.

Figure 1.5
The bits in a digital recording store a discrete amplitude value, and the frequency at which these amplitude values are stored in memory as they fluctuate through time is called the sampling frequency

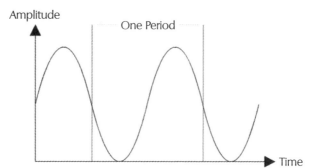

How Sampling Works

In computer terms, the amplitude (or voltage) is measured and its value is stored as a number. The number of bits used to store this voltage value determines the size of this number and the precision of this value. In other words, every bit keeps the value of the amplitude (or voltage) as a binary number. The more bits you have, the more values you have. You may compare this with color depth. When you have 8 bits of color, you have a 256-color palette. A 16-bit resolution yields 65,000 colors, and so on. In sound, colors are replaced by voltage values. The higher the resolution in bit depth, the smaller the increments are between these voltage values. This also means that the more increments you have, the less noise your amplifier creates as it moves from one value to another.

Because the computer cannot make the in-between values, it jumps from one value to the next, creating noise-like artifacts, also called digital distortion. Obviously, this is not something you want in your sound. So, the more values you have to represent different amplitudes, the closer your sound resembles the original analog signal in terms of amplitude variation. Time (measured in Hertz) is the frequency at which you capture and store these voltage values, or bits. Like amplitude (bits), the frequency greatly affects the quality of your sound. As mentioned earlier, Nyquist said that you need two samples per period of the waveform to be able to reproduce it. This means that if you want to reproduce a sound of 100 Hz, or 100 vibrations per second, you need 200 samples. This is called your sampling frequency, and like the frequency of your sound, it is also measured in Hertz. Because in reality, you have complex sounds and high frequencies, you need much higher sampling frequencies than the one mentioned previously. Because most audio components, such as amplifiers and speakers, can reproduce sounds ranging from 20 Hz to 20 kHz, the sampling frequency standard for compact disc digital audio was fixed at 44.1 kHz—a little bit more than twice the highest frequency produced by your monitoring system.

The first thing you notice when you change the sampling rate of a sound is that the more samples you have, the sharper and crisper the sound. The fewer samples you have, the duller and mushier it gets. Why is this? Well, because you need twice as many samples as there are frequencies in your sound, the more samples you have in your recording, the more high harmonics you capture in a sound. When you lose high harmonics, the sound appears duller to your ears. It is those harmonics that add definition to the sound. So, the more samples you have, the sharper the sound. If your sampling rate is too low, you not only lose harmonics, but also fundamentals. And this changes the tonal quality of the sound altogether.

Figure 1.6 shows two sampling formats. The one on the left uses less memory because it samples the sound less often than the one on the right and has fewer bits representing amplitude values. As a result, there are fewer samples to store, and each sample takes up less space in memory. But consequently, it does not represent the original file very well and will probably create artifacts that will render it unrecognizable. In the first set of two images on the top, you can see the analog sound displayed as a single line.

Figure 1.6
Low resolution/low sampling rate vs. high resolution/high sampling rate

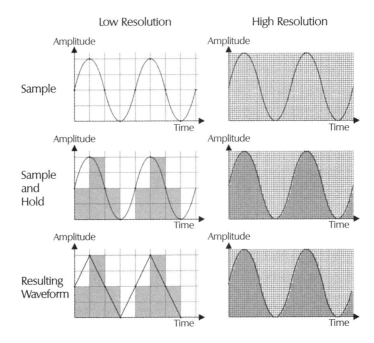

The center set of images demonstrates how the amplitude value of the sample is kept and held until the next sampled amplitude value is taken. As you can see in the right column, a more frequent sampling of amplitude values renders a much more accurate reproduction of the original waveform. If you look at the resulting waveform in the lower set of images, this becomes even more obvious when you look at the line representing the outline of the resulting waveform. The waveform on the right is closer to the original analog signal than the one on the left.

Sampling is simply the process of taking a snapshot of your sound through time. Every snapshot of your sound is kept and held until the next snapshot is taken. This process is called "Sample and Hold." As mentioned earlier, the snapshot keeps the voltage value of the sound at a particular point in time. When playing back digital audio, an amplifier keeps the level of the recorded voltage value until the next sample. Before the sound is finally sent to the output, a certain amount of low-level noise is sometimes added to the process to hide the large gaps that may occur between voltage values, especially if you are using a low bit rate and low sampling rate for digital recording. This process is called dithering. Usually, this makes your sound smoother, but in low-resolution recordings (such as an 8-bit recording), it adds a certain amount of audible noise to your sound. Again, if this dithering wasn't there, you might not hear noise, but your sound might be a little distorted.

So how does this tie into Cubase? Well, Cubase is, in many ways, a gigantic multitrack sampler, as it samples digital audio at various sampling rates and bit depths or resolutions. When you record an audio signal in a digital format, you are sampling this sound. Cubase allows you to sample sound at rates of up to 96 kHz per second and at bit depths of up to 32 bits. How high you can go depends, of course, on your audio hardware.

How Does Cubase Handle MIDI and Audio?

Unlike a tape recorder, Cubase records not only audio information, but MIDI as well. Cubase SX and SL handle MIDI through MIDI ports, MIDI channels, and MIDI tracks and handle audio through audio inputs, audio tracks, mixer channels, and audio outputs (see Figure 1.7).

Figure 1.7
How the MIDI and audio data flows from inputs to outputs in Cubase

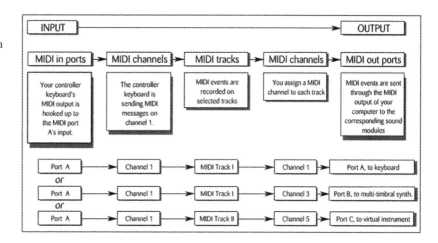

MIDI Port

A MIDI port is a physical or virtual point of entry or point of exit for your MIDI data. The number of physical MIDI ports is determined by your computer's MIDI interface. This can be a stand-alone MIDI interface or MIDI connectors found on your sound card. If you have a sound card that has four MIDI inputs and four MIDI outputs, you will have four MIDI ports available in Cubase. On the other hand, if you are using Cubase to send or receive MIDI information to and from another application inside your computer, chances are you are using virtual MIDI ports.

Why virtual? Because they do not require additional hardware. This is the case when you are using a VST Virtual Instrument (this is discussed in Chapter 5) or when working with third-party software, such as Propellerhead's Reason, Tascam's GigaStudio, or others. When you load these software instruments, they create virtual ports that are available in Cubase for you to use as if they were plugged in to your computer through an actual MIDI port.

The MIDI port determines which physical or virtual MIDI that socket information is coming from and going to (see Figure 1.8). Each MIDI port can carry up to sixteen MIDI channels.

CHAPTER 1

Figure 1.8
Example of a MIDI
input port selection
menu

To view a track's MIDI input and output port setting:

▶   Click the Show Inspector button in the Project window's toolbar (Figure 1.9).

Figure 1.9
The Show/Hide
Inspector button found
on the Project window's
toolbar

Each MIDI track has its own MIDI input port setting and output port setting. This way, you can choose to record MIDI from different MIDI sources directly in your project, just as long as you have a MIDI input device, such as a keyboard, connected to these input ports.

Which MIDI input port appears in your track input port selection field depends on the ports that were set as active in Cubase's MIDI Device Setup window. This is discussed later in this chapter.

MIDI Channel

You have to select a MIDI channel to send information to a particular patch or preset in your MIDI instrument. After your MIDI channel is selected, you can assign a patch to it, such as a bass, for example. A MIDI channel can play only the assigned patch for the instrument with which you want to play or record MIDI. You can change the patch or preset along the way, but you can have only one patch or preset assigned to that channel at a time.

If you run out of MIDI channels for one MIDI port, you need to use another MIDI port to play the MIDI events. Each Virtual Instrument loaded into Cubase's memory creates its own virtual MIDI port, so running out of MIDI channels is unlikely.

In Figure 1.10, you can see that the MIDI In port is set to All MIDI Inputs, which means that any device sending MIDI to Cubase will be recorded. However, the MIDI Out port is set to Nemesys MIDI Out, which also implies that whatever comes in or whatever is already present on this MIDI track will be sent out to this MIDI port.

Figure 1.10
Selecting a MIDI
channel for a MIDI track

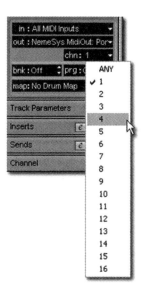

Selecting the MIDI channel causes all MIDI events on this track to be sent to this MIDI channel. In this case, the pointer displays Channel 4 as the new selected MIDI port. Releasing the mouse while this channel is selected causes the check mark appearing next to the number 1 in this list to move to number 4. When you play or record events from this point on, all events are heard through this MIDI port and MIDI channel.

MIDI Track

A MIDI track usually contains MIDI information for one channel at a time. When you play on a keyboard, it sends out MIDI events on a MIDI channel that is recorded on a MIDI track. You then assign a MIDI channel to that track to get the appropriate sound at the output as mentioned previously.

Each track has its own MIDI input and output port setting as well as its channel setting. You can also record from multiple input sources and multiple channels simultaneously on a single track by selecting the appropriate settings for this track; however, it is recommended that you keep each musical part on a separate track for easier editing later. Because you can create as many MIDI tracks as you need in Cubase, you don't really need to worry about running out of them.

Audio Track

An audio track in Cubase is similar to an audio track in an audio multitrack recorder. It has, however, the advantage of being either mono or stereo depending on the audio content you place or record on it. You can create as many audio tracks as you need in Cubase. This said, you are probably limited by your computer's speed, disk access, or memory capacity, so working within these limits is your only concern.

Your project's settings determine the audio bit depth and sample rate recorded in an audio track; however, the mono or stereo selection is independent for each track. After you've decided that a track contains stereo audio files, all files, audio events, or audio parts in this track should be stereo as well. If you decide that a track contains mono events, all events in this track should also be mono. You may later change these settings; however, a stereo audio event on a mono track or vice versa will not play back and Cubase will display a mono/stereo mismatch warning for this audio part on the track.

Audio Inputs

Just like MIDI tracks will record MIDI events from a MIDI input port, an audio track will record events from a selected audio input. In other words, audio inputs are used to feed audio signals to Cubase when recording digital audio, so you need to activate audio inputs for Cubase to record incoming signal. The steps involved in doing this are explained later in this book, but for now, you should understand that you have as many inputs available in Cubase as there are physical inputs available on your sound card or computer system.

Mixer Channel

When you create a track in Cubase, you create a channel in the Track Mixer window. A mixer channel in Cubase is similar to a mixer channel on a hardware mixer with some exceptions:

▶ If you set a track to record or play stereo events, the mixer channel displays information for both channels. On hardware mixers, stereo channels take two channel strips.

▶ If you use a Virtual Instrument such as a software synthesizer, it creates a MIDI channel that allows you to control the MIDI automation for this Virtual Instrument and an audio channel to add audio effects or equalizer parameters. If your Virtual Instrument supports multiple channels, there are as many channels created in the channel mixer as there are output channels for this instrument. For example, loading the LM4-Mark II drum machine creates a set of three stereo channels and six mono channels in your mixer.

▶ Because this is a virtual mixer environment, it is a dynamic mixer as well. In other words, you can create group channels when you need them and add audio channels as well as MIDI channels as you create audio or MIDI tracks in your project.

Mixer channels appear in the Track Mixer panel as shown in Figure 1.11 as well as in the Inspector area of a selected track in the Project window under the Channel section as shown in Figure 1.12.

Figure 1.11
The Track Mixer panel displays all the channels found in your project

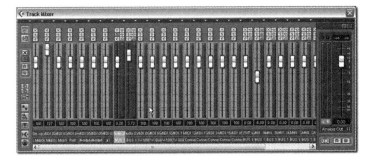

Figure 1.12
The Channel Mixer displays the channel settings, which appear in the Inspector area of the selected track

Audio Output

An audio output is to audio what a MIDI output is to MIDI. Each audio track needs to be forwarded to an audio output at some point in order to hear the content of this track play back. If the sound card in your computer supports only two audio outputs, then all the audio tracks in your Cubase project can and probably will be routed to those outputs. In Cubase, outputs are called busses. You can activate as many busses as you have outputs on your sound card or computer system. In Figure 1.13, the sound card offers ten outputs; therefore, you could enable up to five stereo busses. If your sound card only offers two outputs, you can only activate one stereo bus.

Figure 1.13
The VST Outputs panel allows you to route audio channels to different audio outputs on your sound card

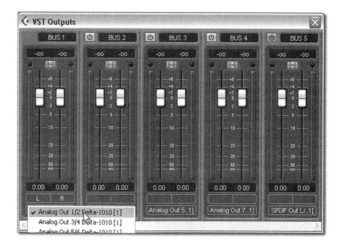

Any effects or equalizer settings you make to a track, as well as automation you might have recorded to an audio track, is rendered to this audio output.

About 32-bit Recording

Most currently available audio hardware supports 16-bit resolution. Some better-quality sound cards also support 20- and 24-bit resolutions. Table 1.1 illustrates the different values that can be stored in their respective resolutions:

Table 1.1
Minimum and maximum values for 16-, 24-, and 32-bit resolution audio signal

Resolution	Minimum Value	Maximum Value	Dynamic Range	Hard Disk Space (min/mono)
16-bit	-32,768	32,767	96 dBFS	5,168 Kb
24-bit	-8,388,608	8,388,607	144 dBFS	7,752 Kb
32-bit	-2,147,483,648	2,147,483,647	193 dBFS	10,336 Kb

But what do these numbers mean? Look at Figure 1.14. With 16-bit resolution, the steps corresponding to voltage values are few and far between. In the 24-bit resolution, there are many more steps (also called Quantum) than in 16-bit recordings. In the 32-bit, the binary word is twice as long, but as you have seen in Table 1.1, instead of having 65,535 steps, you have more than four billion steps. Finally, in 32-bit, floating-point resolution, you still have more than four billion steps; however, they are not fixed but variable points that adjust themselves according to the needs of the audio waveform.

Figure 1.14
Understanding the importance of bit resolution in digital audio recording

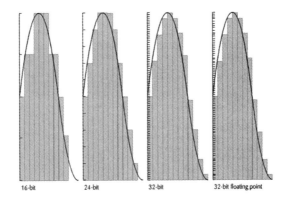

With floating-point resolution, the computer adds a decimal value and can move that decimal point wherever it needs to in order to get greater precision. Here's an example: Let's say you have an analog signal coming in at 1.2245 volts. If you have a system that provides only two decimal points, your resulting value is 1.23 or 1.22. In both cases, this is not very precise, but it's as precise as the recording system can be. Floating-point technology simply adds a decimal value (up to seven) as needed, making the recorded value exactly 1.2245. This kind of technology yields a dynamic range of almost 200 dB! You can configure Cubase to use 32-bit floating point internally, which means that after a sound is recorded at the bit rate allowed by your sound card, a project that is set to 32-bit floating point processes the sound internally—giving you a greater dynamic range. You should still be careful, though, because although there might not be digital clipping in your signal, you might still have digital distortion, which sounds like analog distortion. And any way you look at it, unwanted distortion is never a good thing.

Remember that the bit depth of the mixdown does not have to be the same as the recorded tracks. Cubase allows you to select a different format to mix down your tracks when you are finished working on them. This is because Cubase allows you to record in a format that is superior to the quality available on regular CD players. So, a good rule of thumb to follow is always work with the best quality you can, saving the downgrading for the last step before burning to CD. If your hardware and software can handle it, go for it. But remember this: Audio CD format supports only 44.1 kHz, 16-bit stereo files. So, if you don't convert your audio beforehand, you won't be able to write it in audio CD format, because this format requires that your audio be in 44.1 kHz, 16-bit, stereo channel.

Do I Have the Right Hardware?

To use 24-bit or 32-bit recording, you need to have a 24-bit compatible sound card to actually have better-quality sound. Recording in 24-bit or 32-bit with a 16-bit sound card only makes your file larger; it does not give you better results. Not to mention that your 16-bit sound card might not even be able to play back the audio recorded at 24-bit. This said, you have to understand that 24-bit recordings take up 1.5 times as much space as a 16-bit recording, and that 32-bit recordings take up twice the space of a 16-bit recording and make more demands on the CPU and hard disk performance of your computer. The kind of hard disk and RAM you have in your computer greatly influences the performance of your system when using 24- or 32-bit recording.

On the other hand, if you have a 16-bit sound card but want to get the feeling of analog tape, you can use the TrueTape 32-bit recording technology provided in the Cubase SX version. The TrueTape 32-bit technology encodes the signal in 16-bit using a dithering system. This is different than the 32-bit recording, because it uses software-enabled 32-bit recording rather than true 32-bit recording. The result is similar, but TrueTape allows you to use an interface to control the amount of overdrive you want to add to the sound. This adds the analog saturation feel that occurs when pushing the signal into the red zone of an analog tape. The resulting sound is much more pleasant than if you push a digital signal over the limit, because digital saturation only means you get a nasty clipping sound. This usually occurs when you've hit the ceiling of the digital amplitude; you don't get additional harmonics, instead you get a square wave caused by a series of binary words representing the maximum value they can represent. How to use this and what it does to your audio signal is discussed in Chapter 9.

2

Setting Up Your Environment

Preparing your computer for Cubase requires that your operating system, sound card, and MIDI interface are installed properly and configured for optimal audio operations. Running an application such as Cubase requires a lot of available computer resources, especially when using effects and software instruments. Making these resources available to Cubase helps you get the most out of your working session. Operating systems are designed to look good and do many things. In most cases, you need to change your computer's configuration to emphasize performance rather than looks.

In this chapter, you will:

▶ Choose the right driver for your sound card when working in Cubase

▶ Understand the difference between dedicated, DirectX, and multimedia ASIO drivers

▶ Set up your sound card driver and default MIDI ports in Cubase

▶ Learn how and when to use direct monitoring

▶ Determine what you should consider when running audio applications simultaneously with Cubase

▶ Optimize Windows XP or Mac OS X for audio applications such as Cubase

▶ Determine what you should consider when selecting a hard disk for digital audio projects

▶ Learn how to make sure your hard disk stays healthy

▶ Discover different connection scenarios between Cubase and your studio equipment

▶ Find out why you should organize your media on your hard disk when working with Cubase

CHAPTER 2

Setting Up Your Peripherals

Before you can do anything in Cubase, you must make sure that your software is properly installed on your system. This implies that you have a stable operating system and that the latest drivers for all your peripherals are installed, including peripherals you think are not related, such as video card and network card drivers. If you find that your operating system crashes often for no apparent reason, reinstalling might be a good idea. This may save you from experiencing problems later on. You need to run some tests to allow the software to establish what is the best configuration for its optimal performance. You must then tweak this a bit further before you can establish what is the best configuration for your optimal performance.

The first thing you should set up is how Cubase communicates with the operating system, the MIDI device, and the sound card's driver. Because Cubase uses both MIDI and digital audio, you need to set up both drivers properly.

Sound Cards and Drivers

Because Cubase is a MIDI and audio recording, editing, and mixing environment, one of the most important steps in configuring your computer is to make sure you have the proper drivers installed on your computer. In other words, your sound card's drivers in essence determine the quality of your experience when using Cubase because using the wrong drivers or a sound card that does not provide the proper support for your software will undoubtedly lead to problems when you work on your projects.

For Mac users, it is recommended that you use ASIO drivers for your sound card; however, Cubase does support WDM drivers and it is possible to use a special ASIO driver for sound cards that only have Sound Manager drivers. To install an ASIO driver on a Macintosh computer (if this is not already done), you need to drag and drop your sound card's ASIO icon from its original medium (such as a CD or disk) to the ASIO driver folder found inside the Cubase folder on your hard disk. For PC users, there are three types of drivers supported by Cubase.

ASIO Drivers

ASIO is the acronym for Audio Stream Input/Output, which is a technology developed by Steinberg that allows a sound card to efficiently process and synchronize inputs and introduces the least amount of latency, or delay, between the inputs and the outputs of the sound card. What is latency? It is the time difference between the input and output. The smaller the latency, the shorter the time between what you record and what you hear recorded after the signal has been processed by the computer. High latencies are often troublesome when recording live material because there is always a delay when monitoring the audio. ASIO drivers have a short latency because they do not send the signal into the operating system before sending it to its outputs. Therefore, you can record music while playing back tracks without any noticeable differences. A typical latency for a sound card using a dedicated ASIO driver should be below 10 milliseconds. The greater the latency time, the more noticeable the delay. You should also note that latency also affects the VST Instruments, the LEDs in the Track Mixer, and the response time of faders and knobs inside Cubase.

It goes without saying that this type of driver is highly recommended. In fact, if you went through the trouble of buying this book and Cubase SX, chances are that you are serious about making the most with your audio investment. This also implies that you should use a sound card that has an ASIO driver written especially for it. Most professional sound cards today support this format.

DirectX Drivers

If your sound card doesn't offer an ASIO driver written for it, you need to use the Microsoft DirectSound technology, which is part of DirectX. This DirectX driver should be included with your sound card. When using a DirectX driver, you also have to use the ASIO DirectX Full Duplex driver, which is provided by Steinberg on your Cubase installation CD. This combination of drivers allows Cubase to communicate with DirectX and allows full duplex on your sound card. Full duplex means that you can record and play back at the same time using your sound card (in contrast, half duplex allows only one operation at a time, play or record).

Because Cubase has to communicate with DirectX through the ASIO DirectX driver, and then DirectX communicates with the sound card, expect higher latencies when using this type of driver setup.

For this combination of drivers, you need to use the ASIO Direct Sound Full Duplex Setup window to configure your sound card properly (see Figure 2.1). This window lists all DirectSound compatible input and output ports on your system. Devices that are checked are available inside Cubase. You can find the ASIO DirectX Full Duplex setup utility in a special ASIO folder under the Cubase program folder. To launch it, simply locate its icon or alias and launch it from there.

To configure your DirectSound drivers:

1. To activate a port, check the box found to the left of the device's name. To deactivate it, remove the check mark.

2. The buffer size is used when audio data is transferred between Cubase and the audio card. Larger buffer sizes ensure that playback occurs without glitches, whereas smaller buffer sizes reduce the latency. The default buffer size appearing in this column should be fine in most cases; however, if you want to solve crackling sounds in your audio, you may increase the buffer size by double-clicking in this column and entering a new value. Try to keep these values without increments of 512 samples.

3. If you hear a constant offset (delay) during playback of audio and MIDI recordings, you can adjust the output or input latency time using offset value. In most cases, you should leave this to its default value of zero. If you are noticing a delay at the output, increase the output offset; if you are noticing a delay at the input, increase the input offset.

4. The Sync Reference option lets you determine how MIDI will be synchronized with the audio. You can choose to synchronize MIDI to the audio input or audio output. This also determines which offset value you should adjust as mentioned in the previous item.

5. The Card Options should be left with the Full Duplex option selected; however, if you are noticing problems while this is selected, you can enable the Start Input First option.

Figure 2.1
The ASIO Direct Sound
Full Duplex Setup
window

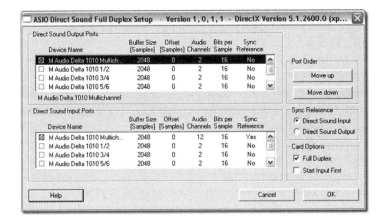

Multimedia Drivers

If your sound card does not have a dedicated ASIO driver or DirectX driver, you need to use the Windows multimedia driver provided by your sound card manufacturer in combination with the ASIO multimedia driver. As with the DirectX configuration, Cubase communicates with your sound card by passing through the ASIO multimedia driver, which communicates to your Windows driver, which communicates with your sound card. That's a long way to go and as you might have guessed, longer delays (latency) are to be expected.

An ASIO multimedia driver is a standard (generic) ASIO driver provided by Steinberg, which allows you to record and play audio through your sound card when using Cubase. You should use this driver only if you don't have dedicated ASIO drivers. Before running Cubase for the first time, you will be asked to profile your ASIO multimedia driver. If you've never done this, now is a good time to start.

You can find the ASIO Multimedia setup utility in the same special ASIO folder as the ASIO DirectX setup utility mentioned earlier, under the Cubase program folder. To launch it, simply locate its icon or alias and launch it from there.

To configure your Windows multimedia drivers:

1.   In the ASIO Multimedia Setup dialog box (see Figure 2.2), you will find a Presets field; start by looking there to see if your sound card is listed. If it is, select it. If it isn't, run the setup in advanced mode by clicking the Advanced Options button.

Figure 2.2
The ASIO Multimedia
Setup dialog box

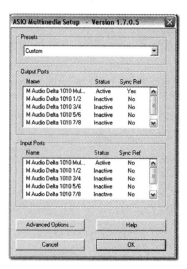

2. As with the DirectX dialog box, you will find all input and output ports for your sound card listed (see Figure 2.3) in the ASIO Multimedia Setup—Advanced Options dialog box. A check mark next to the device's name indicates that a device is available in Cubase. If you want to use your sound card with a different sampling rate than the one indicated in the corresponding field, select the new sampling rate and run a simulation to make sure the buffer size for this device at the selected sampling rate is appropriate.

3. Use the Global Settings section to change the sync reference and card options for your sound card. You should leave these options at their default values unless you run into some problems when checking the buffer size and sync. Avoid using DMA block with any PCI sound card.

4. In the Card Options field, uncheck the Use 16-bit only unless you are sure your sound card does not support more than 16-bit resolution. If this option is checked, you need to make sure not to select 24-bit mode recording once inside Cubase.

5. If you want to test the proper buffer size for each active input and output port, select the port and click the Detect Buffer Size button. It is recommended that you wait for the detection process to be completed before doing anything else on your computer. This provides a more accurate detection of the appropriate buffer size for your device.

6. After it completes, verify your buffer size and sync reference by clicking the Check Buffers and Sync button. If the device passes the test, then run a simulation as explained in the next step. If the test fails, a dialog box appears offering possible solutions to improve your settings.

7. The Run Simulation button allows you to test the current settings for your sound card when using the ASIO multimedia driver in Cubase. It is important that you test your settings whenever you make changes to them.

8. If you are satisfied with your settings, you can store the changes as a preset by clicking the Store button.

CHAPTER 2

Figure 2.3
The ASIO Multimedia
Setup—Advanced
Options dialog box

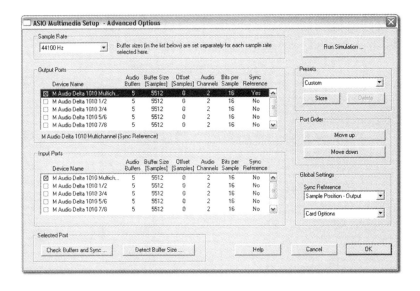

MIDI Interfaces and Drivers

Installing a MIDI card requires you to use the driver that comes with the hardware. This is usually quite simple and is explained in your hardware documentation. Hardware specifics are not discussed here, because there are too many MIDI and audio interfaces out there to cover them thoroughly. However, to make sure everything is set up properly, one good starting point is to verify that your MIDI port appears in your system configuration.

To make sure your MIDI port is installed properly on a PC running Windows XP:

1. Click Start > Control Panel.

2. In the Control Panel, double-click the System icon.

3. Click the Hardware tab to make it active and then click the Device Manager button.

4. Locate the Sound, video and game controller entry and expand the list to view the items under this entry.

5. Double-click your MIDI interface or sound card if you have a MIDI port on it to view its properties.

6. Once again, this opens your device's Properties dialog box. Make the Properties tab active to view if your port is installed properly.

7. In this dialog box, you will also find a Properties button. Select your installed MIDI port and click this button to see if any messages or warnings appear telling you that the device is not installed properly or if this device is in conflict with another peripheral.

At this point, if you have not seen any question marks or exclamation points next to your device and if there is no indication that it is not installed properly, you should be able to use this port in Cubase. If, on the other hand, you have found a problem, you should try reinstalling the driver for this peripheral and follow the installation procedure provided by your device's manufacturer.

If your device is not installed properly, a red X or a yellow question mark is shown on the device's icon in the Device Manager window, as shown in Figure 2.4. If the device is installed, but not working properly, an exclamation point appears over your device's icon in this same list.

Figure 2.4
The Device Manager
window in Windows XP

You might want to consult your manufacturer's Web site for specific settings related to your MIDI or audio device. This Web site will probably provide you with a driver update and tips on configuring your device with Cubase and other software.

Selecting Devices In Cubase

Now that you have made sure your MIDI and audio drivers are installed properly, let's take a look at how you can activate them in Cubase. The Devices Setup dialog box allows you to activate/deactivate MIDI ports, select the appropriate ASIO driver for your sound card, and configure other aspects of Cubase. Among these other settings, you will find the VST System Link, which allows you to network different computers through an S/PDIF, AES/EBU, ADAT, or TDIF digital audio connection, the video player driver used to display video files that you may load in a project, and remote control devices that allow you to control certain aspects of your mixing. However, in this chapter, we discuss only the MIDI and audio settings and leave the other settings for later, as they become relevant.

Selecting the Default MIDI Port

First, you must select which MIDI port you want to use as your default MIDI port. In most cases, this is the MIDI port connected to your MIDI keyboard. The default MIDI port determines which MIDI port is associated by default with a MIDI track when you create one in the Project window.

To set your default MIDI device:

1. Select the Device Setup option from the Devices menu.
2. Click Default MIDI Ports in the list to view its panel on the right side. Notice that there are two tabs on the right side of this dialog box: Setup and Add/Remove. The Add/Remove tab is only used to add remote control devices to your Device Setup dialog box.
3. From the MIDI Input drop-down menu, select the appropriate MIDI input.
4. From the MIDI Output drop-down menu, select the appropriate MIDI output.
5. Click the Apply button.

The Device Setup dialog box also allows you to enable or disable MIDI ports that are present on your system. This might be useful in the event that some MIDI ports are not well-suited for use in Cubase. For example, you might find that after using a specific MIDI port, the timing is off or erratic. This could be the case when using the DirectMusic version of a MIDI port that exists also as a Windows version (provided by your MIDI interface manufacturer). But because both might be present on your system, deactivating one in the Device Setup dialog box hides it from view when selecting MIDI ports in a MIDI track.

Configuring Your Sound Card

To configure your sound card in Cubase:

1. Select the Device Setup option from the Devices menu (if you are not already there).
2. Click VST Multitrack in the list to view its panel on the right side.
3. In the ASIO Driver field, select the appropriate driver for your sound card. If you have a dedicated ASIO driver for your sound card, it is strongly recommended that you use it.
4. If you are using a dedicated ASIO driver, you can set the clock source by clicking the Control Panel button. This allows you to choose if you want your sound card to follow an incoming digital clock source or use its own clock source for digital timing. The clock source, in essence, dictates the sampling frequency. If you don't have any other digital audio devices connected to your sound card, this should always be set to internal. Because each sound card offering a dedicated ASIO driver is different, the options you find in this panel will also be different. (See Figure 2.5.)

Figure 2.5
The control panel for
the Delta-1010 from
M-Audio

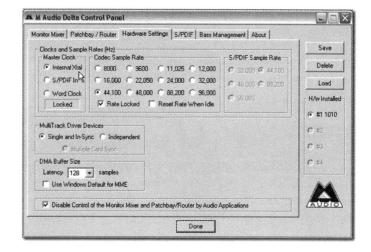

Modifying Disk Buffers

If you run into audio dropouts or if your hard disk performance indicator often peaks, causing audio dropouts, you may adjust the number of disk buffers and their sizes in the Device Setup dialog box. Increasing the number of buffers and their size reduces the load on your hard disk, helping it by loading a portion of the audio in a memory buffer to prevent stuttering in your audio when the hard disk is not quick enough. The reverse effect of this, however, is that higher buffer sizes and additional buffers increase the latency factor. If you don't notice any changes in your audio after increasing these values and you notice that your hard disk performance meter still indicates that your hard disk access peaks, you might need to get a faster hard disk. To view the VST Performance meter panel, press the F12 key on your keyboard or select Devices > VST Performance.

To modify the number of disk buffers and their size:

1. Select the Device Setup option from the Devices menu.
2. Click VST Multitrack in the list to view its panel on the right side.
3. Use the arrows to the right of the values next to the Number of Disk Buffers option or double-click the value and enter the desired value.
4. Use the drop-down menu next to the Disk Buffer Size option to select a different buffer size value.
5. Click the Apply button.

Using Direct Monitoring

If your sound card's driver is ASIO 2.0 compatible, you may use an option called direct monitoring. Direct monitoring allows you to control the monitoring inside Cubase SX, but the actual sound is sent back directly to your sound card's mixer utility. This gives you the opportunity to hear what is coming in Cubase directly through your sound card's outputs without adding any delay between the input and the output. However, direct monitoring bypasses the effects, EQ, and any other parameter found in the Mixer window that does not relate directly to how the signal is routed. This implies that you can't use insert effects and expect to hear those effects in real time as you are recording. When you select this option, you can also set Cubase's monitoring preferences to determine when direct monitoring takes effect and when Cubase's internal routing takes effect.

To set up direct monitoring:

1. Select the Device Setup option from the Devices menu.

2. Click VST Multitrack in the list to view its panel on the right side.

3. Check the Direct Monitoring option, and then click the Apply button followed by the OK button.

4. Select File > Preferences.

5. Scroll down the list on the left and select VST at the bottom of this list (see Figure 2.6).

Figure 2.6
Changing the audio monitoring options in the VST Preferences dialog box

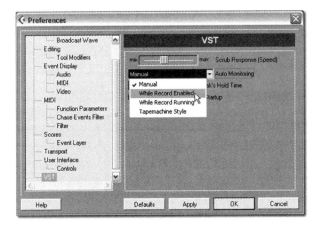

6. On the right side of the dialog box, select one of the four auto monitoring options: Manual, While Record Enabled, While Record Running, and Tapemachine style.

    ▶ **Manual auto monitoring.** Allows you to switch to direct monitoring by pressing the Monitor button in the track's Channel Mixer or the Track Mixer (see Figure 2.7).

Figure 2.7
The Monitor button in the Channel Mixer allows you to switch to direct monitoring when the auto monitoring option is set to manual.

▶ **While record enabled auto monitoring**. Allows you to monitor the inputs when the Record Enable button in the track's Channel or the Track Mixer is enabled (this is the red button above the Monitor button in Figure 2.7).

▶ **While record running auto monitoring**. Allows you to monitor the inputs when you are actually recording audio only.

▶ **Tapemachine style auto monitoring**. Allows you to monitor the inputs when Cubase is stopped or recording audio, but not during playback.

7. Click the Apply button, and then click OK.

Running Other Audio Applications Simultaneously

There is not much to say about running other nonaudio-related applications simultaneously, besides the fact that if you are running applications that require memory and CPU power, these resources won't be available to you in Cubase. Some background applications might perform a hard disk scan in the middle of a recording. A good example of this is Find Fast, an applet that comes with Microsoft Office. If the computer running Cubase is not connected to the Internet, you should remove all Internet-related applications, including virus protection applications.

Any background memory or hard-disk-intensive applications should be disabled when using Cubase. A good rule of thumb is to not run other nonessential applications when running Cubase to improve your performance. If you want to find out what is running inside your Windows system, press Ctrl+Alt+Del. This brings up the Windows Task Manager that shows you which applications are currently running. For example, you can click the Processes tab to view how much memory Cubase uses (see Figure 2.8).

Figure 2.8
The Windows Task
Manager

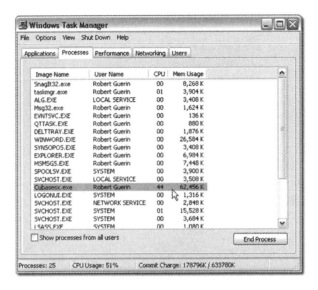

Another good place to look out for is the startup applications found in the Start > All Programs > Startup folder. You should remove any program that you do not want Windows to launch automatically when starting up your computer.

You can end a process or an application (depending if the Applications or Processes tab is active) by right-clicking an item in the list, and selecting the appropriate option. Nothing you do in this dialog box can harm your system in any way. Note that after you reboot your system, the applications that were running before you ended them will be back in business. So, changing the settings for these applications is a good idea. The more icons you have in the bottom-right corner of your Taskbar, the more applications are running in the background, using valuable resources. Make sure you keep those to a minimum. If you can, try to keep your Internet activities apart from the computer you use with Cubase (or any other audio application). Antivirus utilities can use up to thirty percent of your system's resources.

If you are running OS X on a Macintosh computer, you can also view the active processes by accessing the Process Viewer. To access the Process Viewer window, select the Finder's menu, then choose Go > Applications > Utilities Folder > Process Viewer (see Figure 2.9).

Figure 2.9
The Process Viewer
window on OS X

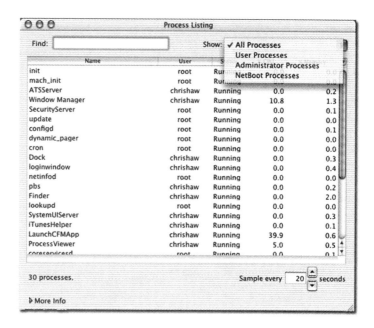

There is a way to deactivate certain applications that are not necessary while running Cubase to free up resources. The most effective way to do this is to choose any program that is loaded on the Dock and then choose the File > Quit option. You can do this is in the Process Viewer; however, you need to be sure you know what you are turning off.

The situation is different if you try to run another audio-related application. To run audio-related applications simultaneously with Cubase, you need a sound card that provides a multiclient driver. What is a multiclient driver? Basically, it is a driver that allows different applications shared access to the sound card. Think of it this way: A single-client driver is like going to the grocery store and having only one cash register open. Everybody has to line up and wait their turn to pay for their groceries. A multiclient driver is like having two or three cash registers opened, where people can go to a second or even a third cash register if the first is busy. Note that if you want to record the output of your Cubase project, you should avoid opening another recording application to do so because you can record the output of Cubase directly from within Cubase.

When Cubase is loaded, it generally takes over the controls of the sound card, leaving it unusable for other applications that would need it as well to run simultaneously, such as a third-party virtual sampler. If you don't have a multiclient driver, there are ways around it; however, they have limitations.

Steinberg provides an engine called Rewire that lets you share audio resources between Steinberg products and other Rewire-compatible products, such as Rebirth and Reason from Propellerheads or Sonar 2.0 from Cakewalk. This is discussed in Chapter 11.

For other types of software, such as Tascam's GigaStudio or GigaSampler, you have to load this software before and set Cubase as your default sequencer from within the GigaStudio or GigaSampler environment. After this is done, you can launch Cubase from the Sequencer button

CHAPTER 2

within GigaStudio or GigaSampler. If you have problems doing this, try disabling audio outputs in GigaStudio that you want to use in Cubase (for good measure, keep outputs 1 and 2 available for Cubase because these are the default inputs/outputs used by Cubase) and disabling audio inputs and outputs that you want to use in GigaStudio in Cubase. By doing this, you are effectively assigning certain outputs of your sound card to Cubase and others to GigaStudio. You should also check the Release ASIO Driver in Background option found in the Device Setup dialog box (see Figure 2.10).

To release the ASIO driver when Cubase is in the background:

1. In the Device menu, select the Device setup option.
2. In the Device Setup window, click to highlight the VST Multitrack option.
3. In the Setup section, check the Release ASIO Driver in Background option.
4. Click OK to complete.

Figure 2.10
Activating the Release ASIO Driver in Background option in the Device Setup dialog box, under the VST Multitrack section

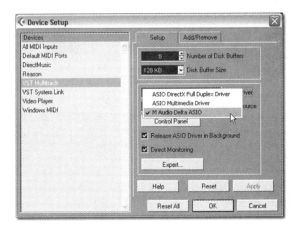

When running such a setup, you are imposing a huge load on your computer resources and are also testing many compatibility issues between the different manufacturers of software and hardware. In a perfect world, everything works, but the computer world is far less than perfect. If you are experiencing difficulties, here are a couple of places to look for information:

▶ Visit Steinberg's site (www.steinberg.net) to see if there is any additional information on the issue you are having.

▶ Visit your other software manufacturer's Web site as well; it also might have some answers for you.

▶ Check your sound card manufacturer's Web site to see if you have the latest drivers for your sound card, and take a look at the support, troubleshooting, or FAQ section to find additional help.

▶ Use discussion forums to share your problems with others; chances are, someone else has had the same problem and might have a workaround for you.

Hardware and OS Setup

Obviously, your software is not alone in this. Without hardware, your Cubase software CD would be a very expensive coaster! It is important that your hardware configuration matches the needs of Cubase. This implies that you have a computer that meets Steinberg's recommended configuration, which includes processor types, RAM, operating system, video display adapter, and CD-ROM drive. But within those specifications, there are some hardware settings that you can apply that will make your operation run more smoothly.

Hard Disk Configuration

Your hard drive is your recording tape. When recording digital audio on it, you are basically using it as a big storage device for this audio, like a magnetic tape does in an analog studio. Although your hard drive is not prone to produce bending, degradation, or hiss like analog tape does, it does have its own problems.

Hard drives come in many sizes, many speeds, and many configurations. If you are planning to buy a new hard drive to record digital audio, you should ultimately use this drive ONLY for audio. Why? Because audio files are usually large files. This is not true for system files or other files required by your applications. When you are recording these large files, your system looks for free space on your hard disk to store them. If it has to find little corners here and there on your disk to place them, it slows down your writing ability, limiting the number of audio channels you can read or write. This is mainly due to disk fragmentation. When using a disk or a partition on a disk only for digital audio recordings, you reduce the amount of disk fragmentation produced by small files that are written by your operating system or by applications you run on a day-to-day basis. If you can afford it, the best solution is, of course, using a separate hard disk dedicated to your audio recording. And, preferably, this disk is on a different E-IDE or SCSI port from your system disk. This allows faster access to the information on your disk, avoiding any issues or degradation of performance due to shared resources. With the price of hard disks coming down, it's an investment worth making if you are using Cubase as a virtual studio environment for your digital audio recordings.

Disk fragmentation is another performance-robbing phenomenon. When working with audio, you write and erase information on your disk frequently; you should defragment at least once a week—yes, once a week. If you are using Cubase as your main working environment for your studio, defragmenting should be done after each recording session. This prevents your disk from unnecessary head movement during intense writing or reading sessions and accelerates the process.

To check your hard disk on a PC for errors and defragment it:

1. Double-click the My Computer icon on your desktop.
2. Right-click the hard disk you want to verify and defragment and select Properties from the context menu.
3. In the Disk Properties dialog box (see Figure 2.11), click the Tools tab.
4. On the Tools tab, click the Check Now button.

CHAPTER 2

5. In the Check Disk dialog box, click the Start button. Windows then performs a check on your disk to make sure there are no errors on it. When it is completed, you can close the Check Disk dialog box and return to the Disk Properties dialog box.

Figure 2.11
The Disk Properties dialog box

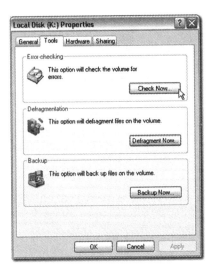

6. Now, you can click the Defragment Now button. The Disk Defragmenter utility appears (see Figure 2.12).

Figure 2.12
The Disk Defragmenter window in Windows XP

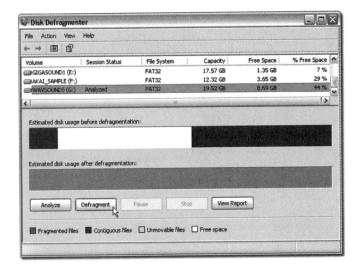

7. Select the appropriate drive in the upper part of the window if it is not already selected and then click the Defragment button at the bottom of the window. Windows analyzes the content of your disk and proposes some choices when it is done. One of these choices is to defragment your disk.

8. Select the Defragment option to begin defragmenting your disk.

If you are running OS X on a Macintosh computer, there is a hard disk utility as with previous versions of Macintosh operating systems, which allows you to verify and set up your partitions, format disks, check for errors, and repair them; however it does not have any defragmenting options. If you want to defragment your disk, you need to purchase a third-party software, such as Micromat's Tech Tool Pro (www.micromat.com) or Symantec's Norton Utilities or SystemWorks (www.symantec.com).

Hard Disk Types and Performance

Now that we've covered how to take care of a disk, let's look at what kind of disk you should get. Hard disks spin at speeds between 5,400 rpm and 15,000 rpm. The faster your disk spins, the more information you can get out of it in a fixed amount of time. What you should look for in a drive is a minimal access time or average track-to-track seek time, which is how much time it takes the heads to move from one cylinder to another. When accessing arbitrary data, first the heads must seek the correct cylinder, then wait until the correct sector spins under the heads, and then read the data. Thus, a small seek time is good, and a fast disk rotation speed is good. A sufficient number to look for is 8 to 9 milliseconds. If it's shorter, it takes less time to find the information.

Another parameter to look for is a sustained data transfer rate, but not a peak data transfer rate. When using digital audio files, your disk reads a sustained stream of information; that's why peak indicators don't matter much, because it is more likely that you will have multiple files of audio data being fed from the disk to the software. If you want to be able to transfer twenty-four channels of digital audio at 44.1 kHz, 16 bits, you need a minimum of 2 MB of sustained data transfer. Now, this is the minimum. What you want to look for is at least two to three times that data transfer, so around 5 to 9 MB per second. Remember that you might have other applications running in the background accessing the hard disk; that twenty-four channels comes and goes pretty quickly when working on a project.

SCSI drives and E-IDE drives today are fairly equal in performance. You might get a 10 percent to 15 percent increase in data transfer rate on a SCSI drive with the Ultra Wide 3 format, compared to the Ultra DMA drives, but the price difference is not worth it. The more recent technologies, such as ATA/100 and ATA/133 drives, render even greater performances.

FireWire drives are quite nice as well, if you can spare your arm and leg over its purchase or if you are also doing video editing. My advice is to evaluate your needs for the next six months and make an educated decision based on those needs. Six months from now, drives will be cheaper, the technology will evolve, and you will be able to reevaluate your needs then.

If your E-IDE hard drive uses DMA or Ultra DMA (UDMA) technology, you should enable this option in your system configuration to improve its performance. You should, in fact, stay away from any drive that does not support DMA for digital audio recording. This affects, among other things, the MIDI-to-audio timing. You should be aware that even though it is virtually impossible to buy a new drive today that isn't DMA, you shouldn't assume it is automatically activated in your system. Inexplicably, often it isn't by default. You can verify this in Device Manager, sometimes under the hard drive itself, sometimes under the IDE Primary and Secondary Controller.

CHAPTER 2

Tweaking Windows for Optimal Performance

If you are running Cubase on a PC, you need either Windows 2000 or Windows XP running on your machine in order for Cubase to run. Both of these operating systems offer a stable working environment and offer superior resource management than did previous versions of Windows. However, there are a couple of things that you can do to make your computer run more effectively when using Cubase.

Here are a few tips to optimize your Windows OS:

▶ Click Start, then right-click My Computer. Select Properties from the context menu and then click the Advanced tab. Under Startup and Recovery, click the Settings button. In the Startup and Recovery dialog box, uncheck the Automatically restart option under the System failure section. Click OK to exit.

▶ Back in the Advanced System Properties dialog box, click the Settings button under the Performance section. In the Visual Effects panel, select the Adjust for best performance radio button. Then, click the Advanced tab and set the Processor scheduling to Background Services. Click Apply, then OK twice to close both windows. You will need to reboot in order for these changes to take place.

▶ Right-click your Taskbar and select Properties from the context menu. Uncheck both Auto-hide the taskbar and Hide inactive icons options (see Figure 2.13).

Figure 2.13
The Taskbar and Start
Menu Properties

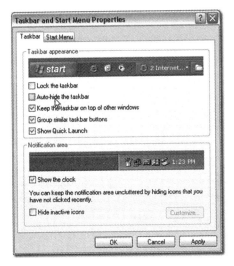

▶ If you are running Windows Messenger, make sure it doesn't load automatically when Windows loads. Open Windows Messenger; select Tools > Options. Click the Preferences tab and uncheck the Run this program when Windows starts and the Allow this program to run in the background options.

▶ Click Start > Control Panel and double-click the Sounds and Audio Devices icon. Select the Sounds tab and choose the No sounds option in the Sound Scheme drop-down list. Click Apply, then OK. If you want to make sure that your sound card is working properly, you could also create a sound scheme with a simple startup sound. This is a convenient way to check that your audio is working properly.

▶ Back in the Control Panel, double-click the Display icon to view its properties. Under the Screen Saver tab, select None from the screen saver's drop-down list. Then, click the Power button. Make sure the Turn off monitor, Turn off hard disks, System standby, and System hibernates options are all set to Never. Click Apply, and then click OK twice.

▶ Also in the Display dialog box, click the Appearance tab. Click the Effects button to disable every option found in this panel.

Hooking Up Your Equipment

There are many ways to hook up your equipment to your computer, and it all depends on what you want to do and what type of equipment you want to hook up. On this topic, there are two major problems you want to avoid:

▶ Having too much sound, which is normally called a feedback loop

▶ Having no sound at all

The following figures represent simple, yet effective ways to hook up your equipment. Obviously, there are many more combinations and you should try drawing out one for your own studio to help you organize your wiring effectively.

Figure 2.14 shows a very modest MIDI setup, using the audio outputs of the keyboard to feed the self-amplified studio monitors. An alternative to this, especially if you want to record the MIDI coming out of your keyboard into a digital format, is to hook up the audio outputs of your keyboard to the inputs of your sound card and the outputs of your sound card to the inputs of your speakers. The way the diagram is shown allows you to use the sound card's input for an acoustic instrument or a microphone. Remember that microphones have a low impedance output (microphone inputs) and that, normally, your sound card's inputs are high impedance (line inputs). You will probably need a microphone preamplifier if you want to use it in this way and avoid using the microphone inputs on a sound card. Note, however, that some sound cards have bad microphone inputs, whereas others have better ones with built-in preamplifiers. If your sound card is part of the latter category, you could use these inputs without worrying; on the other hand, if you find that your microphone inputs are noisy, don't use them.

The MIDI input of the keyboard goes in the MIDI output of the computer, and the MIDI output of the keyboard goes in the MIDI input of the computer.

The way you connect your audio outputs depends on the audio system at hand. If you have powered monitors, you should hook up the audio outputs of your computer or keyboard directly to them, sending the left signal to the left speaker and the right signal to the right speaker. If you are using an amplifier, you should basically do the same thing, but you send the signal to the amplifier first, then distribute the audio signal from the amplifier to the speakers.

Figure 2.14
Simple setup without
any mixer for single-
source monitoring

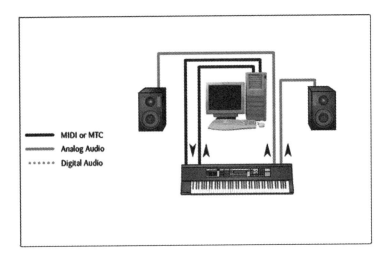

In Figure 2.15, a small desktop mixer has been added. This is necessary if you are using more than one audio source (in this case, the keyboard and sound module). This way, you can have as many audio sources as your mixer has inputs. You then feed the output of your mixer into your computer. This can be a bit tricky if you have only one set of outputs on your desktop mixer. Most desktop mixers have a different volume control for monitoring and master outputs. You should take the audio outputs of the computer and feed them into a separate pair of inputs that can be routed to a signal path that doesn't go back into itself (in this case, the computer), such as a tape return. If you have direct outputs or busses on your mixer, use those to send the signal to your computer rather than using the main outputs. This way, you can monitor independently the sound going to the computer and the sound coming from the computer without having the computer go back into the mix.

Notice that the MIDI Thru of the keyboard is used to echo the output of the computer into the sound module.

Figure 2.15
Simple setup with a
desktop mixer for
multiple-source
monitoring

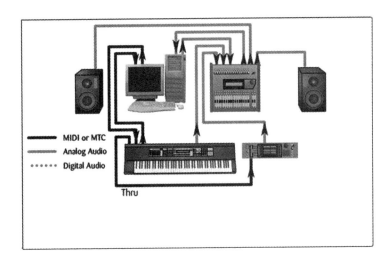

Figure 2.16 shows a setup using a multiple input/output sound card without the use of a mixer. This allows you to use the Cubase mixer as a mixing table. This is not the most flexible way to work, but if you are on a budget and can't afford a mixer, it's a good compromise.

You need to send all the audio outputs to separate audio inputs on the sound card and a pair of outputs from the sound card to speakers for monitoring. A MIDI patch bay has been added to help with the MIDI patching, but this is not necessary. If you don't have a MIDI patch bay, you need to send the MIDI Thru of your keyboard to the MIDI In of the sound module and the MIDI Thru of the sound module to the MIDI In of the drum machine (or other sound module), making the keyboard and computer front and center in your MIDI routing (keyboard's MIDI Out to computer's MIDI In and vice versa).

Figure 2.16
Setup for a MIDI studio using a MIDI patch bay and multiple input sound card without a mixer

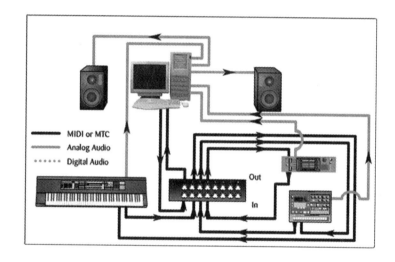

Figure 2.17 shows a setup using a simple digital in/out sound card that feeds and receives information through digital transfer from the digital mixer. As in Figure 2.15, you might want to use an extra pair of audio outputs to monitor the output of your computer without sending it back into the signal of the mixer, creating a feedback loop.

Figure 2.17
Setup for a MIDI or audio studio using a digital mixer and a sound card providing digital inputs and outputs

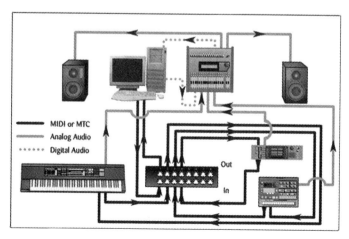

Backing Up and Folder Management

Let's discuss the art of saving files and folders in the event something goes wrong. Yes, it is an art. Why so? Because it takes as much dedication as art does, and most people think it's useless anyway—until their system crashes in the middle of a session and their clients realize they don't have any way of getting back these precious performances.

There are two kinds of computer users: those who have lost information and those who will lose information. So, backing up your information on CD-Rs, CD-RWs, removable media drives, DAT tapes, or any other kind of safety should not be an option for you—it should be mandatory.

The easiest and probably most affordable way to make backups is by saving your files to a CD-R or CD-RW. To do this effectively, you have to be organized and know where all your material is. That's why you have to establish a system when recording MIDI and digital audio information for your projects.

One way to do this is to create a different folder for each project or client on your dedicated audio project hard disk. Fortunately, when you create a new project in Cubase, it prompts you to choose a folder for this project. If the folder does not exist, you can create one. It is a good idea to keep all the files related to a project in the same place. When you create a folder, like the New Song folder in Figure 2.18, Cubase also creates a subfolder called audio where it, by default, places all audio files recorded for this project. When you save your project file, you can place it in the folder you created and all audio files will be in the audio subfolder.

Figure 2.18
Creating a new folder when starting a new project

When you start working on your project, Cubase creates additional folders. One folder contains the fade in, fade out, and crossfade audio segments, another folder contains the graphical information related to your audio files used in your project, and finally the folder created earlier for your audio recordings (see Figure 2.19). When you want to back up a project for later use or simply to keep a safety copy of this project, you should save all the content in these folders. When restoring the content of these folders to your disk, Cubase will be able to find all the information it needs to restore the project file, as it was when you saved it.

Figure 2.19
The folder structure
created by Cubase when
working on a project

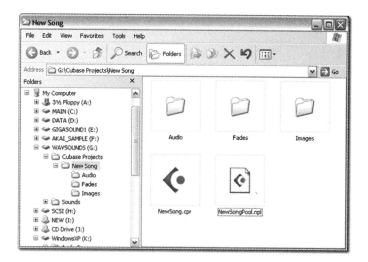

As you find out in Chapter 9, there are additional tools in the Audio Pool found in Cubase that allow you to prepare your audio files for archiving. In effect, this option creates a copy of all the audio files referenced by a project inside the Audio folder of this project, making it easy to save everything in one place rather than looking for audio files across different media and folders.

CHAPTER 2

3

A Guided Tour of Cubase SX/SL

This chapter aims at providing an overview of Cubase SX's and SL's many workspaces. If you are a veteran Cubase user, you will find this chapter useful to find out where things are in relation to previous versions of this software and how to access these windows, dialog boxes, and panels in Cubase SX/SL. If you are new to Cubase, this chapter introduces the software, describes what Cubase looks like, what each window, dialog box, and panel is used for, and how you can get around in Cubase to do what you want to do. Just to make sure you understand the terminology, here's how these elements are defined:

▶ A window contains a toolbar at the top (usually) or on one side and may also have a menu bar at the top of the window. You can edit information inside a window (as with other elements). You don't need to press any buttons to accept or apply changes made to windows. When you make changes to information within a window, they are automatically updated.

▶ A dialog box appears when you want to apply a process or transformation that requires you to accept or apply this process. It is usually associated with a function, such as the Save function or a setting of some sort, such as the Metronome Setup or the Project Setup dialog box. When a dialog box is open, you most likely have to close this dialog box by accepting or denying the changes in order to do something else in your project.

▶ A panel is similar in nature to a front panel of a device. Panels have controls or fields in which you can make selections. Panels do not have any menus or toolbars and do not have any confirmation or cancel buttons. An example of this is the Send Effects panel, which allows you to select an effect, activate it, launch its Editing window, or adjust the effect's level.

In this chapter, you will:

▶ Learn the name and purpose of each window, dialog box, and panel most commonly used in Cubase SX/SL

▶ Learn how to access these windows, dialog boxes, and panels

▶ Get a sense of the different editing environments and how you can use them in your project

▶ Understand how Cubase is organized

CHAPTER 3

The Project Window

The Project window (see Figure 3.1) is your main working area. In Cubase SX/SL, you can load different projects. When you make a Project window active (bring it on top of others by clicking in it), all other project-related windows also update their content to display the settings of this active Project window. The Project window is divided into seven areas:

▶ **Toolbar**. Allows you to access the most common tools and functions used in this window, as most toolbars do. It appears on the top of the Project window, covering the width of the window.

▶ **Event information line**. Displays information on selected events. You can use it to rename these selected events or edit the event's start, end, length, and so on.

▶ **Overview**. Displays the whole project and frames the current portion of the project currently viewed. You can quickly zoom to a specific point or move your point of view using this area.

▶ **Inspector**. Gives you detailed information on a selected track. Each track has different information represented in this area, depending on the track's type.

▶ **Track list**. Displays vertically stacked tracks available in your project. Each track also displays information related to its track type (audio, MIDI, Marker, video, and so on).

▶ **Event display**. Displays events in time as well as automation lanes associated with events on tracks.

▶ **Zoom**. Allows you to view your project in different ways, focusing on a particular section, track, event or simply get an overall view of your project.

Figure 3.1
The Cubase SX/SL
Project window

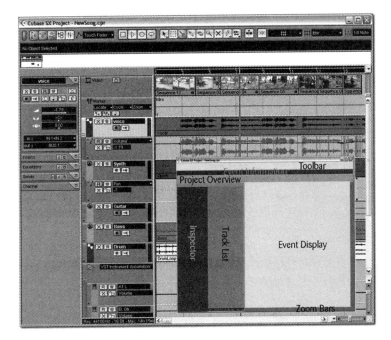

The Transport Panel

The Transport panel (shown in Figure 3.2) allows you to control different aspects of your project, such as the position of your left and right locators, punch-in and -out modes, cycle modes, playback and recording functions, as well as tempo, click, and sync functions.

To view the Transport panel:

▶ Press the F2 key on your keyboard.

▶ Or select Transport > Transport Panel from the menu bar.

Figure 3.2
The Transport panel

Metronome Setup Dialog Box

The Metronome Setup dialog box (see Figure 3.3) allows you to configure your metronome's click. A metronome click is useful mostly when recording events, but you can also use the metronome during playback to make sure the timing of your recorded performance is accurate.

To view the Metronome Setup dialog box:

▶ From the Transport panel, Ctrl-click (or Command-click on a Mac) the Click button.

▶ Or select Transport > Metronome Setup from the menu bar.

Figure 3.3
The Metronome Setup
dialog box

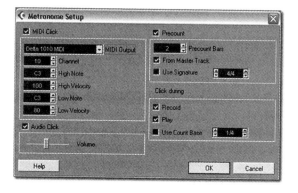

Synchronization Setup Dialog Box

If you are working with video or need to synchronize Cubase with another MIDI device, you can use the Synchronization Setup dialog box (see Figure 3.4) to properly configure Cubase. This allows you to set Cubase as the master or the slave and also allows you to echo synchronization information to various outputs and in different formats.

To view the Synchronization Setup dialog box:

▶ From the Transport panel, Ctrl-click (or Command-click on a Mac) the Sync button.

▶ Or select Transport > Sync Setup from the menu bar.

Figure 3.4
The Synchronization
Setup dialog box

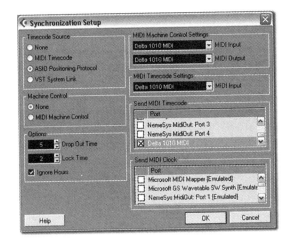

The Devices Panel

You can access many of the different windows and panels allowing you to configure devices in Cubase SX/SL through the Devices panel (see Figure 3.5). When this panel is visible, you can click on any button in the panel to access its content. The content of each panel is also described in this section.

To view the Devices panel:

▶ Select Devices > Show Panel from the menu bar.

Figure 3.5
The Devices panel

MIDI Device Manager

The MIDI Device Manager (see Figure 3.6) allows you to install or remove external MIDI devices in your setup and attach it to a specific MIDI port so that it becomes available in a MIDI track when selecting MIDI ports. It also allows you to configure the patch names for these devices so that you can change the programs on this device directly from Cubase's inspector or track list area.

To view the MIDI Device Manager window:

▶ Click the MIDI Device Manager button in the Devices panel.

▶ Select Devices > MIDI Device Manager from the menu bar.

Figure 3.6
The MIDI Device
Manager window

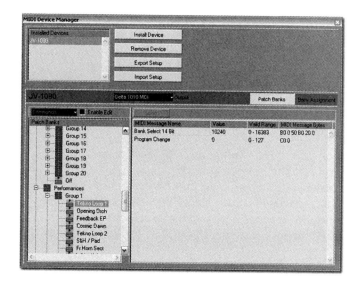

Track Mixer Window

The Track Mixer window (see Figure 3.7) is your virtual mixing console. It allows you to monitor inputs and outputs, adjust levels, assign effects or inserts, adjust the equalization, change the routing of a signal, record and play back mixing automation, as well as finalize your project's mix. Each channel in this mixer can be edited in a separate channel setting window for greater control over this channel; however, the Track Mixer allows you to see what you normally need to see when mixing your project.

To view the Track Mixer window:

▶ Press the F3 key on your keyboard.

▶ Or click the Track Mixer button in the Devices panel.

▶ Or select Devices > Track Mixer from the menu bar.

Figure 3.7
The Cubase SX Track
Mixer window

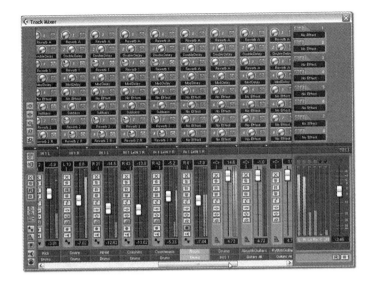

Plug-in Information Panel

Cubase supports three types of plug-ins: VST, DirectX (only on the PC version), and MIDI plug-ins. You can use the Plug-in Information panel (see Figure 3.8) to manage which plug-ins appear in your menu when selecting plug-ins for destructive processing or as a nondestructive process, such as an insert, a send effect, or a master send effect. This panel displays information about each plug-in installed on your system and also allows you to specify the folder containing your shared VST plug-ins.

To view the Plug-in Information panel:

▶   Click the Plug-in Information button in the Devices panel.

▶   Or select Devices > Plug-in Information from the menu bar.

Figure 3.8
The Plug-in Information
panel

Input Effect - TrueTape Panel

Cubase VST 5.0 introduced the TrueTape 32-bit, floating-point input effect, which allows you to simulate an analog tape saturation effect while recording. In Cubase SX (not available in Cubase SL), you can use this recording effect even though you are recording with a 16-bit compatible sound card as it encodes the information as a 16-bit file, adding floating-point information to this file in order to make it compatible with 16-bit sound cards.

To view the Input Effect - TrueTape panel (see Figure 3.9):

▶ Click the TrueTape button in the Devices panel.

▶ Or select Devices > TrueTape from the menu bar.

Figure 3.9
Cubase SX's Input Effect
- TrueTape panel

VST Inputs Panel

The VST Inputs panel (see Figure 3.10) allows you to activate/deactivate audio inputs used in your project and assign specific labels to these inputs in order to identify the inputs in this project. The number of ports displayed in this panel depends on your computer's configuration (mainly your sound card's I/O setting).

To view the VST Inputs panel:

▶ Press the F5 key on your keyboard.

▶ Or click the VST Inputs button in the Devices panel.

▶ Or select Devices > VST Inputs from the menu bar.

Figure 3.10
The VST Inputs panel

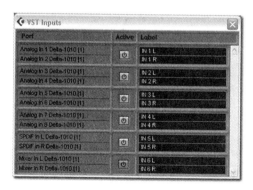

VST Instrument Panel

VST Instruments or VSTi are VST-compatible software instruments that you can load inside Cubase SX/SL. To load, edit, and manage these Virtual Instruments, you can use the VST Instruments panel (see Figure 3.11). After an instrument is loaded into memory, you can use it in a MIDI track to generate the sound produced by recorded MIDI events or record these MIDI events using these instruments in real time. Note that you can load up to thirty-two VST Instruments in the SX version and up to sixteen in the SL version.

To view the VST Instruments panel:

▶ Press the F11 key on your keyboard.

▶ Or click the VST Instruments button in the Devices panel.

▶ Or select Devices > VST Instruments from the menu bar.

Figure 3.11
The VST Instruments panel

VST Master Effects Panel

When finalizing your mix or preparing your master, you can use one of eight available VST master effects available in Cubase SX/SL. These are special effects, which will be applied to any signal routed to the master bus. To manage these plug-ins, you can use the VST Master Effects panel. In Figure 3.12, you can see this panel in a surround sound configuration available in the SX version. Notice also that the last two master effects are post fader and can be used to add dither noise shaping effects when you are converting your projects from 24- or 32-bit to a CD compatible 16-bit file.

To view the VST Master Effects panel:

▶ Press the F7 key on your keyboard.

▶ Or click the VST Master Effects button in the Devices panel.

▶ Or select Devices > VST Master Effects from the menu bar.

Figure 3.12
Cubase SX's VST Master
Effects panel

VST Master Setup Dialog Box

New to Cubase SX is the possibility to create surround mixes. To configure Cubase SX properly for this type of mix, you can use the VST Master Setup dialog box (shown in Figure 3.13), which offers a number of surround sound configurations as well as a basic stereo setup. However, to monitor the surround result, you need a multioutput sound card as well as a surround sound system. Note that surround sound mixes are not available in the SL version.

To view the VST Master Setup dialog box:

▶ Click the VST Master Setup button in the Devices panel.

▶ Or select Devices > VST Master Setup from the menu bar.

Figure 3.13
Cubase SX's VST Master
Setup dialog box

VST Outputs Window

Depending on the number of outputs available on your sound card, you can enable or disable these additional audio outputs in the VST Outputs window (shown in Figure 3.14). Note that if your sound card only has one set of stereo outputs, this is automatically assigned to the BUS 1, which is your master output and it can't be disabled for obvious reasons (well, if you need to know, if you can't hear the only output available, you won't be able to hear your project).

To view the VST Outputs window:

▶ Press the F4 key on your keyboard.

▶ Click the VST Outputs button in the Devices panel.

▶ Or select Devices > VST Outputs from the menu bar.

Figure 3.14
The VST Outputs
window

VST Performance Panel

Cubase SX/SL allows you to monitor the performance of both your CPU and your hard disk. This can be useful to measure when it's time to start creating audio tracks, which contain effects, or create submixes to reduce the load on your computer, especially when your performance indicator shows a high level of activity on a constant basis. If you hear your audio stuttering while playing back your project, take a look at the VST Performance panel (see Figure 3.15). This will probably show you if the CPU is overloaded (top bar), in which case you should unload some of the real-time processes. On the other hand, if the hard disk is overloaded (lower bar), mix down some tracks. If that doesn't work, try increasing the buffer sizes in the ASIO control panel.

To view the VST Performance panel:

▶ Press the F12 key on your keyboard.

▶ Or click the VST Performance button in the Devices panel.

▶ Or select Devices > VST Performance from the menu bar.

Figure 3.15
The VST Performance
panel

VST Send Effects Panel

You can use up to eight real-time effects in Cubase SX and five in Cubase SL through VST send effects. Typically, send effects are processes that you want to apply on more than one channel. To manage, enable, disable, route, or edit these effects, you can use the VST Send Effects panel (shown in Figure 3.16).

To view the VST Send Effects panel:

▶ Press the F6 key on your keyboard.

▶ Or click the VST Send Effects button in the Devices panel.

▶ Or select Devices > VST Send Effects from the menu bar.

Figure 3.16
The VST Send Effects
panel

Video Display Window

When working on multimedia projects or film projects, you can load a QuickTime, AVI (PC only), or MPEG file into your Cubase SX/SL project file. When you import a video file into a project, you should create a video track, place the video file on this track, and the Video Display window should open automatically. However, sometimes you might want to regain access to your desktop's real estate, so knowing how to quickly enable or disable your Video Display window might come in handy.

To view the Video Display window (see Figure 3.17):

▶ Press the F8 key on your keyboard.

▶ Or click the Video button in the Devices panel.

▶ Or select Devices > Video from the menu bar.

Figure 3.17
The Video Display
window

The Project Tools

The project tools are special windows and dialog boxes in which you will find information about settings that affect your entire project, such as sampling format, project tempo, time signature, and Markers, as well as events found in an active project.

Marker Window

Markers and Regions (called cycle markers in Cubase) allow you to identify certain points in your projects, which can be used to easily navigate throughout your project. For example, you can create cycle markers (or Regions) for your chorus, verse, and bridge, and create regular Markers at other places in your project. Each time you create a Marker, it is added to your Marker window, allowing you to go directly to that location using keyboard shortcuts or by selecting it in the Marker track. Also, using cycle markers allows you to zoom in quickly to this 'region' in your project.

To view the Marker window (see Figure 3.18):

▶ Press Ctrl+M (Command+M on Mac) on your keyboard.

▶ Or select Project > Markers from the menu bar.

Figure 3.18
The Marker window

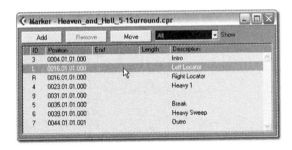

Tempo Track

During the course of your project, you might want to create tempo changes or add meter changes. These changes are stored in a special tempo track (shown in Figure 3.19), which is not visible in your main Project window. However, to access this information, make changes to it, or add values, you need to open the Tempo Track window. After you add information to this window, you need to make sure that the Master button found on the Transport panel is active or you won't hear the tempo changes made in this track. Cubase will, on the other hand, change meter values (time signature) as this information is necessary to properly divide the project in the correct number of bars and beats.

To view the Tempo Track window:

▶ Press Ctrl+T (Command+T on Mac) on your keyboard.

▶ Or Ctrl-click (Command-click on Mac) the Master button found on the Transport panel.

▶ Or select Project > Tempo Track from the menu bar.

Figure 3.19
The Tempo Track
window

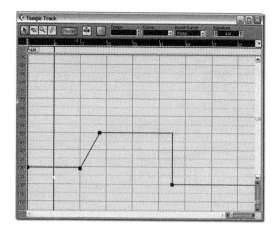

Browse Project Window

If you want to look at all the events found in your project, organized by type of events, the best way to do this is through the Browse Project window (shown in Figure 3.20). Unlike the Audio Pool or the List Editor, this window allows you to view all the events, including MIDI and automation events, Markers, tempo, and time signature changes.

To view the Browse Project window:

▶ Press Ctrl+B (Command+B on Mac) on your keyboard.

▶ Or select Project > Browser from the menu bar.

Figure 3.20
The Browse Project
window

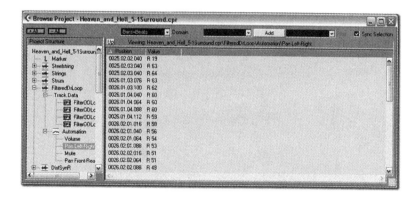

Beat Calculator Window

The Beat Calculator (see Figure 3.21) utility allows you to tap in a tempo, which usually corresponds to the tempo you have in mind for a project, or tap the tempo of an audio file playing in the background to determine the tempo at which the project should be set. This tool can extrapolate the actual tempo and add it to your project, making it easy to determine the correct tempo changes or the speed of a loop, for example.

To view the Beat Calculator window:

▶ Select Project > Beat Calculator from the menu bar.

Figure 3.21
The Beat Calculator
window

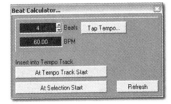

Project Setup Dialog Box

When you begin a new project, you should use the Project Setup dialog box (shown in Figure 3.22) to set the sample rate, bit depth, and the digital audio recording's file type, as well as select the proper display format corresponding to your preference for this project.

To view the Project Setup dialog box:

▶ Press Shift+S on your keyboard.

▶ Or select Project > Project Setup from the menu bar.

Figure 3.22
The Project Setup dialog
box

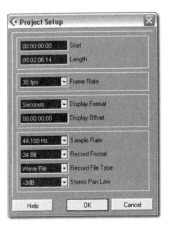

MIDI Editing Windows

Cubase offers different editing environments for MIDI events depending on the type of MIDI events you want to edit. For example, if a track contains melodic or harmonic content, you can use the MIDI editor known as the Key Editor. On the other hand, if the events you want to edit are percussion or drum based, you can use the Drum Editor, which makes it easier for you to associate pitch values to actual percussive instrument names.

Key Editor

The Key Editor (see Figure 3.23) is probably the best-known editing environment for MIDI events, allowing you to modify not only note events, but also MIDI channel messages, such as velocity, Aftertouch, pitch bend, or control change messages. To use the Key Editor, you need to select a MIDI part in the Project window—otherwise, the Key Editor is not available. You can also edit multiple parts simultaneously in the same Key Editor window.

To view the Key Editor window:

▶ Select a MIDI part in the Project window and press Ctrl+E (Command+E on a Mac).

▶ Or double-click on a MIDI part in the Project window.

▶ Or select a part in the Project window, and then select MIDI > Open Key Editor from the menu bar.

Figure 3.23
The Key Editor window

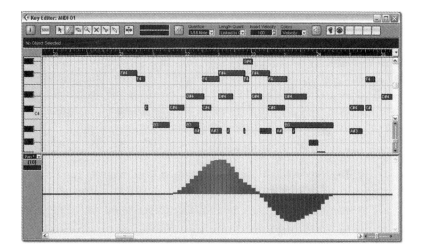

Quantize Setup Panel

Quantizing allows you to match recorded MIDI events to a predefined grid to add rhythmic precision to the recording. You can also use quantizing creatively, adding a swing feeling to a straight MIDI recording for example. The Quantize Setup panel (see Figure 3.24) allows you to configure how quantizing will be applied to the selected MIDI events or parts. You can later save quantization settings to use them in other projects.

To view the Quantize Setup panel:

▶ Select MIDI > Quantize Setup from the menu bar.

▶ Or, from within any MIDI editing window, including the Project window, select the Setup option at the bottom of the Quantize drop-down menu.

Figure 3.24
The Quantize Setup
panel

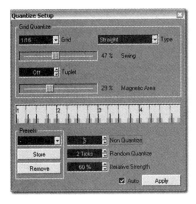

Drum Editor

The Drum Editor, as with the Key Editor, allows you to edit MIDI events; however, in this case, the editor is designed to handle percussions and drum maps. Most drum sounds are short by nature and usually drum patches are laid across a keyboard range, each key playing a different instrument. Drum maps are used to identify each note value (see Figure 3.25). This particularity is well-addressed in the Drum Editor. The lengths of events are not displayed in this editing environment as they are not relevant to editing; however, instrument names are associated to each pitch value to make editing a specific instrument easier.

To view the Drum Editor window:

▶ Select a part associated with a drum map in the Project window and press Ctrl+E (Command+E on a Mac).

▶ Or double-click on a MIDI part associated with a drum map in the Project window.

▶ Or select a part in the Project window, and then select MIDI > Open Drum Editor from the menu bar.

Figure 3.25
The Drum Editor
window

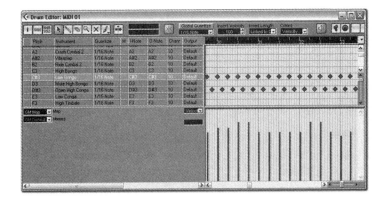

Drum Map Setup Dialog Box

A drum map is a list of percussive instruments associated with pitch values in a MIDI-based rhythmic part or track. You can choose from a list of ready-made drum maps or create your own custom drum maps. The Drum Map Setup dialog box (shown in Figure 3.26) allows you to manage these maps.

To view the Drum Map Setup dialog box:

▶ From the Inspector panel of a MIDI track, select Drum Map Setup from the Drum Map field's drop-down menu.

▶ Or, inside the drum editor, select Drum Map Setup from the Drum Map field's drop-down menu found in the lower-left portion of the window.

▶ Or select MIDI > Open Drum Map Setup from the menu bar.

Figure 3.26
The Drum Map Setup
dialog box

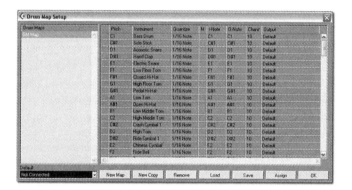

List Editor

The List Editor (shown in Figure 3.27) is another MIDI environment that displays MIDI events in a table (list) format for numerical editing. This list, however, is limited to editing MIDI events. If you want to view any type of events, you may also use the Browse Project window (see Figure 3.20).

To view the List Editor window:

▶ Select a MIDI part in the Project window and press Ctrl+G (Command+G on a Mac).

▶ Or select a part in the Project window, and then select MIDI > Open List Editor from the menu bar.

CHAPTER 3

Figure 3.27
The List Editor window

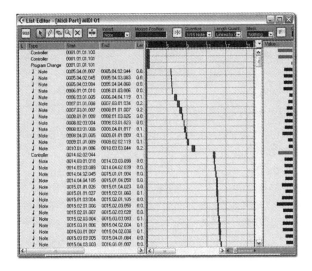

Score Editor

The Score Editor (shown in Figure 3.28), available in the Cubase SX version only, is for musicians who want to convert MIDI events into musical notation, printing the final result on paper for safe keeping or to use in a studio session with live musicians. With the scoring functions, you can create complete scores and individual music sheets for individual musicians. Note that score editing only works with MIDI events, not audio events.

To view the Score Editor window:

▶ Select a MIDI part (or parts) in the Project window and press Ctrl+R (Command+R on a Mac).

▶ Or select a part (or parts) in the Project window, and then select MIDI > Open Score Editor from the menu bar.

Figure 3.28
The Score Editor window

Audio Editing Windows

Because audio and MIDI are two very different types of events, it is normal to see that audio gets its own set of editing tools and windows to manipulate, transform, and process these events. For Cubase veterans, you will find that many of these windows appear similar to previous versions of Cubase; however, Steinberg has added some new features and simplified many tasks involved in audio editing.

Media Pool Window

The Media Pool (see Figure 3.29), previously called the Audio Pool, allows you to see the audio and video files and their associated Regions used in your current project. This window allows you to manage your files, import or export media files, or monitor file use. It also displays file and Region information as well as a graphic representation of these files and Regions.

To view the Media Pool window:

▶ Press Ctrl+P (Command+P on a Mac).

▶ Or select Project > Pool from the menu bar.

Figure 3.29
The Media Pool window

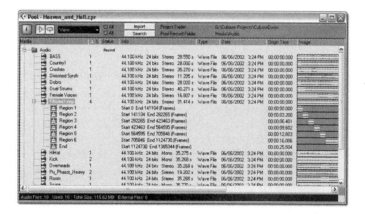

Audio Part Editor

On an audio track, you can have audio parts and audio events. An audio event is a single instance or reference to a file that is self-contained on this track. However, an audio part is a container that can hold several audio events or audio Regions. By default, editing these audio parts is done in the Audio Part Editor window (see Figure 3.30). Here, you can move the audio events the part holds in time, create fades or crossfades between events, and quantize audio events to a quantize grid setting. You can also modify audio events and create new Regions in the Audio Part Editor, which appear in the Media Pool.

CHAPTER 3

To view the Audio Part Editor window:

▶ Select an audio part (or parts) in the Project window and press Ctrl+E (Command+E on a Mac).

▶ Or double-click on an audio part in the Project window.

Figure 3.30
The Audio Part Editor window

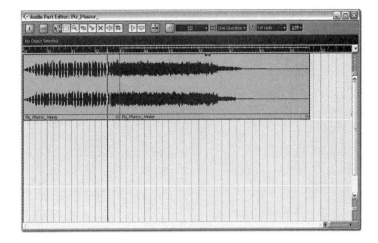

Fade Editor

When working on audio events or parts in the Project window or in the Audio Part Editor, you can use fade envelopes at the beginning or at the end of this event or part to create a fade in or a fade out. This process actually creates an additional audio segment on your hard disk, which contains the actual fade content. By creating an additional audio segment, it allows you to safely create volume changes to the audio file without modifying the original content. You can't, however, create a fade envelope within the Sample Editor and if an audio part in the Project window contains more than one audio event or Region, you need to open this part in the Audio Part Editor to access the fade envelopes before you can access the Fade Editor. How to do this is explained in Chapter 9. The Fade Editor (see Figure 3.31) allows you to choose the type of curve you want to apply to the fade itself.

Figure 3.31
The Fade Out dialog box

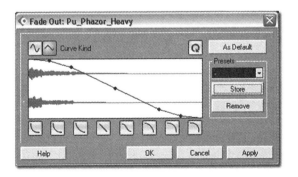

Crossfade Editor

The Crossfade Editor is similar to the Fade Editor in the sense that you can apply fade envelopes to audio events in an audio part. In this case, however, the fade occurs between two overlapping audio events, hence the term crossfade. As with the Fade Editor, you can't create crossfades in the Sample Editor, nor can you create crossfades between two audio parts that contain several audio events embedded into them. You need to access the events from within the Audio Part Editor and open the Crossfade Editor from there. The Crossfade Editor (see Figure 3.32) allows you to select the type of fade out and fade in curves you want to use in the crossfade. How to use the Crossfade Editor is explained in Chapter 9.

Figure 3.32
The Crossfade dialog box

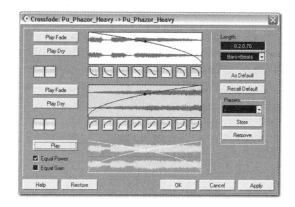

Sample Editor

The Sample Editor (shown in Figure 3.33) allows you to edit your audio file (called audio clip in Cubase SX/SL), process it, and create Regions or hitpoints that can be compared to audio Markers. Hitpoints allow you to slice up your audio file (clip) into Regions corresponding to specific audio elements, such as a kick, a snare, or a crash in a drum loop. You can later quantize these audio slices without affecting the pitch or quality of the audio file. You can also use the Sample Editor to apply destructive editing to your file. Although Steinberg tells us this is nondestructive editing, due to the fact that you can undo any editing you do to a file using the Offline Process History dialog box, it is nevertheless possible to edit the source audio file or clip, and in that respect it is considered destructive editing. So be careful and read the message boxes when they appear on-screen to make sure you don't overwrite your original audio file. This said, with the Offline Process History dialog box, it is possible to revert the file to its original format at any time.

To view the Sample Editor window:

▶ Select an audio clip (file) or audio event in the Audio Part Editor and press Ctrl+E (Command+E on a Mac).

▶ Or double-click on an audio clip (file) or audio event in the Audio Part Editor.

▶ Select an audio clip (file) or audio Region in the Media Pool and press Ctrl+E (Command+E on a Mac).

▶ Or double-click on an audio clip (file) or audio Region in the Media Pool.

CHAPTER 3

Figure 3.33
The Sample Editor
window

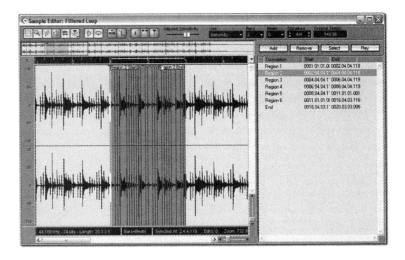

Spectrum Analyzer

The Spectrum Analyzer (shown in Figure 3.34) is a tool available only in the Cubase SX version that provides information about a selected audio event's average amplitude level over a frequency range. This can be useful to pinpoint frequencies that need to be equalized, for example. The Spectrum Analyzer displays this information in an X/Y, two-dimensional graphic, where the X axis represents frequencies and the Y axis represents amplitude values.

To view the Spectrum Analyzer dialog box:

1. Select an audio clip (file) or audio event in the Audio Part Editor or in the Media Pool.

2. Select Audio > Spectrum Analyzer from the menu bar.

3. Adjust the settings or leave as is and click Process.

Figure 3.34
Cubase SX's Spectrum
Analyzer dialog box

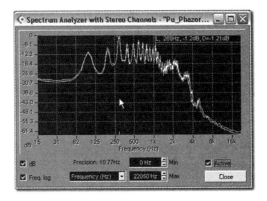

VST Effects and Instruments

Steinberg introduced VST (Virtual Studio Technology) in 1996, allowing Cubase users to include virtual effect processing in their projects, such as equalizers, compressors, and so on, to audio tracks. In 1999, they introduced VST Instruments, which allows Cubase users to insert software synthesizers as sound modules inside the Cubase environment. Cubase SX/SL supports previous VST effects and offers a few new effects bundled with the software.

For example, the new DaTube (see Figure 3.35) VST effect allows you to simulate the effect a tube amplifier provides, adding warmth to an audio channel, either as a send effect or a channel insert. Another new VST effect is the StepFilter (see Figure 3.36). This effect is a pattern-controlled filter that can create rhythmic or pulsating filter effects depending on the filter's settings.

Figure 3.35
The DaTube VST effect processor

Figure 3.36
The StepFilter VST effect processor

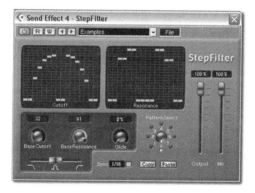

Steinberg also redesigned the VB-1 virtual bass instrument and added the A1 synthesizer (see Figure 3.37), which simulates a two-oscillator polyphonic analog synthesizer. You can add this VSTi (VST Instrument) to a MIDI track's MIDI output port and use a keyboard controller to play the instrument as if it were a sound module in your MIDI track. You can also automate the instrument's parameters just like you can automate VST effect parameters.

Figure 3.37
The A1 VST Instrument

4

Navigating the Project Window

Now that you have Cubase installed and running correctly, it's time to delve into using it. The heart of Cubase is the Project window, which is the main window that appears when you create a new file or launch Cubase. Understanding how the Project window works and what you can do in it is crucial to your work in Cubase—that's why we are going to spend an entire chapter making sure you understand all the nuances associated with it. Anything you do outside this window (but inside Cubase) is always reflected in some way in the Project window. These changes might not appear at first glance, but they certainly affect the project's behavior. For example, if you delete a clip in another window, such as the Media Pool, it shows up in the Project window if the audio clip you deleted in the pool is used in the project. If you change a MIDI channel, that change is reflected in the Project window. It is your main working area.

In this chapter, you will:

- ▶ Learn how to create a new project and configure it for your needs
- ▶ Discover what you can do with the toolbar buttons
- ▶ Understand the different areas in the Project window and how to use them
- ▶ Find out what Markers are and how to use them
- ▶ Learn how to use the Transport panel
- ▶ Understand the Master track
- ▶ Find troubleshooting tips when you have problems with MIDI
- ▶ Discover the Project window's context menus

Creating a New Project

Projects in Cubase SX are the equivalent to documents in Word, Photoshop documents in Adobe's Photoshop, or any other software-specific file format. A project holds all the information needed to re-create the work you have done once you reopen this file, with the exception of media files, which are saved as separate entities on your hard disk and referred to by the project file.

For Cubase VST users, notice that this is a bit different because there are no longer any distinctions between arrangement files and song files. In theory, you can have as many projects opened inside Cubase as you want; however, in practice, your system's resources will most likely dictate how many projects you can simultaneously load into memory. When you have more than one Project window opened inside Cubase, you can drag events from one project to another.

When you launch Cubase, it prompts you to select a new project template (see Figure 4.1) if this is your first time or it asks if you want to open an existing project (see Figure 4.2). Templates are simply project files that were saved as templates inside the Cubase SX program folder. We will look at creating templates in Appendix D.

Figure 4.1
The New Project dialog box, where you select the template you want to use

Figure 4.2
The Cubase SX Open Document options dialog box

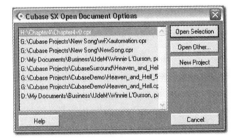

Let's start by creating a new project.

To create a new project:

1. If Cubase prompts you to open an existing document (see Figure 4.2), click the New Project button. Otherwise, you see the New Project dialog box (see Figure 4.1).

2. In the New Project dialog box, select Empty to select an empty project.

3. Click OK. Cubase then prompts you to select a folder. This should be the location where you want to save your project file. Cubase automatically creates subfolders to store audio, image, and fade files inside this folder.

4. For this exercise, select a drive and create a new folder by clicking the Create button (shown in Figure 4.3).

5. In the dialog box, enter the folder name "Chapter 4" and click OK.

6. Click OK once again with the newly created folder selected.

Figure 4.3
The Select directory dialog box allows you to choose an existing folder or create a new one for your new project

Cubase creates an empty project. One thing you should keep in mind is that each project file should be saved in its own folder and setting up your project should take place BEFORE you start working in it rather than after. So, let's set our project up.

Setting Up Your Project

Each project is saved as a CPR file, which is short for Cubase PRoject file. Inside this project file, you can have a number of MIDI, audio, or video event references, as well as automation, effect, and VST Instrument settings. Note that audio or video events are not saved with the project file. References to these media files are kept inside the project file, so when you load the project file later, it finds the media files where you left them. For example, if you delete the folder containing the audio files used in a project file, you can no longer use this audio in your project and Cubase warns you that it could not load certain audio (or video) files.

As for the project settings, they refer to four groups of settings: the duration of the project, the frame rate when working with video, the display format and its display offset value, and the digital audio recording settings.

To set up your project:

1. Press Shift+S (or Project > Project Setup) to open the Project Setup dialog box (see Figure 3.22 in Chapter 3 for a complete image of the Project Setup dialog box).

2. Leave the Start field at its default setting. If you want your project to start at a different time than zero hour, zero minute, zero second, and zero frame, you can enter the proper value in this field. This simply adds the value you enter to the time displayed in your project.

3. In the Length field, click the minute value and enter 01, or if you have a mouse with a scroll wheel, you can scroll forward to increase the value (see Figure 4.4).

Figure 4.4
Increasing the values in a field using a mouse with a scroll wheel

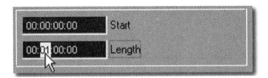

4. If you are working with a video file or synchronizing to an external time code provided by a video tape, you can set the Frame Rate field to the corresponding value of the frame rate of the video or time code format of the external sync signal. This ensures that the time displayed in Cubase in time code format corresponds to the time code format with which it is synchronizing. For now, leave this as is, because you will not work with video in this project.

5. In the Display Format, select Bars+Beats from the drop-down menu. This determines how time is displayed in your project. You can change this later while working in your project.

6. Leave the Display Offset value at its default value. If you are synchronizing your project to an external video that starts at a frame other than zero—for example, if your tape starts at 01:59:45:00—you might still want your project to start at the position 00:00:00:00. In this case, set the Display Offset value at 01:59:45:00 for your start position (00:00:00:00) to correspond to this time.

7. Set the Sample Rate field to 44.100 Hz (see Figure 4.5). After you set a sample rate for your project, you cannot change it later because all the sounds in your project have to be at this sample rate. If you want to import audio files that use a different sample rate, you will need to resample them at the current project's sample rate in order for these files to play correctly in your project.

Figure 4.5
The digital audio project
recording preference
settings

8. In the Record Format field, select 16-bit from the drop-down menu. You may
    select another format if your sound card supports 24-bit recording. Unlike the
    sample rate, you can import or record audio files with different bit rates in a single
    project. However, the record format selected here determines the number of bits
    each sample will use when recording digital audio information in this project.

9. From the Record File Type field, select Broadcast Wave file format. This format
    is identical to the Wave format with one exception: It allows you to enter text
    strings that will be embedded in your audio files. These text strings can contain
    information about you or your project, for example. By using this file type, you
    don't have to enter this information later because it will be done automatically.
    We look at how you can enter this information shortly.

10. In the Stereo Pan Law field, select –3 dB from the drop-down menu. When
    panning a channel, you want the left, center, and right pan position to sound
    equally loud. Selecting a –3 dB setting or –6 dB setting ensures this. Otherwise,
    selecting the 0 dB setting causes the center pan position of a channel to sound
    louder. If this is what you want to achieve, then you can select this setting for a
    subsequent project.

11. Click OK.

Now that your project properties are set up, let's enter the information that will be embedded in
the digital audio recording when using the Broadcast Wave file format as mentioned in Step 9.

To enter information that will be embedded in Broadcast Wave files:

1. Select File > Preferences from the menu bar.

2. Under Audio, select Broadcast Wave. The Audio-Broadcast Wave panel appears
    in the right portion of the dialog box (see Figure 4.6). In this panel, you should
    see three fields: Description, Author, and Reference.

3. Enter any information you want in these fields. Remember that this information
    will be embedded in the audio files. This is a convenient way add your personal
    information to recordings that belong to you.

4. Click Apply, and then click OK.

Figure 4.6
The Audio-Broadcast
Wave panel in the
Preferences dialog box

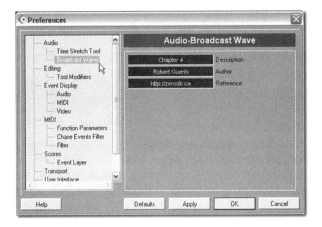

Project Window Options

Now that you have created a new project, set its properties, and entered some text information
that will be added to recorded audio files, let's take a closer look at the Project window. In
Figure 4.7, you can find a quick reference to all the components included in this Project window.

Figure 4.7
The Project window's multiple areas, tools, buttons, and shortcuts

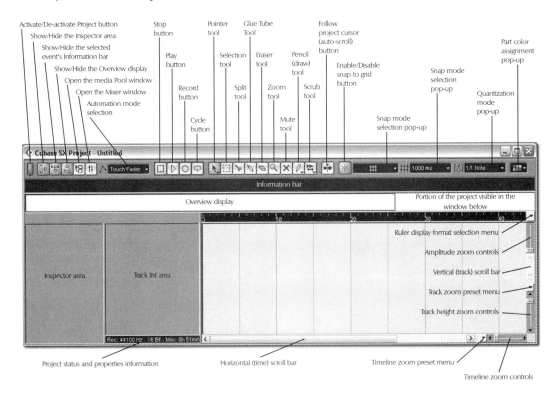

The rectangular button found in the upper-left corner of the Project window is the active project indicator. Because you can have more than one project opened at the same time, the project for which this button is red indicates that it is the active project. It is very important when working with different Project windows that you do not save a project while it is not active, especially if you are using an early version of Cubase SX (in which case you should consider getting the latest update). As Figure 4.8 illustrates, you could have an inactive window on top of an active window.

Figure 4.8
Active and inactive
Project windows inside
Cubase

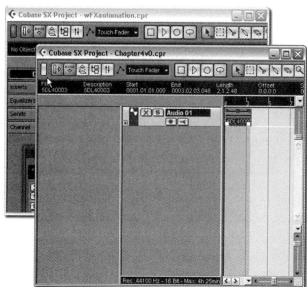

Project Window Display Buttons

The display buttons found in the upper-left corner of the Project window (shown in Figure 4.9) allow you to quickly display or hide certain areas of the Project window or open different windows easily from the Project window.

Figure 4.9
The Project window
display option buttons

> ▶ **Show/Hide Inspector**. Allows you to view the Inspector area of a selected track. The Inspector area displays information on the track's settings. Each type of track displays information relating to its particular type.

> ▶ **Show/Hide Event Information bar**. Allows you to see information for a selected part in the upper portion of the Project window. You can use this area to modify this information.

▶ **Show/Hide Overview**. Displays or hides your entire project, spanning from the left to the right of your Project window. The current visible portion of your project is displayed by a blue outline in the Overview bar. You can use the overview to quickly jump to another section of your project or to zoom to a Region in this project.

▶ **Open Pool Window**. Allows you to quickly open the project's Media Pool window.

▶ **Open Mixer Window**. Allows you to quickly open the project's Mixer window.

Project Cursor Selection Buttons

In the middle of the Project window, you will find a series of buttons, which are shortcuts to cursor tools (see Figure 4.10) that you can also find by right-clicking anywhere inside the Project window. These buttons are new to Cubase SX/SL; however, most of their functions are similar to the tools found in Cubase VST's right-click toolbox.

Figure 4.10
The Project window cursor tool selection buttons

▶ **Object Selection and Sizing tool**. Allows you to select parts by clicking on a part or by clicking and dragging a selection box over several parts when using the tool in Normal Sizing mode. The small arrow on the bottom-right corner of the button indicates that there are different modes to this tool. In fact, there are three sizing modes available (see Figure 4.11): Normal Sizing allows you to resize a part's start or end position, Sizing Moves Contents allows you to resize the start or end position but moves the content inside the part in the direction of your resize, and Sizing Applies Time Stretch time-stretches the events inside a part to correspond to the new size of the part. These modes are discussed further in Chapter 9. The Object Selection and Sizing tool is the default tool in Cubase.

Figure 4.11
From top to bottom, the three sizing modes: Normal Sizing, Sizing Moves Content, and Sizing Applies Time Stretch

▶ **Range Selection tool**. Allows you to click and drag over multiple tracks and multiple parts and then apply different range-specific editing processes, such as delete, cut, insert, or crop, to the selected range. These editing functions are also discussed in Chapter 9.

▶ **Split tool**. Allows you to split a selected part or parts anywhere depending on the grid selection setup.

▶ **Glue Tube tool**. Allows you to join an event or a part to the next event or part in the same track, creating either a continuous event (if you use the Glue Tube tool after splitting an event in two) or a continuous part containing two events (if you either glue two nonconsecutive events or two parts together).

▶ **Eraser tool**. Allows you to erase an event or a part from a track, or multiple parts or events if more than one is selected.

▶ **Zoom tool**. Allows you to zoom in to your project by dragging a selection box around the area you want to view more closely or simply click to zoom in one step closer. You can also zoom out by Alt-clicking or by double-clicking to move back a step.

▶ **Mute tool**. Allows you to mute an event or a part on a track, or multiple parts or events if more than one is selected. This is an alternative to erasing a part or an event. Muted events are not heard during playback; however, they can be unmuted later. If you need to mute all the parts or events on a track, you should use the Track Mute button, which is discussed later in this chapter.

▶ **Pencil tool**. Offers different operation modes (see Figure 4.12). The Draw mode allows you to draw in a part on a track or a series of automation points. The Line mode allows you to add automation by creating a line between two points. The Parabola, Sine, Triangle, and Square modes allow you to create different types of automations, creating automation points that re-create the shape of the selected mode. For example, using the Pencil tool in Sine mode to add automation on a pan creates a panning automation shaped like a sine wave. These editing modes are also discussed in Chapter 9.

Figure 4.12
The Pencil tool's six modes from top to bottom: Draw, Line, Parabola, Sine, Triangle, and Square

▶ **Scrub tool**. Offers two modes from which to choose. The Scrub mode allows you to drag your cursor back and forth over an audio event or part to monitor the audio in the direction and speed your mouse is moving. Or you can choose the Play mode, which allows you to listen to an audio event or part from the point at which you click until the moment you release the mouse (see Figure 4.13).

CHAPTER 4

Figure 4.13
The Scrub tool's two
scrub modes from top to
bottom: Scrub and Play

Project Transport Control Buttons

In Cubase SX/SL, there are two sets of transport controls. The Project window itself holds the basic Stop, Play, Record, and Cycle mode toggle buttons in the window's toolbar (see Figure 4.14) and the Transport panel offers a more complete set of transport controls (which are discussed later in this chapter). However, the Transport panel is a floating panel, and for space ergonomics purposes, it is possible to hide the Transport panel and use the Project window's transport controls if you want to do so.

Figure 4.14
The Project window's
transport control
buttons: Stop, Play,
Record, and Cycle
mode selections

Another button related to transport is the Auto-Scroll button found to the right of the Scrub tool (see Figure 4.15). This button when active (blue state) follows the position of the play line in time as the project moves forward, refreshing your display every time the play line moves past the right edge of the window. If you do not want this to occur, you can deactivate the Auto-Scroll function.

Figure 4.15
The Auto-Scroll or in its
active state

Project Editing Setup Buttons

When working on a project, you will be recording and editing events, parts, and clips in tracks. Moving events around is a task that you will probably do quite often. Determining exactly where you want to move the event is your decision, but helping you in determining the accuracy of this movement is Cubase's task. This is done through a magnetic grid. How this grid works depends on different aspects.

On the Project window's toolbar, to the right of the Auto-Scroll button, are the quantize and snap controls: the Enable/Disable Snap button, the Snap Mode selection field, the Grid Mode selection field and the Quantize selection field. When the Snap to Grid button is enabled, it uses the Snap mode in the field to the right to determine what becomes magnetic. Cubase offers seven such Snap modes:

▶ **Grid**. A grid is defined by the Grid mode setting found in the field to the right of the Snap mode. In Figure 4.16, the Grid mode is set to Use Quantize, which means it will use the value set in the Quantize selection field to determine how the grid will react. In the same figure, the Quantize selection is set to 1/8 Note. In other words, an eight-note magnetic grid will be available when the Grid mode is selected. If, on the other hand, your project displays time values rather than bars and beats, increments of milliseconds are displayed rather than note subdivision values.

Figure 4.16
The project window's
quantize and snap
controls.

▶ **Events**. The start and end of parts or events as well as Markers on Marker tracks become magnetized. So, when you move a part, it snaps to the previous or next event as you move closer to it.

▶ **Shuffle**. This allows you to move events or parts that are adjacent to other parts by switching places with them. In Figure 4.17, the top two tracks are before and after shuffle examples with two consecutive parts. The lower two tracks are before and after shuffle examples with four consecutive parts. As you can see, the Part 01 is the part being shuffled around in both examples.

Figure 4.17
Using the grid in
Shuffle mode

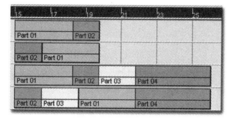

▶ **Magnetic cursor**. When this snap mode is active, the project cursor or play line becomes magnetic. Moving an event or a part close to it causes the part to snap to the cursor's position.

The other snap modes are combinations of these four previous modes:

▶ **Grid + Cursor**. The grid and cursor become magnetized when moving events or parts.

▶ **Events + Cursor**. The events (or parts) and cursor become magnetized when moving events or parts.

▶ **Events + Grid + Cursor**. The events (or parts), the grid, and cursor become magnetized when moving events or parts.

The Grid Mode setting field to the right of the Snap mode field allows you to set a value that determines how far apart each vertical time lines in the grid will be magnetized. These values vary depending on the project's timeline display

▶ If the time is displayed in bars and beats, the grid displays a choice of bars, beats, or quantize value.

▶ If the time is displayed in seconds, the grid displays a choice of millisecond increments.

▶ If the time is displayed in frames, the grid displays a choice of sub-frame, frame, or second increments.

▶ If the time is displayed in samples, the grid displays a choice of sample increments.

When using a bars and beats display along with a Grid mode that uses the quantize value as its setting to determine which values are magnetized, you can select the quantize value in the Quantize settings field to the right of the Grid Mode settings field.

QUANTIZE VALUES

Quantize values divide each bar in fractions equivalent to a note value. Typically, a 1/4 quantize value indicates that there is a grid line at every quarter note. There are three groups of quantize value fractions: normal, tuplet, and dotted. The normal fractions (1/2, 1/4, 1/8, 1/16, and so on) represent note values that can be divided by two. For example, there can be four-quarter notes in each 4/4 bar, eight-eight notes per 4/4 bar, and sixteen-sixteenth notes per 4/4 bar. Tuplet usually means that you can play an uneven number of notes in an even number of non-tuplet note values. For example, a 1/4 T value means that you can have three times 1/4 T notes during the same time equivalent to two regular 1/4 notes. You could also have five times 1/16 T notes during the equivalent time it takes to play four regular 1/16 notes. A dotted quantize value represents one and a half normal quantize value. For example, three quarter notes are equal to two dotted quarter notes.

In Cubase, these quantize value differences are indicated with a T for tuplets, following the quantize value and a D for dotted, also following the quantize value. In Figure 4.18, a piano roll example of different quantizing values shows the different lengths and proportions each note (and silence) takes when changing the quantize value's grid.

Figure 4.18
Example of quantize value lengths and grid size in a 4/4 bar

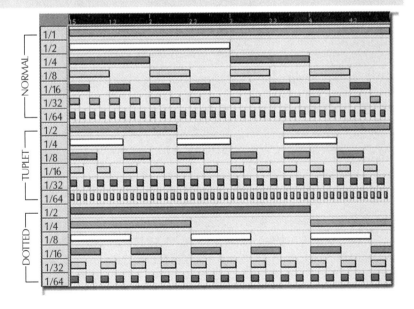

Adding Colors to Parts

Figure 4.19 shows you a simple little option that lets you define colors for each part in the Arrange window's Edit Display area by clicking on the Part Colors option. If this item is checked, the files and segments are displayed with the colors of their respective parts. You can click on a part or select a track, then use one of the colors in the Part Colors option to apply it to your selection. Although adding colors to parts might help you in organizing your events on tracks, they do not add anything to the events because they are merely visual references.

Figure 4.19
The Part Color drop-
down menu

This option can be very useful when working with many tracks. You can group tracks by color or assign a name to each color so that you know what is what later on. For example, your rhythm section can be different shades of green, your wind section different shades of blue, and so on.

To create your own custom colors and associated color names:

1.   Click the Select Colors option at the bottom of the Part Colors option drop-down menu.

2.   Select a color to edit in the Part Colors area.

3.   Type in a new name for that color, as shown in Figure 4.20.

4.   If you want to change the default color, change the color using the color picker options. For example, you can click in the color next to the name for the part you just entered, and then click inside a standard color swatch above. When you click on the Apply button, the selected color will be added to your part. You can also create custom colors by clicking in the Modify Color wheel or by entering values in the field below this wheel. Remember to select your part's color swatch first, choose a color, then apply it.

5.   Repeat the previous steps for another color if you want to create more custom colors and associated names.

6.   Click OK when you are done.

Now that you have created custom colors and names associated with these colors, you can apply these colors to events and parts in your project.

Figure 4.20
You can customize colors and add names to reflect what each color should represent in the Event Colors Setup dialog box

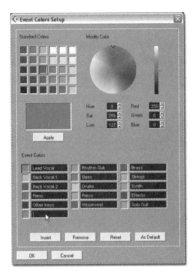

To assign a color to parts and events:

1. In the Project window, select the part(s) or event(s) for which you want to assign a color.

2. Select one of the colors from the Events Colors drop-down menu.

Setting Up a Quantize Grid

We've discussed how quantize grids work and looked at how you can magnetize this grid using the snap, snap mode, grid mode and quantize settings, giving different elements a magnetic quality when moving events in your Project window. In fact, a quantize grid serves not only for moving events but also influences how parts are created and where Markers will be placed. In other words, setting up an appropriate grid before you start working helps you get the result you want more effectively. For example, if you enable the Snap function in Grid mode setting this grid to Bars, the next time you create a new part using the Draw tool or record an event, the newly created part or recorded event will start at the closest bar from its beginning and end at the closest bar after you stop recording or release the Draw tool. In such an example, you can only create parts or events that increase in length by one bar at a time.

To enable and configure a Snap and Quantize settings:

1. Enable the Snap mode by clicking the Snap button.

2. Select the appropriate Snap mode setting. For example, select Grid.

3. Select the appropriate Grid mode setting. For example, if you chose Grid, you could select Bar, Beats, or Use Quantize.

4. If you chose the Use Quantize option in the Quantize Setting field, select an appropriate quantize value you want to use as your magnetic grid; otherwise, your grid setting is complete.

If you choose snap to events, shuffle, or magnetic cursor rather than grid, the quantize value has no effect when you resize or move events.

Working With Markers

Markers are used to define different sections or locations in your project and make it easy to go back to that section or location later in your work. There are three types of Markers in Cubase SX/SL:

▶ The left and right locators are special cycle markers identified by L and R in the Marker track. These locators are used to determine the start and end locations when playing in cycle mode. They also play the role of a punch-in and punch-out location during recording. You can quickly move your play line to the position of the left and right locators using the numbers 1 and 2 respectively on your numeric keypad.

▶ Cycle markers are similar to the left and right locators as they identify the beginning and ending of a range or section in your song. After you create cycle markers, you can quickly move your left and right locators to the position of a cycle marker by double-clicking on it. Cycle markers are identified by numbers within brackets ([1]) in the Marker track's Inspector area or in the Marker window.

▶ Markers identify a single position in your project and they are identified by numbers (without brackets) in the track's Inspector area or in the Marker window. You can quickly move your play line to the position of the first six Markers using the numbers 3 to 9 on your numeric keypad.

The locators are always present in your project; however, it is easier when a Marker track is present in your project when you want to use Markers and cycle markers. This said, you don't have to create a Marker track, but if you want to see where your Markers are without consulting the Marker window, you need to create this Marker track.

To create a Marker track:

1. Right-click (or control-click on a one-button mouse) in the Track List area.
2. From the context menu, select Add Marker Track.

A Marker track appears in your project. If you want to bring this Marker track above the other tracks to quickly find your Markers, you may click in the Marker track's List area and drag the track to the desired position in the same Track List area (above or below the current location).

To manage and view your Markers, you can use either the Inspector area of the Marker track or bring up the Marker window (Ctrl+M or Command+M on a Mac), as shown in Figure 4.21. These two windows display the same information: the Marker's ID number, its position, end and length information if it is a cycle marker, and a Description field to give a descriptive name to your Marker.

CHAPTER 4

Figure 4.21
The Inspector area of
the Marker track and the
Marker window
displaying your project's
Marker information

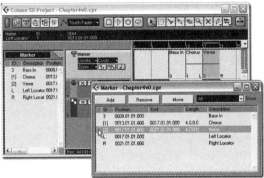

Adding Markers

Before we look at how to use Markers to navigate in a project, let's take a look at how you can
create Markers. There are many ways of creating Markers in Cubase SX, which are described in
detail in the operation manual of the software, so we will look at the easiest way to create both
types of Markers (cycle and normal Markers). This method implies that you have created a Marker
track in your project. So, if you haven't done so already, create a Marker track in your project.

To add cycle markers in a project:

1. Make sure your grid setting is set appropriately (see appropriate section for
    instructions). For this example, you can leave it at Snap to Grid and have your
    grid set to Bars.

2. Above the numbers in the ruler, when the pencil appears, click and drag over
    the timeline to create a blue cycle line over the area you want to define as a
    cycle marker. In Figure 4.22, a line is drawn between bar 37 and 41.

Figure 4.22
Dragging a cycle Region
to define the cycle
marker's boundaries

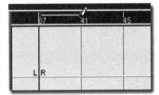

3. In the Marker track's List area, click the Add Cycle Marker button, as shown in
    Figure 4.23.

Figure 4.23
The Add Cycle Marker
button

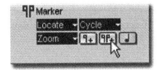

4. Make your newly created cycle marker active by clicking anywhere inside this Marker in the Marker track. The cycle marker's boundaries should become red and two red dots should appear inside these boundaries.

5. In the Event Information line (if you can't see it, click the Show Event Info button in the project's toolbar), click under the field Name and enter a descriptive name for your cycle marker. Figure 4.24 shows that the cycle marker has been named "New Region."

Figure 4.24
Entering a descriptive name for your cycle marker

To add Markers in a project:

1. Make sure your grid setting is set appropriately. For this example, you can leave it at Snap to Grid and have your grid set to Bars.

2. In the Ruler bar, click at the location (bar number) where you want to insert a marker. This should move your play cursor to this location.

3. In the Marker track's List area, click the Add Marker button, as shown in Figure 4.25.

Figure 4.25
The Add Marker button

4. Make your newly created marker active by clicking on this Marker's line in the Marker track. The Marker should become red.

5. In the Event Information line, click under the field Name and enter a descriptive name for your Marker.

Navigating Using Markers

The whole purpose of creating Markers or cycle markers is to give you a tool that allows you to move quickly from one spot to another in your project. Another advantage of using cycle markers is that it also allows you to zoom into a Region of your project. More specifically, you can focus your work on the events found within a cycle marker's range.

To move your play cursor to a Marker position:

▶ For markers with ID numbers between 3 and 9, press the corresponding number on your numeric keypad.

▶ For any markers using the Inspector area of the Marker track or the Marker window, click in the column to the left of the Marker's ID number.

CHAPTER 4

To move the left and right locators to the position of a cycle marker:

▶ In the Inspector area of the Marker track, click in the column to the left of the cycle marker's ID number.

▶ Or, in the Marker window, click in the column to the left of the cycle marker's ID number.

To zoom in to the location of a cycle marker:

▶ In the bottom-right corner of your Project window, to the left of the time magnification bar, click the arrow pointing down and select the desired cycle marker name you want to zoom to, as shown in Figure 4.26.

Figure 4.26
Using cycle markers to zoom in to a Region of your project

Editing Markers

After you've created Markers, you can edit their position, names, and ID numbers as well as remove unneeded Markers. Changing the ID number of a Marker, for example, allows you to optimize your Markers by assigning the ID numbers 3 to 9 to Markers you feel are more important. Because using the equivalent numbers on the numeric keypad allows jumping to the appropriate Marker, you can quickly navigate from Marker to Marker this way.

To rename a Marker (or cycle marker):

▶ From the Marker window, click the name in the Description column and type a new name.

▶ Or, from the Marker track's Inspector area, click the name in the Description column and type a new name.

▶ Or, from the Event Information line, select the appropriate Marker and change the Name field to what you want.

To change the ID number of a Marker (or cycle marker):

▶ From the Marker window, click the ID number in the ID column and type a new number (note that this has little effect on numbers higher than 9 or on cycle markers).

▶ Or, from the Marker track's Inspector area, click the ID number in the ID column and type a new number.

▶ Or, from the Event Information line, select the appropriate Marker and change the ID field to what you want.

You can edit the position of Markers, move cycle markers, or change their range in many ways. However, the easiest way to move cycle markers or Markers around is probably still through the Marker track. You can also edit the position or length in either the Marker window or the Marker track's Inspector area if you prefer. Here's how to edit the position or range of Markers and cycle markers using the Marker track.

To move a Marker:

1. Enable the Snap to Grid option if you want and set the grid property appropriately if you want your Markers to move only to specific bars, beats, or time values.

2. Click and drag the Marker you want to move and drop it in the Marker track at the desired location as shown in Figure 4.27.

Figure 4.27
Moving a Marker by dragging it to the desired location in the Marker track

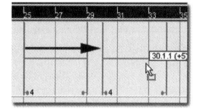

To move the position of a cycle marker:

1. Enable the Snap to Grid option if you want and set the grid property appropriately if you want your cycle markers to move only to specific bars, beats, or time values.

2. Click and drag any red lines that identify the selected cycle marker (don't click on the red dots near the bottom of the vertical lines) and drop it in the Marker track at the desired location as shown in Figure 4.28.

Figure 4.28
Resizing the end (or start) of a cycle marker by dragging its lower edge to the desired location

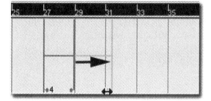

You can also resize a cycle marker by moving its start or end lines instead of simply moving the entire cycle marker range to another location.

To resize the start or end position of a cycle marker:

1. Enable the Snap to Grid option if you want and set the grid property appropriately if you want your cycle markers to move only to specific bars, beats, or time values.

2. Click and drag near the red dots at the bottom of the start or end lines of the cycle that you want to resize and drop it in the Marker track at the desired location.

Removing Markers

When a Marker doesn't serve its purpose anymore, you can remove it from your project.

To remove a Marker (or cycle marker):

▶ From the Marker window, click the Marker you want to remove and click the Remove button.

▶ Or, from the Marker track's Inspector area, select the Marker you want to remove, and then right-click on it to select the Delete option from the context menu.

▶ Or, from the Marker track, select the appropriate Marker (so that it becomes red) and press the Delete key on your keyboard.

The Transport Panel

The Transport panel is a multitask floating panel. There are six areas on the Transport panel, each of which allows you to control an aspect of your session in progress: Record mode, Locators, Pre- and Post-roll, Main Transport, Master and Sync control, and finally Activity.

By default, Cubase displays the Transport panel; however, you can use the F2 key on your keyboard to display or hide this panel. This section steps you through the different areas and their available options on the Transport panel.

Record Mode

The Record mode section allows you to set the Record mode and the Cycle mode as shown in Figure 4.29. The Record mode offers two options: Normal and Merge (both of which determine how Cubase handles overlapping MIDI parts).

Figure 4.29
The Record mode and Cycle mode options on the Transport panel

▶ Normal Record mode means that when you record MIDI events over existing MIDI parts, Cubase creates a new part, which overlaps the existing MIDI part without changing the previous content or location of these parts.

▶ Merge Record mode means that when you record MIDI events over existing MIDI parts, Cubase merges the new content and the existing content into a new merged part.

To change your Record mode on the Transport panel:

▶ Click the mode setting above Rec Mode in the Transport panel to toggle between Normal and Merge mode.

The Cycle mode also offers two options, which determines how MIDI will be recorded. Cycle modes take effect when the Cycle button is active on the Transport panel. When you are in Cycle mode, Cubase plays the content found between the left and right locators in cycle, going back to the left Marker and starting again when it reaches the right locator. Each time Cubase starts again, it is called a lap. How the events you record during a lap are handled depends on the Cycle mode setting. These modes apply to MIDI recording.

▶ **Mix**. Each time a lap is completed, the events recorded in the next lap are mixed with the events from the previously recorded lap.

▶ **Overwrite**. Each time a lap is completed, the events recorded in the next lap overwrite (replace) the events that were previously recorded.

To change your Cycle mode on the Transport panel:

▶ Click the mode setting above Cycle mode in the Transport panel to toggle between Mix and Overwrite mode.

Locators

The Locator section allows you to change your locators, move your play line to the locator's position, and set some of the recording and playback behaviors (see Figure 4.30).

Figure 4.30
The Locator options on
the Transport panel

To position your play line at the locator's position:

▶ Click the L or R found on the left of the locator's address in the Transport panel.

To change your locator's position in the Transport panel:

▶ Above and below each set of digits separated by a period in the location found on the Transport panel, there is a sensitive area. Clicking this sensitive area causes your cursor to change to an arrow with a plus or minus sign. If you click above, the value increases; if you click below, the value decreases. After a series of values is selected, you can also use the scroll wheel on your mouse to increase or decrease these values.

▶ Or, you can click on a value and enter a new position for this value using your keyboard.

You can also change the left and right locators' positions by using the position of the play line as a new left or right locator position.

To change your locator's position to the current play line position:

1. To set the left locator, hold the Ctrl (or Command key on a Mac) and click in the ruler at the desired location where you want to position your locator.

2. To set the right locator, hold the Alt (or Option key on a Mac) and click in the ruler at the desired location where you want to position your locator.

There are four buttons below the Locator fields. The first one on the left is the Auto Quantize button (shown as AQ on the Transport panel's button). When this button is active, it automatically quantizes MIDI events as you record them to the quantize setting found in your Project window. The next button to the right of the Auto Quantize button as well as the last button on the right in this portion of the Transport panel serve as Punch-in and Punch-out buttons. Using these buttons, you can tell Cubase where you want a recording to begin and where you want it to end. The location used for the punch-in is the left locator's location and the punch-out uses the right locator's location. For example, you could start your recording at bar one of your project, but the actual recording process will only begin at bar three and stop recording at bar four if your left locator is set at 0003.01.01.000 and your right locator is set at 0004.01.01.000 while the Punch-in and Punch-out buttons are active. This can be useful to replace events between these two locations (left and right locators). Perhaps the most effective way to use the punch-in and punch-out is in conjunction with the pre- and post-roll fields explained in the next section.

The button found between the Punch-in and the Punch-out buttons allows you to enable or disable the Cycle mode. When this button is active, Cubase continuously plays the events found between the left and right locators. You can quickly enable or disable this by either clicking on the button to toggle its position or by using the forward slash (or divide sign) on the numeric keypad on your keyboard.

Pre- and Post-Roll

The Pre- and Post-Roll function allows you to determine a time value before Cubase goes into Record mode at the punch-in location (pre-roll) and the time it continues playing after it goes out of Record mode at the punch-out location (post-roll). This allows you to configure an automatic punch-in and punch-out on a selected track, while Cubase plays back the project before it starts recording, giving you time to prepare yourself to record the line you want to replace.

To set up automatic punch-in and -out with pre- and post-rolls:

1. Set your left locator to the appropriate time location where you want to punch-in to your existing events.

2. Set your right locator to the appropriate time location where you want to punch-out of the Record mode.

3. Enable the Punch-in and Punch-out buttons on the Transport panel. If you want Cubase to replace all existing events from a specific location, leave the Punch-out button disabled.

4. Set a value for the pre-roll. This is the amount of time, bars, or beats depending on the ruler format displayed, which Cubase plays before the left locator. If the

amount of time exceeds the amount of time that it normally takes for Cubase to reach the left locator's position from the beginning of the project, it simply pauses for that equivalent amount of time. For example, if you enter a value of 10 bars and you want to punch-in at bar five, then Cubase counts five bars before bar one and then starts to play until it reaches bar five, where it goes into Record mode.

5. If needed, set the post-roll time as well, found below the pre-roll time (see Figure 4.31).

6. Disable the Click button in the Transport panel, otherwise Cubase uses the metronome's pre-count setting rather than the pre-roll setting.

7. Check the Transport > Pre-/Post-Roll option from the menu bar.

8. If you want Cubase to stop automatically after the punch-out time, select File > Preferences from the menu bar. Then select the Transport option and check the Stop after Automatic Punchout option.

9. Click Play or Record. Cubase plays until it reaches the punch-in time, and then switches to Record mode. If you have enabled the Punch-out button, it reverts to Play mode at that location. If you have checked the Stop after Automatic Punchout option, it also stops playing after the post-roll time value entered.

Figure 4.31
The pre- and post-roll settings in the Transport panel

Main Transport

The main transport buttons allow you to navigate through your project as a regular transport control panel does. In the upper portion, it displays the current location of the play line. The format displayed depends on the format selected from the drop-down menu found to the right of the time display. In Figure 4.32, the time is displayed in bars and beats. The small plus and minus sign on the left of the time display allow you to nudge the position of the play line one unit at a time. Below the time display is a play line overview display (blue line). This allows you to monitor the location of the play line as your project moves along; however, you can click on the line to grab your play line and move it to any location you desire in the project, or click anywhere in that area to make your play line jump to that location immediately.

To change the time format displayed in a project using the Transport panel:

1. Click the drop-down menu to the right of the time display in the Transport panel.

2. Select the desired time display format.

The transport control buttons allow you to (from left to right): go to the beginning of your project, rewind, fast forward, go to the end of your project, stop, play, and record.

Figure 4.32
The main transport
buttons and the play
line location indicator

Master And Sync Controls

In this portion of the Transport panel, you control over three aspects of your project (see Figure 4.33):

Figure 4.33
The Click, Master, and
Sync buttons on the
Transport panel

▶ **Click.** Allows you to enable or disable the metronome click. Ctrl-clicking (or Command-click on a Mac) brings up the Metronome Setup dialog box, which is explained in Chapter 7.

▶ **Master.** Allows you to enable or disable the Tempo track. Ctrl-clicking (or Command-click on a Mac) brings up the Tempo Track window, which is explained in Chapter 5. When the Master button is disabled, you can change the tempo setting of the project by clicking on the tempo and using your mouse's scroll wheel to increase or decrease the tempo. Otherwise (when Master is enabled), the tempo changes occur in the Tempo track.

▶ **Sync.** Allows you to enable or disable the synchronization functions. Ctrl-clicking (or Command-click on a Mac) brings up the Synchronization Setup dialog box, which is explained in Chapter 14. When this button is enabled, the type of sync Cubase receives will be displayed in the area to the right of the button. The example provided in Figure 4.34 indicates that Cubase is currently locked to a 29 drop frame timecode synchronization signal.

Figure 4.34
Example of a time code
signal being received by
Cubase while the Sync
option is enabled

To the right of these three buttons, you will find the current project's tempo, the time signature and the status of the synchronization signal. If you are not using any sync signals, this field should display as offline. In Figure 4.34, this displays a tempo of 120 BPM, a 4/4 time signature, and, as mentioned above, an incoming time code signal in 29 drop frame format (see Chapter 14 for more details on timecode formats).

CHAPTER 4

ABOUT THE TEMPO TRACK

The Master track is a special hidden track that holds your tempo changes and key signatures. All the tempo changes that you make in the Tempo Track window or the Browse Project window play back when you activate the Master button on the Transport panel. However, the time signature is heard even if the button is not activated. This is logical, because your time signature needs to be activated for MIDI elements to lock with bars and beats throughout the project.

MIDI Activity

The MIDI Activity display (see Figure 4.35) allows you to see if there is any MIDI activity being sent to Cubase or being sent by Cubase to external devices. This is a good way to test your MIDI input and output connections when setting up your system. Note that MIDI metronome information is not displayed in the MIDI output meter. If you are not seeing any MIDI activity when sending messages from an external controller, make sure the selected MIDI track's MIDI Out and In ports are configured properly.

Figure 4.35
The MIDI activity input and output monitors on the Transport panel

MIDI events recorded and sent to a VST Instrument do not show up in the MIDI activity monitors. However, if you are not seeing any MIDI activity when playing recorded MIDI events that are supposed to go to an external device, chances are that this is caused by one of two reasons: There is no MIDI present in your project, or you have not set the track(s) containing MIDI events to play on a physical MIDI port such as your MIDI interface. For example, if your external instruments are not receiving MIDI data, try loading a Virtual Instrument (VST Instrument) and route your MIDI track to that VSTi's MIDI port. If you hear the MIDI going into the VST Instrument, then try reassigning the previous MIDI output port to this track. If you still don't hear MIDI coming from your external instrument, your problem is probably somewhere else.

▶ Make sure your MIDI connectors and cables are connected properly. If they are, try switching them around to see if one of them is not faulty.

▶ Are the MIDI ports you're trying to use properly configured in the Device Setup dialog box?

▶ Is your MIDI interface installed properly?

▶ Is the MIDI Thru active in Cubase? To check this out, select File > Preferences > MIDI in the menu bar.

Customizing Your Transport Panel

Now that you know what each section on the Transport panel does, you can choose to hide certain portions of this Transport panel if you don't need to use them or if you want to free up some valuable desktop space.

To show/hide Transport panel sections:

1. Right-click anywhere on your Transport panel (except where values can be changed with your cursor).

2. From the context menu, check the sections you want to see and uncheck the sections you don't want to see, as shown in Figure 4.36.

Figure 4.36
Customizing your
Transport panel

Context Menus in the Project Window

In the Project window, as in many other windows in Cubase, you will find that right-clicking (Ctrl-click for Mac users) in different Regions reveals a number of options related to the area in which you click, as displayed in Figure 4.37. In many cases, these context menus allow you to choose options that are also available in the Project window's menu bar or toolbar. However, having these options readily available in your workspace makes it easy to stay focused in that area and apply changes to events without having to frequently move your mouse across the screen.

As you can see in Figure 4.37, the default context menu, selected MIDI event, or selected audio event context menus display three parts separated by a line. The top section allows you to change your cursor to a different tool. The middle section offers different functions and sub-functions that you can apply in this context. For example, when an audio event is selected, you can select the Audio > Event as Region option to create a Region in the Media Pool from the visible portion of the event in your project's event list area. The third section will toggle the Info Bar in the project window on or off.

You learn more about these context menus as we learn how to edit events and work with a project.

Figure 4.37
The different context
menus in the Project
window

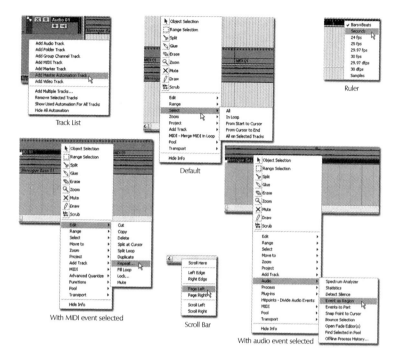

Now You Try It

For information about using the instructions found in this section and to find out where you can get the working files, please consult the section called "About the Exercise Files" in the Introduction section.

It's time to put the topics covered in this chapter into action—you can follow special exercise steps that will help you review what you have learned in this chapter. The exercises are accompanied by a Cubase project file and corresponding media files that you can download from the Muska & Lipman Website at http://www.muskalipman.com.

5

Working With Tracks

In a project, you work with different types of musical or sonic events. These events take place on tracks and occur at the appropriate time in these tracks. Different tracks hold different events or event types. For example, audio tracks hold audio events, marker tracks hold Marker information, and MIDI tracks hold MIDI events. These types of tracks are called track classes and Cubase uses these different track classes to store the different types of events supported within a Cubase project. If you compare this with a multitrack recorder—which allows you to record only one type of information: audio—you can quickly realize how versatile and powerful Cubase really is because all this information is handled by a single software.

Before you can add anything in a Project window, you need to create tracks corresponding to the type of content you want to record and configure the tracks properly to achieve the result you want. Because Cubase is more versatile than a multitrack tape recorder, it's also a bit more demanding. But as you will quickly realize, it's also quite easy to get up and running, creating the music you wanted to do but couldn't with a simple tape recorder.

In this chapter, you will:

▶ Learn how to recognize and work with the different areas in the Project window

▶ Discover the different tools available in the Inspector and Track List areas

▶ Find out what a VST Instrument is and how you can use it in a project

▶ Install and manage external MIDI sound modules through the MIDI Device Manager

▶ How to use the Tempo track to add tempo changes and time signature changes to a project.

Project Window Areas

When you work with tracks in the Project window, most of your time is spent between the Inspector, the Track List, and the Event Display areas of this window. The Inspector area displays information about a selected track and may be divided into several sections, depending on the track class or track type you have selected. This is explained later in this chapter. The Track List area displays all the tracks that are part of your project, stacked one on top of the other. Again, the content of the Track List area for a given track varies depending on its track class. Finally, the Event Display area displays recorded events and automation—the actual audio and MIDI content of the project itself.

The Inspector

As mentioned previously, you will want to use the Inspector area whenever you want to view or edit certain details pertaining to a selected track in your Project window. What you find in the Inspector area also varies depending on the track's class. For example, when a MIDI track is selected, the Inspector area is divided into five sections: the MIDI Track Setup, Track Parameters, Track Inserts, Track Sends, and Track Channel. Each one of these sections allows you to modify a certain amount of information that affects how the events on the track behave or play back. So, in the same example of a MIDI Inspector's area, you can use the Track Parameters section to transpose all the events on the track. Other track classes, such as Folder Tracks (this is also explained later in Chapter 6), do not display as many sections in the Inspector area.

However, you will find elements (such as buttons and fields) that are common to different Inspector areas of different track classes and also with other areas within the Project window. For example, this is the case of the Read/Write Automation buttons, which are found in both the Inspector and the Track List as well as in the Track Mixer panel.

When the Inspector area holds more than one section, the title bar and a control button for that section is always visible. The control button is found on the right of the section's title bar. This button allows you to reveal or hide the content of the selected section. In Figure 5.1, you can see this button, which looks like a little arrow pointing down. This indicates that the section can be expanded or maximized. If the arrow points up, it indicates that you can minimize the panel. In addition, when the button is blue, it indicates that there is an effect active in the section for which the button is blue. Finally, when this button is yellow, it indicates that there might be some effects assigned in the section, but that they have been either bypassed or deactivated.

Figure 5.1
The upper-right corner of this image shows the Control button for this Inspector's area section

By default, when you click on one section to expand it, any other expanded section automatically minimizes itself. When a section is minimized, all the settings you have made in that section remain intact.

CONTROLLING MULTIPLE SECTIONS SIMULTANEOUSLY

If you want to maximize more than one section of the Inspector area at once, hold the Ctrl key (Command key on Mac) down as you click the section's Control button. You can also minimize all opened panels at once by holding the Alt key (Option key on Mac) down while clicking on any one of the section's Control buttons. Inversely, you can maximize all the sections at once using the same key combination.

The Track List

The Track List area allows you to view all of your tracks at once. This makes it easy to enable multiple tracks for recording, for example, or to mute certain tracks while working on your project without having to select each track to use the Mute button in the Inspector area. The content of each track in the Track List area also depends on the track's class. You can use the Track List area to change the order in which your tracks appear or to organize your tracks according to class. You can also use the Track List area to reveal any subtrack automation information. When you want to record or edit automation for a track, the automation data is kept along with the track itself in a subtrack found below the track. Usually, there is one subtrack for each type of automation your track contains. For example, you could have two subtracks to your track, where one contains volume automation and another contains pan automation. Finally, you can also resize each track individually to fit its content on your screen from the Track List area.

To change the order of a track in the Track List area (see Figure 5.2):

1. Click the track you want to move in the Track List area. A red line appears to indicate that Cubase knows you want to move this track as shown in the first image on the left side of Figure 5.2. To select multiple consecutive tracks, click the first track, hold down the Shift key, and then click the last track you want to move. To select multiple nonconsecutive tracks, click the first track, hold down the Ctrl key (Command key on a Mac), and then click on any other track you want to move (note that after the tracks are moved, all the nonconsecutive tracks appear consecutive).

2. Drag the track to the desired location. In the middle section of Figure 5.2, you can see the green line indicating where the track would appear if you released the mouse.

3. Release the mouse button when you are satisfied with the new location. As you can see on the right side of Figure 5.2, the track appears where the green line was. In this case, between Audio 02 and 03.

Figure 5.2
Changing the order of a track in the Track List area

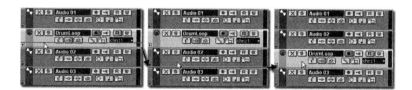

To reveal or hide a track's automation subtracks:

1. Right-click on the track for which you want to see the used automation in the Track List area.

2. Select the Show Used Automation option from the context menu. If you want the used automation visible for all tracks, select the Show Used Automation for All Tracks option instead.

Or:

1. Click the plus sign in the bottom-left corner of the desired track in the Track List area to reveal its automation subtrack. In Figure 5.3, when you click the plus sign, two subtracks are revealed (lower portion of the figure). When you want to view more automation subtracks, you can click the plus sign found in the lower automation subtrack. In other words, clicking the plus sign of the track reveals the last state your subtracks were in and if you click the track's minus sign, it hides all subtracks. Clicking the plus sign of an automation subtrack reveals the next automation subtrack, whereas clicking the minus sign of the automation subtrack hides only that subtrack from the Track List area.

2. Click the minus sign when the track shows its subtrack(s) to hide the subtrack(s). Hiding the subtrack(s) does not remove the automation recorded on this track. It only hides it from view.

Figure 5.3
Clicking the plus sign of a track in the Track List area reveals automation subtracks

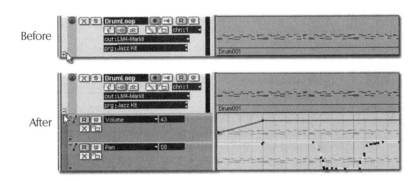

In each automation subtrack, you will find two fields. The first one displays the automation parameter's name used by the subtrack. In Figure 5.3, for example, these are Volume and Pan. The second field represents the value of the automation parameter at the location from the play line's position. In Figure 5.3, the volume is at 43 and the pan is at 58. You can also change the automation parameter displayed in the subtrack if you want.

To change the automation parameter displayed in a subtrack:

1. Expand your track to reveal its subtracks.

2. From the Automation Parameter drop-down menu, select the appropriate automation parameter that you want to view or edit in that subtrack. Note that parameters containing information appear with an asterisk at the end of their name in this menu.

If the parameter you want to view is not in the drop-down menu, select the More option at the bottom of the menu, and then choose the appropriate automation parameter from the dialog box that appears.

To resize an individual track's height:

1. Bring your cursor over the lower edge of the track you want to resize.

2. When your cursor changes into a double-headed arrow (see Figure 5.4), drag your mouse up to reduce the track's size or down to increase its size.

You can also resize the entire Track List's width and height by dragging the right edge of the Track List area when your cursor changes into a double-headed arrow or by dragging the lower edge of a track using the same method (see Figure 5.4). Moving the border to the left reduces the size whereas moving it to the right increases the Track List's width. Note that you cannot resize the left edge of the Track List to increase the space used by the Inspector.

Figure 5.4
Resizing an individual
track's height

The Event Display

The Event Display area allows you to edit and view parts, events, and automation information found in your project. Because most of the work you will do in this area is related to editing, we discuss the functions and operations for the Event Display area in Chapter 9.

For the time being, however, it is important to understand that you will find the content of each track (events, parts, and automation data) in this area.

VST Instruments (VSTi)

VST Instruments—VSTi, for short—are software-based synthesizers that use the ASIO 2 protocol developed by Steinberg to generate or output their sound through the computer's sound card. They are, in essence, audio plug-in effects working within Cubase. These audio plug-in effects generate the sounds triggered by MIDI events recorded in a project. This is done by assigning the MIDI output of a track into the audio VSTi plug-in effect.

This opens up a whole world of exciting possibilities for any music enthusiast as well as for hard core music veterans. VST Instruments are activated through the VST Instrument panel found in the Devices menu. The VST Instrument panel is like an empty rack of instruments in which you load instruments as you need them. You can load up to 32 VSTi per project in Cubase SX (16 in Cubase SL). Each number found on the left of the panel corresponds to an individual instrument slot. The controls for each instrument are identical. By default, these slots are empty. You can click on the instrument list in the VST Instrument panel to access installed VST Instruments on your computer (see Figure 5.5); you can select the VSTi that you want to activate. To install a VSTi, follow the instructions provided by the plug-in manufacturer.

CHAPTER 5

Figure 5.5
The VST Instruments
panel

When selected, the VSTi is also activated by default. You can always deactivate a VSTi without unloading it by pressing the Active/Bypass button next to the number for the VSTi in the VST Instruments panel. When a VSTi is loaded and activated, an additional MIDI port appears when you click on a MIDI track output setting. In Figure 5.6, the a1 VSTi has been loaded, so it is now available as an output device. This means that you can use one of sixteen additional MIDI channels, not to mention that you can also load more than one instance of a VSTi in memory. VSTi MIDI outputs are handled in the same way as regular MIDI output devices.

Figure 5.6
All VST Instruments
that are loaded appear
as an additional MIDI
output

Because VST Instruments are MIDI controlled, yet use your sound card to generate their sounds, Cubase creates two separate, but linked channels in the Mixer window: one MIDI channel to control MIDI-related events and another audio channel to control the audio output. This implies that you can add MIDI effects and automate MIDI control changes through the MIDI track in which you find the VSTi and you can add audio effects, automation, and EQ to the audio channel created in the Mixer window.

Setting Up a VSTi

Using a VSTi is quite simple. The hardest part is usually choosing the sounds for the new project.

To set up a VSTi in your project:

1. Make the VST Instruments panel visible (you can press F11 on your keyboard).

2. From the VST Instruments panel, select the first available slot in the rack and click anywhere on the drop-down menu where it currently says "No VST Instrument." This reveals the installed VSTi on your computer.

3. Choose a VST from this menu to activate it. The blue active button next to the selected instrument reveals that this instrument is ready to be assigned to a MIDI track.

4. Create a new MIDI track or select an empty one.

5. In the MIDI track's setup section of the Inspector area or in the Track List area, select the VSTi you just activated from the MIDI Output Port drop-down menu.

6. If you haven't already configured your MIDI input, you might want to do this before continuing: Click the MIDI input port and choose the MIDI port from which the incoming MIDI events will be sent to the VSTi.

7. You can select a program for the VSTi through the Program field in the Setup section of the MIDI track, from the Track List area, or by clicking on the Edit MIDI Channel button (this button displays an "e" inside the button) at the top-right corner of the Setup section in the MIDI track. This third option might be useful when no default presets are loaded with the VSTi. Clicking this button opens up the VSTi's editing interface panel. On the other hand, if there are presets included, you can also use the left and right arrows found in the VST Instruments panel, next to the Edit VSTi button (see Figure 5.5). These buttons move forward (right button) or backward (left button) in the list of currently loaded presets for this instrument. You can also use the drop-down menu below the VSTi's name in the VST Instruments panel to select a preset program.

WANT TO USE YOUR EXTERNAL KEYBOARD CONTROLLER?
Make sure that the MIDI Thru Active check box is checked in Cubase's preferences (File menu > Preferences > MIDI). Otherwise, you won't be able to use your external keyboard controller to send MIDI events to your VSTi.

With most VST Instruments, you can also create your own preset programs and save them for later use. There are two types of files you can save: instruments and banks. Instruments usually hold settings for a single sound, whereas banks hold a set of sounds, presets, programs, or instruments (depending on the name you call it). You can also load multiple instruments, but you can only load one bank at a time.

To load a bank or instruments in a VSTi:

1. Bring up the VST Instruments panel and its editing interface panel (see Figure 5.7).

2. To the right of both panels, you will find a File menu. Click it to reveal its options.

3. Select the Load Bank or Load Instrument option, depending on what you want to load into the instrument's memory. Remember that if you are using a VSTi sampler, this might require the VSTi to load some samples into memory as well, so it might take a little while. If the loaded VSTi does not need to load samples, then it should be fairly quick because this file only contains parameter setup information.

4.   Browse the folder on your hard disk in which banks or instruments are stored.

5.   Choose the desired program from the corresponding menu in the VST Instruments panel (as mentioned earlier in step 7 in the previous section).

Figure 5.7
The top portion represents the File menu in the VSTi's editing interface panel and the botton represents the VST Instruments panel

To save a bank or instrument for a VSTi:

1.   After making changes to a program or a series of programs in a bank, repeat Steps 1–2 from the previous exercise on how to load a bank or instruments.

2.   From the File menu, simply select Save Bank or Save Instrument.

3.   Select an appropriate folder in which to save your file. It is a good idea to keep your bank and instrument files in the same folder to avoid searching all over your hard disk for these files in the future. If you use a sampler VSTi, you might already have a folder in which samples are stored. You can either save the bank or instrument files in that folder or in a folder above, depending on your folder structure organization.

VSTi Included with Cubase

Steinberg provides you with three VST Instruments when you purchase Cubase.

▶   a1. A powerful dual oscillator with up to a sixteen-voice polyphonic synthesizer

▶   VB1. A four-voice polyphonic virtual bass simulator using physical modeling parameters

▶   LM-7. A twelve-voice/part polyphonic drum machine

Obviously, Steinberg is not the only manufacturer developing VST Instruments. You can find additional resources and links to some manufacturer's websites in Appendix F.

VSTi and Latency

Because VST Instruments play through your sound card, latency plays a great role in how effective the instruments really are. Because latency introduces a delay between the time a sound is played and the time a sound is heard, the shorter that delay is, the more realistic the experience. Make sure your system is configured properly, as outlined in Chapter 2, and always use the ASIO driver provided by your sound card manufacturer. If you have a latency that is equal or greater than 25 milliseconds, you might find it disconcerting to play a VSTi, especially when playing parts with high rhythmic content, because there will always be a delay between the moment you press the keys on your keyboard and the moment you hear the sound. The smallest theoretical latency is 0 milliseconds, but in reality, you can expect at least a 1.5- to 3-millisecond latency, which is pretty good. So, to get a good experience with VSTi, try setting your sound card driver preferences (if you have a dedicated ASIO driver for your sound card) and Cubase to have latency between 1.5 and 10 milliseconds.

If your sound card doesn't provide an ASIO driver with low latency, you can always use a non-VST Instrument to input MIDI events, changing the MIDI output of a track after the events are recorded back to the VSTi output. This way, you don't get the latency delay during recording and because latency does not affect timing, the events are played in sync with other events once recorded.

The Device Manager

As you have seen earlier, it is possible to create program changes or tell a MIDI track to play a specific program and bank from the MIDI Settings section in the Inspector area and the Track List area. When working with a VSTi, this is quite easy to deal with because when you select this VSTi as the MIDI output port for the track, the track's settings adjust themselves to the parameters found for that instrument. So, for example, if you load the a1 VSTi, the Bank Selection field disappears because you can only have one bank at a time. Also, the Program field displays the VSTi's loaded sounds so that you can pick the sound you want to hear by name directly in the track itself.

Working with external MIDI devices is a bit trickier because all the manufacturers do not necessarily offer the same sound architecture or sound name. To access these sounds directly from the MIDI track's setting section in the Inspector, you need to tell Cubase which external device is hooked up to your MIDI output, what MIDI output it uses, and then load which MIDI instructions should be sent to this device (in order to get the name of the patch from this device's LCD display to match with the list inside Cubase's Inspector area). Fortunately, most of these devices already have scripts that you can load from the Cubase CD. However, you do have to install these devices through the Device Manager to let Cubase know what is in your studio and address it properly.

When you open up your MIDI Device Manager for the first time, it will be empty because you have not defined any devices in your setup yet. You can access your Device Manager in a couple of ways:

> ▶ Select the MIDI Device Manager option in the Devices menu.
> ▶ Or, click the MIDI Device Manager button found on the Devices panel if it is visible (Devices > Show Panel).

Adding a MIDI Device

After you have identified your external MIDI devices, you can proceed with their installation inside the MIDI Device Manager.

To add a MIDI device:

1. Open the MIDI Device Manager panel.

2. Click the Install Device button. The Add MIDI Device dialog box appears, displaying a list of existing device definitions (see Figure 5.8).

3. Scroll this list and select the device you want to install and then click OK. Your selected device now appears in the MIDI Device Manager panel.

Figure 5.8
The Add MIDI Device
dialog box

4. Click the device's name in the Installed Devices section to select it. You should see a listing appear in the Patch Banks section (see Figure 5.9).

5. Click the MIDI output to the right of your device in the center of the window and select the MIDI interface to which this device is hooked up. When you select this instrument from the track's MIDI output port, the device's name appears along with the associated MIDI port used to connect Cubase to this device, as shown in Figure 5.10.

6. Repeat this operation for each device in your studio.

7. Close the panel when you are done by clicking the X in the upper-right corner of the window. The changes remain even when the window is not visible.

Figure 5.9
The MIDI Device
Manager panel

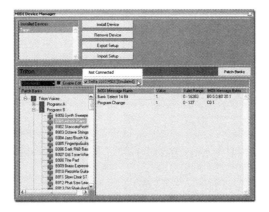

Figure 5.10
The name of an installed device appears in the MIDI output port selection menu with the MIDI port associated with it on the right

If your MIDI device is not included in this list, you might have to create it yourself. Remember, however, that if you are using a MIDI sampler, creating such a device definition in the MIDI Device Manager is pointless because a sampler generally does not have a fixed set of programs it loads by default when you turn the sampler on. In fact, that might be why your device is not listed here!

This said, if you do have a MIDI device with programs and banks that are not defined, you can create your own MIDI device in the Device Manager. Because creating a device from scratch is intricately linked to the device in your setup, you need to refer to your owner's manual and the online documentation (under the MIDI Devices and Patches section) provided with Cubase to find out how to create your own custom device with patch names, banks, and specific MIDI messages associated with it.

Managing a MIDI Device

After a device is installed, you can reorganize its Patch Bank list, export or import other devices, and rename items in the patch banks. For example, the Roland's JV-1080 patch list is organized in patches, performances, and drums. Inside the Patches folder, there are some 20 groups in which all the actual preset names of this MIDI device are found (see Figure 5.11). However, if you've ever used or seen the JV-1080, programs can be grouped by type of sounds rather than taking programs 0 to 31 and putting them in a group. So, you can start from the original instrument definition and create your own structure to better suit your needs; this makes it easier for you when you want to find the right sound for your track.

Figure 5.11
On the left, you can see the original Patch Bank list provided by Cubase; on the right, you can see the modified list that corresponds to the user's preferences

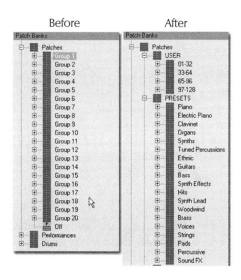

CHAPTER 5

To add a bank to your device's setup:

1. In the MIDI Device Manager panel, select the device for which you want to add the content in the Installed Devices section of the MIDI Device Manager.

2. Check the Enable Edit check box.

3. Select the Create Banks option from the Commands menu if this is what you want to do.

4. A new bank is created called New Bank. Double-click this new entry and type a new name for this bank.

5. If you have more than one bank in your device's Patch Bank list, you will see a Bank Assignment tab appear to the right of your Patch Bank tab. When you click on this tab, Cubase allows you to associate MIDI channels with specific banks. For example, if you have a drums bank, you might want to assign this to Channel 10. This way, when you assign this device to a MIDI output port and select Channel 10, the programs listed in the Inspector correspond to associated banks. Simply select the banks from the drop-down menu next to each channel to associate a bank with a channel.

To add a preset or a folder to your device's setup:

1. In the MIDI Device Manager panel, select the device for which you want to add the content in the Installed Devices section of the MIDI Device Manager.

2. Check the Enable Edit check box.

3. Select the bank or folder in which you want to add the preset or (sub)folder.

4. Select the New Preset or New Folder option from the Commands menu.

5. Double-click the new entry to rename it.

6. If you have added a preset, you need to add the relevant MIDI message information associated with your device in the right portion of this window.

To add multiple presets to your device's setup:

1. In the MIDI Device Manager panel, select the device for which you want to add the content in the Installed Devices section of the MIDI Device Manager.

2. Check the Enable Edit check box.

3. Select the bank or folder in which you want to add the multiple presets.

4. Select the Add Multiple Presets option from the Commands menu. The Add Multiple Presets dialog box appears (see Figure 5.12). In this dialog box, you need to insert the appropriate information relating to the MIDI messages that need to be sent to your MIDI device in order to change the program correctly when a preset is selected. The following steps describe a simple MIDI message containing a list of eight banks and eight presets, for a total of sixty-four possible program changes. This might not be how your device is set up, but you can use these steps to figure out how to get your device to work correctly.

5. By default, the first line shows Program Change. Click this name and select from the pop-up menu the appropriate bank select message for your MIDI device (because this is an example, you might not need to assign a bank message at all).

6. In the Range column, enter "0-7" to create 8 banks.

7. Now click under the bank select message to add a program change message associated with each bank.

8. In the Range column of the program change row, enter "0-7." This creates eight programs in each bank, ranging from number 0 to number 7.

9. In the Default Name field, enter the default name you want to give to the newly created presets. In Figure 5.12, the default name is "Patch." Cubase automatically numbers all the presets created.

10. Click OK when done.

Figure 5.12

The Add Multiple
Presets dialog box

When you select the bank or folder in which you have created these multiple presets, you will find a list of preset names. In our example, there are sixty-four presets numbered from Patch 0-0 to Patch 0-7 for the first bank, then Patch 1-0 to Patch 1-7 for the second bank, and so on. Selecting one of these presets reveals (in the right side of the MIDI Device Manager panel) the actual MIDI message sent to the device.

If you've made some adjustments to your MIDI device listings in the MIDI Device Manager panel, you may want to export these changes to a file so that you can retrieve them later if you ever have to reinstall your software or simply use your device with Cubase in another studio. To do so, use the Export Device function. This allows you to export all the patch bank settings to a file that you can later copy on a floppy disk and carry with you. When you get to the other studio or reinstall Cubase on your computer, you can import your file into the MIDI Device Manager to access your customized settings once again.

To export a MIDI device setup file:

1. In the MIDI Device Manager panel, select the device setups that you want to export to a file.

2. Click the Export Setup button.

3. Choose an appropriate folder and name for your file.

4. Click the Save button. This creates an XML file.

To import a MIDI device setup file:

1. Open your MIDI Device Manager panel.

2. Click the Import Setup button.

CHAPTER 5

3. Browse to the location of the file you want to import.

4. Select the file and click the Open button. This adds the device to your MIDI Device Manager panel.

Adding a new device to a setup does not change or influence how the existing devices are handled, so you don't have to worry about messing things up by installing another device, even temporarily. You can always remove a device you no longer use or need.

To remove a MIDI device from the MIDI Device Manager:

1. Select the device in the MIDI Device Manager's Installed Device section.

2. Click the Remove Device button.

If you made a mistake or are not satisfied with an entry in the patch banks, you can simply click the entry and press the Delete key to remove it from the list. You can also change the order in which items appear and rearrange the list to better suit your needs.

To move an item in the list:

▶ Simply click and drag the desired entry to its new location. You can also move more than one item at a time by using the usual methods: Click the first entry and shift-click the last item to select consecutive entries, or Ctrl-click (Command-click on the Mac) the different entries you want to select.

Using Installed Devices in the Inspector

After you've installed these devices in your MIDI Device Manager, you can use the Program field in the Inspector or the Track List area of a MIDI track to select a program by name. When selecting an entry in this field, Cubase sends the appropriate MIDI message to your external MIDI device in order for you to hear the selected sound.

To assign a program to a MIDI track:

1. Start by setting your MIDI track's output to a device defined in the MIDI Device Manager.

2. In the MIDI setting of the Inspector area or in the Track List area, click the Program field (prg) to reveal its content (see Figure 5.13).

3. This field reveals the patch bank structure as defined in the MIDI Device Manager. Use the Filter field if you are looking for a specific name. In Figure 5.13, the name "Piano" was entered, which reveals all the programs that contain this word in their name.

4. Select the program by clicking on its name. By doing so, Cubase sends a MIDI message to your device causing it to change its program. You can listen to the sound if you want or select another entry if you want to hear another sound.

5. Clicking once again on the selected sound or clicking outside this drop-down menu selects the sound and hides the menu once again.

Figure 5.13
Using the Program field
along with the Filter
option to pinpoint the
sounds you want

About the Tempo Track

The Tempo Track in Cubase essentially allows you to insert tempo and key signature changes to your project. You can access the Tempo Track by Ctrl-clicking (or Command-clicking on Mac) on the Master button found in the Transport Panel, by selecting the Tempo Track option in the Project menu, or by pressing the default key command Ctrl-T (or Command-T on Mac).

The top toolbar in this window (Figure 5.14) offers the following tools:

▶ The first four buttons are the object selection, eraser, magnifying glass, and draw tools. These tools perform the same functions as they do in other editing environments.

▶ The Master button allows you to toggle the tempo track on or off. This button is lit when it is active. When the Tempo track is off, you can set a different tempo in the Transport Panel's tempo field. This provides a way to set a slower tempo for hard-to-play passages when recording in MIDI. Any tempo changes found in the Tempo track will not be reproduced during playback when the Master button is disabled. On the other hand, the time signature changes will still take place as usual.

▶ The Auto Scroll and Snap buttons offer the same functionality as their Project window counterparts.

▶ The Tempo field displays the tempo value of a selected tempo point from the tempo display area below. When a tempo is selected (this only works when a single tempo value is selected, unlike the example found in Figure 5.14), you can use this field to change the tempo value through the up and down arrows to the right of the field, or you can type in a new tempo value.

▶ The Curve field allows you to select how the tempo changes between two selected tempo values. You can choose either Ramp or Jump. When a ramp is created, the tempo will move gradually from one point to another, as displayed between bars 7 and 11 in Figure 5.14. When a jump is created, the tempo will stay the same until the next tempo change, at which point it jumps to the next tempo value in the line, as displayed between bars 2 and 7.

▶ The Insert Curve field allows you to determine how the following tempo changes will relate to other tempo change values along the tempo line. As with the Curve field, you can choose either Ramp (gradual change of tempo from one point to the next) or Jump (sudden change at the location of the new tempo change).

▶ The Signature field allows you to change the value for the selected signature in the Signature bar found below the Ruler bar.

Below the Toolbar you will find the Ruler bar. This bar offers similar functions as Ruler bars in other windows. However, at the left of this bar, you will find a display that shows the current location of your cursor in the tempo display area below. You can use this to locate the desired tempo value when inserting these values in the Tempo track.

The Time Signature bar displays the time signatures in your project. When you start a new project, by default you will find a single 4/4 time signature entry at the beginning of this bar. But as you can see in Figure 5.14, you can add several other time signatures along the project's timeline. This will also change the spacing between each bar to reflect the time signature's value.

The main area of the Tempo track is of course the Tempo Display area. This consists of a tempo ruler displayed vertically along the left side of the window and an area where tempo changes appear along the tempo line. Each tempo change is represented by a square handle along this line. When you insert a new tempo change, the line before and after this new tempo will join the tempo using the current Curve and Insert Curve settings.

In the lower right corner you will find the horizontal and vertical zoom bars, which allow you to adjust the zoom level for the timeline displayed in the Tempo track as well as the tempo precision displayed in the tempo ruler, respectively.

Figure 5.14
The Tempo Track
window

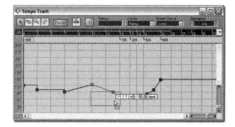

To add a tempo change:

1. In the Tempo track, click on the Draw tool in the toolbar.

2. Select the desired option in the Insert Curve field.

3. Activate the Snap button if you want to position your tempo at the Snap mode's current Grid setting. It is recommended that this be on if, for example, you want your tempo changes to occur at bar changes.

4. Position your cursor in the time and at the tempo height you wish to insert the tempo change. You can use the cursor location field to the left of the ruler to guide you along the tempo value.

To add a time signature change:

1. In the Tempo track, click on the Draw tool in the toolbar.

2. Click inside the Time Signature bar at the location where you want to insert a time signature change. This will add a time signature using the current value displayed in the Signature field.

3. With the new time signature still selected (a red square appears around the selected time signature), change the values in the Signature field to represent the appropriate time signature you wish to add.

To move a tempo change or time signature change:

1. Select the Object Selection tool from the toolbar.

2. Click on the tempo or time signature you wish to move and drag it to the desired location.

You can also move more than one tempo change at a time by dragging a box to select a range of tempo changes. Selected tempo change handles will appear red, as will the lines between these tempo changes.

If you wish to change the curve type between two or more tempo changes, you can select them and then select the desired value in the Curve field. For example, if you have selected three tempo changes, with a jump curve between the first and second tempo and a ramp between the second and third tempo, selecting a ramp will create a ramp between the first and second, leaving the curve between the second and third intact. Note that jump curves are displayed by blue line segments between two tempo changes and ramp curves are displayed by a green line segment between two tempo changes.

To erase tempo or time signature changes:

▶ With the Object Selection tool selected, click on the tempo or time signature you wish to erase to select it and press Delete or Backspace. To erase several events, simply drag a box over the desired tempo or time signature changes and use the Delete or Backspace keys.

▶ Or, select the Eraser tool and click on the events in the Tempo track.

Now You Try It

It's time to put the topics covered in this chapter into action—you can download a practice exercise at http://www.muskalipman.com.

6

Track Classes

When you create a new empty project, as you did in Chapter 4, a blank project appears with no tracks. No matter what you decide to do from this point forward, you need to add tracks to your project to create or record events into them. In Cubase, there are seven types of tracks called classes:

▶ Audio tracks for audio events and automation.

▶ MIDI tracks for MIDI events and automation.

▶ Folder tracks to group other tracks into, such as different takes of a solo.

▶ Group channel tracks, which allow you to group different tracks' outputs into a single mixer channel to control all the channels at once. For example, you could have all the backup singers grouped to the same group fader. When you want the background vocals to go down, you only need to reduce the level of this group fader, rather then reducing the level of all the backup singers' tracks.

▶ Marker tracks, as you saw in Chapter 4, allow you to easily manage your Markers.

▶ The master automation track (there can be only one) holds the automation for the master output channel and the global master effects automation as well.

▶ Video tracks for when you need to synchronize your music to a digital video file and want to see frames appear above audio or MIDI events in your project.

In this chapter, you will:

▶ Explore the different tools available in the track Inspector and Track List areas

▶ Understand what track classes are and what purpose they serve

▶ Understand the differences between MIDI and audio effects

▶ Understand the differences between track insert and send effects

▶ Define the Cubase audio hierarchy in terminology and learn how it applies to your project

▶ Organize your project using folder tracks

▶ Learn when and why you would use group tracks

CHAPTER 6

Adding Tracks

To add a track to your project:

1. Click Project > Add Track from the menu bar.
2. From the Add Track's submenu, select the appropriate type of track you want to add.

Or:

▶ Right-click in the Track List and select the type of track you want to add.

Notice that with both methods, the Multiple option is also available. This allows you to add more than one track of the same class simultaneously. You can't, however, add several tracks of different class (or type) at once.

Now, let's take a closer look at these track classes and their specificities.

MIDI Track

This class of track is for MIDI events. You can use MIDI tracks for any type of MIDI events; however, assigning a drum map to a MIDI track (this is explained later in the chapter) creates events that are associated with the Drum Editor window rather than the Key Editor window. MIDI tracks contain MIDI note events, controllers such as velocity, modulation wheel, pitch bend, and so on. It also contains any type of MIDI automation information generated by the Channel Mixer panel, such as automation for MIDI effects that might be assigned to a track. MIDI tracks can also contain MIDI filters and effects such as MIDI compression, which is also discussed in the next sections. Recorded MIDI events are saved with the project file itself.

When you record MIDI events, such as a musical performance, through your MIDI controller, these events are stored in a part, which appears on the MIDI track's Event Display area in the Project window. You can have many parts containing MIDI events on your track and parts can overlap each other on the track. You can compare a part to a container of MIDI events. In the case of MIDI, these containers can be stacked one on top of the other, playing either different drum instruments, different channels (if the MIDI track is set to play any MIDI channels), or simply as part of your working process.

If you look at the example in Figure 6.1, there are three different parts playing at the same time on the same track, creating a rhythmic pattern. These three parts could be playing over different channels or not. However, you should know that when parts are stacked one on top of the other in a MIDI track, the only visible part is the one on top of the others. If all the parts are of equal length, this might lead to confusion because you will hear the parts playing, but you won't see them unless you select all the parts by dragging your Selection tool over the visible part and opening your selection in the MIDI (Key or Drum) editor.

Figure 6.1
Overlapping MIDI parts
on a MIDI track

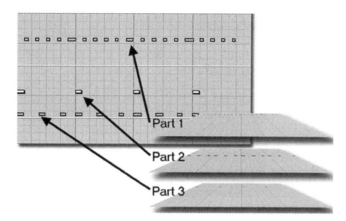

Part 1

Part 2

Part 3

Setting Up a MIDI Track

To use a MIDI track, you must choose a MIDI input port and a MIDI output port. The MIDI input port allows you to record incoming MIDI events on the track. For example, if a controller keyboard is hooked up to your MIDI input port A, you must set your MIDI track to this input port if you want to record events from your controller keyboard. This can be set as follows:

To set your MIDI input port:

1. Make sure the MIDI Thru is active (File > Preferences > MIDI).
2. Select the MIDI track you want to set up for input.
3. Make the Inspector area visible.
4. Make the first panel in the Inspector area visible, as shown in Figure 6.2.
5. Click the arrow to the left of the MIDI Input Port field to reveal the available MIDI input ports.
6. Select the appropriate port.

Notice in Figure 6.2 that a MIDI port is already present. This is because you can set a default MIDI port for your MIDI tracks. Whenever you create a MIDI track, it uses this default setting.

Figure 6.2
The basic track settings
for a MIDI track in the
Inspector area

To set a default MIDI port device for all projects:

1. Select Devices > Device Setup from the menu bar.

2. Make the Default MIDI Ports entry active by selecting it.

3. Click the MIDI Input drop-down menu (the field to the right of "MIDI Input") to select the appropriate default MIDI input port, as shown in Figure 6.3.

4. Repeat this last step for the MIDI output port.

5. Click the Apply button, and then click OK.

Figure 6.3
The Device Setup dialog
box allows you to set a
default MIDI port

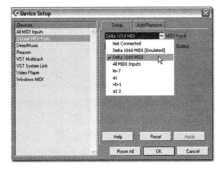

The following three tables describe each element found in both the Inspector's Track Setting area and the Track List area, followed by a description of each element found in only the Inspector, then only in the Track List area.

Table 6.1
Elements found in both the Inspector's Track Setting area and Track List area of a MIDI track

	Mute button Allows you to mute the track during playback.
	Solo button Allows you to solo the track (mutes all other tracks).
	Read Automation button Allows you to read recorded automation on this track.
	Write Automation button Allows you to write automation on this track.
	Record button Allows you to record incoming MIDI events on this track.
	Monitor button Allows you to use the MIDI Thru to hear MIDI messages coming in without recording these messages when in Record mode.
	Lock button Allows you to lock your track from editing
out : Delta 1010 MIDI	**MIDI Output Port setting** Allows you to set the output port for the track. MIDI events recorded on this track play through the device or software connected to this output port. You can also use the output port to monitor incoming MIDI events through a different port.
chn: 1	**MIDI Channel setting** Allows you to set the MIDI channel used by the MIDI output port to play MIDI events on this track.
bnk : Off	**Bank setting** Allows you to set a bank value associated with your MIDI device's preset structure. Typically, programs are grouped in banks of 128 sounds each (this is the maximum number of sounds MIDI can support). To access sounds above this value, banks are created. You can access up to 128 banks of 128 programs using this setting.
prg : Off	**Program setting** Allows you to specify a program number to the MIDI device or software instrument associated to this track.

CHAPTER 6

Table 6.2
Elements found only in the Inspector's Track Setting area of a MIDI track

	Input Transformer buttons Allows you to transform MIDI messages between the MIDI input and output of this track
	Timebase Format button Allows you to switch the track between linear time and musical tempo. When a track is displayed in musical tempo, changing the tempo of the song adjusts the events in the part according to the tempo setting. When a track is displayed in linear time, changing the tempo of the song does not affect the start position of the parts.
	Edit MIDI Channel button Allows you to edit the channel setting if you are using an external device or brings up the VST Instrument's editing interface panel if your track is assigned to one.
	Track Volume setting Allows you to set and monitor volume for the MIDI track. This uses the MIDI control change message number 7 and displays any volume automation for your track.
	Track Pan setting Allows you to set and monitor pan for the MIDI track. This uses the MIDI control change message number 10 and displays any pan automation for your track.
	Track Delay setting Allows you to add a positive or negative delay in milliseconds to your track. Events with a negative delay play earlier, whereas positive values change the timing of events to occur later in time.
	MIDI Input Port setting Allows you to set the input port for the track. MIDI events coming through the input port can be recorded onto the track or monitored through the MIDI output port setting.
	Drum Map setting Allows you to associate a drum map with the MIDI events on this track. This is useful when you record a drum part on this track. You can also use the Drum Map setting in the Track List area.

Table 6.3
Elements found only in the Track List area of a MIDI track

e	**Edit VST Channel button** Brings up the VST Channel panel (does the same thing as the Edit MIDI Channel when assigned to an external device).
	Drum Map button Allows you to associate a drum map with the MIDI events on this track (same as Drum Map setting).
	Bypass Insert button Allows you to bypass (when active) any MIDI inserts you have added in the Track Inserts section of the Inspector area. The button is blue when an insert effect is assigned to the track and yellow when the Bypass button is active.
	Bypass Sends button Allows you to bypass (when active) any MIDI sends you have added in the Track Sends section of the Inspector area. The button is blue when a send effect is assigned to the track and yellow when the Bypass button is active.

MIDI Track Parameters

MIDI track parameters allow you to change how the MIDI in a track is played in real time. In other words, it does not affect the recorded MIDI events, but rather transforms them on their way out to the MIDI output port. It's kind of like looking at yourself in a distorted mirror at the county fair. You do not actually have a big head, small neck, big belly, and small legs, as seen in the reflection. You simply appear like that in the mirror. MIDI track parameters are similar. They transform the data going out. This said, you would understand that, because they don't affect the MIDI data, the track parameters do not appear in the MIDI editors. Also, MIDI track parameters affect all the parts on a track.

These parameters provide a convenient way to try things out without changing the original MIDI messages because you can bypass these parameters at any time by activating the Bypass button next to the track parameter name in the Inspector area (see Figure 6.4). When a track parameter is assigned, the upper-right corner of the Track Parameter section is green. When you click the track parameters' Bypass button, the same corner becomes yellow, indicating that you are bypassing any track parameter settings for this track.

CHAPTER 6

Figure 6.4
The Track Parameters
section found in the
Inspector area of a
selected MIDI track

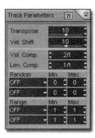

The Transpose field allows you to set a value between -127 to +127. Each value corresponds to a semitone below or above the current. Positive values transpose notes higher; negative values transpose notes lower. This affects all the notes found on this track.

The Velocity Shift field allows you to set a value between -127 to +127 as well; however, in this case these values add or remove the value from the MIDI events' velocity for the selected track. For example, adding a value of "10" causes all MIDI events to play at their recorded velocity plus ten.

The Velocity Compression field uses a multiplication factor, which compresses or expands the velocity of MIDI events on a track by its corresponding multiplication factor. This factor is defined by a numerator (left value) and denominator (right value). The resulting fraction is applied to the track's velocity level. You can see an example of this in Table 6.4.

Table 6.4
How track parameters affect MIDI events

Track Parameter	Note 1	Note 2	Note 3	Note 4	Comment
Before Filters					
Velocity Value	50	70	35	100	Recorded velocities
Vel. Comp. (1/2)	25	35	17	50	Velocities heard after compression
Vel. Shift (+50)	50	50	50	50	Added to the previous velocities when heard
After Filter	75	85	67	100	Resulting velocity that can be heard

The Length Compression field also uses a multiplication factor, which compresses or expands the length of MIDI events on a track by its corresponding multiplication factor. This factor is defined by a numerator (left value) and denominator (right value). For example, a factor of 2:1 means that all notes will be of double length and a factor of 1:3 means that all notes will be one third their original lengths.

Below the Length Compression field, you will find two Random generators with their corresponding fields. These two fields act independently from one another and serve to introduce random values to the position, pitch, velocity, or length of MIDI events on this track. This can be useful with clear rhythmic or melodic parts rather than with tracks containing long sustained notes. In other words, the randomness is more obvious when events occur more often. Under each Random generator is a field that lets you choose what type of randomly generated value you want to add (position, pitch, velocity, or length). You can then set a minimum and maximum value for these random values. A wider range between the minimum and maximum value creates a more pronounced effect, whereas a smaller range creates a more subtle effect. With the position and length selections, you can set the minimum and maximum values from -500 ticks to +500 ticks respectively. For the pitch and velocity, you can set these values between -100 and +100 (this corresponds to semitones when used with pitch). Note that you can't set your minimum value to a higher value than the maximum value.

At the bottom of the Track Parameters section are two Range fields with associated minimum and maximum values that work just like the random minimum and maximum fields. However, in this case, the Range fields, as the name suggests, are used to set a range for which events are included or excluded from processing. There are four Range modes:

▶ **Velocity Limit**. Use this mode when you want all notes to play within a certain velocity range. Any note that plays at a velocity outside the range is either brought to the minimum value in the range if it is below this value or brought to the maximum value in the range if it is above this value. Any other velocity values (which are found within the defined range) play unchanged.

▶ **Velocity Filter**. Use this mode when you want to isolate notes that play within a certain velocity range. Notes outside the range, either above or below, are simply not played back.

▶ **Note Limit**. Use this mode when you want all notes to play within a range of notes. Note values that are below or above this range are transposed an octave up or down respectively in order to play within the range. If your range is too narrow and notes still don't reach the range after transposing an octave up or down, they are transposed to the center note value found within your range. For example, in a range between C4 and G4, A4 is transposed to an E4.

▶ **Note Filter**. Use this mode when you want to isolate certain note pitches within a certain range. Notes with pitches outside the range are not played back.

About MIDI Effects

Before we discuss MIDI track inserts and sends, it is important that you understand the difference between a MIDI effect and an audio effect.

You have probably heard of audio effects and how you can use them to make your audio tracks sound better or different. In this respect, MIDI effects are similar to audio effects. However, the process is quite different with MIDI than it is for audio. When you apply a MIDI effect to a MIDI track, you are not processing the sound generated by the MIDI device (VST Instrument or hardware sound module). In fact, you are using a process that adds or changes the MIDI events that are recorded on your track in real time. For example, when you are adding a MIDI delay to your MIDI track, Cubase generates additional MIDI messages to simulate, using MIDI notes, an echo effect. Because these effects are playing in real time, just as audio effects, you can rest assured that your MIDI events on your track are not modified in any way, except at the output, where the MIDI effect actually takes place.

If you are using a VSTi, you can combine both types of effects: audio and MIDI. This gives you even more flexibility in your creative process. However, you cannot use audio effects on external MIDI devices because the audio of this device is not processed by Cubase until you decide to convert this MIDI track played by an external MIDI device into an audio track. We get to this subject later on, but for now, understand that a MIDI effect can be applied to any MIDI track in two ways: through a MIDI track insert and through a MIDI track send. Both methods instruct your MIDI sound module how to play the MIDI events according to the settings found in the MIDI effect.

You will find more information on what each MIDI effect does and how to use them in Appendix B.

MIDI Track Inserts

Below the Track Parameters section in the Inspector area, you will find the MIDI Track Inserts section. This allows you to add a MIDI effect to your MIDI track (see Figure 6.5). When you are using an effect as an insert, you are sending the MIDI events recorded on this track into a selected effect. This effect then generates the necessary MIDI events through the MIDI output port of the track containing the effect. It is the device's (sound module) job to actually play the resulting MIDI effect along with the original recorded MIDI material. As you can see in Figure 6.5, you can have up to four MIDI effects assigned to each MIDI track simultaneously. When a MIDI effect is selected from its drop-down menu, a panel opens up to reveal its settings. This panel can be found either in the Track Inserts section itself or in a stand-alone window. You may also force Cubase to open the parameters of a MIDI effect in its own window if, by default, they open in the Track Inserts section. You can do so by Alt-clicking (Option-clicking on a Mac) on the MIDI Effect Editing Window button. Here are some of the things you can do with MIDI inserts:

To add a MIDI insert effect:

▶   Select a MIDI effect from one of the four drop-down menus.

To edit a MIDI insert effect's parameters:

▶   Click the MIDI Effect Editing Window button (see Figure 6.5).

To bypass one or all MIDI inserts from playback:

▶   If you want to bypass all effects, click the Insert Bypass button at the top of the MIDI Track Inserts section. When all the inserts are bypassed this way, the MIDI Track Insert section's top-left corner turns yellow, indicating that the effects are bypassed. Because you can always see the top part of the Track Inserts section, you can easily change the status (active or bypassed) of your inserts by using this bar.

▶   If you want to bypass only one effect, click the Activate/Deactivate button above the effect you want to bypass. By default, an effect is activated as soon as you select it from the drop-down menu. By deactivating it, you can do a comparison listening without having to reset your effect each time.

Figure 6.5
The MIDI Track Insert
section in the Inspector
area

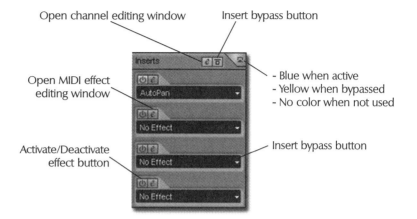

As you can see in Figure 6.6, when you assign a MIDI insert to a track, it only affects the events on this track and you can only use the track's MIDI output port to generate these effects. This said, if you want to use one device to play the original content and another to play the processed information, you can use a MIDI track send. If you want to maximize or minimize this section in the Inspector area, click the button found in the upper-right corner of the insert's title bar.

Figure 6.6
The signal path of a
MIDI track insert

MIDI Track Sends

When you want to send the result of a MIDI effect played through a different MIDI device, you can use the MIDI track sends instead of the MIDI track inserts because the track sends offer an additional setting for MIDI output ports and MIDI channels. As you can see in Figure 6.7, the signal is routed to two different outputs. In other words, if you don't need the effect to play through the same MIDI port and channel, use the track insert. However, if you want your effect to play through another port and channel, or you want to send the MIDI events before or after the volume control setting of the MIDI track, use the track sends.

Figure 6.7
The signal path of a
MIDI track send

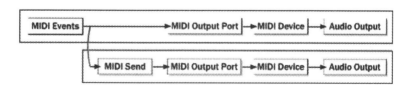

The options for the MIDI track sends are fairly similar to the ones found in the Track Inserts section (see Figure 6.8). In addition to the options explained earlier, a field below the MIDI Effect Selection field lets you choose the appropriate MIDI port for the MIDI events generated by the MIDI effect along with a MIDI channel setting. To the right of the MIDI Effect Editing button above each send effect is a Pre-/Post-fader button, which allows you to choose the point from which the MIDI events are sent to the MIDI effect. In Pre-fader mode, the volume control level of your track has no effect on the MIDI events sent to the effect. However, in Post-fader mode, the volume control level in the track influences how the MIDI events are treated by the MIDI effect if the volume level is part of the effect.

Figure 6.8
The MIDI Track Sends section in the Inspector area

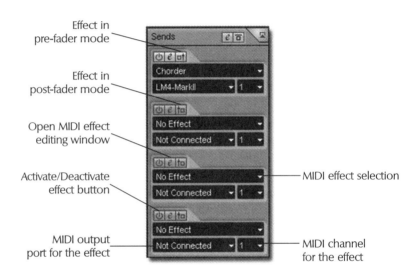

Effect in pre-fader mode

Effect in post-fader mode

Open MIDI effect editing window

Activate/Deactivate effect button

MIDI output port for the effect

MIDI effect selection

MIDI channel for the effect

To assign a MIDI track send:

1. Click the Maximize button in upper-right corner of the MIDI track send's title bar to expand the panel in the Inspector area.

2. From the MIDI Effect Selection drop-down menu, choose an appropriate effect.

3. Under the selected MIDI Effect field, choose an appropriate MIDI port for the output of the MIDI effect.

4. Next to the output port, select an appropriate MIDI channel for playback.

5. Select Pre- or Post-fader mode according to your preference. Note that in Post-fader mode, volume automation on your track may affect how the MIDI events are treated by the MIDI effect.

MIDI Track Channel

The MIDI Track Channel section (see Figure 6.9), found at the bottom of the Inspector area, offers many of the same options as you find in the MIDI Track Setting section of the Inspector area as well as the Track List area for a MIDI track. It also mirrors the information you find in the Track Mixer panel for this specific track class, as well as most of the buttons that we have seen earlier in the Track List and Track Setting section of the Inspector area. You can use this section to set the pan and volume levels of the device associated with this track. You can also use this section to change the MIDI In and Out ports of the track as well as rename the track.

Figure 6.9
The MIDI Track Channel section in the Inspector area

Audio Track

The audio track class is used to hold audio events, audio parts, and automation information. When you record audio on a track, an audio event is created in your project. Each audio track can play one audio event at a time. This implies that if you overlap audio events, you only hear the event on top of the others. You can change the order of these events to hear a different part.

To change the order of overlapping audio parts:

1.   With the Selection tool, click the event (or part) you want to send to back or bring to front.
2.   While the event is selected, right-click and choose the appropriate option under Move To from the context menu.

About Audio Terminology

To work with audio inside a Cubase project, it is important to understand the audio terminology associated with your project. In Cubase, audio is referred to as audio clips, events, parts, Regions, and slices. This section describes how, when, and why these terms are used.

In the Project window, recorded audio is referred to as an audio event. Audio events are the representation of the audio clip, which is the file recorded onto your hard disk. In essence, when you edit an audio event, you edit the audio representation of the audio file or clip inside Cubase without changing the original content found on your hard disk.

You can also create Regions inside an audio event. These Regions are used as a visual reference to define a portion of an audio event. When a Region is placed in your Project window, it behaves exactly as its event. So, when a Region is placed on an audio track, it becomes an audio event. This said, there is one big difference between an audio event that refers to a Region and one that doesn't: When an audio Region is placed on a track, you can change to which Region in the audio event in the pool this event (Region) refers to, allowing you to swap from one Region to another.

Another type of Region found in Cubase is called slices. Slices are used with rhythmic parts, such as drum loops. You can only create slices inside the Sample Editor window. Using the Hitpoints tool allows you to define where important beats or slices occur in rhythmic or percussive musical content. For example, you can cut a drum loop in individual hits called slices. These slices do not appear in the Media Pool; however, when you place a drum loop sample containing slices on an audio track, Cubase creates a part which holds this drum loop sample "sliced" into individual segments. This can be useful when you want to change the tempo of your song and keep the drum loop in sync with the tempo changes. If you take a look at Figure 6.10, you will see a part as it appears when an audio drum loop has been sliced and placed on an audio track. The same content is represented in both portions of Figure 6.10; however, the top portion represents the slices when the project plays at a tempo of 148 BPM, whereas the bottom portion represents the same slices played at a tempo of 79 BPM. As you can see, the beats occur at the same location in the bar/beat grid, but there is space added between each slice when the loop is played at a slower tempo.

Figure 6.10
Example of a drum loop
sliced using hitpoints

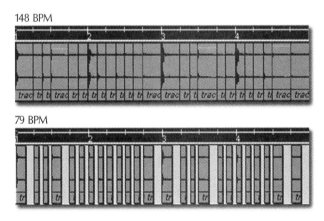

Finally, you can have audio parts in your project. Audio parts are containers of audio events, Regions, or slices. In themselves, they do not refer to any content unless you convert an event into a part or if you place audio content inside an existing part. In other words, audio parts are similar to MIDI parts in that they hold information that can be moved across other audio tracks or in time. Audio parts are useful when you want to move multiple events together, such as the ones found when using slices, for example.

Figure 6.11 is divided into three parts. On the left, you can see where to find the different types of audio terms mentioned in this section. In the center, you can see the hierarchy between the different terms and on the right, a diagram displaying how this hierarchy works in your project. By default, when you double-click in the Project window on a part, it launches the Audio Part Editor. Once inside the Audio Part Editor, you can drag other Regions, events, or sliced events into a part. When you double-click on an event or a Region, it launches the Sample Editor. You can't drag anything in the Sample Editor.

This hierarchy allows for nondestructive editing because what you normally edit is the audio event, its Region, or its slices, not the audio clip itself. When a portion of the audio event is processed, Cubase creates an additional audio clip on the hard disk containing the newly processed section of your audio. The audio parts containing references to processed audio material update themselves to correspond to this new link.

Figure 6.11
The audio terminology's hierarchy

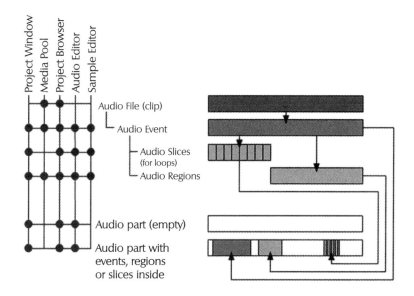

Setting Up an Audio Track

The following tables (6.5 to 6.7) describe the different buttons and control elements found in both the Inspector area and the Track List area for an audio track. It is important to understand what these buttons do as they will be used throughout your work on a project when audio tracks are involved.

Table 6.5
Elements found in both the Inspector's Track Setting area and Track List area of an audio track

	Mute button Allows you to mute the track during playback.
	Solo button Allows you to solo the track (mutes all other tracks).
	Read Automation button Allows you to read recorded automation on this track.
	Write Automation button Allows you to write automation on this track.
	Record button Allows you to record incoming audio events on this track.
	Monitor button Allows you to use the channel's level meters as an audio input monitor. You can't adjust the input level using the channel fader, but you can use this monitor level to adjust it using an external level adjustment.
	Lock button Allows you to lock your track from editing.
	Stereo/Mono Track setting Allows you to set the track for mono or stereo audio events. After a track is set to play mono events, you can only place mono audio events on this track. The same goes for stereo.
	Edit Audio Channel button Brings up the audio Channel Mixer panel for this channel and allows you to edit its settings.
	Timebase Format button Allows you to switch the track between linear time and musical tempo. When a track is displayed in musical tempo, changing the tempo of the song adjusts the events in the part according to the tempo setting. When a track is displayed in linear time, changing the tempo of the song does not affect the start position of the parts.

Table 6.6
Elements found only in the Inspector's Track Setting area of an audio track

	**Auto Fade setting** Brings up the Auto Fade dialog box, which lets you set how fades and crossfades are handled on this track.
 2.40	**Track Volume setting** Allows you to set and monitor the volume level for this track. Automation or volume changes made in the track's Channel Mixer or the project's Track Mixer are displayed here as well.
 0	**Track Pan setting** Allows you to set and monitor the pan position for this track. Automation or pan changes made in the track's Channel Mixer or the project's Track Mixer are displayed here as well.
 0.00	**Track Delay setting** Allows you to add a positive or negative delay in milliseconds to your track. Events with a negative delay play earlier, whereas positive values change the timing of events to occur later in time.
 out : BUS 1	**Audio Output setting** Allows you to set the output port for the track. Audio events recorded on this track play through this output port. You can also use the output port to send the signal to a group channel.
 in : IN 1	**Audio Input setting** Allows you to select the audio input channel used by the track to record incoming audio events for this track.

Table 6.7
Elements found only in the Track List area of an audio track

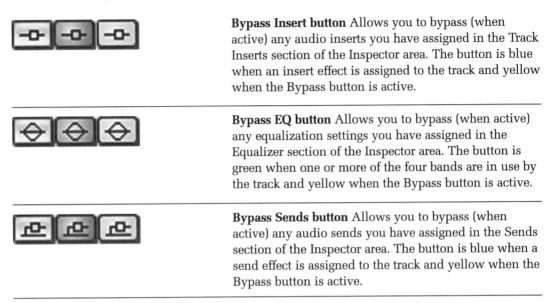

Bypass Insert button Allows you to bypass (when active) any audio inserts you have assigned in the Track Inserts section of the Inspector area. The button is blue when an insert effect is assigned to the track and yellow when the Bypass button is active.

Bypass EQ button Allows you to bypass (when active) any equalization settings you have assigned in the Equalizer section of the Inspector area. The button is green when one or more of the four bands are in use by the track and yellow when the Bypass button is active.

Bypass Sends button Allows you to bypass (when active) any audio sends you have assigned in the Sends section of the Inspector area. The button is blue when a send effect is assigned to the track and yellow when the Bypass button is active.

Audio Track Inserts

In Cubase SX, you can have up to eight insert effects per channel and up to five in Cubase SL. The signal from an audio track is routed through each active insert effect one after another. In other words, the output of one insert effect feeds the next one, and so on, from top to bottom (see Figure 6.12).

TIP
Because each instance of an effect that is loaded into an insert effect slot uses as much processing power and memory as it does in send effects, it is strongly recommended that you use track send effects when you use the same effect on more than one track. This reduces the amount of processing power needed to process the audio and also reduces the amount of memory needed to load each instance. To monitor how your computer is doing in terms of system resources, you can take a look at the VST Performance panel. The default key command to open this panel is F12. You can also open it by selecting its option in the Devices menu. This way, you can make changes to your project before your computer starts to be overloaded.

Figure 6.12
The Track Inserts
section from the
Inspector area of the
audio track

Each insert effect slot has three controls: the Active/Bypass button, the open effect window for editing, and a field to select which effect you want to add to the track. These controls are similar to the ones explained earlier in the MIDI Track Inserts section. You will also find three buttons in the title bar of this section:

▶ The Open Channel Mixer Panel button allows you to make changes to the track's setting.

▶ The Bypass Inserts button allows you to bypass all insert effects found on this track. As with the Active/Bypass button found on each insert, this can be useful to monitor your track with or without effects without having to make changes to these effects.

▶ The Track Insert section's Control button in the upper-right corner allows you to maximize or minimize this section in the Inspector area. As with all other Control buttons in the MIDI track's Inspector, the Control button has three states: light gray means that there are no inserts on this track, blue means that there are inserts on this track, and yellow means that the inserts on this track are bypassed.

Adding an insert effect, bypassing an insert, or all inserts is done exactly the same way as with MIDI track inserts. Please refer to that section in this chapter if you are unsure about the procedure.

Audio Track Equalizer

Below the Track Inserts section, you will find the Track Equalizer section (known as EQ). Each audio track you create has a four-band parametric equalizer (see Figure 6.13). An equalizer allows you to control the gain of a specific band of frequencies, with the center of the band of frequencies displayed in the EQ. How wide the band is on each side of this center frequency depends on a setting called Q. These four bands are called (from top to bottom in the Equalizer section): Hi, Hi Mid, Lo Mid, and Lo.

CHAPTER 6

Figure 6.13
The Equalizer Section
from the Inspector area
of the audio track

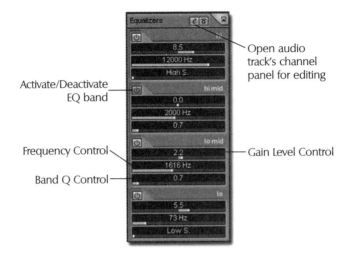

Open audio
track's channel
panel for editing

Activate/Deactivate
EQ band

Frequency Control

Band Q Control

Gain Level Control

Most of the features for each EQ band are similar with the exception of the Hi and Lo bands. In
the Hi band, setting the Q completely to the left creates a high shelf, which means that any
frequency above the center frequency for this band is affected by the gain control. Inversely, if
the Q is set completely to the right, it creates a low-pass filter, where every frequency above the
band's center frequency is reduced. For the Lo band, setting the Q completely to the left
produces a low shelf and setting the Q completely to the right creates a high pass, as shown in
Figure 6.14.

Figure 6.14
The different types of
shelves and pass filters
found in the Hi and Lo
band EQ

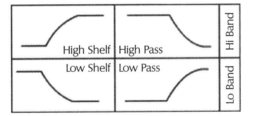

To adjust an EQ band from the audio track Equalizer section:

1. Make the Equalizer section visible for the track you want to adjust.

2. Enable the band you want to use.

3. Find the center frequency you want to adjust by dragging the slider bar under
   the numeric display of the frequency, by clicking on the frequency value and
   using your scroll bar to increase or decrease the value, or by double-clicking on
   the value and entering a new value between 20 and 20,000 (which corresponds
   to the range of each band).

4. Adjust the amount of gain or reduction you want to apply using the gain control
   values. You can adjust these values the same way you can adjust the frequency
   (as seen in Step 3). However, the minimum and maximum values for this field
   are -24 to +24 (which correspond to dB values).

5. Adjust the width of your band by changing the Q value for the appropriate band. Smaller values result in wider bands, whereas higher values result in narrower bands.

6. Repeat these steps for each band in your EQ.

You can bring back each value to its default position in the EQ by Ctrl-clicking (Command-clicking on Mac) on the appropriate field. You can also do a before/after comparison listening by deactivating the band. This acts as a band bypass, keeping your settings intact.

Note that you can also adjust the EQ settings (as well as inserts and sends) through the Track Mixer panel and the Channel Mixer panel. Finally, you can also bypass all bands in the EQ by clicking on the Bypass button in the Equalizer section's title bar.

Audio Track Sends

As with track inserts, the track sends for audio tracks are similar to MIDI track sends. This said, there are a few differences to point out. First, let's start with the title bar. In the MIDI Track Sends section (and in the audio Track Sends section), you have a button that allows you to open the track's Channel Mixer panel to edit its settings. Next to this button, you also have a Bypass All Sends button to monitor your track without sending it to the effects. However, the first button to the left in the title bar (see Figure 6.15) allows you to bring up the VST Send Effects panel.

Figure 6.15
The Track Sends section from the Inspector area of the audio track

Effect in pre or post-fader mode button

Open audio plug-in effect editing window

Activate/Deactivate effect button

Name of the selected effect

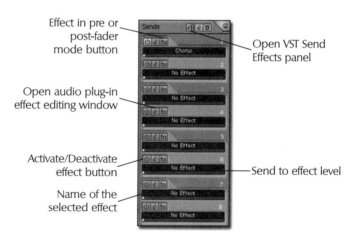

Open VST Send Effects panel

Send to effect level

For each audio track send, you have three buttons above the effect's name which resemble the MIDI track sends: the Activate/Deactivate (or Bypass) button, the Edit Effect Parameter button, and the Pre-/Post-fader toggle button. Below these three buttons, you will find the name of the send effect. The name displayed here represents the effect that you assigned in the VST Send Effects panel. Because you can only have a total of eight send effects per project, you can't change the actual effect directly in this section; however, as mentioned previously, you can open the VST Send Effects panel from the section's title bar.

Below the effect's name is the Send to Effect Level setting. This allows you to control how much signal from this track you want to send to the effect. Remember in the MIDI track sends, you don't have any controls over the amount sent to the effect. That is because you can have eight sends per channel and MIDI effects actually generate MIDI events rather than changing the sound coming from the original sound source (your sound module or VSTi). Audio sent to an audio send effect plug-in is processed at the level at which it is sent. The more signal you send to the effect, the more you hear the processed sound for this audio signal. The idea is to give you control over how much effect you want over each individual track without having to load multiple instances of plug-in effects.

To assign a send effect to an audio track:

1. Make the Track Sends section in the Inspector area visible for the audio track.

2. If there are currently no send effects plug-ins active, make the VST Send Effects panel visible by clicking on the appropriate button in the Track Sends section's title bar.

3. Select the desired send effect from one of the VST Send Effects plug-in selection fields. By default, selecting an effect here activates this effect.

4. In the Send Effect section for the audio track, select Pre- or Post-fader as desired. You can see where the signal is routed in Figure 6.16. In Post-fader mode, the signal sent to the effect is taken after the audio track's channel volume level.

5. In the Send Effect section for the audio track, raise the volume level sent to the effect.

6. Raise the volume of the effect from the VST Send Effects panel to the desired level. This influences the overall level of the effect in the mix.

7. After completing these steps, you need to fine-tune both the Send to Effect Level setting and the return of the effect's signal into the mix to a desired level.

Figure 6.16
The audio send signal path diagram

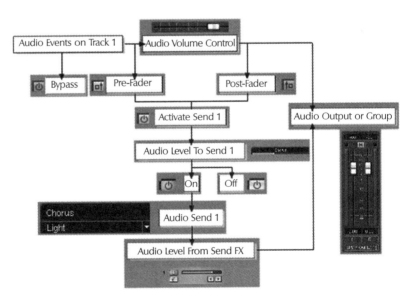

To send the signal of one track to more than one send effect, repeat the same steps as mentioned earlier in this section for another effect. Unlike insert effects, each send effect is processed in parallel, not in series. This implies that the order in which the signal is sent to the send effect does not influence the end result.

As you can see in Figure 6.16, there are many places you can bypass the effect. The following list describes the differences between each one and how you can use them.

To bypass/activate the signal sent to all send effects in a track:

▶ Use the Bypass button found in the Track Sends section's title bar (in the Inspector area of the audio track).

To bypass/activate the signal sent to one send effect in a track:

▶ Use the Bypass/Activate button found above the effect's name in the Track Sends section in the audio track's Inspector area.

To bypass all the tracks sent to the same effect:

▶ Use the Bypass/Activate button found next to the effect in the VST Send Effects panel for this effect.

Audio Track Channel

The Track Channel section (see Figure 6.17) in the Inspector area offers controls over the track's audio channel. Most of these controls are also present in the Inspector's Setup section or in the Track List area. You will find a description of each button found in the Track Channel section in the "Setting Up an Audio Track" section found earlier in this chapter. This said, because these controls are the same as the ones found in the Setup section, the Track List area, the Channel Mixer panel, and the Track Mixer panel, any changes you make in any of these windows is updated automatically in every one of them. For example, if you change the volume level in the Track Channel section, this is reflected in the audio track Setup section as well as in the Channel Mixer and the Track Mixer panels.

Figure 6.17
The Track Channel section from the Inspector area of the audio track

Folder Track

Folder tracks, as you might have guessed, are used as folders in which you can put any classes of tracks, including other folder tracks. You can use folder tracks as you would use folders in your computer, putting different tracks that relate to a specific kind of track inside a folder, identify it, and mute or hide the folder track to give you more working space on your screen. For example, if you have several percussion tracks, you could create a folder, name it "Percussions," and move all the percussion tracks inside this folder track.

When tracks are moved inside a folder track, a folder part is created in the Event Display area, which lets you see the contents of the folder track even when this track is minimized.

The Inspector area of the folder track only contains one section. This section contains the name of the tracks you moved inside the folder track. Whenever you click on the name of a track in this section, the track's Inspector area is displayed below the folder section (also in the Inspector area as shown in Figure 6.18).

Figure 6.18
The Inspector area of a folder track; when a track name in the folder track is selected, Cubase displays that track's Inspector area below

Notice in Figure 6.18 that at the top of the folder track's Inspector area, there are buttons found in other track classes (and explained previously). These buttons affect all the tracks inside the folder track. For example, clicking the Mute button in the Inspector area of a folder track or in its Track List area mutes all the tracks inside the folder track. Similarly, clicking the Lock button locks all these tracks from editing. As you would guess, this makes recording, monitoring, muting, soloing, or locking multiple tracks simultaneously very easy.

HINT
Remember that to add a track of any class to your project, you can right-click (Ctrl-click on a Mac) in the Track List area and choose Add track (of the desired class) from the context menu.

To move tracks into a folder track:

1. Click and drag the track you want to move to a folder track as shown in the top part of Figure 6.19.

2. When a green line appears near your folder track, drop your track into the folder track by releasing the mouse button (as shown in the center image of Figure 6.19).

3. Repeat this process to add additional tracks. You can drag multiple consecutive tracks simultaneously into a folder track by clicking the first track in the Track List area, and then shift-clicking the last track you want to move into the folder track. To move nonconsecutive tracks, use the Ctrl key (Command on Mac) to select your tracks before moving them.

Figure 6.19
Moving tracks into a folder track

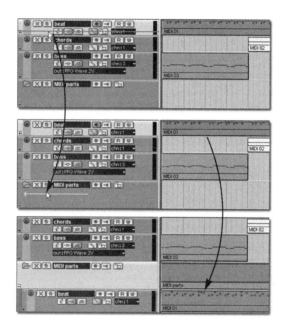

To remove tracks from a folder track, simply move them outside of the folder track, just as you moved them inside of it.

When tracks are added to a folder track, a folder part is created as shown in Figure 6.20. As you can see in the same figure, the folder part displays the position and colors used by the parts on the tracks it contains. In this example, the folder track is minimized, hiding the details of these tracks. You can click the plus sign at the bottom-left corner of the folder track's Track List area to view these tracks once again. You can also rename folder tracks as you would any other tracks through the Inspector area.

Figure 6.20
Folder parts appear in
the folder track

To rename a track using the Inspector area:

1. Click in the name box at the top part of the Inspector area.

2. Type in a new name for your track.

Group Track

A group track allows you to assign the output of different audio channels to a group channel.
You can then add automation or effects to this group, which affect all the audio channels
assigned to this group. For example, if you don't have a multiple output sound card, you could
assign different tracks to group tracks and use the groups as submixes. Typically, you could send
all the drum and percussion tracks to one group, all the back vocals to another group, and the
strings (if you have violins, altos, cellos, and contrabasses, for example) to another group. Then,
if you want to increase the string section, all you have to do is raise the group channel fader
rather than raise the audio channel faders for each string instrument.

Group tracks do not contain any MIDI or audio events and you can't send MIDI tracks that use
external devices for playback, such as a sound module or a sampler. This is because the audio
aspect of these tracks is not handled by Cubase, but rather by the sound module itself. You can
control MIDI automation through the Track Mixer panel, however. This said, if you have
assigned a VSTi (VST Instrument) to your MIDI track, two channels are created in your Track
Mixer panel: one representing MIDI control and another for audio control. Because VST
Instruments use your computer's sound card to generate their sound and Cubase's audio engine
controls your sound card, the audio channels of VST Instruments can be assigned to a group
track.

The Inspector area of a group track offers the same controls as an audio track with a few
exceptions:

▶   You can't record on a group track so there are no record-ready, monitor buttons.

▶   Because group tracks do not contain events (only automation data), you do not
     have a mono/stereo switch, nor do you have an Auto Fade setting button.

▶   Group tracks take their input from other channels you may assign to it, so you
     won't find any input selection field. You can, however, assign the output of the
     group to a desired bus (or even another group) for output.

We take a closer look at how to use group tracks later in Chapter 12.

Marker Track

We've already discussed Marker tracks in Chapter 4, so you should already be familiar with this track class. However, let's take a closer look at the fields found in the Marker track's Track List area: the Zoom, Locate, and Cycle fields. These three fields hold drop-down menus that display the Markers, locators, and cycle markers currently present in your project.

▶ The Zoom field fills the Event Display area with the content found between the selected Markers (cycle markers always hold a left and right or start and end Marker position). You can use this field to quickly change the focus of your work from one Region to another in your project.

▶ The Locate field allows you to move your play line to the location of the Marker you select in this field. If you select a Marker during playback, the play line jumps to that location and continues playing from that point forward. If your project is not playing, the play line simply jumps to this point and waits for your next action.

▶ The Cycle field allows you to move your left and right locators to the location of the cycle marker you select in this field. Moving your left and right locators does not move your play line to the left locator's position, however. This said, you can use the number one key on the numeric keypad as a keyboard shortcut to quickly move your play line to the new location.

Master Automation Track

Each project can contain one master automation track. This track contains automation information for your master and bus output channels as well as master effects. Because we discuss automation later in Chapter 13, it makes more sense explaining how this special track works in that chapter. For now, understand that this track only contains automation information for your busses and sends to master effect input levels. There is no Inspector information for this track's class.

Now You Try It

It's time to put the topics covered in this chapter into action—you can download a practice exercise at http://www.muskalipman.com.

7

MIDI Track Recording and Editing

Now, it's time to start getting some MIDI into our project. This chapter looks at how this process is achieved and how you can set up different parameters to ensure that what you record sounds right. For example, using the Auto-Quantize feature, you can automatically adjust recorded MIDI events so that they match up with a predefined grid. We also take a look at how to set up a metronome click so that you can use this as a reference guide when recording MIDI or even audio events into a project.

You'll also see how easy it is to move around in a project and see either a small section of your project, focusing on a detail in this project, or move out and get the bigger picture. Mastering the zoom tools and options will save you lots of grief and scrolling time because there's nothing more annoying than having to scroll up and down, and left and right all the time to find what you want, where you are, and what just happened.

After these events are recorded, we look at how you can apply different functions to these events to correct errors before we start editing them in a MIDI editor. And, finally, recording is not the only way you can get media into a Cubase project. You can also import audio, MIDI, and video in different formats using the import features included in Cubase SX/SL.

In this chapter, you will:

- ▶ Set up for MIDI recording
- ▶ Adjust MIDI filters to record only the MIDI messages you want
- ▶ Configure a metronome
- ▶ Understand the different quantize methods and how you can apply them to recorded events
- ▶ Work with the different zooming functions, menus, and tools
- ▶ Understand the differences between MIDI functions and MIDI parameters
- ▶ Learn how to import files into a project and how Cubase handles the different formats

MIDI Recording Preparations

In Chapter 4, we looked at the different recording modes available in the Transport panel. In Chapter 6, we looked at the different settings available in a MIDI track to record and play back events that were recorded on that track. Now, it's time to put it all together and look at different MIDI recording situations. For example, do you want to:

▶ Record only one MIDI source?

▶ Record multiple MIDI sources simultaneously?

▶ Record over something you previously recorded?

▶ Tell Cubase to start recording automatically at a certain point and stop recording after it crosses another location in your project?

Before we look at the answers to those questions, you should know that there a few setup preferences that influence Cubase's behavior during the recording process. So, let's start by looking at those.

Setting up Your Editing Preferences

There is an option in Cubase's preferences that allows you to automatically enable a selected track for recording simply by selecting it. When this option is checked, a selected MIDI track automatically record enables itself to record as soon as you click the Record button. If this option is not checked, you need to record enable any track you want to record to manually as you would on a multitrack recorder.

To enable the automatic record enable on selected tracks:

1. Select Preferences from the File menu.

2. In the Preferences list, select the Editing item.

3. In the right area, check the Record Enable on Selected Track checkbox option.

4. Click Apply and then click OK.

You will also find a few recording related options in the MIDI preferences (File > Preferences > MIDI) that we have not yet addressed:

▶ **Snap Record Parts to Bars**. When this option is selected, Cubase automatically extends a part to the closest bar before the part begins and after the part ends when you record on the fly from a location other than a bar's beginning. This makes it easier to move parts later on when you want to edit MIDI events on your track.

▶ **Reset On Record End, Part End, and/or Stop**. When either of these options is selected, Cubase sends a Reset message to all connected MIDI devices. This message sends an All Note Off message and a Reset All Controllers message. You can also send a Reset message to all your MIDI devices if ever an error occurs that causes a MIDI device to sound off a stuck note by using the Reset option found in the MIDI menu.

▶ **Note On Priority**. When your MIDI timing is important, checking this option gives priority to Note On messages rather than continuous Control messages, helping the appearance of a better MIDI timing. Note that the word appearance implies that if your MIDI port is overloaded with MIDI information, you will still experience some delays; however, if these delays occur on Control Change messages, it might not be as audible.

▶ **Length Correction**. When this option is set to a value other than zero, Cubase adjusts the length of two consecutive notes playing on the same pitch and on the same channel to make sure there is a small space between these two MIDI events. The value you enter is the number of ticks found between these two similar notes.

▶ **Solo Record in Editors**. When you want to make sure the events you record go into the part you are editing (when a MIDI editor window is opened), you can enable this option. This record enables the edited track while preventing any other tracks from also recording new events for as long as the MIDI editor is opened.

▶ **Record Catch Range in ms**. When you start recording from a specific point, sometimes you might play a note just a little too early for Cubase to include it in the recording. This results in a missing note at the beginning of a part. To avoid this, you can tell Cubase to catch events that are played slightly before the actual recording begins. The value represents the number of milliseconds Cubase uses as a catch range when a recording is activated.

There are also a few options in the Transport section of the Preferences dialog box that influence the software's behavior during recording.

▶ Return to Start Position on Stop. Returns the play line to the location from which it started when you click Play or Record rather than having it stay at its current stop location.

▶ Deactivate Punch In on Stop. Disables the otherwise enabled Punch-in button whenever you click the Stop button or press the space bar on your keyboard.

▶ Stop after Automatic Punchout. Stops playing automatically right after it hits the punch-out location, or when the post-roll time is played if this setting is also enabled. A pre-roll and post-roll setting is enabled when you've entered a value for either of these fields in the Transport panel and when the Use Pre-/Post-Roll option is checked in the Transport menu.

▶ Always Use MIDI Clock Start. Is only a relevant option in the following case: if you send a MIDI clock to an external device that cannot recognize a Continue command provided by normal MIDI clock transport commands (which includes Start, Continue, and Stop). This might be the case when you are sending MIDI clock information to an external drum machine, for example.

MIDI Filtering

When recording MIDI events, you are recording many different types of MIDI messages. The most obvious type of MIDI message are the channel voice messages, which includes Note On, Note Off, Program Change, and so on. You can decide to record all MIDI messages, or only specific MIDI messages, filtering any other messages from the recording. In other words, you can choose which MIDI events you want to record. This can be useful when you want to avoid recording lots of useless data that can bog down your MIDI output port when passing these events through an already crowded port. Also, some MIDI devices send events that might not be essential to your performance. Cubase allows you to filter out these messages.

To filter MIDI events during recording or playback:

1.   Select Preferences > Filter from the File menu (Figure 7.1).

2.   In the Record section of the MIDI Filter area, check all the types of events you do not want Cubase to record. Events that are already recorded will continue to play.

3.   If you want to filter out events while you are playing as well, check the appropriate types of events in the Thru section. Once again, recorded events will play back, but checked event types in this section will be filtered out from the MIDI input.

4.   In the Channels section, click the MIDI channels from which you do not want to record. In Figure 7.1, messages coming on Channels 11 through 16 will not be recorded.

5.   Finally, if you want to add additional controller messages to the filtered list, use the Controller Selection field in the Controller section to scroll through the types of controller messages and click the Add button to add them to your filtered list.

6.   Click Apply and then click OK when done.

Figure 7.1
The MIDI Filter area in Cubase's Preferences dialog box

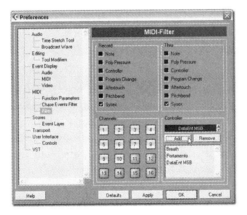

As you've noticed in the previous steps, these settings are optional and in most cases, filtering the System Exclusive (SysEx) messages is all you need to do (which, by default is already filtered). On the other hand, you can deselect the SysEx filter if you want to save your external MIDI device's system exclusive information into a project.

System Exclusive messages are used to transmit parameter settings from and to a MIDI device that are not supported by any other type of MIDI message. In most cases, System Exclusive messages are device specific and are used to recall or store settings that are used by a device to produce a sound or program, such as a reverb type or cutoff frequency setting.

What you just did through the MIDI Filter area influences the general behavior of Cubase. In other words, it applies these settings on all MIDI tracks until you change these settings once again. You can, however, decide to filter out, or even convert, certain MIDI events into other MIDI events in a track as you are recording it. This is done through Cubase's Transformer.

The Transformer comes in two flavors: as a MIDI effect called MIDI Transformer and as a track input called Input Transformer. When used as an effect, it transforms events that are already recorded on a track. When it is used as an Input Transformer, it transforms the events before it records them. You can access the Input Transformer's panel through its appropriate button (described in Chapter 6) found in the MIDI settings section of the Inspector area.

Setting Up Your Metronome

To help you keep the beat while you are recording, you can activate the Click button on the Transport panel. This enables the metronome. You can use either a MIDI device to generate the click produced by the metronome, or your computer's speaker, or both if you want.

To configure your metronome settings:

1. Ctrl-click (or Command-click on a Mac) the Click button on the Transport panel, or from the Transport menu, select the Metronome Setup option. This Metronome Setup dialog box appears as shown in Figure 7.2.

2. Check the MIDI Click and/or the Audio Click check boxes depending on which type of click you want to hear.

3. If you've selected the MIDI Click check box, make sure to select a proper MIDI port connected to the device that will play the MIDI click and the proper MIDI channel (by default, this is set to Channel 10 because this channel is usually reserved for drum sounds and is appropriate for clicks). You may also change the MIDI note value of the high and low notes. High notes are played typically on the first beat of a bar, whereas low notes are played on the other beats. Finally, you can adjust the velocity of these notes in the same area.

4. For the audio click, it's a little simpler because you can only adjust the volume of the click produced by the computer's speaker.

5. Check the Precount check box if you want Cubase to count bars before it begins playing or recording. This is useful when you are not using the pre-roll value in the Transport bar.

6. In the Precount Bars field, enter the appropriate number of bars you want Cubase to sound off before it actually starts playing or recording. If you have deselected the Precount check box, settings in this section are not considered.

7. Because you can set a different tempo for your project when your Master Track button on the Transport panel is disabled, you can choose to keep the metronome click playing at the tempo value determined by the Master track's tempo value by checking the From Master Track option. Because the current tempo when the Master track is disabled is not necessarily linked to the Master track tempo, it is recommended that you deselect this check box.

8. Make sure the Use Signature option is checked because this has a direct impact on how the metronome counts clicks. You can play your project at a different tempo setting when the Master track is disabled, but the signature setting is always active. For example, if your project switches from a 4/4 bar to a 3/4 bar, you want the metronome to correspond to this change as well. If not, deselect this check box.

9. In the Click during area, the two first options determine if the metronome plays automatically only when you are in Record mode, or Play mode, or both.

10. If you want your metronome clicks on a different value than your signature setting, such as every eighth note rather than every quarter note in a 4/4 bar, you can check the Use Count Base option and set the value using the up and down arrows to the right of this check box in order to adjust the beat subdivision for your metronome's click.

11. When you have completed setting these options, click OK.

Figure 7.2
The Metronome Setup
dialog box

Recording MIDI

To record MIDI events on one or multiple tracks:

1. Make sure the MIDI Thru Active option is selected in the Files > Preferences > MIDI dialog box.

2A. Configure each track you want to use during the recording process by setting the MIDI input and output ports. If you only want to record on one track, simply configure that track.

2B. If you want to play the incoming MIDI events through a VSTi as you are recording or if you want to hear a specific sound, configure the Bank and/or Program fields in the MIDI Settings section of the Inspector area or in the Track List area.

3. Select the appropriate MIDI channel for the track's MIDI output.

4. In the Transport panel, set the appropriate Record mode (Normal or Merge).

5. In the Transport panel, set the appropriate Cycle mode if you want to record in cycles (Mix or Overwrite).

6. Set the location of your left and right locators appropriately. For example, if you want to record from Bar 5 Beat 1 to Bar 9 Beat 1, set the left and right locators to Bar 5 and 9 respectively.

7. If you want Cubase to start recording at a specific bar and stop recording at a specific bar without recording in Cycle mode, you can enable the Punch-in and Punch-out buttons on the Transport panel.

8. Activate the metronome click on the Transport panel if you want to hear a click while recording. You can Ctrl-click (Command-click on Mac) to access the Metronome settings (see the appropriate section later in this chapter for a closer look at this dialog box).

9. Select the tracks you want to record and make sure the Record Enable button is active on each track. If you want to monitor a track but not record on it, disable the Record button on this track and enable the Monitor button.

10. Press Record and start playing. If you've enabled the metronome click, the precount value you've entered in the Metronome Setting dialog box determines how many bars Cubase counts before it starts recording.

11. Press the Stop button on the Transport panel (or space bar on the keyboard) when done. If the Punch-out button was enabled, Cubase should stop automatically when it reaches that location.

Now that you've just recorded events on a track or multiple selected tracks, you might want to record over a portion of this recording to correct errors that would be too long to edit in the editor or simply because you feel like it. In the previous steps, you were using the left and right locators as a point of reference to both begin playback and recording as well as to stop recording. You may also use the pre-roll value in the Transport panel to begin playback before you start recording and the post-roll value to have Cubase continue playing after you've stopped recording. The instructions on using the pre-roll and post-roll functions were described earlier in Chapter 4's "Pre- and Post-Roll" section.

Quantizing Your Events

Quantizing information means that you set a virtual grid to which notes or events cling. When you are recording MIDI information, your notes might be recorded a little bit before, or a little bit after, a beat. This is done because humans are not as steady and consistent as the timing in Cubase. Sometimes, this is a good thing, and sometimes it isn't. So, when you want to make sure that everything falls into place, or falls exactly on the beat, you can use the Quantize function to nudge MIDI events to their closest quantize value. For example, if you set your quantize value to quarter note (1/4), every note you record when playing on your keyboard clings to the closest quarter note in the bar where you recorded your MIDI information. Setting your quantizing value higher splits the grid into more subdivisions for each bar in your arrangement.

Quantizing MIDI events affects the way MIDI events are played back, but it does not affect your recorded material; thus, it is not changed permanently and the original position values are kept with the project regardless of the undo history list. At times, however, you might want to requantize a series of events, using the quantized position as a reference. Because quantizing always refers to the original position of the events, you can use the Freeze Quantize function. When you freeze the quantization, you basically tell Cubase that you want to use the new quantized position as a point of reference to requantize your events rather than their original position. Remember, however, that after you use the Freeze Quantize function, you can no longer go back to the original position of the recorded events.

Quantize Methods

The basic quantize method consists, as mentioned earlier, of moving the start of an event to the closest quantize grid value. This is referred to as over quantizing. This said, Cubase offers different quantize methods, which handle events in different way, giving you more control over how notes are affected when applying a quantization.

As displayed in Figure 7.3, the same original content (found in the upper-left corner) has been treated to different quantization methods. All of these examples use the same eighth-note quantize grid.

► **Over quantize method.** Moves the start position of the event to the closest quantize grid setting.

► **End quantize method.** Moves the end position of the event to the closest quantize grid setting.

► **Length quantize method.** Does not affect the start position, but adjusts the length of each event to fit the value found in the quantize grid setting. In this example (Figure 7.3, second row, second column to the right), each note is one eighth-note in length.

► **Iterative quantize method.** Is a looser version of the over quantize method because it moves the start position of an event in proportion with an iterative strength value, which is found in the Quantize Setup panel. Another difference with the over quantize method is that it uses the current location (this could be the quantized location) of the event rather than its original location (unquantized location). This implies that you can quantize an event, and then requantize it differently using the iterative quantize method.

Figure 7.3
Quantize method
examples

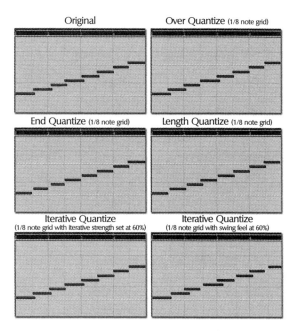

CHAPTER 7

The Quantize Setup panel offers a beefed-up version of the over quantize method, giving you control over a number of different parameters, allowing you to be more creative with the quantization of events. This panel gives you the opportunity to move an otherwise pretty square and static grid around, changing its reference points by different increments. Here are the controls you have over the grid in the Quantize Setup panel (see Figure 7.4):

▶ The Grid drop-down menu allows you to set the quantize reference value for its grid. These represent note subdivisions, as seen earlier in Chapter 4.

▶ The Type drop-down menu offers three options: straight, dotted, and tuplet, which also corresponds to how the grid is separated. This was also discussed in Chapter 4. So for example, selecting the one-eighth-note value for the grid and the tuplet type creates a gridline every 1/8 Tuplet.

▶ The Swing slider allows you to shift the position of a straight grid type, producing a swing or shuffle feeling. This also works best when the Tuplet field is set to Off. As you can see in Figure 7.4, the swing slider is set at 54%. If you look at the display in the middle of the panel, the actual 1/8 grid is shown in pale thin lines above, whereas the swing grid is indicated by the bold lines at the bottom of this same display box.

▶ The Tuplet field allows you divide the grid to accommodate more complex rhythmic patterns, such as triplets or quintuplets. An eighth note quintuplet is as long as an eighth note, but is divided in five. In other words, you could play five notes within an eighth-note value.

▶ The Magnetic Area slider allows you to set the area around which events are affected. In other words, it creates a magnetic field around the grid; any events within that area are pulled towards that gridline, whereas events beyond the magnetic area are not affected. Again, if you look in the middle display, this is represented by the thick pale area around the swing grid mentioned previously (this is displayed as a pale blue color on your screen).

Figure 7.4
The Quantize Setup panel

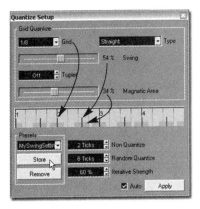

▶ The Grid Display area found in the center of the Quantize Setup panel shows you the result of your settings in the Grid Quantize area above. The entire display area represents a single 4/4 bar.

▶ The Presets area allows you to select different quantize presets that are stored on your computer and allows you to create new ones or remove presets you don't use. You will also see later when we discuss hitpoints, that you can create a quantize preset using an audio drum loop, for example.

▶ The Non Quantize field allows you to set an area around the center of the grid's position where events are not affected. Each tick value represents $1/120^{th}$ of a sixteenth-note. In other words, any note found within this range is left unquantized, creating a more human-like (read "looser") feel to the quantization.

▶ The Random Quantize field, as with the Non Quantize field allows you to humanize the quantize grid by adding or removing small amounts to a quantized note's position. In Figure 7.4, the Random Quantize field adds or subtracts up to six ticks from every note that is affected by the quantization.

▶ The Iterative Strength field allows you to set the strength level of an iterative quantize method. With higher percentage values, events are moved closer to the grid setting. With lower percentage values, events are not moved as close to the grid setting, allowing for more variations.

Setting Up your Quantize

Because the quantize setting influences how events are quantized, no matter which method you use, it's a good idea to start by setting up how you want Cubase to quantize these events before applying a method. This is especially true with the auto-quantize method.

To set up quantize parameters:

1. Select Quantize Setup in the MIDI menu to open the Quantize Setup panel (as shown in Figure 7.4).

Figure 7.5
The Type In Preset
Name dialog box

To remove a quantize setting from the preset list:

1. From the Quantize Setup panel's Presets drop-down menu, select the preset you want to remove.

2. Click the Remove button.

Applying Quantize

There are several ways you can quantize events and you can use any combination of methods to accomplish the task at hand.

▶ You can apply a standard over quantize method to already recorded events. This method simply shifts the start position of selected events to the closest grid line as set in your Project window or editing window (depending on which window is opened when you apply this quantize method).

▶ You can apply an automatic quantize value during the recording process. This records the events as you play them, but places them automatically according to the quantize setting of your project. In other words, you can still unquantize events that were recorded with the automatic quantize (the AQ button in the Transport panel) feature enabled.

▶ You can also use the Quantize Setup panel, which gives you more control over the effect quantization has on your events. For example, using the different parameters available in this panel, you can adjust the strength of the quantization, the swing factor, and the magnetic area of the grid, as well as create a grid for more complex rhythmic values, such as tuplets.

▶ Finally, you can use quantization as a MIDI effect on a track's insert or send effect.

To apply an automatic quantize value during the recording process:

1. Choose the appropriate quantize setup or quantize grid setting.

2. Enable the Auto-Quantize (AQ) button on the Transport panel.

3. Start the recording process.

To apply an automatic quantize value during the editing process:

1. Open the MIDI part you want to edit in the MIDI editor.

2. Open the Quantize Setup panel and choose the appropriate quantize setup.

3. Check the Auto option in the Quantize Setup panel. Any changes you make in the quantize setting from this point forward affect the events in the MIDI editor.

To apply a quantize method to selected events:

1. Choose the appropriate quantize setup or quantize grid setting.

2. Select the events or parts you want to quantize.

3. Press the Q key on your keyboard, or select the appropriate method you want to use from the MIDI menu: over quantize (Q), iterative, or (in the advanced quantize options) end quantize or length quantize.

When you want to quantize the length of MIDI events, you can use the Length Quantize drop-down menu from the MIDI editor's toolbar to determine an appropriate length value for your events. You can't, however, set the length value outside of the MIDI editor.

If you want to apply a quantization on a single track as a track effect, your best bet is probably to use a MIDI insert effect (or a send effect) and select the Quantizer MIDI effect. This MIDI effect is basically a quantize effect with four parameters: a quantize grid selection and a swing factor slider, both of which are identical in function to the Quantize Setup panel's parameter. The following two parameters play similar roles as well. The strength slider determines a percentage of strength, where 100% causes all the events to move to the closest grid line, offering a very tight rhythm. Lower percentages loosen up this rhythm, moving events toward the grid lines, but at a lesser degree. The delay slider inserts with positive values, or removes with negative values, a number of milliseconds to the event's position. This either creates a delayed or anticipated effect depending on the slider's setting, and unlike the delay parameter in the track's Setting section in the Inspector area, this parameter can be automated through time. The advantage of using the Quantizer effect rather than quantizing events allows you to change the quantizing itself in time through automation, creating a more dynamic feel.

To apply a quantize effect as a MIDI track insert (or send):

1. Select the MIDI track you want to use.
2. Make the Track Inserts section in the Inspector area visible.
3. From one of the insert slots available, select the Quantizer effect from the drop-down menu.
4. Adjust the four parameters in the panel or Alt-click (Option-click on Mac) the Edit button to open the effect in a floating window and edit the parameters from there.

Because a quantized note can always be unquantized, its original position is always stored in the project's memory. When you want to start quantizing from the current position of the quantized events rather than using the original position of these events, you can reset the original position to the current, quantized position by using the Freeze Quantize command.

To freeze quantized events:

1. Select the events you want to freeze (replace the original position with the quantized position).
2. From the MIDI menu, select Advanced Quantize > Freeze Quantize.

To undo a quantize on selected events:

1. Select the events or parts you want to unquantize.
2. From the MIDI menu, select Advanced Quantize > Undo Quantize.

About Older Groove Quantize Presets

If you were a Cubase VST user, you might have created groove quantize presets. Unfortunately, Cubase SX/SL does not support these presets at the current time. You can, however, use an alternative, which consists of creating a drum pattern using these groove presets in Cubase VST, exporting the pattern as an audio file, and then importing the audio file in the Audio Pool. From the pool, using the Sample Editor window, you can create a new groove through the Hitpoints function found in that editor. This process is explained later in Chapter 11.

Changing Your Focus

Moving around in a project, finding what you want to edit, focusing on the task at hand, then looking at the project in a more global perspective is as much a part of your work as editing MIDI and audio events themselves. Changing your display, opening, and closing windows is unfortunately part of the computer-based musician's reality. Having two monitors side by side, displaying different parts of your desktop helps, but this is not always a feasible solution. That's why it's important when you work on a project, to know, understand, and use shortcuts that can quickly change your visual perspective to fit the task at hand inside a project.

Fortunately, Cubase offers many options in this respect, allowing you to get to what you need in different ways. The idea is not necessarily to use all these techniques, but to find out what is possible and to use a working method that makes it easy for you to quickly perform necessary tasks.

Using the Overview Panel

When working on a long project, getting a feeling of what you're looking at can be quite handy. That's where the Overview panel comes in handy. This panel displays, as the name implies, an overview of your project. When you click the Overview button in the Project window's toolbar (see Figure 7.6), a white bar spanning the entire length of the Project window appears. This bar contains from left to right, the "mini me" version of your project, tracks, events, or parts on these tracks. Besides displaying the content of your project, a blue box indicates the portion of the project currently visible in the Event Display area of the Project window. You can use this box to navigate throughout your project.

To navigate using the overview rectangle:

1. To draw a rectangle anywhere in the Overview panel, click and drag your mouse in the upper half of the display as illustrated by the number 1 in Figure 7.6. Your cursor should represent an arrow when trying to do this. The size of the rectangle determines the content displayed in the Event Display area.

2. To move the position of the rectangle without changing its size, click and drag inside the lower half of the blue rectangle as illustrated by the number 2 in Figure 7.6. The zoom level remains the same; however, you can use this technique to scroll in time throughout your project.

3. To resize the left or right border of the rectangle, causing the content to zoom in (when you reduce the box) or zoom out (when you enlarge the box), click and drag in the lower half of the left or right edge of the rectangle, as illustrated by the number 3 in Figure 7.6.

Figure 7.6
The Overview panel functions explained

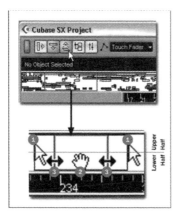

Using Cycle Markers

In Chapter 4, you saw that it was possible to navigate through a project using Markers and cycle markers. You also saw how you could use cycle markers in the drop-down menu found on the left of the horizontal zoom bar to fit the content found within a cycle marker inside the Event Display area. This is one way of traveling from one end of your project to another quickly, while at the same time focusing on the content you want to edit.

Using the Zoom Tools

When it comes to zooming options, Cubase does not leave you out in the cold. There are a number of ways you can control the content displayed on your screen using the different tools at your disposal. Here's a look at these options. Note that each number in the list corresponds to the number in Figure 7.7.

To zoom into your work using the appropriate tool:

1. **The Magnifying Glass tool**. Allows you to zoom into the area found within the rectangle you draw on the screen using this tool. Begin by selecting this tool from the Project window's toolbar, and then click and drag a rectangle around the area you want to zoom into.

2. **The Event and Content Vertical Zoom bar**. Allows you to adjust the vertical axis of the content found inside the events or parts. Drag the handle up to make the events spread out within the event or part's vertical boundary, or drag the handle down to reduce the vertical space these events take within the event or part's vertical boundary.

3. **The Zoom context menu**. Displays a variety of zooming options. (The Zoom submenu is found by right-clicking in the Event Display area, and pointing to the Zoom option.)

4. **The Vertical Zoom menu**. Allows you to set your zoom level to a number of tracks or rows. Selecting the Zoom Tracks N Rows or Zoom N Tracks brings up a dialog box in which you can type in the number of tracks you want to fit in your Event Display area. This menu is available by clicking on the downward pointing arrow found between the vertical scrollbar and the vertical Zoom bar.

5. **The Vertical Zoom bar**. Allows you to zoom in or out vertically, affecting the height of tracks in your Event Display area. You can either drag the handle in the Zoom bar to get the desired height for each track or click on the arrows above and below to increase or decrease by one row at a time.

6. **The Horizontal Zoom bar**. Allows you to zoom in or out horizontally (in time). You can either drag the handle in the Zoom bar to get the desired time frame inside the Event Display area or click the left or right arrows to increase or decrease by the time frame one step at a time.

7. **The Horizontal Zoom menu**. Allows you to select a cycle marker and zoom into it or save a zoom level as a preset that you can recall later. For example, you can create two states, one for a larger perspective and another for a more detailed look at events or parts on your timeline. Then, you can use this menu to toggle between the two (or more) zoom settings. Use the Add option to save the current zoom state to memory and the Organize option to manage the items available in this menu. This menu is available by clicking on the downward pointing arrow found between the horizontal scrollbar and the horizontal Zoom bar.

8. **The Ruler bar**. Allows you to zoom in or out by clicking and dragging your mouse. Click in the lower half of the Ruler bar and drag your mouse down to zoom in or drag your mouse up to zoom out, drag your mouse to the left to move back in time or right to move forward in time. Your zoom always centers on the position of your mouse in the ruler.

Figure 7.7
The various zoom controls

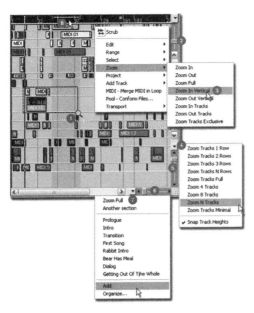

MIDI Menu Options

The MIDI menu is divided into five sections. The first one allows you to open different types of editing windows. The second one is discussed previously in this chapter and relates to quantizing. The fourth section relates mostly to the logical editor functions which are described in Appendix C. The last section is basically a MIDI reset function, which acts as a panic button on a MIDI patch bay, sending out an All Notes Off and Reset Controllers messages on all MIDI channels. You can use this when you experience stuck notes after recording, playing, or editing a track. This leaves us with the central section, which relates to specific MIDI functions.

Transpose

The Transpose option in the MIDI menu allows you to transpose selected MIDI events. Unlike the Transpose field in the Inspector area, this option changes the MIDI note numbers. In other words, after you transpose MIDI events using this option, you actually see the transposition in the different MIDI editors. You can also use this option when you want to transpose only a certain number of events in a part or on a track rather than transposing an entire track using the track parameter setting or a MIDI effect.

Another difference between the Transpose option found in the MIDI menu and the one found in the Track Parameter section in the Inspector area is that you can define a lower and upper barrier for your transposition. When doing so, you tell Cubase that notes above or below a certain value are outside of the desired transposed range possibility, so Cubase transposes the notes that are outside this range in a way that makes them fit inside the range. This is done by octave-shifting these notes. If you look at the example in Figure 7.8, you will notice that a two-semitone transposition will occur and that the Keep Notes in Range option is checked. This makes it possible to set a note value in the upper and lower barrier fields. If the events you want to transpose contain a G6, for example, this note is transposed one octave down, then two semitones up, resulting in an A5 rather than an A6.

Figure 7.8
The MIDI menu
Transpose dialog box

To transpose selected events using the MIDI Transpose option:

1. Select the MIDI part, parts, or events inside a MIDI part you want to transpose.

2. From the MIDI menu, select the Transpose option.

3. In the Transpose dialog box (Figure 7.8), set the number of semitones you want to transpose by using the up or down arrows on the right of the field. If you have a mouse with a scroll wheel, you can click on the number in the field and scroll your wheel up to increase or scroll your wheel down to decrease the value of semitones.

4. If you want to keep the notes within a specific range, check the appropriate check box option, and then set the lower and higher barrier range. Note that if your range is too narrow, some notes will not be transposed with the correct pitch.

5. Click OK to apply your changes.

MIDI Merge In Loop

You've applied different MIDI effects to a track as inserts or sends and you've also assigned different track parameter values to a MIDI part. When trying to edit certain details, you realize that the details you want to edit are played in real time by the various settings you have assigned to this track. If you want to merge these effects with the MIDI track and create a new version of the MIDI events that contains an editable set of MIDI parameter based on the result of the MIDI effects and parameters you've assigned, you can use the Merge In Loop option found in the MIDI menu. Here's an example: You've recorded a piano accompaniment and played certain chords. After recording these chords, you've applied the Track FX MIDI effect using a different scale. When listening back to your new chord coloring, you like the result, but you'd like to change a note in one of the chord, so that it fits better with the rest of the arrangement. But because this is a real-time effect, you can't really change a note that you didn't play to begin with. That's when the merge MIDI In Loop option comes in handy.

To use the merge MIDI In Loop option:

1. Start by identifying the MIDI events you want to merge. This can be a MIDI part on one track or several MIDI parts on several tracks over several channels.

2. After you've identified what you want to merge (or freeze), set the left and right locators to include this content.

3. Mute any other MIDI track you don't want to include in this process.

4. If you want to keep the original content intact, create a new MIDI track.

5. If you have chosen to create a new MIDI track for the merged destination, select it in the Track List area; otherwise, select the desired destination track (this might be the same track as the original content).

6. From the MIDI menu, select the Merge MIDI In Loop option. The MIDI Merge Options dialog box appears as displayed in Figure 7.9.

Figure 7.9
The MIDI Merge
Options dialog box

7. You have three options to enable or disable. The Include Inserts and Include Sends options convert any MIDI messages generated by effects into editable MIDI messages in the new merged part. If you have selected a track that already contains MIDI events as a destination track, you can choose to erase this content by checking the Erase Destination option. If you do not check this option and there is already a part on the destination track, a new part appears on top of it.

8. Click OK after setting your options.

Dissolve Parts

Let's say you have a MIDI file that you want to import into Cubase. You do so using the Import MIDI File option (described later in this chapter), but only to realize that it only contains one track with all the different channel information and events on this single track. If you look at the example in Figure 7.10, the first track named "Original" contains MIDI events on three distinct channels. After dissolved, three additional tracks appear below with the appropriate MIDI channel, program change, and corresponding MIDI events for each channel.

Figure 7.10
The first track has been dissolved into three tracks

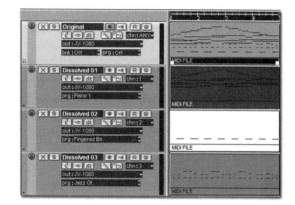

Similarly, you might record a drum pattern in cycle mode using the LM-7 VSTi drum, adding instruments to your pattern every time the cycle begins to get a full pattern. This is probably the simplest way of doing a drum pattern. But after all your instruments are recorded, they are all contained in the same part. If you want to assign a different MIDI effect on the snare drum, this could only be done if each instrument was played on a different channel. Because your drum is already recorded, you can use the dissolve part and select the Separate Pitches option instead of the Separate Channels option. In Figure 7.11, the first track corresponds to the original drum loop. The following tracks represent each pitch (in this case, an instrument of the drum kit). By assigning each instrument on a different channel, you can assign different MIDI effects to each piece of the drum kit while still using only one instance of the VSTi.

Figure 7.11
An example of a dissolve by separating pitches

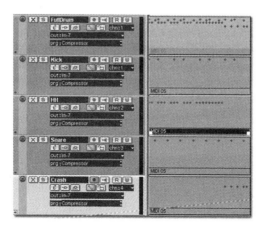

To dissolve a MIDI part:

1. Select the MIDI part you want to dissolve.

2. In the MIDI menu, select the Dissolve Part option.

3. If you have more than one MIDI channel embedded in the selected part, Cubase offers you two choices: Separate Channels or Separate Pitches (see Figure 7.12). Select the appropriate option. On the other hand, if there is only one MIDI channel in the selected part, you can only separate pitches.

4. Click OK to continue.

Note that the original track is automatically muted after dissolved.

Figure 7.12
The Dissolve Part
dialog box

O-Note Conversion

The concept of O-Note is directly related to drum maps. In fact, drum maps use three specific note names to identify a drum instrument: the pitch, the I-note (input note), and the O-note (output note). The pitch is associated to a drum instrument and cannot be modified. So a C1 can be associated with a kick drum, for example. The I-note is the note you play on your MIDI keyboard interface to trigger a specific instrument. In practice, playing a C1 note should trigger a kick drum because that's what is loaded. The O-note is the note sent out by the drum map. Again, in theory, the I-note and the O-note should be the same.

Why all these note names? Well, sometimes, you might want to reorganize which notes triggers which instrument in order to lay out the drum kit more efficiently on your keyboard. This can make it easier, for example, to play a drum part on notes you are accustomed to using. That's when you start playing with the drum mapping, changing the I-note and O-note values. As long as your MIDI part plays this drum, you are fine, but if you want to convert this to a nondrum-mapped track in order to export your file as a MIDI file, you need to convert the drum map appropriately so that the sound you hear corresponds to the output note played by the drum map. And that's when you need to use the O-note Conversion tool. This basically converts the MIDI note number values into whatever O-note mapping you have made, allowing you to play the part as a regular MIDI track while still hearing the appropriate sounds played by the drum kit it was meant for.

To perform an O-note conversion:

1. Select the MIDI part(s) associated with your drum map that you want to convert.

2. From the MIDI menu, select the O-Note Conversion option.

3. A warning message might appear; click Yes if you want to proceed anyway or Cancel if you are not sure this is what you want to do.

About MIDI Functions

The MIDI functions in the MIDI menu play a similar role to the MIDI track parameters. However, there are different reasons that would motivate you to use a MIDI function rather than a setting in the track parameters. For example, track parameters affect all events (parts) on a given track, whereas MIDI functions can be applied to selected parts in the Project window or selected events in a MIDI editor window. Another example is that parameter settings do not show up in the MIDI editor, whereas MIDI functions actually change the appropriate value in the MIDI message, making it visible in the MIDI editor. In other words, if you want to try things out before committing to them, you can use the track parameters, but when you want to affect or change the MIDI events permanently, you are better off using the MIDI functions found in the MIDI menu.

In the MIDI Functions option found in the MIDI menu, you will find a submenu containing various functions. Most of these functions are self explanatory. For example, Delete Doubles deletes any MIDI events that are doubled (two notes playing at the same time and at the same pitch). Some of these functions display a dialog box, whereas others perform their task without needing additional input.

To use a MIDI function:

1. In the Project window, select the parts you want to edit using the MIDI function, or double-click the MIDI part and select the events you want to edit if you don't want to affect all the events in the part.

2. From the MIDI menu, select the MIDI Functions option and then the appropriate MIDI function you want to apply.

3. Change the values needed in the dialog box if one shows up and click OK to complete; otherwise, the function is automatically applied.

Importing Files

When working on a project, you can record events, but you can also import events that are already on your hard disk or use content from another source. All the import functions of Cubase can be found in the File menu under the Import submenu.

About Cubase Documents Imports

You can import documents created in earlier versions of Cubase, such as song, arrangement, or part documents. In each case, however, there are some limitations to what will be imported into your new Cubase SX/SL project. Because none of the previous formats contained any actual audio files, you must reassociate audio events with their audio files on the hard disk if you've moved them since the last time they were saved.

Here's a list of what will be imported when you import a song or arrangement file into Cubase SX/SL:

▶ MIDI events and parts with their MIDI port output settings is imported. If the MIDI output doesn't exist anymore, Cubase displays a "pending output" message in those tracks, allowing you to remap them to a new MIDI output.

▶ The volume and transpose settings found in the MIDI track parameters remain in the new project—any other MIDI track parameter is ignored (such as delay, compression, or shadow tracks).

▶ All the MIDI part parameter settings are included, with the exception of the transpose settings.

▶ MIDI drum tracks are converted to regular drum tracks with a drum map associated. However, MIDI output settings for individual drum sounds are ignored.

▶ The volume, pan, and EQ automation data found in the VST Channel Mixer is imported; however, any plug-in or DSP factory settings are also ignored.

▶ Where multiple audio tracks were routed to the same audio channel, new separate audio tracks are created because Cubase SX/SL always uses one channel per track. A series of separate audio channels are also created in the mixer.

Any other setting is either ignored or removed. Also note that because song files could contain multiple arrangements, you are prompted to choose which arrangement you want to use when importing such a song file. To import all the arrangements in a song, you need to repeat the import process for as many times as there are arrangements in the song. When you import a song or an arrangement, a new project is created. When you import a part, a new track is created in the Project window.

To import a Cubase VST song, arrangement, or part:

1. Select Import and the appropriate Cubase file type (Cubase Song, Cubase Arrangement, or Cubase Part) you want to import from the File menu.

2. Browse the content of your hard disk to locate the song, arrangement, or part.

3. Select the file and click Open.

4. If a Pending Output dialog box appears, assign the missing MIDI outputs to corresponding outputs or temporary ones until the file is imported. You can change these settings after that.

About Audio CD Track Imports

Cubase allows you to grab audio tracks directly from an audio CD using the Import Audio CD option.

There are two ways you can perform this task and which one you choose depends on what you want to do with these imported tracks. In both ways, the Audio CD Import window is the same; however, if you use the submenu option in the File > Import menu, the imported tracks automatically appear in your Project window starting at the current play line's location and on the selected audio track. If you don't have an audio track present, one is automatically created for you. The other option is to import from the Media Pool using this window's right-click (Ctrl-click on a Mac with only one button) and choosing the Import Audio CD option. In this case, the audio track is imported in the pool only and no events appear in the project's Event Display area. This might be the method of choice if you want to import several audio tracks at a time.

To import an audio track or tracks from an audio CD:

1. If you want to place the content of the audio track directly in your project, follow these steps, otherwise, skip to Step 4.

2. Create an empty audio track (for safety) and select it in the Track List area.

3. Position your play line at the location where you want the start of the track to occur.

4. Select the Import Audio CD from the File > Import menu or right-click (Ctrl-click on Mac) in the Media Pool and select the Import Audio CD option found at the top of the context menu.

5. The Import from Audio CD dialog box appears as displayed in Figure 7.13. Choose the appropriate drive containing the audio CD from which you want to import. This field is found in the upper-left corner of the dialog box.

6. Select the transfer speed you want to use to import these files. Note that faster speeds result in a faster transfer, but slower speeds limit the potential for errors that can occur during the transfer.

PREVIEWING CD TRACKS

You can preview a track before importing it using the Play button found in the lower-right portion of the dialog box.

7. If you don't want to grab the entire track, you can move the Grab Start and Grab End arrows found in the Track Display area below the Play button. This changes the value in the Grab Start and End columns in the Track Display above, allowing you to import only sections of the audio.

8. In the Grab column, select the tracks you want to import. If you want to select more than one track, hold the Ctrl key (or Command key on Mac) while you click on nonsequential tracks or select the first track you want to import, hold down the Shift key, and click the last track you want to import to select all the tracks in between.

9. If you want to give a different name to your tracks (the default name being "Track XX," where XX corresponds to the track number), type in a new name in the File Name field.

10. If you want to change the folder destination, click the Change Folder button, browse your computer's hard drive, and select a new destination folder. The folder to which the files will be imported is displayed just under the File Name field.

11. When you are ready, click the Grab button at the bottom of the dialog box. This begins the extraction process. The files appear in the Grabbed Files section when the extraction is completed.

12. When this process is complete, click the OK button.

Figure 7.13
The Import from Audio
CD dialog box

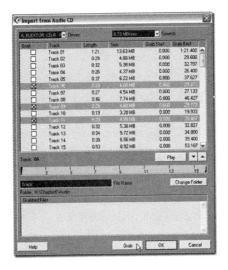

About MIDI File Imports

You can import Standard MIDI files of Type 0 and 1 in a project or create a new project with the imported MIDI files. The difference between a MIDI file of Type 0 and 1 is that in Type 0, all the MIDI events are found in one single track. After importing such a file, you need to make sure the MIDI track hosting this imported track is set to play over ANY MIDI channels. A Type 1 file contains as many MIDI tracks as there are MIDI channels used in the file. Cubase creates as many MIDI tracks as it needs to host the newly imported MIDI file. When importing a MIDI file, it is imported at the beginning of the project.

To import a MIDI file:

1. Select File > Import > Import MIDI File.
2. Browse to the location of the file you want to import.
3. Select the file and click the Open button.

About Audio File Imports

Because sometimes you might want to use prerecorded material in your project, Cubase allows you to import this material in two different ways. The first way is to simply drag WAV, AIFF, WMA (Windows Media Audio), or MP3 files from Windows Explorer (or the Mac's Launcher) onto a track, or below the last track in Cubase to create a new track. The second way is to click the File menu's Import option, and then the Audio File option from the submenu. Note that when importing WMA or MP3 files, Cubase creates a WAV or AIFF copy of this file on your hard disk, rather than using the WMA or MP3 file directly. Just remember that WAV and AIFF files can be much larger than their WMA or MP3 counterparts.

You can also import Recycle files. Recycle files are generated by the software called Recycle, which is also developed by Steinberg. The purpose of Recycle is to cut drum loops into smaller parts, allowing you to reuse these samples at different tempos without changing the pitch. This process is similar to the process used in the Sample Editor.

To import audio files:

▶ From the Windows Explorer window or the Mac Launcher window, drag the compatible files into your project or into the Media Pool.

Or:

1. Select File > Import > Import Audio File.
2. Browse to the location of the file you want to import.
3. Select the file and click the Open button.

NOTE
You can also perform an Import Audio File function from the Media Pool by selecting the Import button or by right-clicking (Ctrl-clicking on Mac) in the pool and selecting the Import Audio File option.

Now You Try It

It's time to put the topics covered in this chapter into action—you can download a practice exercise at http://www.muskalipman.com.

CHAPTER 7

8

MIDI Editing Windows

The main advantage of MIDI over audio can be summed up in one word: flexibility. MIDI is a very flexible and powerful protocol that allows for great control over your music. The MIDI editors in Cubase reflect this fact very well and give you full control over every aspect of MIDI editing. This is, after all, where Cubase earned its first stripes as professional software, and it continues to do so by offering different editing environments to reflect the versatility MIDI offers when it comes to its editable parameters.

In this chapter, you will:

▶ Explore the different areas of the Key, Drum, and List Editors

▶ Learn how to work with the MIDI editing tools available in the MIDI editors

▶ Understand the differences between each editor and the purpose behind them

▶ Learn how to edit MIDI note events and control change events

▶ Discover how to use step recording to enter MIDI events into a project

▶ Find out how to use and create drum maps

MIDI Editor

Before we begin talking about editors, it is important to understand that each track class has its own associated editing window. Events are, therefore, associated with an editor by default. You can change this in some cases; in other cases, there is no way to get around it. The associated editor displays events that are appropriate to the track's class, so it is optimized for the events recorded in its window. Using another editor does not allow you to manipulate the information as easily. However, you can edit events in a non-associated editor by selecting the part(s) in the Project window and selecting the desired editor from the MIDI menu.

There are six MIDI related editors to choose from in Cubase SX or SL:

▶ Edit. Uses the piano roll analogy, where events appear along a strip moving from left to right as you play the events. The pitch is determined by the vertical position of the scrolling events, and the position in time is determined by the horizontal position of these events. The longer an event is, the longer the box in the scroll is, as in a piano roll. The first events in a part being edited appear at the left of the piano roll, and the last events in that part appear at the right of the piano roll. This editor also allows you to edit Control Change messages on separate lanes below the piano roll view. It is the default editing environment for MIDI tracks that are not associated with drum maps.

▶ Drum. Uses the piano roll analogy like the Edit window, but with a small difference: There are no lengths to events; only trigger times (Note On positions) are displayed. Also, instead of a piano layout on the left side representing pitch values, you will find a list of percussion names associated with pitch values. It is the default editing environment for MIDI tracks that are associated with drum maps.

▶ List. Uses a table representation where it displays the raw MIDI data for any edited parts (more on that can be found in subsequent sections).

▶ Score. (Only available in Cubase SX) Uses a traditional music staff display to edit your MIDI parts.

▶ Tempo Track. Allows you to see a graphical representation of tempo changes and meter changes (like the Edit editor). Because this editor does not contain any MIDI events besides the tempo and meter changes, it is associated with the Master Track button found on the Transport panel. You may use this editor to manage and create tempo and meter changes throughout your project.

▶ Browser. Displays not only MIDI events (similar to the List editor), but also displays audio, video, tempo changes, and time signature changes.

Editor Toolbar

There are many ways of editing MIDI events to get what you want. Using the tools available in the Key or Drum Editor's toolbar will most likely always be part of the solution because it holds the tools that you need to select, move, remove, or add events from your Editor window. To help you out in your editing tasks, the editors always contain a context menu available through the right-click (Ctrl-click on a Mac), which holds a copy of the tools available in the toolbar. Finally, you can always use key commands to switch from one tool to another (see Appendix G for a complete list).

The first two buttons on the left of the toolbar are the Information and Solo buttons (see Figure 8.1). The Information button toggles the Information bar on or off. This bar reveals information on the selected event or events and also allows you to modify this information by clicking in the field corresponding to the information and changing the values manually. See Figure 8.2.

Figure 8.1
The Information and
Solo buttons in the Key
and Drum Editor's
toolbar

For example, you could select an event and change its length numerically by clicking in the Length field as seen in Figure 8.2. You could also quickly transpose a series of selected events by changing the pitch value, which corresponds to the pitch of the first selected event in time. Every other selected event would be transposed to their relative pitch. (You can change the pitch value by clicking in the Pitch field and changing the value.)

Figure 8.2
The Information bar in
the Key or Drum Editor

The Solo button allows you to edit a MIDI part without hearing the other parts play in the background, "soloing" the events found in the MIDI Editor.

Next, you will find a series of seven tools that are used to apply different editing operations on MIDI events found in your editor (see Figure 8.3). These tools are not unlike the ones found in the Project window, but also offer editor-specific characteristics.

Figure 8.3
The Key Editor tools,
from left to right: the
Arrow, Draw, Eraser,
Magnifying Glass,
Mute, Scissors, and
Glue Tube tools

▶ **Arrow tool**. Serves as a selection tool and a resizing tool. You can use this tool when you want to move, copy, and select a range of events or when you want to change the start or end position of existing events in your editor.

▶ **Draw tool**. Is a multifunction tool. As you can see in , a small arrow in the lower-right corner of the button indicates that there are additional functions available to this tool. In fact, this tool operates in three basic modes. The Draw mode itself allows you to add events by drawing them in one-by-one inside the editor or to modify controller information in a freehand style. The Paint mode allows you to insert multiple notes by dragging your cursor across the editor. Finally, the Line and Shape mode allows you to either draw a series of events in the shape of the tool (you can switch between line, parable, sine, triangle, and square) or to shape controller information in one of these shapes as well.

▶ **Eraser tool**. Allows you to erase events by clicking on the event while this tool is active or by dragging your eraser over the events.

▶ **Magnifying Glass tool**. Allows you to drag a box over a range so that your current view corresponds to the box's content. In other words, it zooms into the content you want to view. You can also elect to simply click on a note to zoom into that note.

▶ **Mute tool**. Is an alternative to the Eraser tool in the sense that it allows you to mute a note so that you don't hear it, but without erasing it. This provides a way to mute certain events that you're not sure you want to get rid of right away, but you don't want to hear them right now. You can also drag the Mute tool across a number of events to mute them all.

▶ **Scissors or Cut tool**. Allows you to cut selected events at a specific grid line when the quantize grid is active.

▶ **Glue Tube tool**. Allows you to glue notes together. More specifically, when playing at the same pitch value, it glues the event that follows the event you click on.

CHAPTER 8

Continuing our trip along the toolbar, the next button allows you to toggle the Autoscroll function on or off (see Figure 8.4). This only affects the scrolling in the editor because there is also an Autoscroll button in the Project window. The Autoscroll function basically follows the play line in your window. When the line hits the right edge, the page moves to the right, in effect scrolling the content from right to left as the cursor moves forward in time. When the Autoscroll function is off, you can play the events in the editor without worrying if the content in your window will start moving as you're editing events and the play line passes the right side of your window.

Speaking of editing, because the piano roll and the Drum Editor are based on a matrix divided in pitch (vertical axis) and meter or time (horizontal axis), moving your mouse around in this matrix might become difficult, especially when you want to add an event at the far right of the screen where the keyboard reference is far from your mouse's position. That's why the following two fields appear next to the Autoscroll button. On the top, you can see the current location of your mouse in the vertical or pitch axis, whereas the bottom field represents the meter or time position of your cursor. Using these fields when adding events helps you find the exact position to place your mouse in order to add, select, or modify an event.

Figure 8.4
The Autoscroll button and the cursor's Pitch and Meter Position Indicator fields

The quantize fields in the MIDI editor are similar to the ones found in the Project window. You can activate the Snap to Grid button (first button on the left in Figure 8.5) to make the fields to the right of this button active. The Quantize field lets you choose the distance between each grid and influences many operations inside the editor. For example, setting your grid to 1/32 note allows you to move, cut, and insert events at thirty-second note intervals. In other words, the grid quantize setting prevents you from moving, cutting, or inserting events at positions other than the one defined by the field.

The Length Quantize field influences the length of events you add into the editor. For example, when using the step recording technique (covered in detail later in this chapter), if you add notes with a quantize value of 1/4 Note and a length quantize value set to the Linked to Quantize Value, all notes are at quarter note intervals and are of quarter note length. The Insert Velocity field, on the other hand, allows you to determine the velocity of Note On events when adding them with the Draw tools. You can change the velocity either by clicking on the up and down arrows to the right of the field, by clicking inside the field and using your mouse's scroll wheel if you have one, or by entering a numeric value between 1 and 127 (a velocity of 0 represents a Note Off message).

Figure 8.5
The editor's quantize
settings

The Colors field is a visual help option. It does not affect anything in the editor besides the colors that are displayed in your editor. You can choose to give a different color to the different velocities (shown in Figure 8.6), pitches, MIDI channels, or parts. How you choose to use this coloring tool depends on what you are editing. For example, if you are editing events from different channels in a single window, you might want to select the Color by Channel option. On the other hand, if you have selected several parts and opened them in the editor, selecting the Color by Part option might make it easier to locate which events belong to which part.

The Monitor button allows you to hear MIDI notes corresponding to the notes selected with the Arrow tool or when moving a note in time or on different pitch values. This is basically the MIDI equivalent of the audio Scrub tool. When selecting a group of notes, you will be able to hear the note in the group you choose to click on when dragging the selected notes to another location or pitch.

Figure 8.6
The Colors field and
Monitor button

The last series of tools on the toolbar relate to step recording functions. Step recording is meant for the rhythmically challenged, for less-than-proficient keyboard players who have great ideas but just need some help entering them into a sequencer, for creating rhythmically complex patterns, such as machine-like drum fills using sixty-four notes at 120 BPM. It is also useful for musicians who can't enter MIDI events in their computers using VSTi because their sound card's latency is too high. No matter what the reason, step recording means that you can enter notes or chords one by one without worrying about timing.

Figure 8.7
The step recording tools

Table 8.1 describes the function associated with each one of these buttons:

Table 8.1
The step recording buttons found on the editor's toolbar (from left to right in Figure 8.7 and from top to bottom in this table)

Button Name	Button's Function
Step Recording	Enables or disables the step recording options. **Note that when this button is activated, the Autoscroll function is disabled.**
MIDI Connector	Changes the selected note in your editor to the note played (when you press a note on your keyboard with this button active).
Insert	Adds the event you play on your controller keyboard at the position corresponding to the next quantize value following the playback line, pushing the events currently present to the next quantize value (when this option is enabled). When this option is disabled, events added using the step recording insert point are added to the current position of the insertion line, leaving the previous recording content in place. See Figure 8.8 for an example of how this works.
Pitch	Works with the MIDI controller. When enabled, it gives the pitch value of the note you play to a selected event in the Edit window, effectively replacing the current selected pitch with the new pitch from your keyboard controller.
Note On velocity	Works with the MIDI controller. When enabled, it assigns the Note On velocity parameter of the note you play to the selected event in the Edit window. When disabled, the velocity assigned to the note you record comes from the Velocity field in the toolbar. Pressing lightly on your keyboard adds notes with low velocity values, whereas pressing harder adds a higher velocity value to the notes recorded through the step recording method.
Note Off velocity	Assigns the Note Off velocity—otherwise identical to the Note On velocity.

Figure 8.8
An example of the
Insert button's effect on
events recorded in Step
Record mode

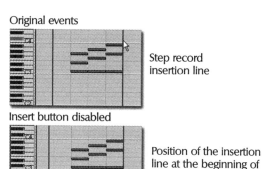

Original events

Step record
insertion line

Insert button disabled

Position of the insertion
line at the beginning of
the step record phase

Insert button enabled

Previous events are
pushed further in time

Key Editor Display Areas

The MIDI editor offers two main display areas—one for the MIDI note events and another for the Control Change messages. In the Note Display area, you will find a keyboard lying sideways. The ruler spanning from left to right represents the time at which events occur. You can change how time is displayed by right-clicking in the ruler and selecting one of the many display formats available. That said, when working with MIDI events, you will probably want to stick with the Bars and Beats display.

USING THE RULER TO CONTROL ZOOM

In the MIDI Editor as well as in all the other windows, when you click in the lower half of the ruler and drag your mouse up or down, you zoom out and in respectively, centering your display on the position where you clicked to start the zoom. Holding down your mouse and moving it left or right moves your window in time. When you release your mouse, your play line snaps to the closest quantize value.

The Controller Display area is a customizable portion of the window that displays one or more controller types, such as volume, pan, expression, pedal, pitch bends, and so on. Using additional controller lanes gives you a better view of the MIDI messages associated with the part you are editing (Figure 8.9).

To add a controller lane to the MIDI Editor:

1. Right-click (Ctrl-click on a Mac) anywhere in the editor.

2. From the context menu, select the Create New Controller Lane option at the bottom of the menu.

3. From the newly created lane, select the controller name you want to display from the drop-down menu found on the left margin of the lane. Note that controllers that contain events are indicated by an asterisk (*) at the end of the name.

4. If the controller you want to view is not displayed in this list, select the Setup option at the bottom of the drop-down menu. The Controller Menu Setup dialog box appears. In this dialog box, you will find two areas: the In Menu area and Hidden area.

5. To add a controller to the menu, select it from the Hidden area and click the double arrow button below the area.

6. To remove a controller from the menu, select it from the in Menu area and click the double arrow button below the area.

7. Click OK when you are finished adding or removing controllers to the menu, and then select the new controller to add its corresponding lane.

8. To remove a controller lane, select the Remove This Lane option at the bottom of the same context menu you used to add one.

Control Change messages found in the Controller Display area are represented by blocks, whereas note velocity values are represented by lines that are aligned with each note. Moving a note moves the velocity value with it, but doesn't move the Control Change messages. The field below the controller's name represents the value of the controller if you were to add this value at the current cursor position. Note that the frequency at which you can add Control Change messages depends on your current quantize value. So, if your quantize grid is set to 1/2 Note, you can only add controllers at half-note distances from each other.

Figure 8.9
The Key Editor with note display on top and three controller lanes below

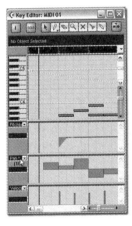

Editing MIDI Events

The main purpose of the MIDI Editor is to edit the MIDI events found in the part or parts you've opened in it. This is done using a combination of tools and functions available to you in the editor. The main tools are available in the toolbar of the editor, but many of the functions you can apply are found in the context menu of the editor (see Figure 8.10). These are available by right-clicking (or Ctrl-clicking on Mac).

In the upper portion of this menu, you will find all the tools available in the toolbar and in the lower portion, you will find a shortcut to the same operations available in Cubase's menu bar.

Figure 8.10
The MIDI Editor's
context menu

Editing MIDI events is not unlike editing text in a word processor. For example, if you want to copy, cut, or move a group of events, you need to select these events first and apply the desired operation on these selected events. That's when you use the Object Selection or Arrow tool.

To select events:

▶ To select a single event, just point and click on it.

▶ To select a group of events, click and drag a selection box around these events.

▶ To select multiple specific events, but not necessarily continuous, hold the Shift key down as you select the events you want.

▶ To select all the notes on the same pitch in a part, hold the Ctrl (Command on Mac) key down and click on the corresponding pitch in the Keyboard Display area to the left of the Event Display area.

After events are selected, you can apply different functions. For example, you might want to move a group of notes to somewhere else in the part. If you want to keep these events in line with the current quantize grid, or to another quantize grid, you should make sure the Snap to Grid button is enabled and that your quantize grid setting is set to the appropriate value. To move one event, you simply need to click and drag it to its new location. To move several events, you select them as mentioned previously and then click and drag one of the selected events to the new destination. You can move both notes and control change values this way, provided that the appropriate controller lane is visible. If you move the velocity value of a note, you will also move the note. This is a good way to move notes in time while making sure your mouse doesn't go up or down, causing the notes to be transposed as you move them. Note that you can also achieve this by holding the Ctrl (Command on Mac) key down as you move the notes. This limits your movement to the horizontal axis. You can also move selected notes by using the up and down keys on your keyboard.

Again, as with text in a word processor application, when you want to paste, repeat, or duplicate events, you need to select them, bring these events into the clipboard, decide where you want the clipboard to put them by placing your insertion point (in Cubase this is the play line), and then apply the Paste, Repeat, or Duplicate function. As with the Project window, it is possible to hold the Alt key (Option key on Mac) down as you move selected events to copy these events rather than move them. You will see a small plus sign (+) appear next to your arrow as you move the mouse. So, if you have never used a computer in your life before, these functions shouldn't be too difficult to understand.

However, Cubase goes a little further, offering additional functions that make editing MIDI easier. For example, you can use the Select options in the editor's context menu or in the Edit > Select submenu to define what you want to select. Using this method, you could position your left and right locators across two bars, click in the Note Display area, use the Select in Loop option, and all the MIDI events found between the locators are selected; now click on a controller event and repeat these steps. This includes both the Notes and the Control Change messages within this range. You can copy these events, position your play line at another location, and then paste the events.

Muting Events

As an alternative to muting an entire track, you may also mute selected events (Notes and Control Change messages) inside the MIDI Editor.

To mute one or several events:

▶ Select the events you want to mute with the Arrow tool and press the Shift+M keys on your keyboard or select the Mute option from the Edit menu.

▶ Or, select the Mute tool and click the note you want to mute.

▶ Or, select the Mute tool and drag a selection box around the events you want to mute. All events within the box's range are muted.

To unmute muted events:

▶ Select the muted events you want to unmute with the Arrow tool and press the Shift+U keys on your keyboard or select the Unmute option from the Edit menu.

▶ Or, select the Mute tool and click the muted events you want to unmute.

▶ Or, select the Mute tool and drag a selection box around the muted events you want to unmute. All events within the box's range are unmuted. If there are events that weren't muted, they are now muted, so make sure you don't include any nonmuted events in your range.

Splitting and Resizing Note Events

Besides moving, cutting, and copying events, you can also split or resize events. These operations can also be applied to a single event, a group of selected events, or a range of events.

To resize a note or a group of notes:

1. To resize a group of notes, start by selecting the events with the Arrow or Object Selection tool.

2. Bring your cursor over the start or end of the events you want to resize. The arrow turns into a double-headed arrow (see Figure 8.11).

3. Click and drag the edge to the desired length. Note that if the snap grid is active, your movement is restricted to the quantize grid setting. If you want to resize the events without turning the Snap to Grid off, you can hold the Ctrl (Command on Mac) key down as you move your mouse.

Figure 8.11
When resizing events, the Arrow tool becomes a double-headed arrow when you cross a resizable zone on the event displayed

If you want to split notes rather than resize them, you can use one of three methods: Use the Scissors tool at the desired location on the note or selected note, use the Split Loop function in the Edit menu or context menu (this splits the notes at the current left and right locator positions), or use the cursor's position to split all note events that cross it. This is also done through the Split at Cursor option found in the Edit menu or context menu. No matter which method you use, the quantize grid setting influences where the split occurs.

Merging Note Events

In physics, what goes up must come down. In Cubase, what can be split can be merged. The Glue Tube tool is the Scissors tool's counterpart. It allows you to glue the following event of same pitch or merge the selected event with the next one in time.

To merge note events:

1. Select the Glue Tube tool from the toolbar or in the context menu.

2. Click the first note you want to glue.

3. Clicking again glues the current note to the next note of the same pitch. For example, in the bottom part of Figure 8.12, the note to the right would be joined with the note on the left.

CHAPTER 8

Figure 8.12
A before and after look at the Glue Tube tool in action

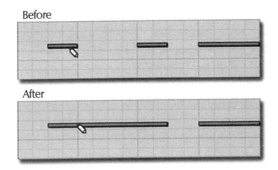

Using the Draw Tool

The Draw tool in the Key Editor window and the Drumstick and Paint tools in the Drum Editor window offer similar options. The difference with the Draw tool is that you can drag a note to determine the length of that note, whereas the Drumstick tool repeats the event using the quantize value to determine the spacing and the insert length value to determine the length of each event in the Drum Editor window. Furthermore, the Draw tools in the MIDI Editor are all grouped under one button, whereas in the Drum Editor, the Draw function is replaced by the Drumstick tool and the other Paint, Line, and Shape tools are found under a separate Draw button. Another difference is that the Draw, Line, Parabola, Sine, Triangle, and Square tools in the Key Editor can be used to add note events in the Event Display area, whereas these tools are only available to modify control change values in the controller lanes of the Drum Editor.

To create notes using the Draw tool in the Key Editor:

1. Set the quantize grid and length values you want to use. The length determines how long each note is, and the quantize grid determines the spacing between the notes.

2. Select the Draw tool from the toolbar, or right-click (Ctrl-click on Mac) in the editor to select the Draw tool or use the key command (by default, this is the number 8 in the Key Editor and 0 in the Drum Editor).

3. Adjust the velocity setting in the toolbar to the desired value.

4. Click where you want to add your note. This adds a note with a length corresponding to the length value in the quantize length setting. However, if you click and drag, you can draw longer notes that increase by length quantize value increments. If you are adding notes using the Drumstick tool (in the Drum Editor) and you drag your drumstick to the right, additional Note On events are added at intervals set by the quantize grid.

In Figure 8.13, the quantize grid is set at sixteenth note intervals, the length for each note inserted is linked to the quantize value. This means that when you click to insert a note, it is one sixteenth note in length. Each inserted note has a Note On velocity of 89 as defined in the Insert Velocity field. In the upper two parts of this figure, you can see how these settings influence how notes are added when either clicking near the quantize grid lines or clicking and dragging over several grid lines. In the lower two parts, you can see the same operation but with the Drum Editor equivalent of the Draw tool, which is the Drumstick tool.

Figure 8.13
Adding note events in
the Key and Drum
Editor using the Draw or
Drumstick tool

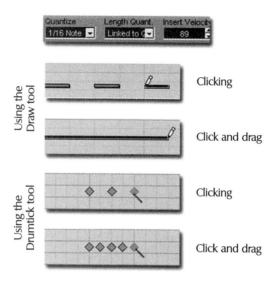

Events are always created with the same MIDI channel as the part you are editing. After you have inserted notes using the Draw tool, you can modify their length by clicking on the existing note and dragging it farther to the right to lengthen the note or dragging it to the left to shorten that note. Remember that note lengths always snap to the next quantize grid value as long as the Snap to Grid button is enabled in the editor's toolbar.

The Draw tool has some limitations; you can change only the end of an event or events using this tool. If you want to modify the beginning, you should use the Selection tool as described in earlier sections of this chapter. You can also modify controllers with the Draw tool. This is described later in this chapter.

Using The Line Tool

The Line tool, like the Draw tool, allows you to insert both note and controller events. However, each type of line has its own particularity in the sense that you can create different shapes using the different tools under the Draw tool. The best use for these tools is to edit control change information, creating MIDI ramps, such as pan effects or fade outs. Here's a look at these tools and their specificities.

The Paint tool allows you to enter notes pretty much anywhere you want. Moving the mouse up and down adds notes on different pitches, whereas moving the mouse left and right adds them at different points in time. When drawing note events, the Paint tool is different from the Draw tool because it adds as many notes as your mouse crosses the grid lines. Where inserting control change events, both tools work the same.

The Line tool allows you to draw a line across the Note Display or the Controller Display area to create events along the line at interval, length, and velocity in the case of notes, determined by the quantize setting. Figure 8.14 displays such lines: in the left half, note events are added and in the right half, controller (Control Change) messages are added. In the case of controller events, you can also use the Line tool to edit existing controller messages to create a linear ramp.

Figure 8.14
Adding note and
controller events using
the Line tool

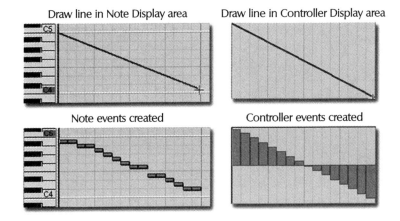

To insert events using the Line tool:

1. Set the quantize values appropriately. You can also leave the snap to quantize grid off; however, this generates a greater number of events, which combined with other dense MIDI tracks, can create a bottleneck in your MIDI stream causing loss of performance.

2. Select the Line tool from the toolbar or the context menu.

3. Click where you want your line to begin. If you want to move this point after clicking, you may hold the Alt+Ctrl keys (Option+Command on Mac) down to move this start point to a new location.

4. Position the mouse where you want the line to end.

5. When you are satisfied, click again to add the events.

The Parabola tool is similar to the Line tool with the exception that it draws a parabolic ramp rather than the linear ramp found with the Line tool (see Figure 8.15). Inserting events or modifying existing events using this tool is done in the same way as with the Line tool, with the following additional options:

▶ Press the Ctrl (Command key on Mac) to change the type of curve created.

▶ Hold the Alt+Ctrl keys (Option+Command on Mac) down after you clicked to insert your start point to move this point to a new location.

Figure 8.15
The different parabolic ramps available when using the Parabola tool

Parabolic ramp

Default   Inversed (Ctrl key)   Direction

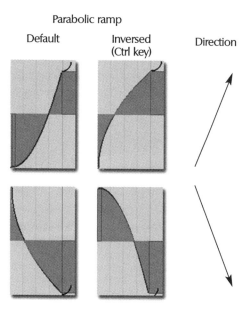

The sine, triangle, and square ramps have similar options as well. However, moving the mouse up creates a more pronounced variation, whereas moving the mouse slightly upwards creates a small variation and dragging your mouse below the start point inverses the shape of the ramp.

To create a ramp using the Sine, Triangle, or Square tools:

1. Select the appropriate tool from the toolbar.

2. Set the quantize grid if you want to use this setting to control how many and where the events will be created. For a smooth curve or change, disable the Snap to Grid option.

3. Click where you want to start inserting the events and drag your mouse to the right.

    ▶ To adjust the frequency of the shape, hold the Shift key down as you move your mouse to the left or right to adjust the period of the frequency to the desired length. After you are satisfied with this period, release the Shift key and drag your mouse to the location where you want the shape to stop inserting events.

    ▶ Hold the Alt key (Option key on Mac) down while dragging the mouse to anchor the position and direction of the curve or shape at the start point.

    ▶ Hold the Ctrl key (Command key on Mac) down while dragging the mouse to anchor the position and direction of the curve or shape at the end point.

    ▶ Hold both Alt and Ctrl keys (Option and Command on Mac) down after having inserted the start point to allow you to move the start point to a new location.

4. Release the mouse button at the desired end point location to insert events corresponding to the current shape setting.

CHAPTER 8

Using Step Recording

As mentioned earlier in this chapter, the step recording functions are available in the toolbar of the Key and Drum Editors. When enabling the step recording functions, a new insert point bar appears in the Note Display area. This line is blue compared to the black play line. You need to keep an eye on the location of this line because events that are inserted appear at the grid line immediately to the right of this insertion point. You can move this line by clicking inside the Note Display area at the location where you want to insert events.

To record MIDI in Step Recording mode:

1. Select or create a MIDI track.

2. Create an empty part in that track using the Pencil tool or by clicking on an existing part to select it.

3. Double-click on this part to open it in the MIDI Editor. If this track is associated with a drum map, the Drum Editor opens. Otherwise, the default editor for MIDI events is the Key Editor.

4. Enable the Step Recording button in the editing window's toolbar. All the step recording buttons should automatically be activated with the exception of the MIDI Connector.

5. Activate the Snap to Grid button.

6. Set the quantize grid and the length quantize value. This influences how far apart each event will be and how long the events will be as well.

7. Position your insertion point where you want to begin your recording by clicking inside the Note Display area of the editor.

8. If you do not want to use the Note On velocity to record the events, turn this option off and set the Insert Velocity field to the desired velocity.

9. Play a note or a chord on your controller keyboard.

    The notes will be recorded as you play them, at intervals set by the quantize grid and the length set in the Length Quantize field. Cubase records the velocity at which you are playing the notes or chords (unless you turned this option off), so try to enter the notes at the approximate velocity at which you want them to play back.

10. If you want to move forward or backward in time, use the left and right arrows on your keyboard. The insertion point where the notes will be added is displayed in the editor's Meter Display Position field in the toolbar.

11. If you want to insert an event between two other events, activate the Insert button in the editor's toolbar, position your insert point (blue line) where you want to insert a note or a chord, and simply play the note or chord. If you want to insert a note without moving the content found to the right of this location, disable the Insert button on the toolbar.

12. When done, don't forget to turn the Step Recording button off; otherwise, Cubase continues to insert events that you play on the keyboard in this part.

Zooming

In MIDI editors (Key, Drum, and List), the zooming functions are similar to the ones found in the Project window with the exception that you do not have a Presets menu next to the horizontal or vertical scroll bar. However, you do have access to the Zoom submenu options found in the context menu (right-click or Ctrl-click) or in the Edit menu.

You can also use the Magnifying Glass tool on the toolbar to draw a selection box around the range you want to zoom into. Clicking inside the editor with the Magnifying Glass tool zooms in one step at a time and Ctrl-clicking (Command-clicking on Mac) zooms out one step at a time.

Editing Multiple Tracks

You can edit more than one track of the same class at a time in the Edit window. When selecting parts on different tracks in the Project window and opening them in the MIDI Editor, you can edit the parts for all the selected tracks at once. This becomes useful when you want to compare events on different tracks in a single editing window. If you select a MIDI track associated with a drum map, the MIDI events for this track are displayed as normal MIDI events without the drum mapping information. In other words, if you want to edit multiple drum mapped events, select only tracks that contain a drum map association.

If you have assigned different colors to different parts in the Project window, you can also see the parts' colors in the MIDI Editor.

To edit more than one track at a time:

1. Click the first part you want to edit in a track.
2. Shift-click the next part you want to edit in another track or with the Selection tool, drag a selection box over the range of parts you want to edit simultaneously.
3. Press Ctrl+E (Command+E on the Mac) or select Open Key (or Drum) Editor from the MIDI menu, or double-click on one of the selected parts.

The editing window appears with multiple tracks displayed, as shown in Figure 8.16. The active part is displayed with its part color and black borders around each event in the window. The title of the editor also reflects which part is active. The other parts are visible but inactive and displayed as gray events.

Figure 8.16
The MIDI Editor can display more than one part at a time

The Information Bar

If you need to quickly determine the start position or the velocity value of an event, the Information bar is your greatest ally. You can modify any parameters of a selected event or events directly from the Information bar by clicking in the Value field below the parameter's name and using the scroll wheel of your mouse (if you have one) to change the value, or entering a new value using your keyboard. When more than one event is selected, the parameter values are displayed in yellow rather than white. You can change parameters of multiple selected events in one of two ways: either relative or absolute. By default, parameters change relatively; however, holding the Ctrl key (Command key on the Mac) down causes the parameter value to become absolute. For example, if you have a G4 with a velocity of 64 and a C5 with a velocity of 84 selected, the Information bar pitch displays the C5's parameters. Table 8.2 shows how this works.

Table 8.2
How relative editing of multiple selected events works in the Information bar compared with absolute editing

Original Parameters (Pitch/Velocity)	Value Entered	Change when Relative (Default)	Change when Absolute (with Ctrl key pressed)
C5/64	D5/84	D5/84	D5/84
G4/104	See above	A4/124	D5/84

MIDI Controllers

Editing MIDI control messages as they appear in the controller lanes is no different than editing note events. The tools that allow you to select or enter new events works the same way here as they did with note events. However, because the quantize grid setting influences the frequency at which these events are inserted when creating new control messages, it is important to make sure that this quantize configuration is set appropriately for the task at hand.

When you are editing Control Change messages, it is important to understand the following principle. When you delete a Control Change message, the value preceding the deleted message replaces the deleted information. For example, if you have three sustain pedal values of 127, 0, 127 and decide to delete the second value, then you only have two values of 127 in your lane, as shown in Figure 8.17.

Figure 8.17
A before and after look at what happens when you remove intermediate values in controller lanes

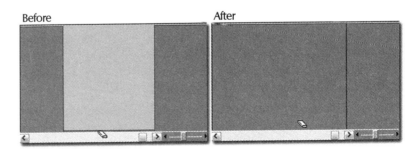

Drum Track Editor

What you have just read about the Key Editor applies for the most part in the Drum Editor as well. The Drum Editor window treats every single drum or percussion instrument with its own parameters. One of these parameters is the quantize value associated with each instrument. The Drum Editor can either treat them separately or apply a general quantize value to all of them depending on the state of the General Quantize button found in the title bar. For example, you can set a different quantize value for the kick drum and the hi-hat. This can be very useful when using the step recording method. The quantize value determines the spacing between each entered event. When the General Quantize option is disabled, the individual quantize settings take over. When the General Quantize option is enabled, the quantize value set in the toolbar dictates the quantize grid for each instrument in the part. This said, changing the quantize value for an instrument does not affect the general quantize value you set in the Drum Editor, but affects the frequency at which events are added when using the Drumstick tool (same as the Draw tool in the Key Editor). You will notice that the Drumstick tool has also replaced the Draw tool, but they play a similar role in both editing windows.

Try this out by creating a drum track. Set the quantize value for the kick drum at quarter notes and the hi-hat's quantize value at sixteenth notes. Disable the General Quantize button in the toolbar. Now, use the Drumstick tool to draw events on these instruments by simply dragging it from left to right, holding the mouse button down. You will see that a kick is added on every beat and a hi-hat on every sixteenth note.

Another small difference is that when you add an event with the Drumstick tool, clicking it a second time removes it, unlike the Draw tool, which usually edits the note by dragging the event to make it longer or shorter. Because you can set an individual length for each instrument in a drum track, you can't extend the length in the Event Display area. There is a very simple reason for this treatment: Most percussive sounds are, by nature, quite short or without any sustained material, and they also are not looped. So, it really doesn't matter if you extend the event, because most instruments play the sound until the end and the MIDI Note Off event's position has little or no effect on this note, no matter how long you hold it. Unlike a guitar or keyboard note, the position of the attack, or Note On event, is more relevant in this case than the actual end of the event. As a direct result of this, there are no Scissors or Glue Tube tools in the Drum Editor.

Drum Editor Display Areas

As with the Key Editor, the Drum Editor is divided into task specific areas. In this case, it is divided into five basic areas which are described next.

The toolbar and Information bar as mentioned earlier in this chapter are quite similar and offer minor differences. Most of these differences have already been addressed; however, there is also an additional Solo Drum button in the toolbar, which lets you solo a specific instrument within the Drum Editor.

The drum sound list and its columns replace the keyboard display of the Key Editor. The number of columns displayed here (see Figure 8.18) depends on the drum map associated with the track. This represents individual parameters for instruments that are defined in your drum map.

Below the drum sound list, in the left corner are the Map and Names field. The Map field allows you to select a map from the drum map list or set up a new drum map if you haven't already done that. The Name field allows you to select from a drop-down menu, the names of instruments associated with different pitches when you don't want to use a drum map. So, this field is grayed out when a drum map is selected.

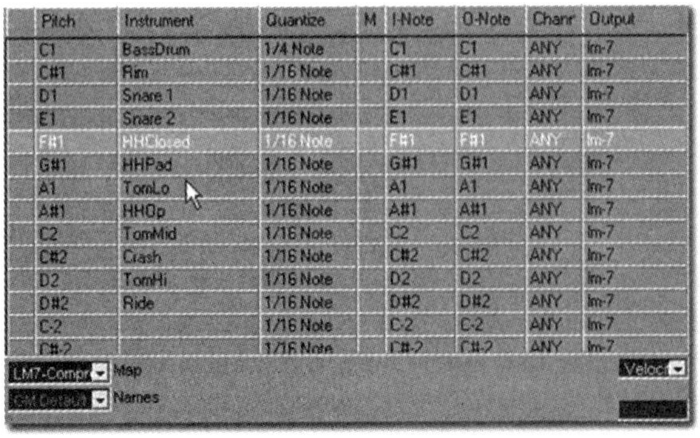

Figure 8.18
The drum sound list and at the bottom-left corner, the active Map and Name fields

If you drag the divider line between the Note Display area and the Drum List area to the right, you will see some of the columns that might be hidden. The drum list can have up to nine columns, each representing a control over an instrument.

▶ The first unnamed column allows you to select the instrument and hear the instrument associated with this pitch. By selecting an instrument, you can also view the velocity values associated with Note On events for this instrument in the controller lane.

▶ The Pitch column represents the pitch associated with a particular instrument. This cannot be changed because most instruments are already preprogrammed to play a certain instrument on an assigned pitch value.

▶ The Instrument column represents the name of the sound associated with this row's pitch. The name that appears in this column depends on the drum map you have associated with this part or the name list you have selected in the Name field below the Map field if no drum maps have been associated with the track.

▶ The Quantize column represents the quantize value setting for each instrument. You can change this setting by clicking on the current value and selecting a new one. You can also change all the instruments' quantize value by holding the Ctrl key (Command on Mac) down as you make your selection. The list that appears offers the same options as the editor's Quantize Grid drop-down menu.

▶ The M column controls whether an instrument is muted or not. To mute an instrument, click in the instrument row in the M column. To unmute that instrument, click for that instrument once again.

▶ The I-Note column stands for the Input Note value, or the note as recorded from the controller keyboard or drum machine. This is important to understand when we discuss the Drum Map feature in the next section. You can use the scroll wheel on your mouse to change this value, or click in the field and enter a new value.

▶ The O-Note column stands for Output Note Value, or the note that plays back the sound you want to map. By default, the O-Note is the same as the I-Note, but you can remap the input to another output when using drum maps. Again, this is discussed in the next section. You can change the value of this column the same way as in the I-Note column.

▶ The Channel column lets you select the MIDI channel you want to assign to the instrument in a particular row. Each row can be played through a different MIDI channel. Again, for this to work, your drum track has to be set to play the Any setting in the Project window. You can use the scroll wheel on your mouse to change this value, or click in the field and enter a new value.

▶ The Output column allows you to assign an instrument to a different MIDI output port. Each row or instrument in the drum part can be assigned to a different MIDI output if desired. To change the output, click the appropriate row in the Output column and select a new MIDI output from the pop-up menu. Each note in a drum track can be assigned to a different instrument. For example, you could have the kick drum played by a GM device, the snare played by the VSTi LM-9, and so on. For this to work, you need to set your track's MIDI channel in the Track List area of the Project window to the Any setting; otherwise, all the sounds in the track are played by the same instrument.

To the right of the drum sound list is the Note Display area (see Figure 8.19). The horizontal axis represents different instruments or pitches according to the information found in the drum sound list on the left and the time line divided by the quantize setting. Rectangles are replaced by diamonds, each of which represents a Note On event. Notes are inline with the quantize grid when the grid line crosses the diamond in its center.

Below the Note Display area are the controller lanes. Whereas the Key Editor displays the velocity of every note, the Drum Editor only displays the velocity of the selected instrument. In Figure 8.19, the current selected instrument is the HHClosed. Therefore, the velocity values you see represent the velocities associated with the Note On events of this instrument. For every other Control Change message, the editor behaves the same way as in the Key Editor described earlier.

Figure 8.19
The Note and Controller Display areas of the Drum Editor

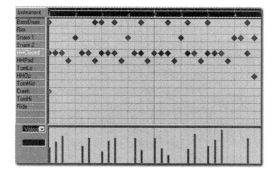

Working With Drum Maps

Because not all instruments are created equal, they all operate differently, assigning different sounds to different keys. For example, one instrument's drum setup could use all the notes in a C scale to map its drum sounds, whereas another instrument might use every chromatic note to map its drum set. This is fine when you know which note is playing which sound. But, what if you want to try a different drum set or drum machine? Do you need to rerecord all your beats because C1 is not the bass drum anymore? Well, not really. That's where drum mapping becomes very handy.

As you read in the previous section, in the Drum Editor, you have two columns that display Input notes and Output notes. This is used to remap what was recorded on one note but now will play as if it were recorded on another note, remapping the event to correspond to a new drum instrument map. To do this, you can either create your own drum map or load one that has already been programmed. Cubase comes with ready-made drum maps on its CD; before you start creating your own drum map, check your CD or your Drummaps folder if you've installed them on your computer.

Drum maps are essentially a list of 128 sound names associated with a pitch, Note In, and Note Out event. You can assign one drum map per track. For obvious reasons, if you use two tracks with the same MIDI output and MIDI channel, you can have only one drum map assigned to that instrument. Finally, you can assign only one Note In instrument per note name or note number, but you can have more than one Note In assigned to the same Note Out.

Because your drum map is a way of reassigning the keys you play to other keys at the output, remember that each note in a drum map corresponds to a pitch value. Each pitch value (note number) can be associated with an instrument name, such as Kick Drum 1, Snare, Hi-hat, and so forth. You can then assign the played note to that named instrument, which in turn is associated to a pitch, such as C1 (or note number 36). For example, you could create your perfect drum kit layout where you position on the keyboard (or other MIDI interface) the instruments the way you want them. Take, for example, the left portion of Figure 8.20. This could be your permanent drum layout setup that you use as a template for all drum parts. You could base this on your favorite drum layout if you wanted. From this point forward, you want all your drum sounds to map to the notes that are associated with the sounds on this layout. In the drum map on the right, you can see that the bottom half does not need remapping because the sounds in this setup are similarly positioned to play the same notes. Things change when you get into the cymbal sounds. Where you want the Ride 1 sound, the current drum setup plays a Crash 1 and your Ride Cymbal 1 sound is associated with another pitch. The solution: You remap the I-note in the drum map of the currently loaded instrument to C#4 and the O-note to D4. This way, you can play the C#4 and hear the Ride Cymbal. Because the C#4 is associated with the D4 pitch value, a D4 is actually recorded onto your MIDI track. Now, if you have a D4 recorded on your track, which in this drum map is a Ride Cymbal 1, what happens when you load another drum kit where D4 is a cowbell? Well, let's say that your ride is now on E5, all you need to do is set the O-note of the pitch D4 to E5 and you will hear the ride sound once again.

Figure 8.20
Example of a drum map
in action

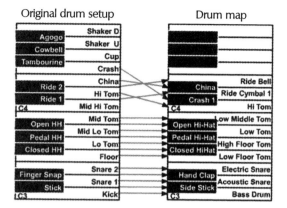

Assigning a Drum Map to a Track

To load a drum map and assign it to a drum track:

1. In the MIDI Setup section of the Inspector area, in the Map field, select the Drum Map setup option. This opens the Drum Map Setup dialog box (see Figure 8.21).

Figure 8.21
The Drum Map Setup
dialog box

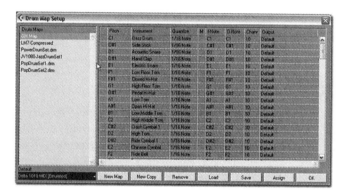

2. In the Drum Map Setup dialog box, click the Load button.

3. Browse to the folder containing your drum map files (*.drm), select it, and click the Open button.

4. Select your newly loaded drum map from the drum map list.

5. In the Default field below the drum map list, select the default MIDI port associated with this drum map.

6. Click the Assign button to assign this drum map to the current track.

Or:

1. Assign the generic GM Map to the MIDI track containing the drum parts.

2. Double-click on a part in the Event Display area for this track to open it in the Drum Editor.

3. From the Drum Editor, below the drum list, select the Drum Map setup option.

4. From this point forward, follow Steps 2–6 from the previous list.

Creating a Drum Map

As mentioned earlier, you can create your own drum maps or start from existing ones and edit them. The editing process takes place inside the Drum Map Setup dialog box.

To create a drum map:

1. Click the New Map button.
2. Select the new map in the Drum Map field to rename it.
3. Next to each pitch in the list of instruments, enter an appropriate instrument name. It is a good idea to have the drum kit loaded so that you can hear the sounds as you are entering instrument names.
4. Adjust the Quantize, the I-note, the O-note, the Channel, and the Output fields if needed.
5. Repeat these steps for all the sounds available in your drum kit.
6. Click the Save button when you are satisfied with your current settings.
7. Name the file and browse to the location where you want to save the file, then click Save once again.

Later on, if you feel you have loaded drum maps that you don't want to use anymore, you can select the unnecessary drum map, and then click the Remove button from the Drum Map Setup dialog box.

List Editor

The List Editor, like the Key and Drum Editors, allows you to modify your MIDI and audio events. The difference with the List Editor is that all the events are "listed" in rows of information and sorted by the order in which they were recorded. This is different than the Key or Drum Editors in the sense that you can have three notes displayed at the same place in a piano or drum roll, but in the list they all have their own row. This makes it a good place to look for glitches like note doubling (two notes playing the same channel and the same key at the same time), or consecutive patch changes that you've entered by mistake and that make your sound module behave erratically. When you want to edit notes and change velocity levels or edit controllers, the Key and Drum Editors are better suited for these tasks.

List Editor Display Areas

Before we take a look at the values in the columns and what they mean, let's look at the different parts of the List Editor, as shown in Figure 8.22. The toolbar offers some similarities with the other MIDI editors. You will find, however, some new elements. The Insert menu allows you to select the type of event you want to insert, for example.

Figure 8.22
The List Editor; from
left to right: the List
area, the Event Display
area, and the Value area

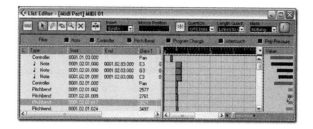

The other difference in the List Editor's toolbar is the Filter button represented by the letter F. This is different from the Information button in the Key Editor, but displays or hides a bar beneath the toolbar. This bar represents elements that you can filter from the display areas below. They are hidden from your view, but any modification you make can affect these events as well, unlike the Mask. But not to worry, usually, if you can see it, it's hard to erase it. The Mask field, contrary to the Filter toolbar, allows you to view only the type of event or controller selected. It filters events as well, but events that do not correspond to the selection you make in this field. Both filter and mask options are there to help you isolate and manage the events displayed in the areas below, making it easier to focus your editing on the events you want to edit in this window.

To filter a type of event in the List Editor:

1. Make the Filter bar visible.
2. Click in the check box next to the event type name in the Filter bar.

Below the toolbar, there are three areas giving information: the List area, the Event Display area, and the Value area (see Figure 8.22).

The Value area shows the Data 1 value from the List area. This value can be edited by using the Draw tool. In fact, as soon as you enter the area, your tool changes to the Draw tool automatically. When you make a modification to the value in this area, the change is reflected in the column titled Data 1.

The start, end, and length columns in the List area appropriately display the start time of the event, the end time of an event when this event has one, and the length of the event, again when the event has a length. Where it becomes a little bit less obvious is when you look at the Value columns. Table 8.3 describes what each column represents depending on the event's type.

Table 8.3
Description of information present in the List area

Type	Data 1	Data 2	Comment
Note	Pitch of the note	Note On velocity	
Poly Pressure	Note number	Pressure amount	
Control Change	Controller type	Change amount	
Program Change	Patch number		
Aftertouch	Pressure amount		
Pitch bend	Fine value of bend	Coarse value of bend	
System Exclusive			The SysEx message

The Event Display area shows events as they occur in time, like the Key or Drum Editors. The difference is that the vertical axis of the display shows the order in which these events occur rather than the pitch itself. If you move an event to the left, before another event occurs, it also moves up in the list as Cubase refreshes its display after you release the mouse button.

To modify events in the Event Display area, select the events you want to move and drag them to the left or right to move them in time where you want the event or events to occur.

Creating And Editing Events

To insert an event in the List Editor window:

1. Select the type of event you want to insert from the Ins. ?? menu.
2. Right-click in the right area of the List Editor window where the events appear and select the Pencil tool from the toolbox.
3. Click where you want to insert the event. The horizontal ruler on top represents the time and each row represents an event at that time.
4. If you want to move your event in time, use your Selection tool and move the event left or right by dragging it. The Column view reflects that change.

To edit several events at once:

1. Select the first event you want to edit in the Column Display area.
2. Ctrl-click the last event in the list you want to edit, thus selecting all the events between the two. If you want to edit nonsequential events, Shift-click each event.
3. Press and hold the Alt key down before you make your modifications to all the selected events. If you want to modify a series of events proportionally, hold the Ctrl+Alt keys down before making the changes.

Now You Try It

It's time to put the topics covered in this chapter into action—you can download a practice exercise at http://www.muskalipman.com.

9

Audio Recording and Project Editing

In Chapter 8, we look at how to record MIDI and edit these events in the Project window. This chapter looks at similar functions related to audio. You will probably find some similarities between the two types of events because many of the tools used for MIDI are also used for audio. In other cases, you will find tools specifically designed to handle digital audio in a multitrack environment.

We start by looking at how to record audio, then venture into the different processes that can be applied to this recorded audio, and discuss the different methods involved in processing these audio files.

In this chapter, you will:

▶ Learn how to set up Cubase to record digital audio

▶ Learn how to record in Cycle mode

▶ Understand the differences between audio events, Regions, and parts

▶ Discover how to work with fade envelopes attached to objects in the Project window

▶ Determine the differences between destructive and nondestructive editing

▶ Find out what you can do with the audio objects in your Project window

▶ Learn how to edit events and parts inside the Event Display area of the Project window

Recording Audio

At this point, let's assume that you have already configured your studio for audio recording and that you understand how audio goes into your computer through the sound card and comes out of it into an external audio monitoring system (self-powered studio monitors or headphones, for example). If you have not configured your audio connections already, you should do so before proceeding because you might want to test things out as you read the information found in this chapter.

Before you begin recording audio, you should configure the project's sample rate and format through the Project Setup dialog box (the default key command is Shift+S) if you haven't done so already. After you start recording in one sampling rate, you can't change it. In other words, all audio files in a project have to be recorded (or imported) at the same sampling rate. You should also make sure that the digital clock of the audio card is set up correctly if you are using a digital input to record your audio. The digital clock defines the exact sampling frequency of the sound card. If your sound card is receiving its digital clock information from an external digital audio device, your sound card should be set to follow this device's sampling frequency.

To configure the digital clock on your sound card:

1. Select the Device Setup option in the Devices menu.
2. In the Device Setup dialog box, select the VST Multitrack option.
3. In the VST multitrack option, click the Control Panel button to access your sound card's configuration panel.
4. In your sound card's configuration panel, set the master clock (digital clock) appropriately. If your external device is set as master (or internal), you should set your sound card to follow the external device's digital clock using the appropriate option for your card (you might have to consult your sound card's documentation if you are unsure how to do this). This said, it is recommended that you use your sound card's digital clock to control other devices rather than have other devices control your sound card. In this case, make sure that the external digital audio devices follow your sound card's digital audio clock by setting them appropriately. You will find more information on this in Chapter 14.
5. When done, close your sound card's configuration panel.
6. Back in Cubase, click Apply and then OK to close the Device Setup dialog box.

Note that if you don't have any digital connections with other devices in your studio setup, you most likely don't have to worry about the digital clock of your sound card because it is probably set appropriately to follow its internal clock.

To record a single track of audio in Cubase:

1. Right-click (Ctrl-click on a Mac) in the Track List area and choose Add Audio Track from the context menu. If you already have audio tracks in your project, you don't need to create a new one, just select an existing empty audio track.
2. In the Name field for the new track, or the existing track if you didn't create one, name your track appropriately. When audio is recorded, Cubase names the audio file according to the name of the track. This makes it easier to manage audio clips later on.
3. Enable the Record Ready button in the audio track to which you want to record. You can do this either through the Track Setting section in the Inspector or in the Track List area.
4. Also in one of these two previously mentioned areas, select the type of audio you want to record by clicking on the Mono/Stereo button. Remember that after you record audio in one of these formats, the rest of the track has to stay in that format. If you change your mind later on, you have to create a new track or convert your current files from one format to another.

5. Press F5 on your keyboard, or select VST Inputs from the Devices menu, or select VST Inputs from the Device panel if it is visible.

6. In the VST Inputs panel, enable the inputs you want to use during the recording process.

7. In the Inspector area of the selected track, open the audio channel section.

8. At the top of the audio channel, select the input you want to use to record audio.

9. Still in the audio channel, enable the Monitor button. This allows you to monitor the level of input in this channel before you begin recording (see Figure 9.1).

Figure 9.1
When the Monitor button is active, the level meters next to the fader become input level monitors

10. Start playing as you would during recording to adjust the input level of the audio. Remember that the fader in the audio channel does not influence the input level, only the output level. If you need to adjust the input level, you need to use one of the following alternatives: Adjust the level coming out of your instrument, adjust the level coming out of the mixer (if your signal passes through a mixer before heading to Cubase), or adjust the input level from your sound card's control panel applet if it allows it.

11. In the Transport panel, select the appropriate recording mode. When recording audio, Normal is usually the appropriate choice.

12. If you want to start a recording at a specific point in time and stop recording at another specific point in time, adjust the left and right locators appropriately and enable the Punch-in and Punch-out buttons on the Transport panel.

13. If you want to hear a metronome click while you are recording (but not in the recording signal), make sure that the metronome click is not routed into the recorded signal. You can configure your metronome click through the Metronome Setup dialog box (Ctrl-click or Command-click on Mac on the Click button in the Transport panel). After your settings are made, close the dialog box and enable or disable the metronome click from the Transport panel (the default key command is C).

14. Place your play line at the position where you want your recording to begin.

15. Click the Record button and begin recording the audio.
16. Click the Stop button to manually stop the recording if you haven't enabled the Punch-out button.

Using TrueTape

The SX version of Cubase offers the possibility to record audio using an analog tape saturation simulator called TrueTape. This is an input effect that records the audio using a 32-bit, floating point format compatible with 16-bit sound cards that produces the feel produced by saturating the analog tape. This effect does not increase the actual volume beyond the limit of digital recording; it merely gives the impression that it does. You activate the TrueTape recording and adjust the drive slider to the desired level. You can monitor the output produced by this effect through Cubase's mixer. To hear the effect of the TrueTape, you need to turn the Direct Monitoring option off.

To use the TrueTape effect in a recording:

1. Begin the recording process as described in the previous steps until you get to Step 9, then continue on with these steps.
2. From the Devices menu, select TrueTape. This brings up the TrueTape Input Effect panel as displayed in Figure 9.2.
3. Adjust the drive slider on the TrueTape Input Effect panel to get the desired saturation level for your recording. You can't cause the input to digitally clip using this effect, but you should make sure that the level going into your input does not clip (pass the 0 dB limit of a digital signal); otherwise, you get a distorted sound that does not like analog saturation.
4. When you are satisfied with the level of saturation, proceed to Step 10 of the previous list for your digital audio recording.

Figure 9.2
The TrueTape Input
Effect panel

The TrueTape effect has only one parameter to control, and that's the level of saturation you have just adjusted. You can also select one of the presets available in the Presets menu of the interface, but they only set the drive slider to different drive levels.

Recording Audio in Cycle Mode

Sometimes, you want to record a solo that throws everybody on the floor when they hear it. Working in Cycle mode allows you to run a section of your song over and over again. While this section plays, you can try different things out and record them. When you're done, you can try either to reproduce the best ideas you had while practicing, or simply use portions of the different takes you've just made if you were recording what you just did. That's the whole point behind cycle recording.

In Cubase, when you are recording in Cycle mode, it means that you are looping a portion of the project found between the left and right locators. When you record audio in this mode, Cubase records a long audio file but can define events and/or Regions within that file corresponding to the section found between the locators. What it actually defines depends on the current setting found in Cubase's preferences (see Figure 9.3).

Figure 9.3
The Cycle Record Mode options found in the Cubase Preferences dialog box

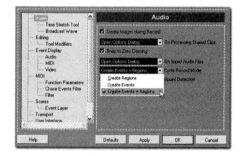

Cubase can identify each recorded lap in two different ways when you record in Cycle mode: events or Regions (or both).

▶ When you record in Cycle mode and create events, Cubase creates a single, long audio clip, but each time a lap (a cycle) is completed, an event is inserted on the track. The event that appears when you stop recording is the one recorded during the last lap (or cycle). All the other events are still on the track but under this last event. Because you can only hear one event at a time on a track, you need the To Front option found in the Project window's context menu as shown in Figure 9.4. This option appears when you right-click (Ctrl-click on Mac) over the overlapping events. You should create and work with events when you want to split the events up to create an edited version using parts of each take.

Figure 9.4
Selecting which take
you want to bring to the
front after a cycle
recording

▶ When you record in Cycle mode and create Regions, Cubase creates a single, long audio clip where a Region defines each lap (cycle). The difference here is that there is only one event on your track, but using the Set To Region option (also displayed below the To Front option in Figure 9.4), you can choose which Region you want to display in this event. Because Regions are created, you can also see the defined Regions in the Media Pool (see Figure 9.5) and in the Sample Editor somewhere else in the project. You should create and work with Regions when you want to select a take from an entire Region in your event.

Figure 9.5
The Regions created
during cycle recording
are named Take *,
where the asterisk
represents the number
of the lap/take

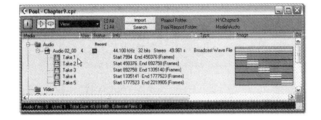

▶ Finally, you can set Cubase to create both events and Regions. This places a number of overlapping events on your track and creates identical Regions in the Media Pool. By doing this, if you decide to go back to a take and modify it, you can place the Region from the Media Pool onto a track. This said, you should beware of mixing both methods of editing (events and Regions) when working on a track. When using the Scissors tool to split an event, you split all the overlapping events. Selecting an event in one portion and a Region in another might not give you the result you were going for.

To change your Cycle recording mode preferences:

1. Select Preferences in the File menu.

2. Select Audio in the Preferences dialog box.

3. Select the desired option in the Cycle Record Mode drop-down menu (see Figure 9.3).

4. Click Apply, then OK to close the dialog box.

To choose which event you want to hear when editing a track:

1. Start by listening to each take one after the other, identifying the segments you want to keep in each take. To bring a different take to the front, right-click (Ctrl-click on Mac) over the track and select the appropriate take from the list as shown in Figure 9.4.

2. Adjust your Grid setting in the project toolbar to the desired value, especially if you don't want to be restricted to splitting at bar intervals.

3. Select the Scissors tool and split the event where you want to switch from one event to another (see the top part of Figure 9.6).

4. Select the Object Selection tool from the toolbar or the Project window's context menu.

5. Right-click on each new event to select the appropriate take to bring to front (see the bottom part of Figure 9.6).

Figure 9.6
Using the Scissors tool splits all overlapping events on a track, allowing you to create a new version using different takes

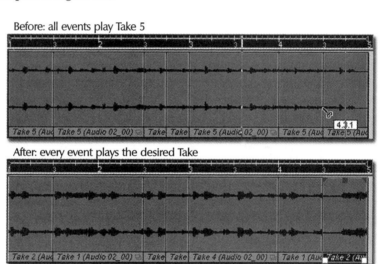

Before: all events play Take 5

After: every event plays the desired Take

Destructive and Nondestructive Editing

Sometimes, we like to take risks or try things to see how they sound. If you don't like it, it's nice to be able to put things back like they were at the beginning. If only life could be so easy! In Cubase, it is. The idea of being able to make changes and then being able to undo these changes is not new to computers. Most of us have used the Undo command time and time again. When you are typing an e-mail to a friend, you can undo operations many times over until you get it right. However, if you save the e-mail, open it later to change things, and save it once more, you are replacing the original e-mail with the new one unless you saved the new version under another name.

Working with audio files is quite similar in the sense that a Cubase project refers to files as clips. These clips are on the hard disk inside a project subfolder appropriately called audio. When you save a project file, the project itself does not contain the audio, but merely a link to the original audio clip. When you split an audio event and place it somewhere else, you are changing the reference points found in the project file to the audio clip, but are still not editing or transforming the original clip in any way. The same applies for effects or volume changes you might add to a project; all of these transformations are not affecting the original audio file. This type of editing is referred to as nondestructive editing.

If we push the editing further and decide to apply a time stretch, a normalize, or fade out to a portion of an audio clip, Cubase still does not touch the original content of the file because it creates additional files in another folder inside your project folder. If this is not enough to convince you that Cubase is a completely nondestructive environment, you can also use multiple undo levels through the History option in the Edit menu. In addition, there is a feature called Offline Process History in the Edit menu, which allows you to select a processing you applied on an audio file, let's say seven steps ago, and edit the parameters of that processing without affecting the other six steps you did after that.

Destructive editing, on the other hand, has one advantage: It is not as space consuming. Whenever you are working on large files, every processed audio bit in your project stays there unless you decide to clean up the audio through another function called Remove Unused Media which is discussed later. Keep in mind, however, that a project can quickly grow in size and you should prepare sufficient hard disk space when working with a digital audio multitrack project when using 32-bit recordings. If space is not an issue, then enjoy the benefits of working in an environment that allows you to undo mistakes and to take creative risks with the audio files you record.

Working With Events, Regions, and Parts

As mentioned previously in this chapter and in Chapter 6, Cubase uses different levels of audio references. The basic recording is saved as an audio file, which is referred to as an audio clip inside Cubase. An audio event is automatically created in your Project window after a recording. Cubase can also create Regions, which are portions of an audio clip that you can reuse somewhere else in a project. You can also convert audio events into a Region or a part. Because Regions can be reused elsewhere and parts can contain more than one Region or event, making it easy to move a number of events at a time, you might find it easier in certain instances to convert your events into Regions or parts. All three types of audio objects offer different editing properties when placed on a track. Knowing how differently they behave can help you choose which type of object is best suited for your needs. Table 9.1 takes a look at how different these objects are:

Table 9.1
Differences between events, Regions, and part objects on an audio track

Events	Regions	Parts
You can modify the length of an event on a track, but you can't extend the event beyond the limit of the file it refers to.	You can modify the length of an event on a track and can extend it beyond the limits of the Region itself but not beyond the limit of the file the Region refers to.	You can extend the boundaries of a part as much as you want because a part does not refer to a particular audio clip, event, or Region.
Audio events have envelopes (fade in, sustain level, fade out). You can use these envelopes to control the level of the event. The envelope is locked with the event, so when you move the event, the envelope follows.	Audio Regions also have envelopes (fade in, sustain level, fade out). You can use these envelopes to control the level of the event (see Figure 9.7). The envelope is locked with the Region, so when you move it, the envelope follows.	Audio parts do not have envelopes associated with them, but the events and Regions they contain have individual envelopes that can be edited inside the Audio Part Editor.
The default editing window for events is the Sample Editor.	The default editing window for regions is the Sample Editor.	The default editing window for parts is the Audio Part Editor.
On an audio track, you can convert an event into a Region or a part using the Events to Part option found in the Audio menu.	On an audio track, you can convert a Region into a part using the Events to Part option found in the Audio menu. Also, if you have resized an object beyond the original Region's boundaries, you can bring back the object to its original Region's size using the Events From Region option found in the Audio menu.	You can dissolve an audio part containing several events and Regions to create independent objects on a track using the Dissolve Part option found in the Audio menu.

Figure 9.7
Comparing audio events
(top), audio parts
(middle), and audio
Regions (bottom)

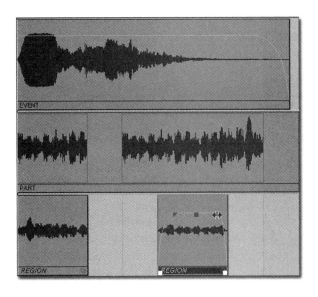

Project Window Editing

The Project window is your main working area. This is where you record audio and MIDI events and edit different track parameters through the Inspector or Track List area. However, the Event Display area is where you will do most of your editing tasks. When you can't do it in there, that's when you open an editor to fine-tune these editing decisions.

Because the editing capabilities of Cubase are quite extensive, you need to understand that the options available at any given time depend on the context itself. In most cases, this context is determined by the currently selected objects. For example, if you select a part, the Dissolve Part option is available but the Events to Part option is not. When you select an event, the Dissolve Part option is not available, but the Events to Part option is available.

There are different ways to select what you want in the Project window. When you want to select objects, you can use the Object Selection tool; when you want to select a range, you can use the Range Selection tool. In some cases, you can use items found in the Select submenu options (Edit > Select). For example, you can use the Select from Cursor to End option, which selects all objects crossing the cursor's location or appearing after it in the Project window.

Let's take a look at how you can manipulate objects inside the project.

Using Edit Menu Options

The editing options inside the Project window are available in one of two places: in the Edit menu or through the Project window's context menu in the Edit submenu. This is where you will find the basic Cut, Copy, and Paste options, which work the same way as in any other application. In addition, you will find other options specifically designed to give you more control over project editing tasks.

Splitting

When you want to divide objects in the Project window, you have several options at your disposal.

Using the Scissors tool, you can click on an existing event. The position of the split is determined by the Snap to Grid settings if it is active or by the location of your click. You can also use the cursor's position to determine where the split will occur.

To split objects at the cursor's location:

1.   Position the cursor at the desired location.
2.   Select all the objects crossing the cursor at this location that you want to split. All nonselected objects will not be split.
3.   From the Edit menu, select the Split at Cursor option.

If you want to quickly create a loop section with the objects (parts or events) between the locators, you can use the locators' position to determine where a split will occur. After these objects are split, for example at Bar 5 and Bar 9, you can select only the objects that occur in this range and copy them elsewhere.

To split objects at the locators' position:

1.   Position the left and right locators at the desired position.
2.   Select the objects you want to split.
3.   From the Edit menu, select the Split Loop option. Selected objects crossing the left or right locators are split as displayed in Figure 9.8.

Figure 9.8
Using the Split Loop option

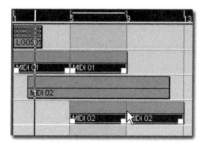

Another quick way to split objects is to use the Range Crop option. This allows you to select a series of objects and remove the area that is outside of the selected objects in the range. (See Figure 9.9.)

Figure 9.9
A before and after look at the Range Crop function applied on a selected range

To set the Range Crop function to a desired range:

1. Select the Range Selection tool.
2. Click in the upper-left corner where you want your range to begin and drag over the range and tracks you want to include in this range.
3. In the Edit menu, select the Range > Crop option.

Using the Range tool with the Split option, you can also achieve an effect similar to the Split Loop option. In this case, however, all the objects within the selected range would be split at the start and end position of this range.

To split a range of selected objects:

1. Select the Range Selection tool.
2. Click in the upper-left corner where you want your range to begin and drag over the range and tracks you want to include in this range.
3. In the Edit menu, select the Range > Split option.

In other instances, you might want to insert an amount of time in the middle of recorded events, but don't want to have to select all the events and split them, then move all the events after the split to a new location. This operation can be done in one easy step by using the Insert Silence option in the Edit > Range submenu. All the events in the selected range are split and the objects crossing the start point of the range are split and then moved at the end point of this range (see Figure 9.10).

Figure 9.10
A before and after look at the Insert Silence option applied on a selected range

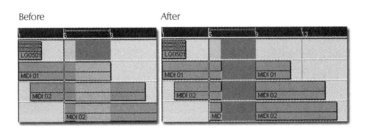

Inversely, if you want to remove the time, including events recorded within this range, you can use the Delete Range option from the Edit > Range submenu. This deletes events within a selected range and deletes the time, moving all events following the range to the start point of this range.

Still using the Range tool, you can copy the content found inside a range and paste it back into the project using the Paste Time or Paste Time at Origin. This is different than the regular Paste function because the Paste Time option pushes existing events forward, effectively adding the contents of the clipboard at the cursor's location, whereas the regular Paste function pastes the contents of the clipboard over any existing events. The Paste Time at Origin function works like the Paste Time but pastes the contents of the clipboard at the original time it was copied from.

Duplicate

When you want to make a single copy of selected events or parts, you can use the Duplicate function from the Edit menu. This function works with the Object Selection or the Range Selection tools. The result varies depending on the objects you select or the range you select.

When using the Object Selection tool, duplicated events appear after the end point of the latest object selected. For example, looking at Figure 9.11, you can see that three parts were selected, ranging from Bar 1 to Bar 9. The duplicated events start at the closest snap grid location (if this option is active) after Bar 9.

Figure 9.11
A before and after look at the Duplicate function while using the Object Selection tool to determine the duplicated content

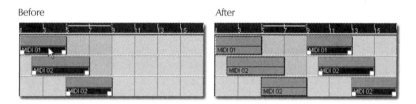

When using the Range Selection tool, only the portion found within the range is duplicated. This means that new events are created to conform to the selected range. In Figure 9.12, the events in the first and second track before the selection are not duplicated. Duplicate events from the selected range appear after the end point of the current range. In both cases (using a range or objects), if there are objects where the duplicated objects are suppose to be pasted, these events are left in place but overlap with the new content. So, you should make sure that there is no content where duplicated events will appear.

Figure 9.12
A before and after look at the Duplicate function while using the Range Selection tool to determine the duplicated content

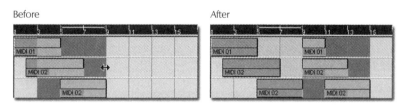

To duplicate objects using the Object Selection or Range Selection tool:

1. Select the appropriate tool (Object Selection or Range Selection).
2. Select the objects or range you want to duplicate.
3. From the Edit menu, select the Duplicate option.

CHAPTER 9

Repeat

If you want to make more than one duplicate copy of selected objects or a selected range of objects, you should use the Repeat option from the Edit menu. This is a great way to repeat looped material several times instead of copying it several times over. In this case, Cubase asks you how many copies you want to make of the selected objects or range. If you are repeating objects, you will also be asked if you want to create shared or real copies. Remember that when you edit one instance of a shared copy, all the subsequent instances share this editing. If you want to only edit one copy of the repeated material, you should either choose to create real copies or select the shared copy you want to edit and transform it into a real copy using the Edit > Convert To Real Copy option.

The Repeat option follows the same behavior as described in the Duplicate option. As you can see in Figure 9.13, selected events appear after the last end point of the selected objects. In Figure 9.14, the portion outside of the range is not repeated. Also, Cubase assumes you want to create real copies when you are using the Range tool to repeat this content.

Figure 9.13
A before and after look at the Repeat function while using the Object Selection tool to determine the repeated content

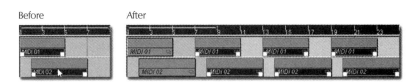

When using the Repeat function, you will also notice that the position of the left and right locators have no effect on the placement of the repeated material. On the other hand, the Snap Grid settings play a role on where your repeated objects appear if you have selected objects that do not start or end on bars.

Figure 9.14
A before and after look at the Repeat function while using the Range Selection tool to determine the repeated content

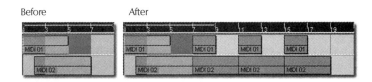

To repeat selected objects or range over time:

1. Select the appropriate tool (Object Selection or Range Selection).
2. Select the objects or range you want to repeat.
3. From the Edit menu, select the Repeat option.
4. Enter the number of times you want this selection to be repeated.
5. If you have selected objects rather than a range, check the Shared Copies option if you want to do so.
6. Click OK.

Fill Loop

Another variation on copying events is offered through the Fill Loop option also found in the Edit menu. This allows you to determine a cycle Region between the left and right locators in which events will be repeated. If events cannot fit completely inside this area, the last copy is split (see example in Figure 9.15).

Figure 9.15
A before and after look at the Fill Loop function while using the Object Selection tool to determine the content that is repeated until the right locator's position

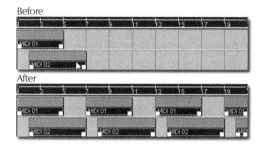

As with the Duplicate and Repeat options, you can also use the Range Selection tool to determine which range will be used to fill a loop section (see example in Figure 9.16). This is a great way of creating a section structure inside a project where all selected objects are repeated until they arrive to the right locator position.

Figure 9.16
A before and after look at the Fill Loop function while using the Range Selection tool to determine the content that is repeated until the right locator's position

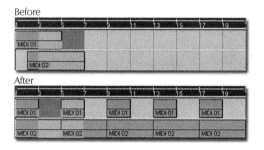

To fill an area with selected objects using the Fill Loop option:

1. Select the appropriate tool (Object Selection or Range Selection).
2. Position your left and right locators to the desired locations where you want the fill to begin and end.
3. Select the objects or range you want to use in the fill.

Normal Sizing

Different objects have different sizing restrictions. For example, you can resize an audio event, but not beyond the extremities to which the original audio clip refers. The same restriction goes for audio Regions: You can expand the audio Region's event in the Project window beyond this Region's boundaries, but not beyond the original clip's boundaries. In terms of audio or MIDI parts, you have no restrictions because a part does not actually refer to any content; it only acts as a container for this content. This being said, you might want these objects to react differently to the sizing you apply. Normally, when you change an event by moving its start or end point, the content within the event stays in place and only the start or end points move, as illustrated in Figure 9.17. Moving the end of the MIDI part in this case (middle segment) moves the end point back in time, whereas moving the start point inward causes the events occurring before the new start point to be ignored during playback. But the events playing during Bar 3 in the original version are still playing at Bar 3 in the resized version.

Figure 9.17
Resizing an event using the Normal Sizing tool (which doubles as the Object Selection tool)

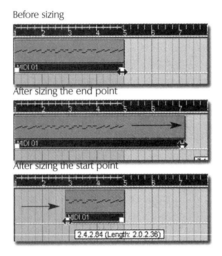

Before sizing

After sizing the end point

After sizing the start point

To resize objects (events or parts):

1. In the Project window's toolbar, select the Object Selection tool (a.k.a. Normal Sizing tool).
2. Select an object to view its resizing handles.
3. Move the handles in the desired direction.

Sizing Moves Contents

In other instances, you may also want to move the content inside of the object (event or part) when resizing it. Looking at the top of Figure 9.18, you can see the original content. In the middle segment, the start point has been moved forward in time, but as you can see, the MIDI events displayed are the same at the beginning as the original event. Similarly, in the bottom segment, the end point is moved back in time, adding extra time at the beginning of the event. This is done when the Sizing Moves Contents option is selected from the Object Selection tool's pop-up menu.

Figure 9.18
Resizing an event using
the Normal Sizing tool
(which doubles as the
Object Selection tool)

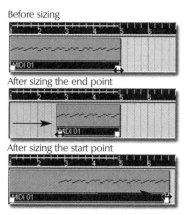

Before sizing

After sizing the end point

After sizing the start point

To resize objects while moving its contents:

1. In the Project window's toolbar, select the Sizing Moves Contents option from the Object Selection's pop-up menu.

2. Select an object to view its resizing handles.

3. Move the handles in the desired direction.

Sizing Applies Time Stretch

The last option available in the Object Selection's pop-up menu allows you to time-stretch objects so that the events inside fit in the new object's size. This stretching can be applied to both audio and MIDI events. Figure 9.19 displays both types of events being stretched. In the top portion, MIDI events' note length values are adjusted to fit within the new proportion. If you stretch in a proportion that changes the quantizing of events, you might have to do a bit of editing inside the MIDI Editor to get the MIDI events to work with the quantize grid. In other words, if you don't want too much hassle with this, try stretching in a proportion that is suitable to the time subdivision currently used in your project. Using this option on audio is a great way to make a drum loop, for example, fit inside a specific number of bars—especially when the tempo difference is minimal. If you look at the audio example in Figure 9.19, you can see that the original content is less than one bar long. Stretching it allows you to loop it properly using the Fill Loop or Repeat options described earlier in this chapter. You may select the quality applied to audio through the Files > Preferences > Audio > Time Stretch Tool panel. The option you select in this dialog box is applied to all audio events that are being stretched using this tool.

CHAPTER 9

Figure 9.19
Resizing an event using
the Sizing Applies Time
Stretch option

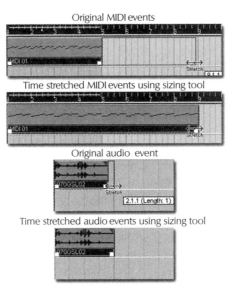

To stretch the content of an object while resizing it:

1. In the Project window's toolbar, select the Sizing Applies Time Stretch option from the Object Selection's pop-up menu.

2. Select an object to view its resizing handles.

3. Move the handles in the desired direction.

You should know that applying time stretching on an audio file in a large proportion will probably create some major artifacts in the sound itself. You should avoid using time stretch in a proportion greater or less than twenty-five percent of the original content's length. As for MIDI events, because the only thing that changes when time stretching an event is a value in a field, there are absolutely no restrictions in this respect.

Shifting Events Inside Object

Cubase also offers you the possibility of shifting events inside an object without moving the object's position. This is done by offsetting the position of the audio clip inside the object's start and end points, as illustrated in Figure 9.20. You can also shift MIDI events inside a MIDI part. In both cases, there is only one condition that applies: The object in which the events are found has to be smaller than the events themselves. For example, if you have MIDI events at Bar 1, Beat 1 and Bar 3, Beat 4 within a MIDI part that spans from Bar 1 to Bar 4, you cannot shift these events inside because the container covers the same area as the events inside the container.

Figure 9.20
Shifting event's position
within an object

Original audio event

Contents slided forward in time

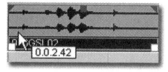

To shift events inside an object:

1. In the Project window's toolbar, select the Object Selection tool.

2. Select the object you want to shift.

3. Hold down the Ctrl+Alt keys on a PC or Command+Option keys on a Mac and drag the content to the left or right.

You can use this technique creatively by shifting a drum loop, for example, trying out different beat combinations when playing a shifted event along with other events in the same time line.

If you want to fine-tune, or edit the shift offset values, you can access these parameters inside the Project Browser window, which is covered in Chapter 10.

Muting Objects

When trying out things inside the Project window, you might want to mute a track using the Mute button found in the Inspector and Track List area. However, if you only want to mute a number of events, you can do so by selecting these events followed by the Mute option found in the Edit menu. The default key command to mute events is Shift+M. After an object is muted, you can unmute it with the Shift+U key command or by selecting the Unmute option—also found in the Edit menu.

Lock

If you've worked hard at positioning events in the time line, you can lock them in place to prevent time-consuming mistakes. When an object is locked, a tiny lock icon appears in the bottom-right corner of the object next to the end point handle. You can lock selected events by using the Lock option in the Edit menu (Ctrl+Shift+L or Command+Shift+L). After objects are locked, you cannot move or edit them from the Project window. To unlock objects, select the corresponding option in the Edit menu, or press Ctrl+Shift+U or Command+Shift+U.

Disabling Audio Tracks

After you start recording audio inside a project, you will gather many more audio files than you'll probably use in the final project because you will most likely have different takes from which to choose. You might also create several working tracks along the way that are not used anymore. Simply muting these tracks only mutes the output level, but the information on these tracks is still read, causing your hard disk to look for them and load them anyway. After a while, these muted tracks might start dragging your project down. To avoid this kind of situation, you can disable tracks that are not currently being used in your project. This offers the advantage of shutting down all disk activity related to the audio content found on these tracks, while still remaining in your project in case you need them later on.

To disable audio tracks:

1. Right-click (Option-click on Mac) in the Track List area.
2. From the context menu, select Disable Track.

You can enable a track after it has been disabled by repeating this operation. The option in the context menu is replaced by Enable Track instead.

10

Browsing and Processing Options

One of the newest additions to the Cubase editing window family is the Browse Project window. This window provides you with a complete list of all the events found in your project, making it a perfect environment to troubleshoot all kinds of objects as well as a tool that lets you quickly edit details within a project. For example, you can rename a number of events directly from the Browse Project window. Any changes you make here are reflected in all other windows.

We also look at offline (not in real time) processes inside Cubase and the advantages they may provide over online processes (processed in real time) when you need more processes than your computer can handle. Because Cubase offers a nondestructive editing environment, making changes to processes applied directly to audio objects has never been easier.

In this chapter, you will:

> ▶ Understand and use the Browse Project window
> ▶ Use the Offline Process History panel
> ▶ Use the Edit History panel
> ▶ Learn how to use offline audio processes to control different aspects of your sound
> ▶ Learn how you can use VST and DirectX plug-in effects without taxing your computer's CPU

The Browse Project Window

When you want to see every type of event found in your project in a single window, the Browse Project window is the one for you (see Figure 10.1). This window is similar to the List Editor described earlier in the sense that events are displayed in list format, but this is where the similarities end. Because the Browse Project window displays all types of events in list format, it also implies that you can modify them using the different fields it displays for each type of data.

Browse Project Window Areas

The Browse Project window is divided into two areas and a toolbar. In the left area called the Project Structure, you will find a tree with the file name for the current project as its root. Linked to the file are all the tracks available in the current project. In other words, each type of track currently present in your project is displayed here. If the track contains data (this could represent events, Regions, parts, or automation parameters), it is displayed under the track's name. The details for the events or data found on a track are visible in the List area found on the right side. The behavior of the browser is very familiar to Windows Explorer—in which selecting a folder on the left reveals its content on the right.

The toolbar offers a few options:

▶ The Domain field allows you to select how time line values are displayed. Changing the format in this field changes all values in columns displayed below.

▶ The next drop-down menu works with the Add button that follows it. You can use this field to select the type of event or object you want to add, and then click the Add button to add it to the list. What you can add depends on what is selected in the Project Structure area.

▶ The Filter drop-down menu actually works like the Mask function in the List Editor. You can use this to select the type of MIDI events you want to see. For example, selecting the Controller option from this menu displays only the Controller messages found in the track. The only other type of track that supports this field is the Marker track. You have the option to view the cycle markers, regular Markers, or both.

▶ The Sync Selection check box is a very convenient option that allows you to select in the Project window, the event you select in the Browse Project window, and vice versa. If you want to troubleshoot an object in your project, you can open the Browse Project window and check this option. Next time you select an object in your project, when you open the Browse Project window, this object is displayed in the List area.

Figure 10.1
The Browse Project
window

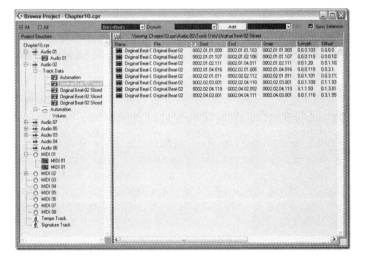

The List area on the right of the Browse Project window adapts its content to the selected objects in the hierarchy structure on the left. For example, if you select an audio track on the left, its events are displayed on the right. If you select one of those events in the Project Structure area, the details for this event appear in the list on the right.

After you can see an event's details, you can make any modifications you want in the appropriate column. At the top of each column are the column headers. You can click and drag a column header to move it to another location to change the order in which these columns appear. You can also click in the column header to change the sorting order. The column that is used for sorting displays a arrow pointing up or down, depending on the type of sort used.

To expand the entire project structure or to hide the details in each track, you can use the +All/-All buttons found in the upper-left corner of the window.

Understanding the Information

Although it is possible to add events in the Browse Project window, because of its list nature, its environment is more appropriate to editing existing events. When you want to make changes to events in the Browse Project window, it's important to understand what each column represents. In most cases, the column header describes well what its content represents. However, some columns might appear ambiguous; the following list describes the columns that aren't so obvious.

▶ **Snap column**. Represents the absolute position of the snap point for this object (audio event). This can be different from the start point because the snap point is used to adjust the position of an event with the grid setting of the project or editor. Changing this value does not change the position of the snap point in relation to the event's start, but rather moves the snap point (and its event) to the location entered in this field.

▶ **Length column**. Represents the length of the event. Editing the value affects the length of the event, moving its end position, not its start position.

▶ **Offset column**. Represents the location in the audio clip (in the audio event or Region and in the MIDI and audio part) that corresponds to the start of the event. When you change this value, the part or event stays in place on the audio track, but the content inside the part or event slides forward or backward in time.

As for the other columns, you can change the values by entering data directly in the appropriate row and column juncture.

The Offline Process History Panel

When you apply a process to an audio object or a portion of this object through offline processing, an entry is made in this event's Offline Process History panel. Remember that offline processes mean that the effect is not calculated during playback (online), but when the project is stopped (offline). Each process is displayed on its own row. You can decide to modify the settings of a process if it's available.

For example, you could select the Normalize process and change the amount of normalizing within this process. If a process does not have any parameters to modify, such as the Reverse process for example, clicking the Modify button simply displays a warning telling you this process cannot be modified. You can also replace one process with another. For instance, you could select the Reverse process and select another process in the drop-down menu below the Replace by button. This brings up the new process' dialog box. Once replaced, the old process is removed from the list and the new process takes its place. Before letting you replace a process, Cubase asks you if this is what you really want to do. Finally, you can remove a process from the list by selecting it and clicking the Remove button.

If you have the SX version, you can also use the Offline Process History panel with any plug-in effect (VST or DirectX). This means that you can apply any kind of offline process from the plug-ins installed on your computer and cancel or modify the parameters inside that plug-in.

There is only one instance in which it is not possible to remove a process: If you change the length of an audio clip through time stretching, cutting, deleting, or copy/pasting, you can only remove or modify this process if it is the last one in the list. In this case, this is indicated in the Status column (see the Delete action in Figure 10.2).

Figure 10.2
The Offline Process
History panel

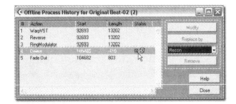

To modify, replace, or remove an action from the Offline Process History panel:

1. Select the event containing offline processes you want to modify.

2. From the Audio menu, select the Offline Process History option.

3. Select the process you want to modify (A), replace (B), or remove (C).

4A. Click the Modify button and edit the parameters inside the process' dialog box, and then click the Process button to update the Offline Process History panel.

4B. Select the new process you want to use instead of the currently selected one in the drop-down menu below the Replace by button, click the Replace by button, make the necessary adjustments in the process' dialog box, and click Process to update the Offline Process History panel.

4C. Click the Remove button to remove this process from the list. When you have completed modifying, replacing, or removing the processes, click the Close button.

Because the history of each offline process is saved with the object affected, you still have access to this history after you close Cubase and reload the project into memory. This is not the case for the Edit History panel described in the next section.

The Edit History Panel

When you apply a transformation, such as deleting an object, moving, and so on, each action is saved in a list. This allows you to undo several actions. You can do this by using the Undo function in the Edit menu if you only have a few steps to undo; however, if you want to look at all the steps and undo a whole bunch in one go, you can use the Edit History panel, which is also found under the Edit menu (see Figure 10.3).

This panel displays the actions on the left and the target object for this action on the right. The latest actions appear at the top of the list, whereas the earliest actions appear at the bottom. The panel is separated by a blue line. Clicking on this line and dragging it down creates a selection. All the actions that are included in this selection will be undone. This means that you can undo from the last edit to the first one, unlike in the Offline Process History panel, in which you can edit any action in the list.

You should know that when you save and close your project, the Edit History panel is reset and is not available until you start editing again. However, only saving your document without closing it keeps this list available.

Figure 10.3
The Edit History panel

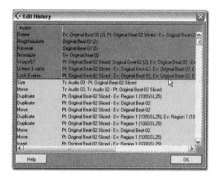

Audio Menu Options

After an audio clip is recorded and its event displayed on the audio track, most of the operations you can apply to this event can be found in one of two places: the Audio menu in the Project window or in the context menu (through right-click or Ctrl-click on a Mac) of the same window.

Using Audio Editing Options

The audio editing options are found in the Audio menu in the Project window and under the Audio submenu option in the context menu of the Project window when an audio object is selected in the window. These options relate to editing functions of audio objects on a track and display the currently available options depending on the object selected.

Spectrum Analyzer and Statistics

The two first options in this category are the Spectrum Analyzer and Statistics functions, which are available only in Cubase SX. These functions allow you to look at and analyze an audio object to find problem areas, such as identifying a noise frequency, or determining if there is any DC offset in an audio file. A DC offset can occur when a sound card adds DC current to a recorded audio signal. This current results in a recorded waveform that is not centered on the baseline (-infinity). Glitches and other unexpected results can occur when sound effects are applied to files that contain DC offsets. The Statistics dialog box in Figure 10.4, for example, reveals that this value is set at -75.88 dB; in other words, not at minus infinity. From the information the Statistics dialog box provides, you can correct the situation by applying the Remove DC Offset process to the audio object.

Figure 10.4
The Statistics dialog box

To use the Spectrum Analyzer (Cubase SX only):

1. Select the audio object you want to analyze. If you select a part with multiple events or Regions inside, Cubase opens an analysis window for each object inside the part.

2. The Spectrum Analyzer's Analysis Options dialog box appears. Because the default settings give the best results in most cases, leave these settings as is and click the Process button.

3. The various options inside the Spectrum Analyzer result window allow you to view the content of the analysis in different ways. Clicking the Active check box allows you to analyze another audio object and replace the current analysis window with the new analysis. Otherwise, a new window opens and this window remains open until you close it.

To use the Statistics function (Cubase SX only):

1. Select the audio object you want to analyze. If you select a part with multiple events or Regions inside, Cubase opens an analysis window for each object inside the part.

2. The Statistics dialog box opens showing you the results of the statistics (see Figure 10.4). Close the dialog box when you are finished reviewing the information.

Detect Silence

The main purpose of the Detect Silence function (see Figure 10.5) is to create different Regions from a long audio event that may contain silent parts. For example, if you record a vocal track, the singer might sing in certain parts and be silent in others. If you chose to record the performance from beginning to end, you end up with a recording that contains both usable and useless content. To automate the Region creation process, the Detect Silence function allows you to set an audio level threshold where events below this threshold are considered as silent. Then, in the same dialog box, you can determine how long this silence has to be before considering it a silent part. After you have set up your preferences appropriately and are satisfied with the result displayed in the preview area, you can create sequentially numbered Regions that appear in both your Media Pool and in the Project window, replacing the current object with the newly created Regions. This operation does not remove any audio content from the original audio clip; it merely creates Regions that hide the unwanted portions of your audio.

Figure 10.5
The Detect Silence
dialog box

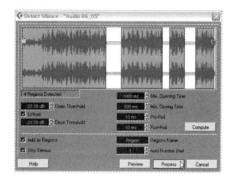

To create Regions using the Detect Silence function:

1. Select the audio event or Region (this doesn't work on parts) for which you want to create Regions.

2. Select the Audio > Detect Silence option from the context menu (right-click or Ctrl-click on the Mac), or select Detect Silence from the Audio menu.

3. The Detect Silence dialog box appears (Figure 10.5). Start by setting the Open Threshold level by clicking and dragging the green box found to the left of the display area. You should set this low enough to make sure that the content you want to keep becomes part of the Region, but high enough that the noise or silence is left out of the Region.

4. Set the Minimum Opening Time to an appropriate value in milliseconds. Remember that 1000 milliseconds is equal to one second. How you set this up will depend on the actual content you are trying to process.

5. Repeat the same operation for the Minimum Closing Time field.

6. Click the Compute button to preview where the Regions will appear and click the Preview button to hear the result.

7. If you are not satisfied with the result after previewing, continue tweaking the settings in this dialog box until you are satisfied with the preview's results.

8. Make sure the Add as Regions and the Strip Silence check boxes are selected. This creates the Regions and removes the silence from the Regions it creates.

9. If you want to give a specific name and number to the Regions this function creates, you can use the Regions Name field to enter a new name and the Auto Number Start field to adjust the number of the first Region Cubase creates.

10. Click the Process button to create the new Regions and hide the silent (unwanted) portions of the audio clip.

Converting Audio Objects

As discussed earlier in the topic discussing event, Region, and part objects, it is possible to convert one object type to another in the Project window. Cubase is very flexible when working with objects and wanting to create a Region from an event, or convert a part in individual event objects after moving the part to another part of your project, for example.

To convert one audio object type into another:

▶ **Convert an event into a Region**. Select the event or events. In the Project window's context menu under the Audio submenu, select the Event as Region option.

▶ **Convert an event into a part**. Select the event or events. In the Project window's context menu under the Audio submenu, select the Event to Part option.

▶ **Convert a Region into a part**. Select the Region or Regions. In the Project window's context menu under the Audio submenu, select the Event to Part option.

▶ **Convert a part into independent objects (Regions or events)**. Select the part or parts. In the Project window's context menu under the Audio submenu, select the Dissolve Part option.

Bounce Selection

Let's say you've just used the Detect Silence function and you've created a Region that excludes the silent parts of the original content. You might want to create a new audio file with only the content of this new Region. In this case, use the Bounce Selection function to create a new file or audio clip from the selected object on your track. You can also create a new audio file from a part containing several objects inside. We discussed the possibility of creating the perfect take out of portions of different takes using the Set to Region and To Front options with events and Regions. After you are satisfied with this final take, it is possible to select the resulting events or Regions, glue the objects together, creating a part with multiple objects inside, and then bounce all the events to a new file.

To bounce audio objects to a new file:

1. Select the objects you want to bounce to a new file.

2. You may adjust the fade handles (see the next section for more details) if you want to include these fades in the new file.

3. From the context menu or the Audio menu, select the Bounce Selection option.

4. Cubase asks you if you want to replace the current selection in the Project window with the newly created file. Select Yes if you want to do so, or No if you simply want the file to appear in your pool.

CHAPTER 10

Working With Fade Envelopes

In Cubase, you can create two types of fades and crossfades. You can opt to have Cubase process fades in real time using the fade envelopes or you can process these fades, creating small fade segments that are seamlessly integrated into your project. Either way, you get the same result. However, using real-time fades means your computer calculates these fade curves every time you click Play. If you are short on computer resources, you might want to opt for the processed version (more details later in this chapter). This section describes how to use real-time fade envelopes found on Region and event objects.

When selecting a Region or an event on an audio track, you will notice the appearance of little boxes and triangles. Those found at the bottom of an object are resize handles that can be used to resize an audio Region, event, or part. However, the ones found on the top of the event and Region objects are meant to control the fade in or out properties of this object and the handle found in the middle is used to control the overall sustain level of the object between the fade in and out. In Figure 10.6, this handle is shown at its maximum value (default). Clicking this blue box with the Object Selection tool allows you to control the overall output level of this object. This offers a different form of automation because this envelope (similar to an Attack-Sustain-Release envelope) moves along with its object, whereas track automation is not associated with the object on the track.

You can control the fade curve for both the fade in and fade out on Region and event objects.

Figure 10.6
Control handles found
on Region and event
objects in the Project
window and Audio Part
Editor

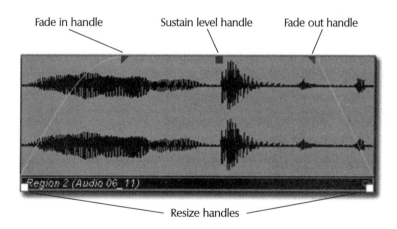

Fade in handle   Sustain level handle   Fade out handle

Resize handles

To change the fade curve type of an audio object:

1. Select the event or Region you want to edit.
2. Adjust the fade in and/or fade out using the appropriate handles.
3. To modify the fade type, select Open Fade Editors in the Audio menu or Audio submenu of the context menu, or double-click on the fade in the part itself . This brings up both Fade In and Fade Out dialog boxes (see Figure 10.7).

Figure 10.7
The Fade Out dialog
box

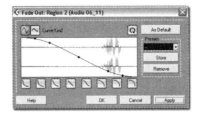

4. Select the spline or linear curve type you want to use with your object.

5. You can choose from different curve types below the display or use these as a starting point, editing the curve by clicking and dragging the handles inside the display.

6. If you want to store this curve for later use, click the Store button, type in a name, then click OK.

7. Click the Apply button to accept your changes, and then click OK.

8. Repeat this operation for the other fade curve if necessary.

If you want to apply a default type of curve to all the objects in your project, you can use the Auto Crossfade Settings button found besides the track's name in the Inspector area. After you've changed the default crossfade setting, all new fades will use this curve setting unless you change it on an object.

To change the default crossfade (fade) settings:

1. Click the Auto Crossfade Settings button to the left of any track's name in the Inspector area.

2. The Auto Fades dialog box appears. Click the Fades tab.

3. Select the appropriate settings on this tab. These settings are applied by default afterward.

4. Click the Crossfades tab.

5. Select the appropriate settings on this tab as well.

6. Selecting the Auto Fade In, Auto Fade Out, and Auto Crossfade options applies the same settings to all subsequent fades in your project from this point forward.

7. Clicking the As Default button saves your settings as the default value for subsequent projects as well.

8. If you do not want your fade settings to be the same on every track, deselect the Use Project Settings check box. However, if you do want all the tracks to use these settings, keep the check in the box.

9. Click OK.

You can also apply a fade to objects on several tracks at once using the Range Selection tool. When your range crosses the start point of an object, a fade in is created over that range (see the lower-right Region in Figure 10.8). When your range crosses the end point of an object, a fade out is created over that range (see the lower-left Region in Figure 10.8). When your range doesn't cross either the start or end position, a fade in and out will respectively end and begin at the borders defined by the Range Selection tool (see the upper Region in Figure 10.8). Notice that all the curves types for the fade ins and outs are identical. This is because the project uses a default auto fade setting.

Figure 10.8
Using the Fade to Range function

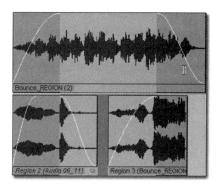

To apply a fade over selected objects in a range:

1. Click the Range Selection tool in the toolbar or in the Project window's context menu.
2. Drag a selection box over the desired range.
3. Select the Adjust Fades To Range function from the Audio menu, or press A (default key command), or select the same function in the context menu's Audio submenu.

If, after all this, you decide you don't want a fade on this event or Region, you can either move the handles back to their default position (no fades), or select the events and then choose the Audio > Remove Fades function.

Finding Your Objects

As your project starts to grow in size, you will want an easy way to find events in the pool. When the pool gets crowded, it can be time-consuming to look for this object's name in the pool. That's why you can use the Find Selected in Pool function, which does just that.

To find a selected object in the pool:

1. Select the object you want to find.
2. Then select the Audio > Find Selected in Pool function.

This brings up what you were looking for, highlighted in the pool.

Audio Processing Options

Audio processing, as with audio fades, can be applied to audio in two different ways: You can apply effects that are processed in real time, allowing you to automate these effects; you can change the parameters or effect altogether; or you can apply processing to an audio Region, event, or even slice and seamlessly integrate the result in your project. When adding a real-time effect or process, the audio passes through an insert, send, or master effect that is processed by your computer. The effect itself is not saved to an audio file, though the effect's parameters are saved as part of your project. Every time you click Play, the computer starts processing once again. This is why you can change parameters easily. On the other hand, it can add a serious load on your computer that can slow it down to a grind when your real-time processing needs exceed the computer's capabilities.

Processing files offline, changing the portion of the audio and saving this processing with the file, allows you to create the effects without changing the original file's content and does not require any processing time during playback because the files are simply read from the hard disk. The disadvantage is that you cannot automate this processing using automation in real time. There are many instances, however, where automation is not needed. When you want to optimize a file or add an effect to a portion of an audio clip, event, Region, or slice, processing this portion and writing the effect to a file might be more effective than using real-time effects, not to mention reducing the load imposed on your computer. Pitch shifting and time stretching operations are notoriously known to be heavy computer resource consumers, so using them in offline processes is highly recommended.

You can apply real-time effects and processes through the insert effects, send effects, and master effects. You can apply processes and plug-in effects through the Plug-ins or Process submenus found in the Audio menu, or through the same submenus in the Project window's context menu.

Using Audio Processes

In audio terminology, any effect applied to an audio signal is referred to as an audio processing. However, in Cubase, processes refer to a specific type of processing. In fact, all processes in Cubase are meant to change audio without adding effects to it, such as reverbs, chorus, and delays.

You can apply processing to an entire selected audio event or Region in the Project window, or apply it to a portion selected using the Range Selection tool. You can also apply processing to the same elements that are found inside a part after you open them in the Audio Part Editor. Selecting an event or Region in the pool applies the processing to the entire selected object. Finally, you can apply a process to a selected portion of an event or Region in the Sample Editor as well. All processes in any of these situations are found in the Process' submenu in the Audio menu or in each window's Process submenu options.

Because some objects may be shared (used more than one time in the project's time line) when applying a process to one of them, Cubase asks if you want to create a new version or change all the instances of this object across the project's time line. If you opt to create a new version, the selected object is the only one affected by this process and the processed version of the object replaces the original content in the Project window (not on your hard disk). If you want all the shared instances of this object (event or Region) to change, then you can select the Continue button (see Figure 10.9). This replaces the currently selected object rather than creating a new version, which causes all shared occurrences to change as well in the project.

Figure 10.9
Cubase can replace the
selected object or create
a new one

About Pre- and Post-CrossFade Options

In some processes, you will find a Pre-CrossFade and Post-CrossFade option under the More
button in the process' dialog box. These options allow you to apply the process gradually over
time (pre-crossfade) and end the process also gradually over time (post-crossfade). As displayed
in Figure 10.10, this process would take 410 milliseconds before completely implemented and it
would start reverting from processed signal to nonprocessed signal over the last 217
milliseconds of the object. So, if this were applied to the Gain process, for example, it would
take 410 ms to reach the Gain setting in the Process window and would go back to the original
gain over the last 217 ms of the object being processed.

To access these options, you can click the More button found in the process' dialog box and
check the options you want to apply after setting the parameters to the desired value. If you
don't want to see these options (but still apply them if the options are selected), click the Less
button.

Figure 10.10
The Pre- and Post-
CrossFade options

Envelopes

The Envelope process (see Figure 10.11) allows you to create a volume level envelope using a
fade-like display to control the amplitude of the signal.

To apply an envelope process to a selected object:

1. Select the desired object.
2. Select the Envelope process from the Process option in the Audio menu.
3. Select the type of curve you want to use for the envelope.
4. To add handles, click along the envelope line where you want to insert the
   handle, and drag it to the desired position.
5. To remove handles, drag the handle outside the display area.
6. To store or remove a preset, click the Store or Remove buttons.
7. To preview the result, click the Preview button. You can make changes to the
   envelope as you are previewing. To stop the preview, click the Stop button.
8. When satisfied with the settings, click the Process button. Click Cancel if you
   want to cancel the process.

Figure 10.11
The Envelope process
dialog box

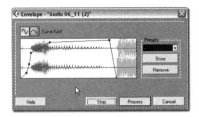

Fade In and Fade Out Processes

The controls in the fade in and fade out processes are identical to the auto fade controls described earlier. The only difference is that fade processes are saved with the audio in a new file. You can apply this process using the Fade options available in the Process menu rather than using the fade envelopes on events and Regions in the Project window.

Gain Process

The Gain process allows you to add or remove gain from the currently selected object or objects. Moving the slider to the right adds gain, whereas moving the slider to the left reduces it. You can also enter the desired amount of gain in the Gain field by typing in the appropriate value. When clicking the Preview button, Cubase indicates if this gain change causes the object to clip (digital distortion), as displayed in Figure 10.12. If this occurs, reduce the gain until Cubase displays "No Clip Detected."

To apply a Gain process to a selected object:

1. Select the desired object.
2. Select the Gain process from the Process option in the Audio menu.
3. Make the appropriate adjustments in the dialog box.
4. To store or remove a preset, click the Store or Remove buttons.
5. To preview the result, click the Preview button. You can make changes to the envelope as you are previewing. To stop the preview, click the Stop button.
6. When satisfied with the settings, click the Process button. Click Cancel if you want to cancel the process.

Figure 10.12
The Gain process dialog
box

Merge Clipboard Process

This process allows you to merge the audio content that has been previously copied to the clipboard with the currently selected object. Besides the Pre- and Post-CrossFade options available under the More button of this dialog box, the Merge Clipboard process (see Figure 10.13) allows you to set the proportion of each material through a percentage slider. On the left side, you can see the proportion of the original (selected) object and on the right side, the proportion of the audio previously copied in the clipboard.

To merge the content of the clipboard with a selected object:

1. Select the desired object.

2. Select the Merge Clipboard process from the Process option in the Audio menu. This implies that you have previously selected audio in the Sample Editor and have copied this content to the clipboard.

3. Make the appropriate adjustments in the dialog box. To preview the result, click the Preview button.

4. When satisfied with the settings, click the Process button.

Figure 10.13
The Merge Clipboard process dialog box

Noise Gate Process

The Noise Gate process (see Figure 10.14) allows you to remove sound from an audio signal that is below a threshold level by muting it. Imagine a gate that opens when a signal is strong enough (above threshold) and closes when the signal is not strong enough (below threshold). You can use this to silence portions of an audio signal during silent passage. For example, you can use a noise gate to remove a guitar amplifier's humming noise from a recording during passages where the guitar player is not playing. A noise gate does not remove the noise when the guitarist is playing because the signal will most likely be loud enough to pass the threshold, but the noise at that point should be less noticeable because it blends in with the guitar sound. If the noise level is too loud even when the guitarist is playing, you should consider using a noise reduction plug-in or rerecording this part.

The attack time represents the time it takes for the gate to open, letting the sound through, and the release time represents the time it takes for the gate to close after the signal goes below the threshold level. The minimum opening time defines the minimum amount of time the signal has to be over the threshold before the gate can close again.

To apply a Noise Gate process to a selected object:

1. Select the desired object.

2. Select the Noise Gate process from the Process option in the Audio menu.

3. Make the appropriate adjustments in the dialog box. To preview the result, click the Preview button. If the signal you are processing is stereo, you can select the Linked Channels check box to determine how the Noise Gate process will treat the signal.

4. When satisfied with the settings, click the Process button.

Figure 10.14
The Noise Gate process
dialog box

Normalize Process

Normalizing an audio signal affects its overall amplitude level by adjusting its highest peak to the value set in the Normalize process dialog box. It is similar to the Gain process in the sense that it acts on the level of the signal, but instead of calculating the level generally, it brings these levels up in proportion to the highest peak found in the signal, making sure that there is no clipping in the signal as a result of the level change. You can set the level value you want to assign to the highest peak level in this object by adjusting the slider or entering a value in the Maximum field.

To apply a Normalize process to a selected object:

1. Select the desired object.
2. Select the Normalize process from the Process option in the Audio menu.
3. Make the appropriate adjustments in the dialog box (see Figure 10.15). To preview the result, click the Preview button.
4. When satisfied with the settings, click the Process button.

Figure 10.15
The Normalize process
dialog box

Phase Reverse Process

Reversing a phase does not change the shape of a sound file but it changes the direction this shape takes. For example, the slopes going up will now go down and vice versa. When you mix different sound files, phase cancellation can occur. This produces a hollow sound. Inverting the waveform on one of the files can prevent this phase cancellation from occurring. In other words, if the phase of the current audio file does not sound correct, changing the direction of the phase might help to restore this problem. A good way to monitor this problem is to monitor the audio in mono. If you can barely hear the signal, then you might have phase cancellation occurring. In Cubase, you can reverse the phase of both channels in a stereo file, or only one or the other. You should preview the result before applying this process.

To apply a Phase Reverse process to a selected object:

1. Select the desired object.
2. Select the Phase Reverse process from the Process option in the Audio menu.

3. Make the appropriate adjustments in the dialog box (see Figure 10.16). To preview the result, click the Preview button.

4. When satisfied with the settings, click the Process button.

Figure 10.16
The Phase Reverse
process dialog box

Pitch Shift Process

The Pitch Shift process allows you to change the pitch of a selected object throughout the duration of this object or apply a change of pitch that varies through time using an envelope to determine when the pitch is shifted upwards or downwards.

At the top of the Transpose tab (see Figure 10.17), you will find a keyboard layout that can help you set the relationship between the pitch of the original audio content and the pitch-shifted one. In this example, the original content played a pitch equivalent to D3, so the pitch shift base area is set to D3, making this note appear red on the keyboard display. Clicking another note changes the pitch shift settings automatically to match the value needed to get this pitch. In this case, B2 is pressed and displayed in blue on the keyboard. If you want to create a multivoice effect, creating several pitch shifts simultaneously, you can enable the Multi Shift option. This allows you to add other notes to the process. Remember that the base note, unless selected as a shifted note as well, will not be part of the multishifted signal. You can use the Listen Key or Listen Chord button to hear the notes you selected.

The Pitch Shift Mode area allows you to set accuracy values. For example, moving the accuracy slider toward the left favors sound quality over rhythmic accuracy. Moving it toward the right does the opposite. In other words, the content being shifted determines how this setting should be applied. If you are shifting vocal content, you should check the Formant Mode option, which helps to keep the qualities associated with voice when shifting it. The Algorithm drop-down menu offers three types of algorithms in Cubase SL and a fourth type in Cubase SX (MPEX Algorithm). When you want to preview the result, you should use the Quick algorithm and avoid the MPEX algorithm because it is not designed to preview pitch shifting in real time. However, when processing to file, you should always use the best quality possible (better quality algorithms only take longer to process).

The Time Correction option allows you to change the pitch without changing the time it takes to play the shifted content. If this option is not selected, events shifted upwards play faster and events shifted downwards play slower.

Figure 10.17
The Pitch Shift process'
Transpose tab

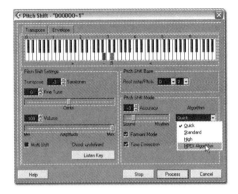

Clicking the Envelope tab at the top of the dialog box reveals the envelope settings for this process (see Figure 10.18). Using an envelope rather than a keyboard allows you to change how the audio is shifted through time. In this example, the Pitch Shift Setting's Range field is set to two semitones, which means that at the top of the display area, events are shifted upward by this amount and downward at the bottom. The Transpose value setting represents the currently selected handle's value. In this case, the area found under the cursor, and from that point forward is transposed upwards by two semitones. So using these settings, the pitch shift transposes the first portion of the audio two semitones below the current note at the beginning of the object, and halfway through pitch shifts two semitones above the current note played by the original file. The Pitch Shift Mode options are identical to the Transpose tab. Notice, however, that the accuracy settings are not available in both tabs when the MPEX Algorithm is selected.

Figure 10.18
The Pitch Shift process'
Envelope tab

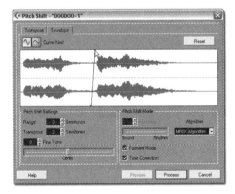

To apply a Pitch Shift process to a selected object:

1. Select the desired object.

2. Select the Pitch Shift process from the Process option in the Audio menu.

3. Make the appropriate adjustments in the dialog box. To preview the result, click the Preview button.

4. When satisfied with the settings, click the Process button.

DC Offset, Reverse, and Silence Processes

These three processes offer very different results; however, they do not offer any settings. The purpose of the DC Offset process was explained earlier in this chapter in the "Spectrum Analyzer and Statistics" section. This process allows you to remove any offset that might be present in your audio signal. If you have Cubase SX, it might be a good idea to look at the statistics of a file. If you need to remove a DC offset, run the process on the file. The Reverse process simply reverses the data horizontally, making it sound as if it is playing backwards. The Silence process brings all the samples in a selection to a zero value, creating an absolute digital silence.

Stereo Flip Process

The Stereo Flip process (see Figure 10.19) can be applied on stereo objects only because it manipulates the stereo channels of the selected object. You have four modes available in this process, which are available in the Mode field. For example, you can merge both channels together to create a mono sounding file, or subtract the left channel from the right channel to get a karaoke-like effect.

To apply a Stereo Flip process to a selected object:

1.   Select the desired object.
2.   Select the Stereo Flip process from the Process option in the Audio menu.
3.   Make the appropriate adjustments in the dialog box. To preview the result, click the Preview button.
4.   When satisfied with the settings, click the Process button.

Figure 10.19
The Stereo Flip process
dialog box

Time Stretch Process

Time stretching allows you to change the duration of a selected object without changing the pitch or rhythmic integrity. In the Time Stretch process dialog box (shown in Figure 10.20), there are several ways you can attain that goal.

In the Input area, you will see information on the selected object such as the Length in Samples field, Length in Seconds field, and a field where you can enter the tempo in BPM if you know it. You can also enter the number of bars and time signature. So, if you want to know the BPM (beats per minute), you can listen to the segment, count how many bars and beats pass, and enter the time signature of the event. Cubase calculates the tempo automatically. You can then use the Output area to determine the result of the Time Stretch process.

Let's look at some practical examples. If you want to change the tempo of a drum loop using this process, figure out how many bars and time signature the selection represents and then enter the new BPM in the Output area's BPM field. This also determines the correct amount of samples, seconds, and range this new processed file will cover. If you are preparing a TV jingle and your spot has to be exactly 29.5 seconds, you can enter this amount in the Output area's Seconds field. Now, let's say your current object is just short of a five-bar area, between Bars 12 and 17. If you want it to cover this range, set the locators to Bars 12 and 17, select the object, and apply the Time Stretch process. When this dialog box opens, click the Set to Locators Range button to enter this value as the output length (five bars in this case).

This process changes the quality of the audio to a certain degree. The more time stretching you apply, the worse your result is. Optimally, you should stick within a plus or minus ten percent range; otherwise, you might start to hear some undesirable artifacts in the sound. In fact, if you don't select the Effect check box found to the right of the Time Stretch percentage, you can only apply a plus or minus twenty-five percent change. If, on the other hand, you want to create an effect, check this option to change the factor anywhere between ten and one thousand percent.

As with the pitch shifting process, you can adjust the focus of the accuracy towards the sound quality or the rhythmic accuracy. The algorithms used also influence the end result. Selecting higher algorithms takes more time to process but yields better results. You will also find an algorithm specifically designed for drum tracks.

On the other hand, if you are trying to adjust the tempo of an audio drum loop to match with your project's tempo, you might want to consider using hitpoints to create slices in the Sample Editor. You will find more about this in the next chapter.

Figure 10.20
The Time Stretch
process dialog box

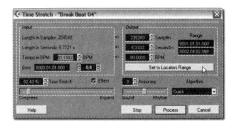

To apply a Time Stretch process to a selected object:

1. Select the desired object.
2. Select the Time Stretch process from the Process option in the Audio menu.
3. Make the appropriate adjustments in the dialog box. To preview the result, click the Preview button.
4. When satisfied with the settings, click the Process button.

Using VST and DirectX Plug-Ins

VST or DirectX (PC version only) plug-in effects, as you saw earlier in this book, can be added as an insert, send, or master effect on an audio track or on the master outputs. When doing so, you are processing the audio in real time, as described at the beginning of the section discussing audio processing options. You can also apply VST or DirectX plug-in effects available on your computer to a file directly if you want to affect only a portion of a track or if you don't want to add an additional load on your computer's processor.

Remember that when you apply one of these effects to a selected object, the processed result is saved in a special file, leaving your original file intact. This new file is seamlessly integrated into your project. In other words, you won't even feel or see it's a different file, besides the fact that this portion is processed.

Because VST and DirectX plug-in effects vary from one computer to another, we will not discuss the specific settings of these plug-ins, but understand that you can use these effects in an offline process (non-real time) the same way as you would use them in an online process (real time). The only difference is that you can't automate changes in the effect during the offline processing time.

To add a plug-in effect to a selected object:

1. Select the desired object.

2. Select the desired plug-in from the Plug-ins submenu in the Audio menu (see Figure 10.21). DirectX effects available on your computer are available under the DirectX submenu.

3. Make the appropriate adjustments in the dialog box. To preview the result, click the Preview button.

4. When satisfied with the settings, click the Process button.

Figure 10.21
The Plug-ins submenu options; the More Plug-ins submenu holds additional plug-ins when the current submenu can't display them all

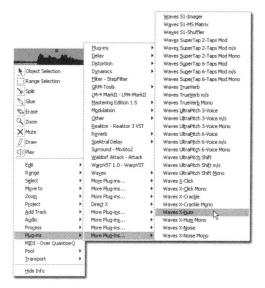

Optimizing Projects After Processing

When you process several files using offline processes, a number of additional files are created on your hard disk in the Edit folder. These files are necessary to preserve the original audio clip intact while providing the option to change an applied process. For example, as described earlier in this chapter, you can change the settings of a process, or with Cubase SX, you can also change the parameters or replace a process with another process. For each offline process line created in the Offline Process History dialog box of a selected object, there exists an equal number of processed files representing the portion of this object that has been processed on your hard disk. This makes it very convenient, but you should also realize that asking Cubase to move back and forth from one file to another and managing several tracks with multiple edited portions costs you in overall performance.

If you start noticing that your performance meter for the CPU or the hard disk starts to creep up, causing Cubase to feel slow or unresponsive, you should consider performing the following steps to help get things back to a more fluid working environment:

▶ Use the Save Project to New Folder option in the File menu. When Cubase prompts you to enter a name for the new project's version, make sure to check all the options in the Save to Folder Options dialog box (see Figure 10.22).

Figure 10.22
The Save to Folder
Options dialog box

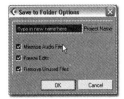

▶ If you don't want to save your entire project to a new folder, you can select audio events that contain the most editing done through offline processes and choose the Freeze Edits from the Audio menu. Cubase asks you if you want to create a new file or replace the existing one. Choose the appropriate option. Either way, this improves the performance because Cubase doesn't have to skip from one file to another.

▶ Make sure that your disk is defragmented regularly to avoid slowing down your computer because of inefficient disk reading caused by fragmented files.

Now You Try It

It's time to put the topics covered in this chapter into action—you can download a practice exercise at http://www.muskalipman.com.

11

Audio Editing Windows

As with MIDI, audio has its own editing environment. Actually, audio has three different editing environments: the Media Pool allows you to manage your audio objects and doubles as a resource center for media content, the Sample Editor lets you manipulate recorded or imported audio and create Regions and slices, and finally the Audio Part Editor lets you edit and position a group of events and Regions.

The Browse Project window, on the other hand, allows you to manage the content found in your project, where tracks in Cubase become like folders inside your computer—containers that can hold objects and other folders. In Cubase, tracks are containers that hold events or parts, which are themselves containers that hold events. Every time you add an event or change automation, this information is added to the Browse Project window.

In this chapter, you will:

▶ Take a look at the Media Pool and how it operates

▶ Find out how you can optimize the audio content in your project

▶ Create a backup copy of your audio content and project files

▶ Use offline processes in different audio editing environments

▶ Learn how to create, edit, and manage Regions

▶ Learn how to create and use hitpoints

▶ Understand the Audio Part Editor and its relation to the Project window

The Media Pool

Commonly known as "The Pool," it is the audio and video file managing window and it is similar to Windows Explorer or Apple Launcher (see Figure 11.1). All references to audio clips that were recorded or imported into a project are represented in the pool. Each project has its own pool, which can be saved separately and have its contents imported into another project. The pool also allows you to view your audio clip references (called events) and corresponding Regions. You can use the pool monitor and manage these references.

You will find three default folders in the pool: the Audio, Video, and Trash folders. You can create any number of new folders within these folders, but you can't rename or delete them. There are many ways to access the Pool window as seen in Chapter 3. The simplest method is to use the Open Pool button on the Project window's toolbar.

Figure 11.1
The Pool window

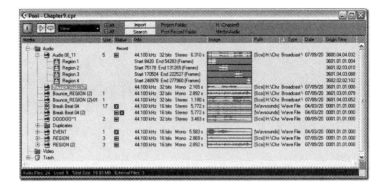

The Pool Areas

The pool is divided into two main areas: the toolbar and the main display area. A third, less obvious but very important, area to the pool is its menu options found under the Pool menu and through a right-click (Ctrl-click on Mac). Most of the operations besides monitoring audio objects are done through this menu.

To the left of the menu bar is the Information bar button. Enabling this button reveals the Information bar at the bottom of the pool. This is where you will find the current status information of your pool. In Figure 11.1, you can see that the pool holds 24 audio files, 9 of which are used in the current project, the total size of the files in the pool takes up 19.93 MB on the hard disk and there are 3 files that are not saved inside the project's Audio folder.

The two buttons to the right of the Information bar button can be used to hear a selected object found in the Media column. The Play button starts playing the file and the Loop button (next to it) loops the playback. To stop the playback, you can click the Play button again.

The View field allows you to select which column is displayed in the pool below. There are a total of eight information columns available. Adding a check next to a name (by selecting it in the View drop-down menu) adds this row to the columns displayed in the pool. Selecting the Hide All option hides every column to the right of the Media column.

Next to the View field are two little buttons displaying plus (+) All or minus (-) All. As in Windows Explorer or Apple Launcher, this allows you to expand the tree found under the Media column. When a plus sign appears to the left of an object, it means that there are other objects inside this one. This could be Regions inside an event, events inside a folder, or objects inside one of the three default folders if you've minimized the displayed content using the minus all button.

The Import button allows you to import media files from your hard disk into the pool. You can use this button to import any media format supported by Cubase.

To import media files into the pool:

1. Click the Import button in the pool.

2. Browse the hard disk to find the location of the file you want to import. After a file is selected, you can preview it using the Play button found below the File Display area in the Import Options dialog box.

3. Select the file and click the Open button to import it to the current pool.

4. If the file you want to import is not currently in the Audio folder of your project, Cubase prompts you to select different import options (see Figure 11.2). If the file you want to import does not correspond to the current project sample rate and bit depth, you are asked if you want to convert these files. Remember that in order to use a file in your project, it has to have the same sample rate as this project. You can have different sample size rates, but it is recommended that you keep all your files at the same sample size whenever possible.

5. Click OK when you have finished making your selections. This adds the current file or files to your pool.

Figure 11.2
The Import Options
dialog box

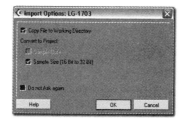

The Search button, found below the Import button, allows you to search the content of hard disks to find files you might want to import in your project. Clicking this button opens the search panel at the bottom of the pool. This interface is similar to any search tool on your computer. It allows you to enter a name of a file you want to search for or use wildcard characters to find multiple files containing specific strings of characters (see the example in Figure 11.3).

To search for files you want to import:

1. Click the Search button in the pool's toolbar.

2. In the Name field of the search panel, type in the name of the file you want to find. You can use wildcard characters to widen your search criteria.

3. In the Folder field, select the drive or drives you want to look in or select a specific path to look in at the bottom of the drop-down menu.

4. Click the Search button. The search results appear in the list to the right.

5. Check the Auto Play check box if you want to automatically preview the files found by the search. To preview a file, select it in the list. If the Auto Play option is not activated, you can click the Play button below the Search button in this panel. You can also adjust the level of the preview using the preview level fader.

6. To import the selected file or files, click the Import button.

7.   Cubase brings up the same Import Options dialog box as when you use the Import button in the toolbar. Make the necessary selections and click OK to import the files to your pool.

Figure 11.3
The search panel found in the pool when the Search function is activated

To the right of the Import and Search buttons, you can see the project folder's path and its associated pool record folder. By default, the pool record folder is found inside the project folder and is called Audio. This allows you to easily create a backup file of your project, including the media files associated with it.

Directly below the toolbar, above the columns, you will find column headers for each column in the pool. You can use the column headers to sort the information the column holds by clicking on the header. This adds a little arrow pointing up or down depending on the sorting order, next to the column's header, indicating that this column is used for sorting purposes. You can also use the column headers to change the columns' order by dragging the header horizontally to a new location. The header is inserted to the right of the column found on the left edge of the header's border when you drag it.

Understanding the Information

The Media column displays the names and types of media used in the project as well as folders that you might have created inside the pool to organize your media files. You will find three types of icons displayed next to the name (see Figure 11.4); these represent an event object, a Region object, and a sliced event object. Region objects are positioned under the event object it refers to. You can click on the plus sign to expand an event object to reveal its defined Regions.

Figure 11.4
Icons associated with different objects in the Pool window

Folder   Record folder   Event object   Region object   Sliced event object

To rename objects in the pool:

1. Select the object you want to rename. A light blue box appears around it.
2. Click again to make the blue box change into a frame as shown in Figure 11.5.
3. Type in the new name for the object.

Figure 11.5
Renaming an object in
the Pool window

The Use column displays the number of times the object in the row appears in the project. In other words, how many times you've used it. Objects that aren't used in the project have no value in the Use column. You will notice that a sliced object increments its use value by the number of slices found in the object every time you repeat, copy, or duplicate the corresponding part in the Project window. For example, if your drum loop is divided into eight slices, the Use column displays sixteen if you used this object twice in the project, even if these are shared copies of the same object.

The Status column offers information on the status of the objects inside your pool. The following table describes each icon's meaning in this column.

Table 11.1
Understanding the Status column's icons

Icon	Its Meaning
Record	Represents the content found in the pool's record folder; found next to the Audio folder. If you create a folder in the pool, you can click in the Status column next to this folder to make this the new record folder. Subsequent recordings appear under this folder. This does not create a new folder on your hard disk, but helps you manage the appearance of your files in the pool. For example, you could create a folder for a vocal session called "Vocals." By clicking in the Status column next to this folder, the record moves next to it and all recordings made from this point on appear in this pool folder.
R	Represents events that have been recorded since the last time you opened the project, making it easy to find newly recorded material.
X	Represents events that are not located in the pool record folder. These events might have been imported from another location on your hard disk. This occurs when you have not selected the Copy to Project Folder option when importing them. In other words, if you were to save your project's folders, these files would not be included, unless you use the Prepare Archive function described later.

	Represents events that have been processed offline. In other words, there are some references made to both the original clip and the portions that have been processed and saved in the Fades or Edits subfolders found in your project's folder.
	Represents files that have not been found when loading the project. You can use the Find Missing File function to scan these missing files. This is explained later in this chapter.
reconstructible	Represents files that have been processed in some way using offline processes or effects and for which some of the processed portions have been lost or misplaced. Cubase displays this indication in the Status column when it can reconstruct the missing portions.

To create a folder in the pool:

1. In the Pool window, select the Audio or Video folder or another existing folder, depending on where you want your new folder to appear.

2. Right-click (Ctrl-click on Mac) and select the Create Folder option. You can also find the same option in the Pool menu.

3. Name your folder appropriately.

The Info column displays one of two things: either the file format and length details or a Region's start and end locations.

The Image column displays a graphical representation of the event or the Region within the event's boundaries. You will notice that all the events have the same length; however, Regions are represented as a proportion of this length. You can quickly preview the content of an object by clicking on its image representation.

To preview an audio object using the Image column in the Pool window:

▶ To begin playback, click anywhere in the image. Playback occurs from the point you clicked until the end of the object or until you stop the playback.

▶ To skip to another portion of the same object, click approximately where you want to hear in the display before the preview ends.

▶ To stop the playback, click beside the Image column next to the image, or click the Play Preview button in the toolbar.

▶ To loop the playback, click the Loop button in the toolbar. The object loops from the point where you click in the image to the end or until you stop the playback.

The Path column displays the path to the original clips (audio files) on your hard disk. Note that processed files refer to a different file, but this is not displayed in the path. This measure is taken to ensure that you don't even have to think about the fact that additional files are created when you process a portion of the audio using an offline process (not real time).

The Date column tells you when the clip was originally created.

The Origin Time column corresponds to the original position in time where this object was placed or recorded in the project. You can change this time directly in the column. Doing so may become useful because you can use the origin time or the locator time as a point of insertion when using the Insert Into Project option found in the Pool menu (or context menu). This function allows you to insert a selected object at the origin or cursor location.

To insert an object at its origin time or cursor location in the project:

1. Select the audio track in which you want to insert the object in the Project window. If you want to insert the object using the cursor location, position the cursor (play line) at the desired location.

2. In the Pool window, adjust the origin time value appropriately by typing the new value in the object's row or by using your mouse's scroll wheel to adjust the values for the time. You don't need to adjust the origin time if you are using the cursor location option.

3. Select the Insert Into Project > At Origin or At Cursor option in the Pool menu.

Pool Functions

Generally speaking, the pool is not something you worry about or use the most at the beginning of a project. When your project is taking shape, you will probably also want your pool to take shape by organizing it and using it as an effective "pool" of audio source material.

We've already discussed certain managing functions related to the pool through the creation of folders in which to put additional media objects, or renaming existing objects. Let's take a look at other typical pool functions.

Dealing with Missing Files

When you save your project and reload it later, it may happen that Cubase can't find files it used in this project. You might have deleted them by mistake, or purposely deleted them because you didn't need them anymore, but forgot to update your pool before saving it, so the reference to a missing file still exists. This section discusses different situations that can occur and how to deal with them.

When references to files are found, but the files themselves are not found in the specified folder, you can use the Find Missing Files option from the Pool menu. This might occur if you moved the files since you last saved your project, or if you renamed the files outside Cubase. Missing files are identified with a question mark in the Status column.

To find missing files in the pool:

1. From the Pool menu, select Find Missing Files. The Resolve Missing Files dialog box appears (see Figure 11.6).

Figure 11.6
The Resolve Missing Files dialog box

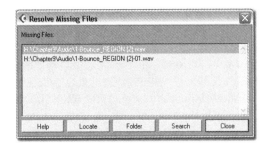

2. If you want to locate the files yourself, click the Locate button. If, on the other hand, you want Cubase to attempt to find them, click the Search button. If you want Cubase to look for them in a specific folder, click the Folder button and choose the desired folder.

3. Depending on the option selected in Step 2, you are offered different solutions or results. However, if you have chosen the Search option, a new dialog box appears, allowing you to change the name of the file you are looking for. This might be helpful if you remember renaming the file after saving it with the project. Simply enter the new name in the appropriate field and then click the Start button to begin the search process.

4. If the search successfully found the missing files, you need to select the file you want from the list displayed and accept it by clicking the Accept button. This updates the link to the file in your pool.

In the event that a file is missing, even after a search (or you don't want Cubase to keep referring to a file because you've erased it anyway), you can use the Remove Missing Files option from the Pool menu. This affects any object in the pool with a question mark in the Status column.

In some cases, a portion of a file that has been processed might become corrupt or missing, just like any other file. But because this represents a portion of an audio clip that's been processed, the actual settings or processing history is saved with the project file and available through the Offline Process History dialog box. Because this processing history is saved, you can reconstruct the missing portion of the processed audio clip using the Reconstruct option in the Pool menu (see Figure 11.7). Cubase tries to reconstruct the processed portion using the original clip and the settings available in the Offline Process History dialog box. For this option to be enabled, the Status column of the object needs to display the word "reconstructible."

Figure 11.7
Cubase indicates clips for which portions of processed events are missing by displaying the word "reconstructible" in the Status column

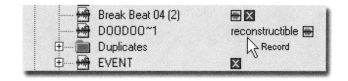

Optimizing the Pool

Many of the pool related functions allow you to optimize the content of the clips it holds. When you are working on a big project, the pool can quickly get crowded and overwhelming. When you are editing, you don't want to worry about how the pool looks and how much space is used by your pool, until you start running short on space, or get tired of looking for sounds in a pool that contains many useless audio clips at this point in the project.

We've already discussed how you can create folders to organize your clips. You can also drag and drop objects inside a folder to organize your files. When you delete events or Regions from the pool, they often end up in the Trash folder. This means that the files are still using space on your computer. You can use the Empty Trash option in the Pool menu to free up some of that hard disk real estate. When using this function, Cubase prompts you once again to make sure you really want to erase the files from the hard disk or only remove them from the pool (see Figure 11.8). If you choose to erase the files, you cannot get them back because this function can't be undone. This is one of the only ways you can actually erase audio clips from your disk within Cubase itself.

Figure 11.8
Cubase offers you a last chance to keep the files on the computer or completely erase them from your hard disk

Besides the trash you've collected, there might be some files that were used at the beginning but aren't being used any longer. If you don't need them, you can use the Remove Unused Media option in the Pool menu. This time, you are prompted to choose if you want to remove these files from the pool completely (the files are still on your hard disk) or just send them to the Trash folder. Note that if you remove them from the pool and don't need them, these files still take up space on your computer. It is, therefore, recommended that you always use the Trash folder as a transitional stage when optimizing your pool. When you are done, empty the trash.

When you record a long segment that includes useless audio, you can create Regions, resize or split the events in the Project window to hide unneeded portions. However, this does not remove them from your hard disk. The Minimize File option in the Pool menu looks at your current project and produces new files (audio clips) for the audio portions of the selected object that are used in the project. This effectively removes unused portions from the original file on the hard

CHAPTER 11

disk and initializes the offline process history for this file. Before using this option, it might be advisable to consider another option available in Cubase that allows you to minimize the file sizes of all audio clips for your project. This can be achieved by using the Save Project To New Folder option in the File menu. This option allows you to save all the files referenced in a project as well as the project file itself to a new folder, minimizing the space used by the project. However, by doing this, you still have the original content in the original folder where you began the project. If you want to revert to this project at a later date, the files will still be there.

To minimize file sizes in your project:

1. Select the files you want to minimize in the Pool window.
2. Choose the Minimize File option from the Pool menu.
3. When completed, Cubase prompts you to save the project so that the new file references take effect. Click the Save button.

Archiving and Exporting a Pool

When you want to save a backup of your project or use it in another studio, it is important that you have access to all the files that are used in this project. Saving the project using the Save command updates the project file, but chances are, you might have files that are in different folders or on hard disks inside your computer. Make sure you have everything you need in the audio project folder—this operation makes a copy of all the audio clips used in your project to the audio project folder and it allows you to freeze all offline processes you might have applied to an audio file, which prevents you from having to copy the content of the Edit folder onto a backup disk. After this operation is completed, you can simply copy the project file, its Audio folder, and any video file referenced in the project to a backup CD, for example.

To prepare a project for backup:

1. Select the Remove Unused Media option from the Pool menu.
2. Click the Trash button when prompted to choose between trashing and removing from the pool.
3. Select the Empty Trash option from the Pool menu.
4. Click the Erase button when prompted once again. This removes whatever files are not used in your project and erases them from your drive.
5. Select the Prepare Archive option from the Pool menu.
6. Because this is a backup, you can either opt to freeze the edits or not. If you choose not to, make sure to include the Edit folder on your backup media inside the project's folder.
7. Save the project file.
8. When you are ready to back up your files, be sure to include the project file, its Audio subfolder, and the video files you might have used with the project on the backup medium.

If you are in the final stages of a project and want to save a final version of the project files, you can do so by repeating the previous steps with the addition of a couple more steps to save only the necessary material. Before heading on to Step 3 from the previous list, you can use the Conform Files option from the Pool menu to change all audio files in your project. This converts all of your files to the current sample rate and word length set for your project. You can use the Minimize Files option, as described earlier, to reduce each file to the size it's actually used for in the project. Then proceed until Step 7, and use the Save Project To New Folder option in the File menu instead.

When working between projects, you might want to use the pool from one project in another project. This is possible through the use of the Export and Import Pool options, allowing you to save the status of objects in the pool and retrieve them from another project. Note that the pool itself does not contain the audio files because these are located in the Audio folder. But you can save the references, Regions, slices, and other pool-specific settings.

To export or import a pool:

1. Prepare your pool by making sure all your files conform to the project's format, removing or searching for missing links, and emptying the trash.

2. From the Pool menu, select the Export Pool option.

3. Type a name for your pool.

4. Click the Save button.

5. To import the saved pool inside another project, select Import Pool from the Pool menu.

Pool Interaction

Beyond the inner pool functions, you can also use the pool to drag events from it into the Project window as shown in Figure 11.9. When you drag an object from the pool into the Project window, the location of this object depends on two variables:

▶ The snap and quantize grid settings

▶ The position of the snap point inside the audio event or Region; because the snap point can be anywhere in the event, the event snaps the snap point to the closest grid line in the Project window

The location displayed above the cursor as you move the selected object over a track indicates the position at which the snap point or start point of this object will be placed (depending on the variables mentioned). When the blue line next to the cursor and location display the desired location, simply drop the object into place.

Figure 11.9
Dragging a Region from the pool into an audio track in the project

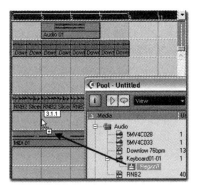

When you drag an object onto an empty audio track, this track adjusts its format (mono/stereo) to the format of the inserted object. However, if an existing object already exists on a track, make sure it has the same format (mono/stereo) as the object you are inserting; otherwise, a mono/stereo mismatch warning appears and Cubase will not play these events.

You can also create a new audio file from a Region in the Pool window by highlighting this Region and then selecting the Bounce Selection option in the Audio menu. This prompts you to choose an appropriate folder for the new file. After you save, it is added to your pool as a new event.

Offline Processes in the Pool

When you apply any type of offline process (from the process, VST, or DirectX plug-ins) to an object inside the pool, this processing affects the entire object. For example, if you apply a delay effect to a Region, the whole Region is affected. If you want to apply a process to a portion of a Region, use the Sample Editor instead. Offline processes in the Pool window can be viewed in the Offline Process History panel found in the Audio menu, as is the case with processes applied in the Project window or Sample Editor.

To apply an offline process to an object from the Pool window:

1. Select the object in the Media column.
2. From the Audio menu, select the desired process you want to apply.
3. Make the appropriate setting in the process' dialog box.
4. Click the Process button.

Sample Editor

The Sample Editor is the default editor associated with audio events and Regions. It allows you to perform many types of editing tasks in a nondestructive environment. It is in this editor that you can create Regions within an event or process an event using offline processes and effects. You also use the Sample Editor to work with hitpoints.

Hitpoints are special Markers that you can add to an audio event, which allow you to create audio slices representing individual beats in the event. After you have created slices from hitpoints, you can use the event in the project and change the tempo of this project without affecting its pitch, or use the timing of the audio event to determine the tempo of a project. You can also use this timing to create a groove map that can be applied to other audio or MIDI events through the Quantize Setup panel.

Sample Editor Areas

The Sample Editor is divided into two areas (see Figure 11.10): the Sample Display area (on the left in the figure) and the Region Display area (on the right in the same figure). It also displays a number of bars as with the other editors: the toolbar, the Sample Overview bar, the Status bar, the ruler, and the Level Scale bar.

Figure 11.10
The Sample Editor
window

The first five buttons in the toolbar are used to perform different operations in the editor, such as selecting a range, zooming in or out, editing the waveform, performing audio playback, or scrubbing. We discuss these tools later on as we talk about the operations available in this window. Following the sample editing tools is the Hitpoint Editing tool, which is a multitool button allowing you to edit hitpoints when you are in Hitpoint mode.

The Play and Loop buttons have the same properties as in the Pool window and the Autoscroll and Status buttons act the same way in this window as they do in the Project window.

When you open an event by double-clicking on it in the Project window, the Show Event Borders button appears in the toolbar. If, on the other hand, you load an event by double-clicking on it from the Pool window, this button is not visible. The Show Event Borders button enables or disables the event border display. When visible, you can use these Markers to alter the start and end point of an event inside the Audio Part Editor.

To edit the start and end of an event in the Sample Editor:

1. In the toolbar, activate the event border display.
2. Select the Range Selection tool in the toolbar.
3. Click the start or end event point Marker and drag it in the desired direction. For example, moving the start point to the right shortens the event and moving it to the left lengthens it. Note that you can't extend these Markers beyond the limit of the audio clip the event refers to.

Changing these Markers also affects the event as it appears in the Project window.

Using the Show Regions button reveals the Region area as shown in Figure 11.10 and also displays Region Markers if there are any. This area allows you to create a Region from a selection in the Sample Display area, remove an existing Region, select the highlighted Region in the Sample Display area, and play the highlighted Region.

If the Region Display area is not visible, you can use the Show Region Display Area button in the toolbar of this window. Unless you have recorded audio in Cycle mode with the Create Region option, events do not normally contain any Regions when recorded or imported. It is through editing options or preference settings that Regions are created, or, as we see later in this chapter, through the Sample Editor's Region Display option buttons.

The Overview area displays a thumbnail view of the current event loaded in the Sample Editor. Using this Overview area is identical to the Overview area found in the Project window. You can only have one event loaded in this editor at a time, so this overview only displays one event or several Regions defined in this event.

The Sample Display area displays one or two channels of audio depending on the event's type (mono or stereo). The waveforms are displayed around a zero axis at the center of each waveform and displayed in the level scale on the left of this area. Each lane displaying the waveform displays two halfway lines above and below the zero axis line. You can customize the elements displayed in this area by right-clicking (Ctrl-clicking on Mac) in the Sample Editor, selecting the Elements option at the bottom of the context menu, and checking or deselecting elements found in this submenu. You can also change the level scale representation from dB to percentage display, or decide to hide the level scale altogether by right-clicking (Ctrl-clicking on Mac) in the level scale area itself and choosing the appropriate option in this context menu.

Basic Editing Functions

It goes without saying that the Sample Editor allows you to cut, copy, and paste audio data inside the Sample Editor. These basic editing functions are similar to any other type of application. For example, cutting and pasting audio can be summed up in four basic steps:

1. Select what you want using the Range Selection tool.
2. Apply the desired function, such as Cut or Copy from the Edit menu.
3. Position the cursor to place the content of the clipboard if you want to paste what you have just cut or copied.
4. Paste the content (Ctrl+V on a PC, Command+V on a Mac).

You can also insert silence within an existing audio clip. This might be useful when you want to add pauses between specific audio content.

To add silence in an audio event:

1. With the Range Selection tool selected, drag a selection box over the area where you want to add silence.
2. Adjust the start and end point if needed by dragging the edge of the selection.
3. Select Edit > Range > Insert Silence (this is also available in the editor's context menu or by pressing Ctrl+Shift+E on a PC or Command+Shift+E on a Mac).

Working with Regions

Regions allow you to define portions within an audio event that you can reuse several times in a project. For example, you could create Regions from a sixteen-bar groove played by a drummer, naming each Region appropriately: intro, beat, break, fill, ending. Then, you can drag the Region from the Region Display area in the Sample Editor into the Project window, just as you did when dragging objects from the pool into the Project window.

To create a new Region:

1. With the Range Selection tool, click and drag over the area in the Sample Editor that you want to include in the new Region. At this point, you don't need to be precise.

2. When you have a good idea of the range, right-click (Ctrl-click on Mac) and select Zoom > Zoom to Selection. This allows you to view your selection close up. Note that the selection appears in a light teal color, whereas a selected Region appears as a darker shade of teal because a Region is usually displayed in a darker shade of gray.

3. You can edit the start or end of your selection to fine-tune the Region by clicking and dragging the edges of your selection. Your cursor becomes a double-headed arrow when you can modify the selection without losing it (see Figure 11.11).

4. Enable the Loop button and click the Play Preview button in the toolbar to hear the selection. Make any necessary modifications to your selection.

5. When you are satisfied with the selection, enable the Region Display area if you haven't done so already.

6. Click the Add button.

7. Type in a name in the Name field for your new selection.

Figure 11.11
Fine-tuning your selection by dragging the edges when the Range Selection tool displays a double-headed arrow

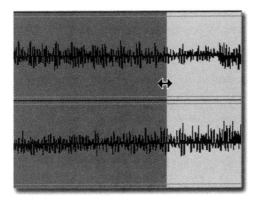

USING THE SNAP TO ZERO OPTION

When you are making a selection, it is a good practice to keep the Snap To Zero option enabled. This option makes sure the amplitude of the audio signal is at its lowest possible value (the zero axis), reducing the chances that glitches might occur during playback due to an abrupt change in amplitude. When this option is enabled, you will notice that your selection might skip over areas in the Sample Display area. This is because Cubase cannot find a proper zero crossing in that portion of the audio.

To modify an existing Region:

1. Click in the column to the left of the Region you want to edit in the Region Display area. This column does not have a name, but allows you to move the Sample Display area to the area of this Region.

2. Click the Select button. The Region's start and end Markers appear.

3. Right-click (Ctrl-click on Mac) and select Zoom > Zoom Selection to center the selection in the display area.

4. With the Range Selection tool, drag the Region's start or end point to the new desired location.

You can also change the start and end location numerically by changing the values manually in the Start and End columns in the Region Display area.

To add a Region to a project from the Sample Editor:

▶ Click in the empty column to the left of the Description column in the Region Display area and drag the Region to the desired location in the Project window.

The same rules apply here as when dragging files from the Pool window.

About the Snap Point

The snap point is to audio what the Note On time is to quantizing. Because audio events or Regions don't necessarily begin at a specific quantize value, you can change the location of the sensitive area that is used to snap to the current quantize grid. This is called the snap point and is displayed as a blue line with an S in a box found in its center. In Figure 11.12, you can see that the event begins earlier, but the actual audio occurs later in time. If this corresponds to a strong rhythmic division, you can move the snap point to this location. When moving the event on the track in the Project window or in the Audio Part Editor, the object snaps to the grid using this location rather than the event start position. If you don't change this, by default, the snap point is placed at the event start point.

To edit the snap point's position:

1. Open the event or Region in the Sample Editor.

2. Make sure the audio event elements are visible in the window. If not, select Elements > Audio Events from the editor's context menu.

3. Zoom to view the current snap point and the place where you want to place it.

4. For more precision, you can use the Scrub tool or the Play tool to find the exact place where the snap point should go.

5. Click and drag the S (in the box on the snap point line) and move it to the appropriate location.

Figure 11.12
The audio event snap point

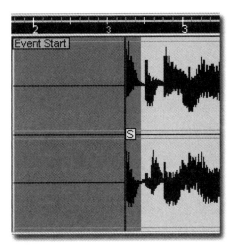

Working with Hitpoints

In Cubase SX or SL, the main purpose of hitpoints is to define individual beats in a rhythmic part and use the location of these special Markers to slice up this part into separate beats, replacing a single audio event by a series of audio slices in an audio part.

Let's take a look at Figure 11.13 as an example. Here, we have the same drum beat played in three different ways. Although there are four representations of this beat in the figure, the original beat never changes speed when played at different project tempo values. It stays constant and the number of bars it covers at different tempo values varies because the number of bars passing when the tempo is higher also increases. The upper portion of both pairs represents the sliced version of the same beat. As you can see, in both cases, the part ends at the beginning of Bar 2, whereas in the original version, it ends after Bar 2 when played slower and before when played faster.

The same drum beat has been placed on two tracks: in the upper track, a sliced version of the beat and on the lower track, the original version. A screenshot was taken while the project was set at 120 BPM (upper couple of tracks) and another at 90 BPM (lower couple of tracks). Notice how the sliced version in both tempos ends at the beginning of Bar 2, whereas the original content spreads across Bar 2 when the tempo is at 120 BPM and doesn't reach Bar 2 when the tempo is set at 90 BPM. That's because slicing up the beats creates a snap point at the beginning of each, which follows the beat position in the bar/beat grid.

CHAPTER 11

Figure 11.13
Using sliced parts
instead of original audio
at various project speeds

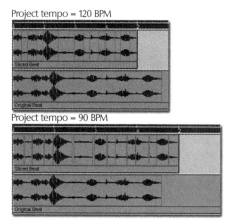

Another useful way of using hitpoints is when you have an audio segment for which you want to determine the exact speed. Because hitpoints allow you to identify beats within an audio sample, it also calculates the tempo value automatically after you tell Cubase how many bars and beats are included in the selection.

Using hitpoints, however, works best with audio content with strong attacks. You can still get tempo values out of sustained material, but the result this produces when you change the pitch can be disappointing.

Creating Hitpoints

The best way to work with hitpoints is to load a drum beat or rhythmic content in the Sample Editor. There are two basic methods you can use to create hitpoints: using a sensitivity slider to determine where the hitpoints should occur or using a quantize grid value. Both methods offer advantages and disadvantages; however, because beats are usually fairly regular, using the quantize value seems to offer a more consistent result.

To create hitpoints:

1. Open the audio event to which you want to add hitpoints in the Sample Editor. You can open an event from the pool or the Project window. If the event is inside a part, this opens the Audio Part Editor; double-click on the event from the Audio Part Editor to open it in the Sample Editor.

2. If the area in which you want to create hitpoints for is shorter than the object itself, start by selecting a range that defines a clear, loop-friendly beat, such as a one, two, or more bar segment.

3. Preview the selection by enabling the Loop option and clicking Play in the Sample Editor.

4. Adjust the start and end position of the selection if you have created one; otherwise, you don't need to adjust any selection.

TIP

Try counting how many bars and beats are in your loop, if you can feel the beat subdivision; for example, the HiHat might play sixteenth notes. You can use this as your hitpoint quantize value later.

5. Enable the Hitpoint mode from the window's toolbar button. Cubase calculates a temporary position for the hitpoints. After it's done, several hitpoints (how many depend on the actual content you loaded) appear in the Sample Editor.

6. Using the bar counting you did earlier, see if the value in the Bars field (see Figure 11.14) matches your count. If the number of bars, beats, and time signature is not properly displayed, adjust any value to make it accurate.

Figure 11.14
The hitpoint fields on the Sample Editor toolbar appear when the Hitpoint mode is enabled

The Bars field represents the number of complete bars found in this object. If there are additional beats outside the bar or bars, such as a pick up, change the value found in the Beats value using the drop-down menu. Finally, if the time signature is not 4/4, adjust these values using the arrows on each side of the field. For example, if your looped beat represents two bars of 4/4 and two additional beats, you should set both bars and beats at two. Because it is recommended that you use loop-friendly content, it is, therefore, not recommend that you slice an event that uses additional beats outside the bars because this makes it harder to use the slice content in a loop context. However, because there are no rules cut in stone that say you can't use a six-beat loop, for example, in a 4/4 project, it is up to you to decide if you want to do this.

7. Under the Use field, select an appropriate quantize value.

Taking our previous example of a loop involving a HiHat playing sixteenth notes, use the 1/16 value from the drop-down menu. This places a series of hitpoints at sixteenth-note intervals. For this to work, however, you need to make sure the Bars, Beats, and Time Signature fields are set up properly. You can also use the sensitivity slider to adjust the number of hitpoints displayed if the quantize grid doesn't work well with your loop. Sliding it to the left removes less important hitpoints and sliding it to the right adds sensitivity, thus creating additional hitpoints. Note that you can't use both quantize and sensitivity methods simultaneously.

8. Click the Speaker tool in the toolbar to select it.

9. Click between hitpoints to preview the result of each slice.

10. Make changes to the quantize value or the sensitivity slider, depending on the method you used to improve the result.

At this point, it is possible that each slice found between hitpoints is perfect. However, in most cases, you need to fine-tune these hitpoints.

CHAPTER 11

Editing Hitpoints

You can move, erase, or create new hitpoints manually when in Hitpoint mode. The best way to move a hitpoint to an appropriate location or to create a new one is to zoom into the audio display area in order to properly position your hitpoint. When you preview a slice, it is important that each slice (space between two hitpoints) contains only one "hit," such as a kick, snare, or combination of instruments on the same beat subdivision. It is also important that the end of the slice does end in a glitch. This is usually the case when the next hitpoint arrives just after the sound has started.

If you look at the example in Figure 11.15, you will notice that the hitpoint occurs directly on the beat. The instrument will probably sound like it does as well because its peak is heard around this area as well, but as you can also notice, the attack begins before the hitpoint location. This causes the previous slice to play the beginning of the attack for the next slice, resulting in a glitch-like sound at the end of the slice. Moving the hitpoint a bit to the left, in this case, prevents this glitch from happening even if it means placing the hitpoint slightly before the quantize value. This only adds to the feel of the beat itself. We see how you can create a groove map later on, using the hitpoint locations as the template for this groove.

Figure 11.15
The hitpoint is placed at a quantize value, but the sound begins before the quantize value

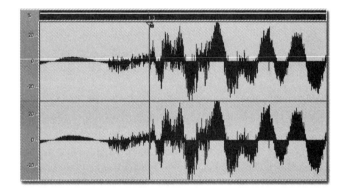

To move a hitpoint:

1. Enable the Snap to Zero Crossing button on the toolbar.
2. Zoom into the area you want to edit.
3. Select the Move Snap button from the Hitpoint tool. This button has three functions: Disable Hitpoint, Lock Hitpoint, and Move Hitpoint. You can also move the hitpoint using any other tool except the Draw tool.
4. Click the hitpoint's handle and drag it to the desired location.
5. After you are satisfied with the location of this hitpoint, you can lock it.
6. Repeat this operation for other hitpoints if necessary.

Locked hitpoints can be moved, but they remain visible if you choose to change the sensitivity slider later.

To insert a hitpoint manually:

1. Enable the Snap to Zero Crossing button on the toolbar.

2. Zoom into the area you want to edit.

3. Select the Draw tool from the toolbar.

4. Click at the location at which you want to add a hitpoint. If you hold your mouse button down as you add the hitpoint, you can position it exactly where you want it if the original location isn't exact.

To remove hitpoints:

1. In the Hitpoints tool, select the Disable Hitpoints option.

2. Click the hitpoints you want to remove (disable).

Creating and Using Audio Slices

After you've created hitpoints and are satisfied that each hit in your drum loop or rhythmic content is identified correctly with a hitpoint, you can create the audio slices that will be used in the Project window. Slices are similar to small Regions, but are not handled as Regions by Cubase in the sense that a sliced event does not display a number of corresponding Regions in the pool as does an event with Regions as described earlier in the "Working with Regions" section.

To create audio slices:

1. This requires that you have previously created hitpoints and have properly positioned your hitpoints in the audio object.

2. While the Hitpoint mode is still active, select Hitpoints > Create Audio Slices from the Audio menu (or the editor's context menu).

To use the sliced loop, you can drag a sliced object from the Pool window to an audio track in the Project window. When you place a sliced event on an audio track, an audio part is automatically created with the corresponding slices inside this part. From this point on, when you want to edit the slices in the part, the Audio Part Editor opens. This allows you to move the slices around in the part, apply a different quantize setting, or reorganize your loop to create variations of it.

After you've placed a sliced event on a track, you might notice that changing the tempo to a value lower than the original tempo of the loop might create audible gaps between each slice. You can solve this problem by using the Close Gaps function available in the Audio menu. This function can also be used in other instances; however, this is probably the best use for it. As Figure 11.16 displays, the small gaps that occur between each slice are removed after Cubase time stretches each slice to compensate for the missing audio content. Note that extensive use of this over large gaps alters the sound quality of your audio content, so you should use this function on small gaps only.

To close gaps between slices in a part:

1. Select the audio part in the Project window.

2. From the Audio menu, select the Close Gaps option.

Figure 11.16
A before and after look
at how the Close Gap
function affects slices

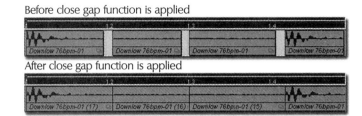

Creating and Using Groove Maps

When creating hitpoints in a drum loop, you are placing Markers where important beats and beat subdivisions occur in this loop. By doing so, you are, in essence, creating a rhythmic blueprint that holds the rhythmic feel of your loop and this can be applied to other audio or MIDI events through the Quantize Setup panel. This rhythmic extraction is called a groove map.

To convert hitpoints into a groove map:

1. Create hitpoints in an audio loop as described earlier in this chapter.
2. When satisfied with the result, from the Hitpoints submenu found in the Audio menu, select the Create Groove Quantize option.

Note that this works better if you use at least one slice per eighth-note; otherwise, your map will be very coarse and will only affect events on beats.

To apply a groove map to events:

1. Select the events you want to quantize. This can be in the Project window, the MIDI Editor, or the Audio Part Editor.
2. Press the default Shift+Q key command to bring up the Quantize Setup panel, or select Quantize Setup from the MIDI menu.
3. Click the Presets drop-down menu and select the corresponding quantize groove. By default, the groove map is given the name of the event used to create it. You can, however, rename it by selecting the preset, double-clicking on the name in the Preset field, and type a new name for it.

You see how the events will be quantized by looking at the quantize preview display in the center of the Quantize Setup panel.

Audio Part Editor

This editor is the audio equivalent of the MIDI Editor and many of the functions you can apply in it can also be applied in the Project window. The main purpose for this editor is to edit events inside an audio part because the Project window allows you to edit events and Regions. You can look at the Audio Part Editor as a mini version of the Project window, where all edits are made for a single part found in the Project window.

To create an empty audio part in the Project window:

▶ Double-click between the left and right locators on an audio track.

▶ Or, with the Pencil tool selected, click and drag a range on an audio track.

To create an audio part from existing events in the Project window:

▶ With the Glue Tube tool selected, glue two or more events together on the same track.

▶ Or, select an event on a track, and then select the Audio > Events To Part option.

Because this is the default editor for audio parts, double-clicking on an audio part in the Project window opens the Audio Part Editor. If you have created shared copies of a part you open in the editor, any editing you do is applied to all copies. If you don't want this to happen, you should convert your shared copy into a real copy beforehand. Shared copies display the name at the bottom of the part in italics and real copies display the name in regular font style.

HIDING OR SHOWING THE EVENTS NAME
You can change how events appear by selecting the appropriate options in the File > Preferences > Event Display options. You will find different options, one of them called Show Events Name. If this option is not selected, you will not see the difference between shared and real copies.

To convert a shared copy into a real copy in the Project window:

1. Select the part you want to convert in the Project window.

2. From the Edit menu, select the Convert to Real Copy option.

Shared copies are usually created when you hold the Alt+Shift keys down when dragging an event to create a copy.

Audio Part Editor Areas

The Audio Part Editor's toolbar offers much of the same options found in the Project window. The tools used to edit events in a part are the same and work the same way here as they do in the Project window. The Play Preview and Loop Preview buttons allow you to hear the content of a part in a loop or play the content of a selected event in a part in a loop when this button is active. The Information bar and ruler also offer the same options as in the Project window.

The Audio Part Editor, on the other hand, offers the possibility of using lanes to place and organize audio events on a track. In Figure 11.17, you can see that there are two events located below the others. The area on which they are placed is called a lane. You can have as many lanes as you want in an Audio Part Editor, but only one audio event can be heard at any time. This means that when events overlap on the same track, the one on top is heard, cutting off the one below. When events overlap across different lanes, the event on the lowest lane gets priority. For example, at Bar 4, Beat 2, the event placed on the lower lane (in Figure 11.17) cuts off the event placed on the higher lane from this point forward. You can bring an event to the front when they overlap on the same lane in much the same way as you do in the Project window: by using the To Front option in the context menu (right-click on a PC or Ctrl-click on a Mac).

Figure 11.17
The Audio Part Editor

To hear the content of an event in the Audio Part Editor:

▶ Activate the Solo button and start playback normally. The Project window's locators and play line's position determines what is heard.

▶ Or, click the Play Preview button in the editor's toolbar. Activating the Loop button plays the content in a loop.

▶ Or, select an event and click the Play Preview button to hear only the selected event.

▶ Or, choose the Speaker tool and click where you want to start the playback. Cubase plays from the location where you click until the end of this event in the editor.

▶ Or, choose the Scrub tool, and click and drag the mouse to the left or right. The playback plays in the direction and at the speed you move your mouse.

Audio Operations

Because the operations in this editor are identical to the ones available in the Project window, please refer to that section in Chapter 9 for details on these operations. However, here is an alternative to editing events as separate objects in the Project window. As mentioned earlier in Chapter 9, it is possible to record multiple takes in a single audio clip, creating several Regions or events within this clip. By creating a part on a track and placing several takes inside this part, you can edit them inside the Audio Part Editor using the different lanes to create your perfect take.

As you can see in Figure 11.18, four takes are used to create the final version of this part. Using different lanes at the beginning to place your events, the Scissors tool to split the events where you want (the snap and grid settings influence where you can split), the Mute tool to mute the portions you don't want to hear, and snap points to reposition your events along an appropriate grid, reorganizing musical ideas becomes very easy. When you move events on lower lanes to hear them, you can hold down the Ctrl (Command on Mac) key to restrict your movement to the vertical axis. This is useful when you don't want to move an event in time. You can also apply auto fade and crossfade options as well as offline processes to events inside the Audio Part Editor.

Figure 11.18
Assembling takes in the
Audio Part Editor

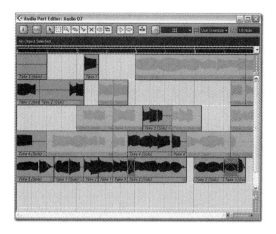

Importing Audio into an Audio Part

You can import audio events or Regions into the Audio Part Editor just as you would do when dragging events or Regions from the Sample Editor or Pool window.

Now You Try It

It's time to put the topics covered in this chapter into action—you can download a practice exercise at http://www.muskalipman.com.

CHAPTER 11

12

Mixer and Channel Settings

Up until now, we have explored both the Project window and the editing environments provided for MIDI and audio tracks. This chapter discusses the mixing environment inside Cubase and ways you can edit settings applied to a channel. The Mixer window in Cubase offers an interface that resembles a typical desktop mixer. In this Mixer window, you will find a replica of settings that have been described in Chapter 6 as well as functions described in Chapters 8 and 9 when discussing MIDI and audio recording respectively.

So, why this fancy mixing window? Instead of having to select tracks in the Track List area, then expanding the Channel section of the Inspector area for each channel you want to view, and then switching to the Inserts section or Send Effects section, everything is available to you in a single window. This not only makes it easier to see the settings applied to all your tracks, it also makes it easy to automate the mix for an entire project, as you will see later.

In this chapter, you will:

▶ Explore the different areas of the Mixer window

▶ Learn how to save channel settings and apply them to other channels inside the Mixer window

▶ Find out how to customize your Mixer window to fit the tasks at hand

▶ Learn how to use additional audio outputs by activating busses

▶ Understand what channel EQs are and how to use them

▶ Understand what dynamic control is and how to use it

▶ Learn how to use groups to create submixes and monitor mixes

Mixer Areas

The Mixer window offers a common window for all types of channels present in your project (see Figure 12.1). A channel for each audio, MIDI, and group track is represented in the Mixer window, offering controls, such as volume, pan, mute, solo, and read and write automation. To help you with this process, a panel on the left of the Mixer window allows you to control common elements found in the mixer. Cubase SX users can extend the Mixer window to display online (insert and send) effect settings as well as EQ settings for audio and group channels.

Figure 12.1
The Mixer window

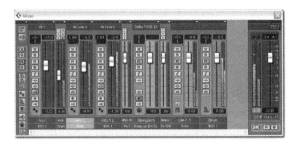

Common Panel

The Common panel found on the left of the Mixer window (see Figure 12.2)controls global settings for your Mixer window as well as its appearance and behavior. Here's a look at each item in the panel from top to bottom.

Figure 12.2
The Common panel found on the left of the Mixer window

The area at the top displaying an arrow pointing down holds a View Options drop-down menu (see Figure 12.3). This menu is divided in three sections (in Cubase SX). The first section allows you (in Cubase SX version only) to change the Mixer view from Normal to Expanded. When in Expanded mode, the mixer can display different insert, EQ, or send effects settings for each channel. The Narrow and Wide options allow you to change the width of all the channels displayed in the Mixer window. Each channel has its own width setting; however, when selecting an option in the Common panel, all the channels are affected. When a channel is displayed in Narrow mode, all its functions remain active; however, some of the controls are hidden away. The following five of the remaining six options allow you to choose which types of channels are displayed in the Mixer window. You can also change these settings through buttons found at the bottom of the Common panel. The sixth option allows you to display "hideable" channels. You can set a channel's display property to hideable (explained later). When deselecting the Hideable option in the View Options menu, all channels that use the hideable property are hidden from view while remaining active.

Figure 12.3
The Common panel's
View Options menu

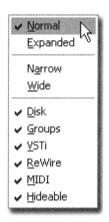

Below the View Options menu are two display control buttons (only one in Cubase SL). The top one toggles the Extended mode on or off and the bottom one displays the master output channel at the right edge of the Mixer window.

The following four buttons are also found on each channel: solo, mute, read and write. However, in the Common panel, they serve as a master control and monitor the current status of channels available in the Mixer window. When one or more tracks in the Mixer window are muted, the Mute button is lit. Clicking this button cancels all current mute settings, returning all channels in the Mixer window to their nonmuted state. The Solo button plays a similar role in the sense that it appears lit when one or more tracks are in Solo mode. Clicking this button cancels the solo monitoring in all affected channels in the Mixer window. The Read and Write buttons allow you to activate or deactivate the read or write automation on all channels by changing the state of the button in the Common panel. If one or more channels are already in Read or Write mode, the Mixer window is lit as well to indicate that a channel is currently actively reading or ready to write automation.

If you want to copy the settings of a selected track to another, you can use the following three buttons. For example, if you want to have the same EQ, inserts, and sends settings on several vocal tracks, you can make the settings on a first channel and when you are satisfied with these settings, copy and paste them to one or more channels. Subsequently, all the channels to which you copied these settings will be the same.

To copy a channel's settings to another channel:

1. Adjust the settings of the channel you want to copy.
2. Make sure this channel is selected in the Mixer window. If not, click the channel's name below the fader to select it, or select it from the Channel Selection drop-down menu in the Common panel.
3. Click the Copy Channel button. The Paste button becomes active.
4. Select the channel to which you want to paste the copied settings.
5. Click the Paste Settings button in the Common panel.
6. You can repeat this paste operation to any number of channels by selecting it and clicking the Paste button again.

The following five buttons allow you to hide or show the channel types associated with each button. These are, from top to bottom, audio channels (disk-based digital audio recording), group channels, VSTi channels, Rewire channels, and MIDI channels. As mentioned previously, you can also select or deselect these types from the View Options menu at the top of the Common panel.

The last button in the Common panel lets you save a set of mixer display options as a preset and retrieve it later from this menu. Using these presets, you can create custom mixer displays, such as an EQ display, a MIDI display, an audio channels only display, and so on. When you want to work on the mix or settings of a specific set of items, you can quickly change the entire Mixer window to suit your needs.

To create a channel mixer view set:

1. Set up the mixer view options appropriately so that it displays the information to which you want to have quick access.

2. From the View Channel Set drop-down menu, select the Add option.

3. Enter a name for your preset, for example "Audio EQ" if you selected to display only audio channels with their EQ settings in the Extended panel.

4. Click the OK button.

You can remove view sets by first selecting a view set and then selecting the Remove option from the same menu. Cubase offers two different Mixer windows. You can take advantage of this feature to organize your mixing environment in a way that suits you best. For example, you could choose to display all MIDI channels in one mixer and display audio channels in another. You can access the second Mixer window through the Devices menu.

Extended Panel

The Extended panel is visible to Cubase SX users when selecting the Extended view option in the Common panel's View Options menu or by clicking on the Display Extended Panel button.

This panel offers five display options. When selecting a display option, all channels in the Extended panel display this selection. You can, however, change the displayed Extended panel for a specific channel by selecting a different display option for this channel.

The bottom of Figure 12.4 displays each button found in the Common panel and above them the panels that are displayed through these buttons. You will notice that there are no MIDI EQ settings in the Extended panel. When you choose to display the EQ for other channels, the MIDI channel's Extended area keeps displaying whatever was there before you chose the extended EQ display.

The MIDI insert's Extended panel displays the four Inserts settings. Each insert has the following fields:

▶ Enable/disable the Insert button

▶ Open the Edit window for the Insert button

▶ The Insert Effect selection menu

Audio inserts have the same controls as the MIDI inserts; however, the list displayed in the Insert Selection menu is different.

Both extended EQ display options offer the same controls in different display options.

▶ An On/Off button to enable or disable the EQ band

▶ A gain control (top slider in Slider mode and inner knob in Dial mode)

▶ A frequency control (second slider in Slider mode and outer knob in Dial mode)

▶ A Q setting (third slider in Slider mode and lower small knob in Dial mode)

The MIDI sends in the Extended panel display the following settings for each of the eight (in Cubase SX) or five (in Cubase SL) send effects:

▶ An On/Off button to enable or disable the MIDI sends

▶ An open effect's editing panel button

▶ A pre- or post-fader selection button

▶ An effect selection menu

▶ A MIDI output port selection menu for the output of the effect

▶ A channel setting for the output of the effect

The MIDI sends Extended panel is the same for both versions of the audio sends Extended Display mode. The audio sends offer the following controls:

▶ An On/Off button to enable or disable the MIDI sends

▶ An open effect's editing panel button (only in Slider mode)

▶ A pre- or post-fader selection button (only in Slider mode)

▶ An effect selection menu

▶ A send to effect level (represented by a slider in Slider mode and dial in Dial mode)

The setting displayed in the Extended panels are the same settings that are available in the Inspector area of each track, so if you don't have Cubase SX, you can still modify these settings in the Inspector area of the channel, or you can click on the "e" button next to the channel's level fader to open that channel's additional settings panel.

Figure 12.4
The Common panel's extended functions in Cubase SX

Audio Channels

In the Mixer window, audio tracks, VSTi, and group channels offer similar settings and are considered as audio channels.

Disk Channels (Audio Tracks)

Let's take a look at the controls found in the audio track channel. In the Mixer window, this is referred to as the disk channel to distinguish it from other channels that are handled as audio channels, such as the VSTi and group channels.

▶ **Channel View Options menu**. As with the Common panel discussed earlier, the top of the audio channel offers a Channel View Options drop-down menu. Making a selection in the channel only affects the current channel, not the other channels. For Cubase SL users, this choice is limited to Wide or Narrow view because there are no extended display modes (see Figure 12.5 for an example of the audio channel's Wide and Narrow view). For Cubase SX users, you can select which Extended panel you want to see for this channel. These choices were described in the "Extended Panel" section earlier. At the bottom of this list, however, is a hideable property. When a channel displays a check mark next to this option, it is hidden when you choose to not display the hideable channels in the Common panel's View Options menu as discussed earlier. This is an easy way to switch tracks on and off, regardless of their type in the Mixer window.

▶ **Audio Input Selection field**. Below the View Options menu is the audio Input Selection field. This allows you to select the input used to record or monitor audio through this channel.

▶ **Pan Control and Peak Margin indicator**. The Pan field displays a numeric and graphic representation of the pan setting for this channel. Ctrl-clicking (Command-clicking on Mac) brings the pan back to its center position, which is represented by a C in the numeric display (as shown in Figure 12.5). To the right of the pan display is the margin display. This represents the distance between the highest audio peak in this track to the maximum digital audio level. In this case (Figure 12.5), the peak was at -11.3 dB. This value resets itself if you move the channel's fader.

▶ **Channel Setting Option buttons**. The buttons found below the pan display and to the right of the fader are the same buttons found in the audio Channel section in the track's Inspector area. Whatever settings you made in the Inspector are displayed here and vice versa. These functions are Mute, Solo, Read, Write, Open Channel Editor panel, Insert Bypass, EQ Bypass, Send Effect Bypass, Record Enabled, and Monitor. Remember that when the Monitor button is active, the level indicator to the right of the channel fader becomes an input level indicator. Below the Monitor button is the audio channel icon. This corresponds to the same icon found on the show/hide audio channels in the Common panel of the Mixer window. When you deselect this button in the Common panel, all channels with this icon are hidden away.

▶ **Channel Fader and Level indicator**. The channel fader control's the output level of this channel, except when you are in Monitor mode. The numeric display below the fader tells your exact position along the fader. To bring the fader to its default 0 dB position, hold the Ctrl (Command on Mac) key down as you click on it. If you want to move the fader by smaller, more precise increments, hold the Shift key down as you move the fader. This is very useful when you want to create slow and precise fade effects with automation.

▶ **Channel's Name**. You will find the name of the channel below the fader. You can use this area to select the channel, or change the name by double-clicking on it. When a channel is selected, this area appears in reverse color (a light beige color in this case). You can select more than one channel at a time by holding down the Shift key as you make your selection.

▶ **Channel's Output Setting**. The bottom of the audio channel displays the current output assigned to this channel. You can click in this area to change the output of a channel at any time. If you have groups in your project, you can send your signal to a group channel instead of a bus.

Figure 12.5
The audio channel in its Wide (left) and Narrow (right) modes

Sharing Resources with Rewire

Rewire is a software-based technology that lets you share application resources inside your computer—more specifically, Rewire-compatible ones. Developed by Propellerhead and Steinberg, Rewire is compatible with most products sold by either company.

What Rewire does is quite nice, and it's simple to use. It patches the outputs of one software application into the inputs of another software application and synchronizes them. This has the same effect as a VSTi, except that Rewire instruments or Rewire software applications are not running inside Cubase, as a VSTi is. When you activate Rewire channels, you add these channels to the channel mixer in Cubase. This allows all Rewire-compatible applications to share the same sound card, assigning each Rewire instrument a different output if you want, and also providing a common transport control and timing base; you can control playback for all applications from Cubase.

To use Rewire:

1. Launch Cubase first. It is important that your other Rewire applications are launched after Cubase; otherwise both applications run independently.

2. Make sure the Release ASIO Driver in Background option is not selected in Devices > Device Setup > VST Multitrack.

3. In the Devices menu or the Devices panel, select the Installed Rewire Application option. If you don't have any Rewire applications installed, you will not have this option. The Rewire panel appears, as shown in Figure 12.6. What appears in this panel depends on the Rewire-compatible applications installed on your computer. In this example, Reason is installed.

Figure 12.6
The Rewire panel; active channels appear lit

4. Click the green buttons in the Active column next to the channels you want to activate in Cubase. Each active channel creates a channel in the Mixer window.

5. If you want to rename a channel, click in the VST Label column and type in the label you want to use.

6. Launch your Rewire application.

At this point, the Transport bars in both applications are linked together. This means that you can start and stop your playback within any application, and the others follow. If you record events, this is recorded in the application that is active, or, in other words, the recording takes place in the application in which you clicked the Record button. So, recording is independent, but playback follows and if you use cycle playback or recording, all applications follow this loop. When you have a loop playing in Reason, for example, this loop stays looped. Cubase always sets the tempo setting when the Master track is active. If you change the tempo in Cubase's Master track, the other applications follow the lead. If you are not using the Master track, you can change the tempo setting in either application and the playback reflects it. In other words, if you start playback at 100 BPM in Reason and Cubase is not set to play the tempo from the Master track, it plays at 100 BPM as well.

All Rewire channels containing recorded events that are not muted when you export your mixdown from the File > Export > Audio mixdown option are included in this output file.

One thing to look out for is the sample playback rate. Make sure both applications are set to a compatible sampling rate. If your Rewire application doesn't support Cubase's sampling rate, the Rewire application might not play the right pitch.

VSTi and Rewire Channels

MIDI tracks that are assigned to a VSTi (see Figure 12.7) or Rewire (see Figure 12.8) MIDI output port are represented by two channels in the Mixer window: one MIDI channel to control MIDI-related settings associated with the Rewire or VSTi and one audio channel that can be processed just as the disk audio channel described previously. There are, however, some differences in an audio VSTi or Rewire and a disk audio channel:

▶ You can't assign an audio input to a VSTi or Rewire audio channel.

▶ There is no Record Enable buttons on this audio channel because the events are recorded through the MIDI channel instead (see the "MIDI Channels" section for details on this).

▶ There is no Monitor button because there are no audio inputs to monitor.

▶ Below the Bypass Send Effect button, you will find an Edit VSTi button that allows you to open the VSTi interface to change settings in the instrument. Because the Rewire instrument is not inside Cubase, you need to access that application to make changes to the instrument's settings.

▶ The icons for VSTi or Rewire channels are associated with VSTi or Rewire types respectively. When you choose to hide these types of channels (VSTi or Rewire) from the Common panel on the left of the Mixer window, all channels with these icons are hidden from view.

▶ The color behind the fader is different from the audio disk channel.

The MIDI channel of the VSTi and Rewire offers the same settings as the MIDI channels described later in the "MIDI Channels" section. It is the presence of the VSTi or Rewire audio channel that makes it possible for Cubase to process these types of MIDI tracks as audio channels as well and export the audio created by the instrument to a file without having to use the Record function in the Transport panel, because in a way, the audio is generated by your sound card.

Figure 12.7
The VSTi MIDI (left) and audio (right) channels

Figure 12.8
The Rewire MIDI (left)
and audio (right)
channels

As you will probably notice, some VSTi have multiple output support, creating as many audio channels in the Mixer window as they offer. The HALion sampler VSTi, for example, offers eight audio channels, configurable as pairs or mono outputs.

Group Channels

When a group track is created in the Project window, a group channel is added to the Mixer window. Groups are used as outputs only, where you can assign other channels to play through a group channel and then process all the channels sent to that group as one entity in the group's channel settings. For example, if you have several tracks for your drum kit, you can assign all the individual tracks to play through the group channel, and assign a reverb to this channel. This applies the same reverb level to all the parts of the drum kit instead of applying an individual reverb level on each track. Here are some differences between the audio disk channel and the group channel:

▶ You can't assign an audio input to a group channel because it only serves as an output.

▶ There is no Record Enable buttons on this audio channel because there are no inputs.

▶ There is no Monitor button because there are no audio inputs to monitor.

▶ The icon for group channels is associated with this channel type (see Figure 12.9). When you choose to hide this type of channel (group) from the Common panel on the left of the Mixer window, all channels with this icon are hidden from view.

▶ The color behind the fader is different from the audio disk channel.

Figure 12.9
The group channel in its
Wide (left) and Narrow
(right) modes

MIDI Channels

A MIDI channel is added to the Mixer window each time you create a MIDI track in the Project window. As you saw in the "VSTi and Rewire Channels" section, even if these instruments are considered as audio plug-in effects, you still need MIDI to record events that will be played by these audio effects, and as such, they are also MIDI-triggered instruments needing a MIDI channel. The MIDI channel in the Mixer window displays an exact replica of the MIDI Channel section in the Inspector area. The only difference is found in the View Options menu of the Mixer window because this is not present in the Inspector area.

The View Options menu, located at the top of the channel in the Mixer window (in Normal View mode for Cubase SX users), offers three options in the SL version and five in the SX version. The Narrow or Wide modes let you minimize or expand the channel in the Mixer window as with other types of channels (see Figure 12.10 for an example of wide and narrow displays). Adding a check mark next to the hideable item adds this property to the channel. When you deselect this type in the Common panel's View Options menu, any hideable channel is hidden from view.

The two other options available with Cubase SX allow you to display the MIDI insert and send effect settings in the extended portion of the Mixer window. Cubase SL users can access these settings by clicking on the "e" button in the channel, just below the Write Automation button. This opens the channel's settings. Note that any settings made in the Inspector area are reflected in this panel and vice versa.

You should also be aware that the fader's default position is set at 100, which represents the MIDI control change volume's value. You can hold down the Ctrl (Command on Mac) key as you click on the fader's handle to bring it back to this value. You can also hold the Shift key down while moving your fader to get a greater level of precision. The level display on the right of the fader, unlike the audio channels, does not represent the output level of the instrument.

This level cannot be monitored because the sound of the MIDI instrument is not monitored through the MIDI channel itself. In fact, this represents the velocity value of Note On and Note Off messages. Changing the volume level with the fader to the right does not, therefore, affect the level displayed in this bar and no digital clipping can occur because of high velocities being monitored by this display.

Figure 12.10
The MIDI or Rewire channel in its Wide (left) and Narrow (right) modes

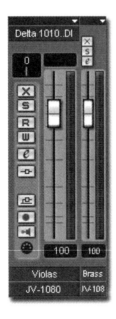

Master Output Channels

To view the master output channels in the Mixer window, you have to enable it in the Common panel. You can also view the master output channels by selecting the VST Outputs option from the Devices menu or by pressing the default key command F4.

The master outputs are your main outputs (see Figure 12.11). Depending on how you set up your system or how many outputs your sound card has, you will generally use the two main outputs of your sound card to monitor the output in your sound system. If you have more than two outputs (and probably inputs), you can use these additional outputs for additional busses or if you are using Cubase SX in a surround sound setup, you will need these additional outputs to monitor each additional channel in your surround mix.

Let's say your sound card has eight inputs and eight outputs. You can assign Outputs 1 and 2 to the Master output. This is your monitor mix output, or what you want to hear in your speakers. Outputs 3 and 4 can be used by Bus 2; Outputs 5 and 6 can be used by Bus 3; and Outputs 7 and 8 can be used by Bus 4. This way, you can send four different pairs of signals to an external multitrack recorder—external effects, different monitor mixes, and so on. In a surround sound setup using a 5.1 surround configuration, you need at least six outputs to monitor these channels: left, right, left surround, right surround, center, and subbass.

The master outputs can also have up to five different assignable effects in the SL version and eight in the SX version. These master effects are very useful for final dynamic control over the entire mix, or noise reducing effects. Because master effects are applied to any channel going to the master output, you probably won't want to use anything else here.

When a project's sample record format is set to 32-bit floating point, you don't need to worry about digital clipping on audio channels after the channels are recorded and there was no clipping at the input. That's because the processing inside Cubase is done using this 32-bit format and makes it very difficult to actually get digital clipping using this format. However, after the signal is sent to the output, it is converted to the sound card's format; in many cases, this is 16-bit. Because the output is 16, 20, or 24-bit depending on your sound card, digital clipping becomes a very real possibility if the clip indicator lights up above one of the master channel's level displays. You should try to avoid any clipping, especially when it comes to your master outputs.

At the top of the master outputs, you will find two small buttons on the right side. These buttons allow you to open the VST Master Effects Setup panel (the "e" button) or bypass effects in the Master Effects section using the Bypass button to the right. Below the output level monitors in the stereo setup, you will find an Output Selection field. This allows you to change the sound card's output used by the master output. In a surround sound setup, you need to access the VST Output panel to make changes. You will notice, at the bottom of each level indicator, a small letter identifying the purpose of this channel. In a stereo setup, the usual L/R is displayed to indicate the left and right channels. In a surround setup, this can be displayed in several ways depending on your surround setup. Typically, you will find the following abbreviations: L for left, R for right, Ls and Rs for left and right surround, C for center, and LFE for subbass.

Figure 12.11
The Master channel in its stereo (left) or Surround (right) configuration; note that surround is only available with the Cubase SX version

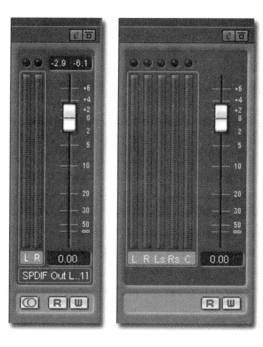

VST Master Effects

The master effects found in the VST Master Effects panel are routed directly into the signal path of the master output. This means that they operate in much the same way as an insert effect. They are pre-fader, so the position of your master fader has no consequence on the output of the effect. Because it is applied to all audio channels passing through the master fader, the type of effect you use here should be limited to dynamic control over the entire mix and noise reduction processes. This doesn't mean you can't use a reverb on the entire mix, but if you do, understand that you won't be able to prevent any audio channels from passing through this reverb, including channels that are already assigned to reverbs through send effects, for example. On the other hand, you might use less reverb on individual tracks and add a subtle reverb on the master output to make all the instruments sound as if they were in the same room. But the key word here is "subtle." It is easy to drown your mix in reverb unnecessarily. If you want to save a file as streaming audio content for the Web, you might want to use a final brick-wall equalizer to limit the frequencies of your mix before converting it to RealMedia, QuickTime, Windows Media, or MP3 files.

To add a master effect to the master fader:

1. Click the VST Master Effects button in the Devices panel, select this option in the Devices menu, or press the default key command F7. The VST Master Effects panel appears (see Figure 12.12)

2. Select the desired effect from the drop-down list in the Effect menu.

3. Click the Edit Effect button if you want to change the effect's settings (the "e" button on the right of the panel).

PREPARING A 16–BIT MIXDOWN

If you are preparing your project for a final CD mixdown and want to convert the files from 32- or 24-bit to 16-bit, you should apply the UV22 dithering plug-in effect as your last master effect in the chain.

Figure 12.12
The VST Master Effects panel for Cubase SX (there are only five master effects in SL)

VST Outputs

The main purpose for the VST Outputs panel is to activate and configure additional outputs if needed and if available, meaning that if your sound card offers only two inputs and two outputs, you have, by default, only a master output. This master output will be your Bus 1 in the VST Outputs panel. On the other hand, if you have a multi I/O sound card, you can configure which physical outputs are assigned to busses as well as activate them inside this panel (see Figure 12.13). This figure shows a setup with five busses (Bus 1 is by default the master bus) because there are ten outputs on the system used to create this figure. The total number of busses available depends on the total number of physical outputs available on your sound card. Therefore, if you have twenty-four outputs, you will have a total of twelve stereo busses. By default, busses are linked in pairs, and moving one output level fader affects the other. It is possible to have individual control over each output level by breaking this link; however, this does not affect the output configuration. In other words, you can't change the output of one bus output without changing the other output for the same bus.

Figure 12.13
The VST Outputs panel

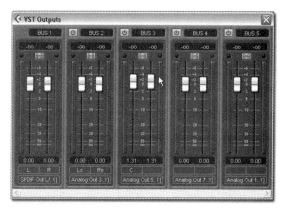

To activate a bus:

▶ In the VST Outputs panel, click the button to the left of the Name field for the desired bus. A bus is active when the button is lit.

To change the physical output assigned to a bus:

▶ In the VST Outputs panel, select the desired output from the available outputs at the bottom of the appropriate bus.

Note that you cannot use an output on more than one bus. Changing the output on one bus that is already assigned to another active bus automatically changes the bus to which this output was assigned as well.

After a bus is active, it becomes available at the bottom of the audio channels in the Mixer window. You can send any audio channel (disk audio, VSTi, Rewire, and group channels) to any active bus (see Figure 12.14). You should understand, however, that the master effects assigned in your project only affect signals passing through the master bus, which is always Bus 1.

Figure 12.14
Selecting a bus in the
Mixer window's audio
channel Output
Selection field

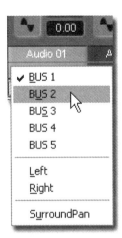

To unlink a bus output fader:

1. Open the VST Outputs panel.
2. Click the Link/Unlink button found between the bus' output level faders.

You can also rename busses inside the VST Outputs panel by clicking where the current bus name exists and entering a new name for this bus.

Saving Mixer Settings

Besides saving the mixer's layout described earlier in the Mixer window's Common panel, there are a few other mixer settings you can save. After a setting is saved, you can load it later, applying these saved settings elsewhere in the Mixer window. Saving mixer settings applies only to audio-related channels: disk, VSTi, Rewire, and groups. These options are available by right-clicking (or Ctrl-clicking on Mac) over an audio channel in the Mixer window. These options include:

▶ **Save Selected Channels**. Saves all the selected channel settings including bus routing.

▶ **Save VST Master, Sends, and VSTi.** Saves the Master setup, VST output bus levels and active status, master mix level, and all assignments and settings in the VST Send Effects and Master Effects panels.

▶ **Save VST Master FX.** Saves the current master effects configuration and settings.

▶ **Save All Mixer Settings.** Saves everything in the current mixer setup.

To load saved mixer settings, you simply need to select the appropriate channel, select the load setting option desired, look for the file on your hard disk, and load it in the Mixer window.

In the same menu, you also have the option to link or unlink channels. When channels are linked, the volume, EQ and send effect settings, the bypass insert, and the bypass send effect settings you apply to one channel also affect all the other channels linked to this channel.

To link or unlink channels in the Mixer window:

1. Select the first channel you want to link. To select a channel, click on its name above the channel Output Selection field.
2. Shift-click on the other channels you want to link with this first channel.
3. Right-click (Ctrl-click on Mac) over one of the selected channels.
4. Select the Link Channels option from the context menu.
5. To unlink them, select one of the linked channels and select Unlink Channels from the same context menu.

You can also customize the behavior of VU-Meter found on audio channels. There are two

▶ **VU-Meter Fast**. Causes the VU-Meter to respond very quickly to peaks in the signal.

▶ **VU-Meter Hold**. Causes the VU-Meter to hold the highest peak detected in the channel for a defined amount of time. How long this time represents depends on your preferences. To change these preferences, select File > Preferences > VST, and then change the value in milliseconds found in the Change VU-Meter Peak's Hold Time field. This can be any value between 500 and 30,000 milliseconds.

Working With Effects

Chapter 6 discusses how you can apply insert effects, send effects, and EQ to a channel through its Inspector area. Working with effects in the Mixer window is no different. The only difference is that all the channels are side by side, making it easier to adjust the different settings of several tracks.

When working on a mix, it is important to understand that the more effects you have running simultaneously in real time (online as opposed to offline), the more processing power it requires from your computer. With this in mind, it is highly recommended to use the send effects as much as possible rather than using the inserts because you can apply the same effect to several channels simultaneously, which uses less computer resources than if you were to use the same effect on several channels as an insert effect.

When you want to see all the effects and EQ settings assigned to a single channel, you may use the Channel Settings panel or the Extended panel in the Mixer window (Cubase SX only).

Channel Settings Panel

The Channel Settings panel offers a convenient way of editing all channel settings in a single window. You can access a Channel Settings panel through the Edit button in the Inspector's Channel section, the Track List area, or in the Mixer window (see Figure 12.15).

Figure 12.15
The Edit button opens
the Channel Settings
panel

Audio Channel Settings

The audio Channel Settings panel for every audio channel offers the same five areas (see Figure 12.16). Here they are from left to right:

▶ The Common panel displays a Mute and Solo button that allows you to see if there are any other tracks that are muted or soloed. If one of these buttons is lit, clicking on it unmutes or removes the Solo mode for all channels. Below these two buttons are the copy channel settings, paste channel settings, and Channel Selection menu. You can use this menu to open another channel from the drop-down list. This replaces the current channel settings with the new selected channel settings. At the bottom, you will find an Initialize Channel button. This brings all channel settings to their default position and removes any active inserts or send effect assignments for this channel.

▶ The audio channel display offers identical settings to the ones found in the Mixer or Channel section of the Inspector area in the Project window. Any changes you make here or anywhere else are reflected in all parts of the project. The options available in this area will vary depending on the type of audio channel displayed.

▶ The audio inserts display the current inserts settings for this channel. As with the audio channel settings, any changes you make here or in any other window in the project update the channel's settings in all windows.

▶ The EQ settings offer a graphical display of the four-band parametric EQ available for each audio channel. See the following section for more information on this area.

▶ The Send Effects Setting panel, as with the inserts, displays the current settings for this channel.

Figure 12.16
The audio Channel
Settings panel

Channel EQ

"EQing" (pronounced "ee-queing") is part of the recording and mixing process in probably 99 percent of recordings today, and at some point in your creation process, you will find it to be a very useful tool. This said, it can be used correctively or creatively. Too much equalization and you might lose the purity of the well-recorded original sound; then again, maybe this is what you were going for. You can use an EQ to increase or decrease specific frequencies to help the general quality of the sound, to correct certain flaws in the recording due to poor microphone performance, to remove noise generated by fluorescent lighting or air conditioning, and in more ways than this chapter allows us to mention. In Cubase, you have four bands of parametric EQ per channel.

The only channels you don't have EQ control on are the master outputs, the busses, and MIDI channels.

Each EQ band gives you control over gain, frequency, and Q.

▶ The Gain control is the amount of gain or reduction that you apply to a frequency. You can add or reduce from + or -24 dB.

▶ The Frequency control determines what frequency is affected by your gain or cut. You can set each band to any frequency between 20 Hz and 20,000 Hz.

▶ The Q is the control you have over the width of the frequency band you want to affect. The lower the numeric values for this field, the larger the width; the higher the numeric values for this field, the narrower the width. Narrow Qs are useful to isolate a problematic frequency, such as a 60 Hz cycle that is often associated with electrical equipment. Use wide Qs to enhance or reduce a large area of the harmonic structure of a sound, such as boosting the high end of the sound.

To adjust the EQ settings for an audio channel:

1. From the Track List area, the Channel section in the Inspector area, or the Mixer window, click the Edit Channel button.

   This launches the Channel Settings panel. Note that Cubase SX users can also adjust EQ settings directly in the Mixer window by displaying the Extended panel of the Mixer window and selecting the EQ panel for the desired channel. The following steps describe the procedure within the Channel Settings panel.

2. To activate a band, click the On button (see Figure 12.17) over the desired EQ band. If you don't activate the band, the changes you make have no effect on the sound.

Figure 12.17
An EQ band is active when the On button is lit

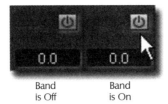

Band
is Off

Band
is On

3. To select a frequency, click and drag the outer ring above the frequency display window for the active band. You can also click in the frequency display to type your frequency or click on the graph above the bands, moving the square handle next to the number corresponding to your band. If you have a scroll wheel on your mouse, you can also use it to change the values inside the numeric field after it is selected.

NOTE
Moving the band's control handle left or right changes the frequency; moving it up or down adds or removes gain from that band. If no band control handles appear, it's because you haven't activated any bands. You can kill two birds with one stone by clicking on the green line to activate the band corresponding to the area where you click and moving the control handle that appears to where you want it.

4. Adjust the gain by clicking and dragging the inner ring above the frequency display or, again, by using either the box in the graph or by clicking in the gain area and typing your value. You can enter a maximum value of - or +24. This corresponds to a cut or boost of 24 dB.

5. To change the Q for the band, you need to use the Q dial found over the Q display. Drag it up to increase or down to decrease the value. You can also click in the Q display area to type your Q value. You can enter any number between 0 and 12. The lo and hi bands have additional settings that were described earlier in Chapter 6.

To hear the sound without the EQ active, and to make sure that the settings you are applying actually help your sound, you can use the EQ Bypass button in the Channel section of this panel.

After you are happy with the result, you can store your settings for later use.

To store an EQ as a preset:

▶ Click the Store button below the hi band. This button displays a folded page with a plus sign inside.

You can recall a preset by clicking the Presets drop-down menu and selecting the desired preset from the list.

To rename a stored EQ preset:

1. Select the preset from the list.

2. Double-click on its name.

3. Type the new name and click OK.

If you want to remove a preset from the list, select it and click the Remove button. This button displays a folded page with a minus sign inside and is to the right of the Store button.

Using Dynamics

Using processing to control the dynamic of an audio channel is very common in today's music production studios. Cubase users who have experienced previous versions of Cubase, such as Cubase VST, will probably remember that dynamic controls were integrated to every disk audio channel. However, in Cubase SX, this has to be added through an insert effect (dynamic control is an exception to the rule that you should use an insert effect rather than a send effect due to the nature of its effect on sound).

Because this is an important part of the mixing and music production process, we look at its application in Cubase. You will find two varieties of dynamic controls included with the software, both of them found under the Dynamics submenu in the plug-ins selection menu: Dynamics and VST Dynamics.

The Dynamics plug-in offers three dynamic controls, including a compressor, an autogate, and a limiter. The VST Dynamics plug-in offers the same controls as its Dynamics counterpart, but with two additional modules: the Auto Level and Soft Clip controls. It also has a fixed signal flow, whereas the Dynamics offers different signal flows through a series of signal flow selection buttons. Finally, the VST Dynamics has a higher inherent latency, so the signals passing through it are delayed. Cubase compensates for this latency when it is used as an insert effect for an audio track, but not as a group, VSTi, or Rewire channel. Therefore, it is recommended that you only use the VST Dynamics plug-in as a master effect and use the Dynamics plug-in instead as an insert effect. If you need the Soft Clip or Auto Level functions of the VST Dynamics plug-in, you can use it as an insert on disk audio channels, just avoid the previously mentioned types of audio channels if you don't want the timing to suffer due to latency or processing issues that might arise as a result.

WHAT IS DYNAMIC CONTROL?

A dynamic control in audio implies that you can modify the peaks and valleys of the amplitude of a sound by adding boundaries, such as a ceiling or a floor. The basic parameters of dynamic controls include:

▶ **Threshold**. This is the point from which a signal is affected. Signals below or above this level are not affected depending on the type of dynamic control you are using.

▶ **Attack**. This determines how quickly the processing is applied to the sound. It acts like an attack part of an envelope; the value you set determines the time it takes for the effect to go from not processing the sound to processing the sound, and it does this gradually. Longer values mean longer attack time; shorter values mean shorter attack time.

▶ **Release**. This determines how long the process lasts after the signal has passed the threshold, has been affected by the processing, and then moves out of the threshold area. Like the attack, this is the tail end of an envelope, and the value you set determines how much time it takes before the processing ends completely. It is also a gradual process. Longer values mean longer release times; shorter values mean shorter release times.

▶ **Ratio**. This determines the amount of processing applied to the sound. As you will see, there are more parameters in the Dynamic Controls window, but these are basic dynamic parameters.

As mentioned before, the Dynamics plug-in offers three different types of dynamic control:

▶ Compress. This is the core of the dynamic world. Use a compressor to reduce the dynamic range between different amplitudes. Amplitude that passes a set threshold is "compressed" at a determined ratio level, such as 2:1, which means that for every two decibels that pass over the threshold level, only one comes out. Therefore, if you have a sound going in a compressor at -2 dB with a threshold value set at -20 and a ratio of 2 to 1, the resulting sound is -11 dB instead (20-2 = 18 dB above the threshold, 18/2=9 dB after the compression ratio is applied, -20+9=-11 dB). The attack time determines how fast the compressor reacts—for fast, aggressive percussive sounds (such as kick drums, snares, and so on), the faster the better. The release time determines how long it should take before the compressor stops compressing between threshold points. Always use your judgment when setting compressor parameters, because your ears are the best tools in setting the compression process properly, as with any other dynamic effect.

▶ AutoGate. With the AutoGate module, you can reduce the amount of low-level noises or sounds. By setting a threshold, you tell the processor to close the gate (or the amplifier), making that sound silent. When the threshold is passed, the gate opens and the sound emerges. Use this dynamic process when you want to remove a noisy guitar amplifier buzzing from a recording when the guitar player is not playing. You will still have the amplifier "buzz" when the guitar player plays, but it will be less noticeable because, hopefully, the guitar sound hides it within its harmonics. With the AutoGate processor, you can set a specific range of frequencies to look for.

▶ Limiter. A limiter makes sure nothing goes beyond the threshold value, and it makes sure that the volume (amplitude) doesn't exceed that prespecified threshold level. Imagine that the limiter is a wall. When a sound attempts to pass through this wall, it bangs into it and stays there. So, if your volume is always near the limiter's threshold, you will not pass the 0 dB limit, but you might hear some distortion.

Figure 12.18
The Dynamics plug-in effect available in the Dynamics submenu of the plug-in selection field

To assign the Dynamics plug-in to an audio channel:

1. Click the insert plug-in selection field in the desired audio channel. This can be done in the Mixer window through the Extended panel, the audio Channel Settings panel, or in the Inserts section of the Inspector area.

2. From the Plug-in drop-down menu, select Dynamics > Dynamics.

You should know at this point that, no matter which dynamic process you are using, it is always a good idea to listen to the result while making your settings. So, set your playback in Cycle mode to loop the area you want to edit.

To set your compressor:

1. Click the Compressor button to activate this module in the Dynamics plug-in.

2. Set your threshold value for the compressor like any other field in this window. Remember that the threshold is the point from which the sound will start to be compressed.

CHAPTER 12

3. Set your ratio to the desired value. You can set this value from 1:1 to 8:1, meaning that for every 8 decibels passing the threshold, only one comes out.

4. Set your attack value to the desired level. This determines how quickly the compressor kicks in after the threshold has been reached. If you're not sure, experiment with this setting while listening to the track.

5. Leave or assign the Release button to Auto. This determines the best release time. If you think of a compressor as a muscle contraction, the release time is the time it takes for your muscle to feel relaxed after a contraction.

6. The MakeUpGain dial allows you to add gain to your output after it has been compressed. This is useful when the amount of compression brings down the sound considerably. You can set this to a value of between 0 dB of compensation up to 24 dB of gain. As a result, your music sounds louder because the lower levels are brought up and the higher levels have been compressed previously by the compressor.

To set the AutoGate process:

1. Start by enabling the AutoGate function by clicking on its button, shown as highlighted (active) in Figure 12.18.

2. Set the slider with a handle under the Trigger Frequency Range area to its Listen position by clicking on the handle and dragging it to the right. This slider has three positions: Off, On, and Listen.

3. Set your low and high frequencies to determine the range for your gate trigger by dragging the vertical handles. You can press Play on your Transport bar to listen to the range being filtered as you are modifying this range.

NOTE

The Trigger Frequency Range slider allows you to select a range of frequencies that can trigger the gate to open. For example, if you don't want to hear a singer's headphone leaking into the microphone, you might want to exclude the high- and low-end frequencies from the gate's trigger frequency range. Any frequency inside the frequency range has the potential to trigger the gate to open, whereas the frequencies outside this range do not affect the gate, keeping it closed, as it should be in this example. The trigger frequency range is located between the two vertical lines and is displayed in green. This range triggers your gate to open.

4. Now that you have set the range, bring the slider below the trigger frequency range to the On position. If you have a constant, low-level noise in your recording, you can use the Calibrate button under the Threshold knob found in the AutoGate function.

5. Start the playback of the project where there are no actual instruments recorded and click the Calibrate button to determine the optimized threshold level to remove (gate) the noise from the sound. If you find that it cuts into your desired program material, change the value manually by clicking the Threshold knob and dragging it up or down.

6. Set the attack function to Predict mode. The button is lit when activated, as shown in Figure 12.18. This optimizes your attack speed—the speed at which the amplifier opens when the threshold has been reached.

7. Set the hold value by dragging the mouse over the Hold knob to have the gate hold the doors open for the time set in the numerical display below this button. If you set this value too high, the gate stays open and you might hear noise from the original sound coming in.

8. Set the release to auto by clicking the Auto button. This determines the best release time, or in other words, the optimal amount of time it takes for the gate's doors to close.

TIP

You can use AutoGate in Listen mode to get EQ effects resembling a very narrow band-pass filter, such as a 1930s radio or telephone line simulation. Note that you cannot automate this parameter.

To set the Limit:

1. Click the Limit button to activate it.

2. Set the threshold value for the limiter. This is the uppermost amplitude value your signal will reach. Any part of the sound that was recorded over this threshold setting is limited at the output. Note that too much limiting might create distortion in your signal.

3. Set the Release to Auto.

MIDI Channel Settings

The MIDI Channel Settings panel offers a convenient way to edit all MIDI channel settings for a selected MIDI channel in a single window. You can access a Channel Settings panel through the Edit button in the Inspector's Channel section, the Track List area, or in the Mixer window (see Figure 12.15).

The MIDI Channel Settings panel offers four areas (see Figure 12.19). Here they are from left to right:

▶ The Common panel displays the same options as the audio Channel Settings panel. Please refer to that section for more details.

▶ The MIDI channel display offers identical settings to the ones found in the Mixer or Channel section of the Inspector area in the Project window. Any changes you make here or anywhere else are reflected in all parts of the project.

▶ The MIDI inserts displays the current inserts settings for this channel. As with the MIDI channel settings, any changes you make here or in any other window in the project update the channel's settings in all windows.

▶ The Send Effects Setting panel, as with the inserts, displays the current settings for this channel.

Figure 12.19
The MIDI Channel
Settings panel

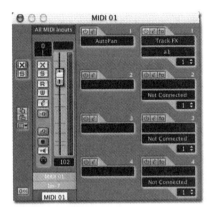

Using Groups

The benefits of using groups were described earlier in this chapter. This section describes how to use a group in a mix situation.

A group channel appears in the Mixer window whenever a group track is created. After a group track is created, you can assign the output of other tracks to a group channel in the Mixer window. Group channels can, therefore, be useful to create submixes, in which a series of related tracks are mixed and sent to a group. You can then use the group's fader as a general level control for all tracks routed to this group.

To use a group as a submix group fader:

1. Start by creating a group track in the Project window.
2. Name this group appropriately. In Figure 12.20, the group is called DrumKit.

Figure 12.20
Naming your group
helps to identify it later
when assigning
channels

3. Open the Mixer window.
4. Select the channel you want to send to the group channel.
5. At the bottom of the selected channel, select the group's name from the channel's Output Selection field. In Figure 12.21, the Toms channel is sent to the DrumKit group.
6. Repeat Steps 4–5 for all the channels you want to send to this group.

Figure 12.21
Selecting a group as the
output for a channel

Now that you have assigned different channels to a group, you can adjust their relative level and use the group's channel fader to adjust the overall level being sent to the master fader.

You can also create a monitor mix that can be sent to a headphones amplifier through the channel settings send effects plug-in selection field. Instead of sending the signal of this channel to a plug-in, you can route the signal to a group channel, and then assign the output of this group channel to another available bus. Using this method allows you to send each channel to two sets of outputs, giving you an independent control on levels being sent to each output. Note that you need at least two sets of outputs on your sound card to use this effectively.

To use a group as a monitor mix (for headphones or external effect processing):

1. Start by repeating the first three steps from the previous technique: create a group track, name it, open the Mixer window, and select the channel you want to send to a monitor mix.

2. Click the channel's Edit button. Cubase SX users can also use the Extended panel in the Mixer window and display the Send Effects panel for each channel.

3. In the Channel Settings panel, select an empty send effect slot.

4. In this empty effect slot, select the appropriate group as the send effect destination. In Figure 12.22, the group is named DrumKit.

CHAPTER 12

Figure 12.22

Assigning a group
channel as a send effect

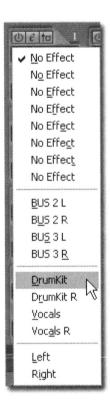

5. Adjust the level being sent to the send effect (in this case, the group output channel).

6. If you want to send another channel to a send effect assigned to a group, use the Select Channel menu in the Channel Settings' Common panel. If you are in the Extended panel (Cubase SX users), simply select another channel.

7. Repeat Steps 3–6 for each additional channel you want to send to this subgroup mix.

8. Go back to the Mixer window.

9. Select the output bus for the group at the bottom of the Channel Settings panel. If you want to use this as a separate mix, you should not assign your group's output to Bus 1, especially if the channels being sent to it are assigned to this bus.

10. Adjust the level of the group being sent to this bus. You can also adjust the output level of bus.

TIP

If you don't want to have to assign individual channels to a group through send effects in each channel, you can create a submix group. Let's take our previous example of the DrumKit group; you assign all channels to this group. Then, you create a second group that you call something like "Headphone Mix." All you need to do is assign the send effect for the DrumKit group to the Headphone Mix output, and then you assign the Headphone Mix output to another bus, and voilà! (See Figure 12.23 for a diagram of this example.)

Figure 12.23
Example displaying how the signal travels when using a group as a headphone submix

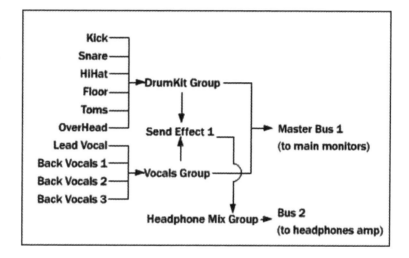

Now You Try It

It's time to put the topics covered in this chapter into action—you can download a practice exercise at http://www.muskalipman.com.

13

Working With Automation

Mixing a recording is an art form unto itself—the art of listening. Being a great musician doesn't mean you're going to be a great mixing engineer, and being a great mixer doesn't mean you will be a great musician.

No matter what your speciality, the goal is to get everything in perfect balance. The mixing process inside Cubase is not unlike the traditional mixing process in the sense that external mixer desks have many of the same features as Cubase offers. Where Cubase shines is through its integration of traditional mixing techniques and the addition of real-time effect processing and automation.

Cubase provides support for VST effects that come with the program or those bought as plug-ins, and it also provides support for third-party DirectX effects (under the Windows environment). These can produce the same result as VST effects, but are a little more CPU intensive than their VST counterpart because they were written using different standards. Because VST plug-ins have been written for Cubase (but are also compatible with Logic), this type of plug-in is more effective inside Cubase than DirectX. On this note, be aware that to use DirectX effects, you need to have a DirectX-compatible computer and the latest DirectX support available. You also need to install those third-party DirectX effects on your computer.

TIP
Make sure to consult Steinberg's Web site to find out which DirectX version you need and to verify that the other plug-ins you have support the same DirectX drivers. DirectX technology applies only if you have the PC version of Cubase.

In this chapter, you will:

▶ Learn to use the Mixer window to record mix automation events

▶ Learn to use the automation subtracks to record mix automation events

▶ Find out how to create and edit plug-in parameter automation

▶ Discover how to edit recorded automation

▶ Learn how to use SysEx to automate external MIDI devices

▶ Find out how to use external MIDI remote controllers with Cubase in a mix automation setting

Mixer Automation Settings

The channel mixer automation affects the way audio events are played, and the computer is responsible for this processing, whereas MIDI automation is processed by the MIDI instrument. There are three sets of automation that you can apply: MIDI channel settings automation, audio channel settings automation, and global settings automation. The audio setting affects the channel, and the global setting influences any channels that are routed through this setting. Table 13.1 displays a list of what you can automate in the Mixer window:

Table 13.1
Parameters available for automation in the Mixer window

MIDI Channel Settings	Audio Channel Settings	Global Settings
Volume	Volume	Master volume controls
Pan	Pan	Master send effect input levels
Mute	Mute	Program selection and parameters of send effects
Track parameter EQ on/off switches	Bypass button	Program selection and parameters of master effects
Transpose	The settings for up to 4 EQ modules	Program selection and parameters of VSTi
Velocity shift	Effect send activation switch	One plug-in automation track for each automated send and master effects, as well as VSTi
Random settings	Effect send levels	
Range settings	Effect send pre/post switch	
Insert effects bypass switches and parameters	Effect send bypass switch	
Send effects bypass switches and parameters	Insert effect program selection	

Cubase is a multitrack recorder and a MIDI sequencer that integrates both types of channels inside the same mixing environment as described in Chapter 12. Because some MIDI tracks might be assigned to VSTi or Rewire compatible applications, this creates additional channels inside your Mixer window: one for the MIDI volume level and another for audio related controls, which also includes a volume level fader. To avoid confusion when mixing levels for these specific channels, you should only use the audio channel to control pan and volume levels when mixing VSTi and Rewire instruments. Otherwise, it is difficult to pinpoint exactly where to change things if you start automating both MIDI and audio volume levels.

We have discussed the Mixer window before, so its options should be familiar to you by now. However, we have looked at how to move faders or pans and how to add effects, but not how to automate these movements. Unlike traditional mixers, Cubase VST allows you to record most of the manipulations you make inside the mixing environment, including, to a certain degree, effect automation.

Track Automation Settings

Automating inside Cubase is not limited to the Mixer window. You can also add automation to the automation tracks available in each track in the Project window (see Figure 13.1). Automation parameters can be displayed in several ways:

To view automation subtracks:

▶ Click the plus sign in the lower-left corner of the desired track in the Track List area of the Project window.

▶ Or, right-click (Ctrl+click on Mac) over the track in the Track List area and select the Show Automation, Show Used Automation, or Show Used Automation for All Tracks options from the context menu.

Figure 13.1
Automation subtracks are always displayed under the track they are associated with; an automation line is displayed over a background representation of the content currently playing in the track

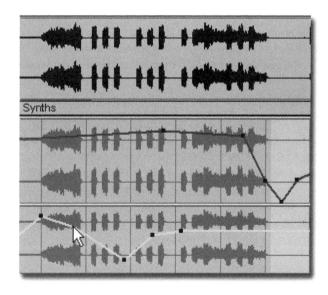

Automation recorded in these subtracks is not different than the automation recorded in the Mixer window. The only difference is the way you record these events. When automation is recorded or edited in one location, it is updated in the other location as well.

Cubase offers three types of automation tracks: channel track automation, plug-in track automation, and Master track automation. Each track type displays a number of subtracks associated with its type. The subtracks available depend on the settings available. For example, a MIDI track does not have the same automation subtracks as an audio channel because you can't automate the same parameters. The automatable parameters are described in the previous section, "Track Automation Settings."

▶ Channel track automation. You will find channel automation subtracks for each audio, MIDI, group, VSTi, or Rewire track created in a project. Each automatable parameter has its own subtrack. Channel track automation includes all track parameters including insert effects, but excluding send effects parameters. However, the send level to send effects is included in this type of track automation.

▶ Plug-in track automation. There is an additional automation track created for each automated plug-in parameter assigned as a send effect or master effect, as well as for VSTi parameter automation. In other words, if you automate parameters for three send effects plug-ins, two master effects, and five VST Instruments, you have a total of ten additional plug-in automation tracks. Each one of these automation tracks has as many automation subtracks as there are available automatable parameters.

▶ Master track automation. There is only one master automation track in a project. As with other automation tracks, it contains a number of additional subtracks to represent each automatable parameter, such as the additional bus output levels and master send effects input levels (levels that are sent from the master output to the input of master effects).

Figure 13.2 displays at the top, the Master Automation folder, which contains the VST Mixer automation track. The Effect Automation folder contains the plug-in send effects automation tracks. In this case, the Chorus send effect plug-in has two subtracks shown—one for the Mix parameter and another for the Delay parameter. At the bottom is the VST Instrument Automation folder, which holds the automation tracks for the VST Instruments you automated parameters for. The LM-7's volume slider, inside the LM-7's interface, and the Vol1 parameter, which represents the volume level for the first pad on the LM-7, offer different controls over volume. In the LM7's case, you have four separate volume automation controls: one through the MIDI track's volume, another through the audio channel's volume control inside the mixer, a third one through the LM-7's volume fader (which is treated as a VSTi parameter), and a fourth volume control for each pad or instrument in the LM-7 itself. This gives you great freedom over automation control, but with freedom comes great responsibility. You have to make decisions when handling automation and find a method that suits you and stick with it; otherwise, you will generate automation events that add confusion to your mixing process, not make it simpler, as it was intended to be.

Figure 13.2
Examples of the master, effect, and VSTi automation tracks

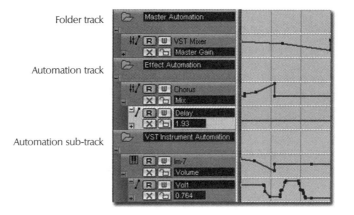

Folder track

Automation track

Automation sub-track

Recording Automation

Because you can record automation in the Mixer window as well as by using automation tracks and subtracks, we look at these two methods separately. If you are using an external control surface to control specific parameters inside Cubase, you will probably find that recording automation is easier when done through the control surface rather than adding events in the automation tracks associated with each channel in the Project window. On the other hand, editing previously recorded automation might be easier if done through the Project window.

Before heading into the automation section itself, let's point out that you can set the levels and pans of audio channels in the VST Channel Mixer without using automation, just as you would on a normal mixer desk, to monitor your tracks appropriately. As long as the Write or Read Automation buttons (found in the Common panel on the left of the Channel Mixer window) are not activated (not lit), the faders, pan, and any other effect settings stay at the same position.

Using Read and Write Buttons

To record your mix automation using the Mixer window, the Channel Settings panel, or the Channel section found in the Inspector area, you need to use both Read and Write Automation buttons to achieve your goal. To activate the automation writing process, click the Write Automation button of the desired channel. Clicking this button in any of the mentioned areas activates the same function in all subsequent windows where the channel is represented (the Inspector area, the Track List area, the Channel Settings panel, and the Mixer window). By clicking the Write Automation button directly in the channel, you activate the writing automation functions for this channel only. On the other hand, if you want to activate the write channel automation for all channels at once, you can use the Global Write Automation button found in the Common panel of the Mixer window, as demonstrated in Figure 13.3. Which one you use depends on what you want to achieve.

Figure 13.3
The difference between the channel's Write Automation button and the Global Write Automation button in the Common panel of the Mixer window

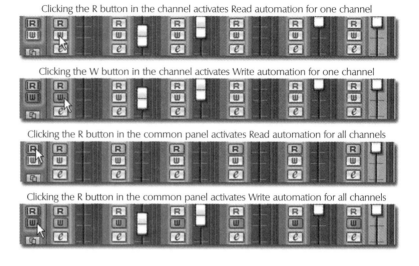

Clicking the R button in the channel activates Read automation for one channel

Clicking the W button in the channel activates Write automation for one channel

Clicking the R button in the common panel activates Read automation for all channels

Clicking the R button in the common panel activates Write automation for all channels

After you have recorded automation, you need to activate or enable the Read Automation button for Cubase to read whatever automation you have recorded. Otherwise, the information is present, but your automation is not read. As with the Write Automation button, the Read Automation button is found in several windows inside your project and enabling it on a channel in one window enables it in all the other windows as well. The Global Read Automation button found in the Common panel of the Mixer window also activates the read option for all channels in the mixer at once.

Recording Channel Track Automation

This section describes how to record channel track automation. This includes any channel settings mentioned earlier in this chapter, including MIDI and audio channel settings. The actual settings you can record are determined by the track type itself.

To record channel automation:

1. Open the Mixer window (F3 is the default key command).
2. Activate the channel's Write Automation button. This button is lit when active.
3. Position your playback cursor and click the Play button on the Transport bar (or press the space bar).
4. Move the appropriate faders, knobs, switches, and so on (this includes any settings mentioned in Table 13. 1 in the Channel Settings column).
5. Stop the playback.
6. Activate the Read Automation button.
7. Click the Play button to see (and hear) your recorded automation.

After your automation is recorded, you can use the channels' automation subtracks to view each setting that was automated. We get into this a little later in this chapter.

CHAPTER 13

Recording Plug-In Automation

Recording parameter changes in a plug-in effect, such as a VSTi or send effect, is quite similar to recording channel settings in track automation. However, these automation events are recorded in separate tracks and subtracks, created automatically as soon as you move one of the controls of an effect or VSTi when the Write Automation button is activated inside the plug-in itself (this can be a VSTi or VST effect plug-in; PC users cannot automate DirectX effect plug-in parameters). This type of automation is normally used to change the parameters of effects or a VSTi, creating dynamic changes in the plug-in through time during playback. For example, you can automate the Cutoff frequency by moving this parameter in the VST Instrument's panel (provided there is such a parameter on the instrument itself).

To record plug-in parameter automation:

1. Open the desired effect's panel.

2. Activate the Write Automation button found inside the panel. This button is lit when active.

3. Position your playback cursor and click the Play button on the Transport bar (or press the space bar).

4. Move the appropriate faders, knobs, switches, and so on. You might need to consult the documentation provided with the effect itself to find out which parameters are automatable as this varies from one effect to the next (see an example in Figure 13.4, featuring the a1 synthesizer VSTi plug-in).

5. Stop the playback.

6. Activate the Read Automation button inside the effect panel.

7. Click the Play button to see (and hear) your recorded automation.

Figure 13.4
Moving the Attack parameter in this example while the Write Automation button is active and the project is playing records the changes through time to this parameter

Recording Master Track Automation

The principal behind recording Master track automation and the previous two types of automation remains the same. Recorded automation for the master output, any active busses, and any effect send to effect levels within the Master Effects section is added as automation tracks (and subtracks) inside a Master Automation folder in the Project window.

To record Master track automation:

1. Make sure the Master button on the Transport panel is active (lit).
2. Open the Mixer window (F3 is the default key command).
3. Activate the Master output's Write Automation button. This button is lit when active. You can also use the Global Write Automation button in the Common panel of the Mixer window.
4. Position your playback cursor and click the Play button on the Transport bar (or press the space bar).
5. Move the appropriate faders, knobs, switches, and so on (this includes any settings mentioned in Table 13. 1 in the Master Settings column). To automate the bus outputs, open the VST Outputs panel (F4 is the default key command).
6. Stop the playback.
7. Activate the Read Automation button.
8. Click the Play button to see (and hear) your recorded automation.

About Automation Modes

In Cubase SL, there is only one automation mode available. This is called Touch Fader mode. In this mode, the program starts writing automation as soon as you click a control, such as the volume fader, and stops writing when you release the mouse button.

In Cubase SX, there are two additional automation modes: Autolatch and X-Over. In Autolatch mode, the program starts writing the automation as soon as you click a control, such as the volume fader, and stops writing when you deactivate the Write Automation button. In other words, the last automation value is continuously written until you turn off the Write Automation button within the channel mixer found in the Inspector area or in the Mixer window. This mode is useful if you want to write over a long section that contains previously recorded automation that you want to replace. It is also useful when using an external control surface to control your mix. Because the software has no way of knowing which control you want to rewrite, it starts writing as soon as you move a control and keeps the value sent by this control until you stop playback or you switch the Write Automation button off. Make sure, however, that you don't touch any other controls when doing this; otherwise, you might end up replacing automation by mistake.

X-Over mode works much like the Autolatch mode, with one exception: When you cross a previously recorded automation curve, the write process is automatically turned off.

To change the automation mode (in Cubase SX only):

1. In the Project window, click the Automation Mode Selection field in the toolbar (see Figure 13.5).

Figure 13.5
The Automation Mode
Selection field in the
Project window's
toolbar; this option is
only available in Cubase
SX

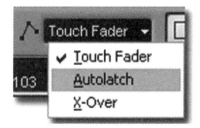

2.   Select the desired automation mode from the drop-down menu.

Using Automation Tracks

An alternative to using the Write Automation button is offered through automation tracks and subtracks associated with each channel in a project. This method of adding automation to events in a track allows you to see the events on the track; therefore, you can more easily insert automation at specific locations by drawing them in using the tools at your disposal. Because you are actually drawing in this automation, we call the following sections discussing how to add automation accordingly.

After automation has been added to a track, you need to enable the Read Automation button for the track containing this automation, otherwise, Cubase does not reproduce the events recorded.

Drawing Channel Track Automation

This section describes how to add automation to any audio, MIDI, VSTi, or Rewire channel automation or group channel settings automation.

To draw channel settings automation values in an automation track:

1.   In the Project window's Track List area, select the track for which you want to create automation events.

2.   In the bottom-left corner of the selected track, click the Show/Hide Automation button (plus sign) to reveal the first automation subtrack (as shown in Figure 13.6).

Figure 13.6
Revealing automation
tracks in the Project
window

3.   Select the desired parameter you want to automate from the Parameter field (in Figure 13.6, this field displays the Volume parameter). If the parameter you want to automate doesn't appear in this list, click the More option to display a dialog box revealing additional automatable parameters available for this track, select the one you want, and click OK to return to the subtrack. At this point, the Parameter field should display the selected parameter.

4. If there are currently no automation values that have been added to this parameter, a black horizontal line appears next to this subtrack in the Event Display area. Click the Draw tool to select it.

5. To add a handle, click near the location inside this lane where you want to add an automation value. The line automatically becomes blue and the Read Automation button is active. If you want to create a ramp between two points, release the mouse. However, if you want to create a curve, drag your mouse to the next desired location and value (see Figure 13.7).

Figure 13.7
An example of a ramp created between two separate points (left) and a curve created by additional handles added as a result of dragging your mouse (right)

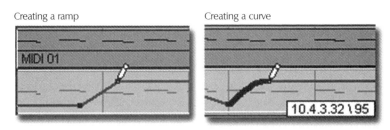

Creating a ramp

Creating a curve

6. Repeat Step 5 to add more automation handles along this parameter's subtrack.

If you want to create automation events to another parameter for the same channel, you can either select another parameter from the Parameter field to display a new parameter in the same subtrack or click the Append Automation Track button as displayed in Figure 13.8. When the new subtrack is visible, repeat Steps 3–6 from the previous list.

Figure 13.8
Clicking the plus sign in the lower-left corner of an automation subtrack reveals a second automation subtrack for this channel, effectively appending the automation track

Note that choosing a different parameter in a subtrack that already contains automation does not remove or cancel the automation it holds. When a parameter contains recorded automation events, an asterisk appears after this parameter's name in the Parameter field of the automation subtrack.

Figure 13.9
Parameters with
recorded automation
events appear with an
asterisk in the Parameter
field

After you've recorded automation on a track, you can select the Show Used Automation option available in the Track List's context menu (right-click on PC or Ctrl-click on Mac). So, you can add automation to several parameters using a single subtrack, changing the parameter's name to view or add new automation, and after you are done, reveal all automation events. Each parameter has its own subtrack.

Using Draw Shapes

Under the Draw tool are several shape tools: the Line, Parabola, Sine, Triangle, and Square tools. As described in Chapter 8, these tools can be used to create automation values, such as pan effects. However, using the Parabola and Line tool, you can create consistent automation curves instead of drawing handles freely.

Figure 13.10
Using the Draw tools (in
this example, the
Parabola tool) to create
automation curves

Using the parabola to draw a fade

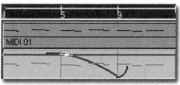

Resulting automation

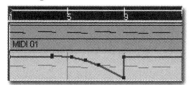

Drawing Plug-in Track Automation

To draw plug-in track automation, you need to enable the Write Automation button on this plug-in, otherwise, there won't be any tracks for you to draw in new automation values because an automation track for plug-ins is automatically created when the Write Automation button is enabled. If the Write Automation button is not enabled, a plug-in will not have an automation track.

1

plug-in automation values in an automation track:

1. Click the Write Automation button in the Plug-in panel for which you want to create an automation track, or add a plug-in to this existing folder track if you already recorded plug-in automations. In the example provided in Figure 13.11, there are two plug-in effects containing automation events and both of them are visible in the Inspector area when selecting the Effect Automation folder track. You can also see that both tracks in the Track List area are appropriately named Flanger and StepFilter, which represents the name of the effects that are currently automated. If you don't see the tracks inside a folder, click the Expand/Collapse Folder button of the folder track.

Figure 13.11
Each plug-in automation track is placed inside the Effect Automation folder track

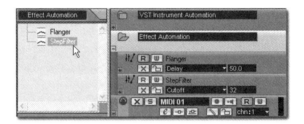

2. Select the desired parameter you want to automate from the Parameter field (in Figure 13.11, the Flanger's Parameter field displays the Delay parameter). If the parameter you want to automate doesn't appear in this list, click the More option to display a dialog box revealing additional automatable parameters available for this track, select the one you want, and click OK to return to the subtrack. At this point, the Parameter field should display the selected parameter.

3. Select the appropriate tool from the Project window's toolbar.

4. Click in the automation track to add automation points. This is done exactly the same way as with channel track automation.

5. Repeat Step 4 to add more automation handles along this parameter's subtrack.

Drawing Master Track Automation

To add Master track automation by drawing events in automation tracks:

1. Right-click (Ctrl-click on Mac) over the Track List area.

2. Select the Add Master Automation Track option. If your project already has one, Cubase warns you that you can't create a second one. In this case, locate the folder track containing the Master automation tracks.

3. Proceed exactly as described in Steps 2–5 from the previous description.

Hiding and Removing Automation Subtracks

When working with automation, you can hide automation tracks that you don't need to see to clear up your working area. Hiding automation subtracks does not prevent automation from being read. If you don't want to hear the changes made by automation, simply turn the Read Automation button off. At any time, you can also mute a specific type of automation by clicking the appropriate Mute button in the subtrack's Track List area. For example, Figure 13.12 displays the Pan parameter automation as muted, whereas the Volume parameter automation is not muted. This means that the track plays the volume automation, but not the pan automation.

Figure 13.12
Muting only one
parameter using the
subtrack's Mute button

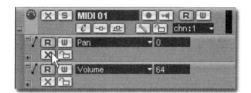

To hide automation subtracks:

▶ To hide all automation subtracks, select the Hide All Automation option from the context menu that appears after right-clicking (Ctrl-clicking on Mac) over the Track List area.

▶ To hide all automation for one track, click the Show/Hide Automation button for this track (the minus sign in the lower-left corner of the track containing the automation subtracks).

▶ To hide only one automation subtrack, click the Show/Hide Automation button of the subtrack above it (the minus sign in the lower-left corner of the subtrack containing the automation you want to hide).

To remove automation subtracks:

▶ To erase all automation events for a subtrack's parameter, select the Remove Parameter option from the Parameter field of this subtrack.

▶ To remove unused subtracks that might have been left behind after editing, select the Remove Unused Parameters option from the Parameter field in one of the subtracks.

Editing Automation

After you've recorded automation, editing it is not very different. You can use the Mixer window to edit this automation through the Write/Read Automation buttons or by editing the recorded automation parameters in their respective automation subtracks. As mentioned earlier when describing the automation modes, Cubase SX users can switch between these modes to use the mode that best suits their editing needs.

To view the automation previously recorded:

1.   In the Project window, right-click (Ctrl-click on Mac) in the Track List area.

2.   Select the Show Used Automation option from the context menu.

You will probably notice that some parameters do not allow intermediate values. This is the case for switch type parameters, such as a Mute, Bypass, or Foot Pedal MIDI message. Because these parameters are either on or off, there are only two acceptable values: 0 or 127. When editing their automation, you can only enter these values.

Using Write Automation

To edit already recorded automation using the Write Automation button on a channel, you just need to write over the automation again. As soon as you touch the control (by clicking on it and holding it or moving it to a new location), the old automation is replaced by the new one, until you release the mouse. At that point, if the Read Automation button is also active, Cubase continues reading the automation as it appears on the parameter's automation subtrack.

Using Automation Tracks and Subtracks

When you open a parameter subtrack containing recorded automation, you will notice that points appear along the automation line. Here's a look at how you can edit the points on this line:

To edit recorded automation in a parameter automation subtrack:

▶   **To move an existing point**. In the Project window, select the Object Selection tool and move the point to a new location by clicking and dragging this point to the new desired location. Note that the quantize grid settings, if the Snap to Grid option is active, influence where in time you can move this automation.

▶   **To move several automation points simultaneously**. With the Object Selection tool, drag a selection box over the points you want to move. The selected points become red. Click and drag one of the selected points to the new location. You can also Shift-click on several points if you want to edit noncontinuous points instead.

▶   **To draw over an existing automation**. In the Project window, select the Draw, Line, Parabola, Sine, Triangle, or Square tool from the toolbar and click where you want to start drawing over the existing automation and drag your tool until the point where you want to stop replacing the existing automation. The first and last point where you draw this automation automatically creates a connection to the existing automation line. You can use the different options associated with each tool to create different shapes, for example, use the Ctrl (Command on Mac) key to invert the parabola curve.

▶   **To erase existing automation points**. Click on the point or drag a range over several points using the Object Selection tool. After the desired points are red, press Delete or Backspace on your keyboard to erase them.

▶   **To move or erase all automation points on a subtrack**. Right-click (Ctrl-click on Mac) over the desired subtrack's Track List area and select the Select All Events option from the context menu. After selected, you can move or erase these points. Note that if you want to remove all automation for a parameter, you can also use the Remove Parameter option from the subtrack's Parameter field.

You can also use the Browse Project window to edit automation as you would edit any other events in your project (see Figure 13.13). Simply expand the track to reveal the automation events, and then select the automation parameter in the Project Structure panel to reveal the list of events it holds in the right panel. Then, you can select a value and change it in the list. If the Sync Selection option is checked in the Browse Project window's toolbar, Cubase displays the event you are editing in the Project window as well.

Figure 13.13
Editing automation in the Browse Project window

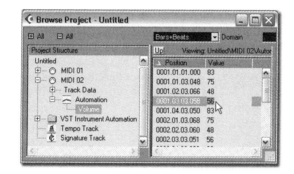

Using SysEx

SysEx (System Exclusive) is used to send data that is specific to a MIDI device, such as a dump of its patch memory, sequencer data, waveform data, or information that is particular to a device. In other words, SysEx is used to change MIDI device parameters that no other MIDI message can because it is the only way MIDI can retrieve or send parameter data from and to a device.

When working with Cubase, SysEx can serve two main purposes:

▶ You can save all the parameters of a MIDI device used in a project using a bulk dump procedure.

▶ Because you can't automate the parameters of an external MIDI device using automation tracks, you can use SysEx to record parameter changes on your device's front panel into Cubase, and then have Cubase play back these parameter changes through MIDI.

You could say that SysEx allows you to control *how* sounds are produced, whereas other MIDI events allow you to control *when* sounds are produced. You do have some control over how a note is played with MIDI events, such as the control provided by Control Change messages; however, this does not affect, in most commonly used situations, how the sound is produced by your MIDI device.

It is important that a direct MIDI connection between the sender and the receiver be made. You can work with SysEx messages even with devices in a daisy chain; however, this requires extra precautions, such as assigning a different device ID number for each device in the chain, making sure that the base MIDI channel in your external MIDI device is also different from one device to the next in this chain. These precautions help make sure that the MIDI device you meant to communicate with only processes the SysEx messages.

Recording SysEx

There are two reasons you would record SysEx. The first reason is to save all the values that make up, for example, one program, or all programs in the instrument or device so that when you play a project, it remembers the external device's setup. This includes how the device's parameters are configured, especially when you've made changes to the original sounds provided by the manufacturer. This allows you to recall the device's parameters, as they were when you saved the song. The next time you load your project, you won't have to change anything on your device when you load the project because the parameters were stored with the project file using SysEx. This is called a bulk dump.

The second reason is to store codes that instruct the instrument to change one of its settings, such as the cutoff frequency of a filter, or the decay of a reverb during playback or at the beginning of the project. System Exclusive can be used as a last resort for things that can't be done with regular MIDI messages. This is done through SysEx parameter changes.

Recording a Bulk Dump

Usually, you will find a function or utility button on the front panel of your MIDI device, which allows you to send a bulk dump. This means that you will be sending SysEx messages. From that point, you can choose what kind of information you want to send. For example, you might send user patches, performances, or system settings. If there are no such buttons on your device, there are two workaround solutions:

▶ Get an editor/librarian software that identifies your device and initiates a SysEx bulk dump request from this application. This allows your software to receive the appropriate SysEx information from your external MIDI device.

▶ Find out what message to send to the device to make it dump its settings via a MIDI output. Use the List Editor in Cubase to insert that message in a MIDI track. Writing such a SysEx string is fairly complicated, and requires an extensive study of the fine print in the operation manual; so if in doubt, stick with the first method and get an editor/librarian—it'll save you lots of headaches.

Because your MIDI device stores values for its parameter in its memory, changing these values results in changing the parameter's settings as well. Usually, your MIDI device can send all or some of these parameters to Cubase using what is called a bulk dump. This action is performed using SysEx messages.

After your device's SysEx has been dumped into Cubase, you can send it back to the device later to reset all the parameters to the way they were when you saved them. Most hardware MIDI devices have specific functions that allow you to send a bulk dump of all or some of your device's parameters. To find out which function or where this function is, you need to consult your device's documentation.

To record a SysEx bulk dump from an external MIDI device into Cubase:

1. Make sure the MIDI Out of your device is connected to the MIDI In of your computer or Cubase.

2. Inside Cubase, select the Preferences option in the File menu. This brings up the Preferences dialog box (see Figure 13.14).

3. Deselect the SysEx check box under the Record section and leave it checked (default) under the Thru section. This allows you to record it and play it back normally, but does not echo the SysEx events back to the MIDI device as it is transmitting it. Otherwise, it creates a SysEx MIDI loop that could corrupt the transport.

4. Click Apply, and then click OK to close the dialog box.

Figure 13.14
The MIDI Filtering
option in Cubase

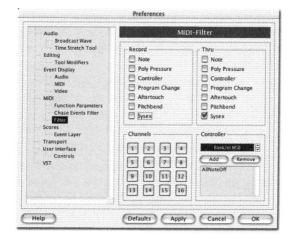

5. Create a new MIDI track in your project. This track should be used only for the SysEx events.

6. Assign the MIDI input port appropriately. This should be the port used by the MIDI device to send SysEx to Cubase.

7. Position your cursor at the beginning of your project. Make sure the Metronome click and Cycle Recording mode are disabled.

8. If you already have events recorded in this project, mute all the tracks. When recording a bulk dump of your device's parameters, the SysEx messages require a large portion of your MIDI bandwidth.

9. Click the Record button on the Transport panel.

10. Press the appropriate buttons on your MIDI device to initiate the bulk dump. You might notice during the transmission that your device displays a special message on its LCD screen telling you it's currently transmitting SysEx. When the device is finished with its transmission, you should see a message, such as "Done" or "Completed."

11. When the external MIDI device has completed the bulk dump, you can stop the recording. Depending on the information you transmitted in this bulk dump (if it's just a few parameters or the entire set of parameters in your device), this process might take a few seconds or a few minutes. This creates a single MIDI part, which contains all the SysEx messages.

12. Save the project.

13. Mute this track to avoid having the SysEx retransmitted every time you click Play, or select the Not Connected option from the MIDI Output Port selection field in the Inspector or Track List area for this track.

Here are some tips when recording SysEx bulk dumps:

▶ Just record the parameters you need to record. Usually, you can tell your MIDI device what type of bulk dump you want to perform. This saves space in your sequencer and speeds up the SysEx transfer back to your MIDI device. In a live performance, you don't want to wait too long between projects for SysEx to be uploaded to your MIDI devices, so keeping things to a minimum is useful.

▶ If you only want Cubase to send parameter information and patch information to your external MIDI device before a song starts to play, put the SysEx information before the first bar if possible, or before the occurrence of MIDI events in your song. This prevents you from having lags in MIDI sent to your devices caused by a long SysEx message being sent simultaneously with other MIDI events.

▶ If all you want to do is change the sound settings (program) during playback, you might be better off creating two different programs and using a program change during playback rather than using a SysEx message. Program changes are more efficient in this case and take less time to update your external MIDI device.

▶ Avoid sending SysEx bulk dump from Cubase to several external MIDI devices simultaneously.

▶ Make sure when you record a bulk dump, that you are using the same Device ID number as you will use when sending this bulk dump back to the MIDI device. Otherwise, the device might not accept the SysEx bulk dump.

▶ Certain sequencers allow you to send a SysEx bulk dump automatically whenever you load a MIDI file. Use this feature to configure your devices appropriately for each song.

Recording Parameter Automation Through SysEx

If you only want to record certain parameter changes, you can proceed in a similar way. This is useful if you want to change a parameter during playback. Remember that MIDI is transmitted over a serial cable, which implies that information is sent one after the other, not side by side. In the case of SysEx, the entire SysEx message has to be transmitted before the rest of the MIDI messages can resume their course. So, if you want to record SysEx parameter changes as you are playing notes, the more SysEx messages you are sending, the longer it takes for the other events to be transmitted. So keep your SysEx events as short as possible, or if you can, make sure not to overload your MIDI port with this type of message.

To record parameter changes into Cubase during playback using SysEx messages:

1. Make sure the MIDI Out of your device is connected to the MIDI In of your computer or sequencer.

2. You might need to disable any SysEx filters from your sequencer's MIDI filter options as mentioned in the bulk dump procedure described earlier.

3. Create a new MIDI track in your project where you want to record the SysEx. You could record SysEx parameter changes in the same track as the rest of your MIDI messages being sent to this device, but it is not recommended.

4. Chances are, if you want to update parameters during playback, you probably already have a MIDI track with recorded events. At this point, you'll want to hear this track if you want to update the parameters for the sound used in this track, so make sure this track is not muted.

5. Position your cursor at the appropriate location and click the Record button on the Transport panel.

6. Make the changes to your external MIDI device's parameters when it is appropriate in the project.

7. Stop the recording process when done.

8. Rewind and start playback to hear the result.

Because you recorded the SysEx events on another track, if you are not satisfied with the result, you can always erase these events and start over without affecting the other types of events recorded for this part. For example, let's say you have a synth line playing on MIDI port A, channel 1, and you want to change the cutoff frequency of the sound used to play this line as it evolves in the song. You would have one track that contains the notes played by the synth and another track that performs the change in the cutoff frequency using SysEx. Erasing the SysEx events does not affect the notes because they are on separate tracks.

Transmitting Bulk Dumps

After your bulk dump is recorded in your project, you will probably want to send it back to your MIDI device when the time comes to restore the saved information. This is fairly easy to do because you already know how to do a bulk dump in one direction. The following list describes the steps you should take when transmitting the information back to your external MIDI device.

To transmit recorded SysEx bulk dumps to your external MIDI device:

1. Assign the appropriate MIDI output port for the track containing the SysEx bulk dump events. This should be the output port connecting to the MIDI input of your external device.

2. If your MIDI device can deactivate its SysEx reception, make sure this option is disabled. In other words, you want your MIDI device to respond to incoming SysEx information.

3. Solo the track that contains the SysEx data. This might not always be necessary, but it's a good precaution to take, because you might have more than one SysEx data track or might have other events that will cause the transfer to interrupt abruptly.

4. Click Play on the Transport panel to begin transmitting a SysEx part to the external MIDI device. You should see some information on the front panel of your external MIDI device to the effect that it is receiving SysEx.

As when your project is receiving SysEx, you should take the same precautions when sending SysEx to your MIDI device. For example, try not to send more data than required. If all you need to recall is a single program's parameters, avoid sending full bulk dumps to your machine. If the bulk dump serves to set up your device for a project, try putting your SysEx in the count-in bars before the actual song starts.

Using a Remote Control Mixer

It is possible to use a MIDI remote control device to record and edit automation inside a Cubase project. Recording automation using such a device is no different than using the controls inside the Mixer window in Cubase. However, editing recorded automation events is a little different. If your remote control MIDI device does not have touch sensitive controls, Cubase does not have any way of knowing if a control is sending information or not once you moved it. As a result, when you activate the Write Automation button in the Mixer window and move a control on your MIDI controller, all following automation is replaced until the moment you stopped playback or disabled the Write Automation button once again. This said, to avoid recording over automation by mistake, you should only enable the Write Automation button on the channels you want to overwrite automation, or avoid moving controllers associated with automation that you want to keep.

Setting Up a Remote Control Mixer

To use a controller device with Cubase, you have to install it in the Device Setup panel.

To install a MIDI remote control device:

1. Select the Device Setup option from the Devices menu.
2. Click the Add/Remove tab on the right side of the dialog box (see Figure 13.15).
3. Select the appropriate device from the supported devices list. If your device is not in this list, select the Generic Remote device.
4. Click the Add button in the bottom-right corner of the dialog box. This adds the selected device to your list on the left.
5. Click the Setup tab on the right side of the dialog box.
6. Select the appropriate MIDI input and output ports connecting the controller to Cubase.

Figure 13.15
Adding a MIDI device
controller to your device
setup

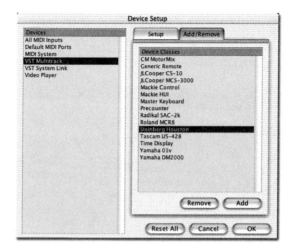

You can now use your controller with Cubase. How this controller interacts with Cubase
depends greatly on the controller itself. You need to refer to this controller's documentation for
further details.

Most remote control devices can control both MIDI and audio channel automation in Cubase SX
even if their parameter setups are different; however, when audio specific parameters are
associated with MIDI tracks, such as EQ parameters, they are then ignored by Cubase.

Now You Try It

It's time to put the topics covered in this chapter into action—you can download a practice
exercise at http://www.muskalipman.com.

14

Working In Sync

Synchronizing Cubase to other devices is one of the most important, yet underused, tasks in a typical recording environment. Synchronization is often something we have to deal with, but resist because it can lead to all kinds of problems. On the other hand, when done properly, it can save you lots of time (which usually converts itself into money) and allow you to accept new and interesting projects, such as film and video sound tracks or sound design and editing.

In this chapter, you discover a technology developed by Steinberg that allows different host computers to share resources using the digital audio hardware you already have. In fact, the VST System Link can transform your second computer in an impressive VSTi rack and a third computer into a processing power house, all linked together, mixing everything inside your first computer.

In this chapter, you will:

▶ Understand the difference between a Word Clock, a timecode, and a MIDI Clock
▶ Learn how and when to use a specific timecode
▶ Learn how and when to use a MIDI Clock
▶ Understand what MIDI Machine Control is and how you can use it
▶ Determine why digital clocks are important when using digital audio devices
▶ Find out what VST System Link is and how you can use it
▶ Learn how to synchronize devices together using different synchronization methods
▶ Determine how you can deal with events that need to stay synchronized to time, whereas others are synchronized to bars and beats
▶ Find out how to work with online video files

About Word Clock, SMPTE, and MIDI Clock

Before we start looking at how Cubase handles synchronization, it is important to understand the different types of synchronization, its terminology, and the basic concept behind these terms. The idea behind synchronization is that there will always be a sender/receiver relation between the source of the synchronization and the recipient of this source. There can only be one sender, but there can be many receivers to this sender. There are three basic concepts here: timecode, MIDI Clock, and Word Clock.

Timecode

The concept behind timecode is simple: It is an electronic signal used to identify a precise location on time-based media, such as audio, videotape, or in digital systems that support timecode. This electronic signal then accompanies the media that needs to be in sync with others. Imagine that a postal worker delivering mail is the locking mechanism, the houses on the street are location addresses on the timecode, and the letter has matching addresses. The postal worker reads the letter and makes sure it gets to the correct address the same way a synchronizing device compares the timecode from a source and a destination, making sure they are all happening at the same time. This timecode is also known as SMPTE (Society of Motion Picture and Television Engineers) and it comes in three flavors:

▶ **MTC (MIDI Timecode).** Normally used to synchronize audio or video devices to MIDI devices such as sequencers. MTC messages are an alternative to using MIDI Clocks (a tempo-based synchronization system) and Song Position Pointer messages (telling a device where it is in relation to a song). MTC is essentially SMPTE (time-based) mutated for transmission over MIDI. On the other hand, MIDI Clocks and Song Position Pointers are based upon musical beats from the start of a song, played at a specific tempo (meter-based). For many nonmusical cues, such as sound elements that are not part of a musical arrangement but rather sound elements found on movie sound tracks (for example, Foley, dialogue, ADR, room tones, and sound effects), it's easier for humans to reference time in some absolute way (time-based) rather than musical beats at a certain tempo (music-based). This is because these events are regulated by images that depict time passing, whereas music is regulated by bars and beats in most cases.

▶ **VITC (Vertical Interval Timecode).** Normally used by video machines to send or receive synchronization information from and to any type of VITC-compatible device. This type of timecode is best suited when working with a Betacam or VTR device. You will rarely use this type of timecode when transferring audio-only data back and forth. VITC may be recorded as part of the video signal in an unused line, which is part of the vertical interval. It has the advantage of being readable when the playback video deck is paused.

▶ **LTC (Longitudinal Timecode).** Also used to synchronize video machines, but contrary to VITC, it is also used to synchronize audio-only information, such as a transfer between a tape recorder and Cubase. LTC usually takes the form of an audio signal that is recorded on one of the tracks of the tape. Because LTC is an audio signal, it is silent if the tape is not moving.

Each one of these timecodes uses an hours: minutes: seconds: frames format.

ABOUT MOVIE SOUND TRACKS

The sound track of a visual production is usually made up of different sounds mixed together. These sounds are divided into six categories: Dialogue, ADR, Foley, Ambiances, and Sound Effects and Music.

The dialogue is usually the part played by the actors or narrated off-screen.

The **ADR (Automatic Dialogue Replacement)** refers to the process of rerecording portions of dialogue that could not be properly recorded during the production stage for different reasons. For example, if a dialogue occurs while there is a lot of noise happening on location, the dialogue is not usable in the final sound track, so the actor rerecords each line from a scene in a studio. Another example of ADR is when a scene is shot in a restaurant where the atmosphere seems lively. Because it is easier to add the crowd ambiance later, the extras in the shot are asked to appear as if they are talking, but in fact, they might be whispering to allow the audio boom operator to get a good clean recording of the principal actors' dialogue. Then, later in a studio environment, additional recordings are made to recreate the background chatter of people in this restaurant.

The **Foley** (from the name of the first person who used this technique in motion pictures) consists of replacing or enhancing human-related sounds, such as footsteps, body motions (for example, noises made by leather jackets, or a cup being placed on a desk, and so on), or water sounds (such as ducks swimming in a pond, a person taking a shower or drowning in a lake).

Ambiances, also called room tones, are placed throughout a scene requiring a constant ambiance. This is used to replace the current ambiance that was recorded with the dialogue, but due to the editing process, placement of camera and other details that affect the continuity of the sound cannot be used in the final sound track. Take, for example, the rumbling and humming caused by a spaceship's engines. Did you think that these were actually engines running on a real spaceship?

The **sound effects** in a motion picture soundtrack are usually not associated with Foley sounds (body motion simulation sounds). In other words, "sound effects" are the sounds that enhance a scene in terms of sonic content. A few examples are explosions, gun shots, the "swooshing' sound of a punch, an engine revving, a knife slashing, etc. Sound effects aren't meant to mimic but to enhance.

And last but not least, the **music**, which comes in different flavors, adds the emotional backdrop to the story being told by the images.

CHAPTER 14

Frame Rates

As the name implies, a frame rate is the amount of frames a film or video signal has within a second. The acronym for frame rate is "fps" for Frames Per Second. There are different frame rates depending on what you are working with:

▶ **24 fps**. This is used by motion picture films and in most cases, working with this medium will not apply to you because you likely do not have a film projector hooked up to your computer running Cubase to synchronize sound.

▶ **25 fps**. This refers to the PAL (Phase Alternation Line) video standard used mostly in Asia and SECAM/EBU (Sequential Color And Memory/European Broadcast Union) video standard used mostly in Europe. If you live in those areas, this is the format your VCR uses. A single frame in this format is made of 625 horizontal lines.

▶ **29.97 fps**. Also known as 29.97 non-drop and may also be seen as 30 fps in some older two-digit timecode machines (but not to be mistaken with the actual 30 fps timecode; if you can't see the 29.97 format, chances are the 30 format is its equivalent). This refers to the NTSC (National Television Standards Committee) video standard used mostly in North America. If you live in this area, this is the format your VCR uses. A single frame in this format is made of 525 horizontal lines.

▶ **29.97 fps DF**. Also known as 29.97 drop frame (hence the DF at the end). This can also be referred to as 30 DF on older video timecode machines. This is probably the trickiest timecode to understand because there is a lot of confusion about the drop frame. To accommodate the extra information needed for color when this format was first introduced, the black and white's 30 fps was slowed to 29.97 fps for color. Though not an issue for most of you, in broadcast, the small difference between real time (also known as the wall or house clock) and the time registered on the video can be problematic. Over a period of one SMPTE hour, the video is 3.6 seconds or 108 extra frames longer in relation to the wall clock. To overcome this discrepancy, drop frames are used. This is calculated as follows: Every frame 00 and 01 are dropped for each minute change, except for minutes with 0's (such as 00, 10, 20, 30, 40, and 50). Therefore, two frames skipped every minute represents 120 frames per hour, except for the minutes ending with zero, so 120–12 = 108 frames. Setting your frame rate to 29.97 DF when it's not—in other words, if it's 29.97 (Non-Drop)—causes your synchronization to be off by 3.6 seconds per hour.

▶ **30 fps**. This format was used with the first black and white NTSC standard. It is still used sometimes in music or sound applications in which no video reference is required.

▶ **30 fps DF**. This is not a standard timecode protocol and usually refers to older timecode devices that were unable to display the decimal points when the 29.97 drop frame timecode was used. Try to avoid this timecode frame rate setting when synchronizing to video because it might introduce errors in your synchronization. SMPTE does not support this timecode.

Using the SMPTE Generator Plug-In

The SMPTE Generator is a plug-in that generates SMPTE timecode in one of two ways:

▶ It uses an audio bus output to send a generated timecode signal to an external device. Typically, you can use this mode to adjust the level of SMPTE going to other devices and to make sure that a proper connection between the outputs of the sound card associated with Cubase and the input of the device for which the SMPTE was intended.

▶ It uses an audio bus output to send a timecode signal that is linked with the play position of the project currently loaded. Typically, this tells another device the exact SMPTE location of Cubase at any time, allowing it to lock to Cubase through this synchronization signal.

Because this plug-in is not really an effect, using it on a two-output system is useless because timecode is not what you could call "a pleasant sound." Because it uses an audio output to carry its signal, you need to use an audio output on your sound card that you don't use for anything else, or at least one channel (left or right) that you can spare for this signal. Placing the SMPTE Generator on an empty audio track is also necessary because you do not want to process this signal in any way or the information the signal contains will be compromised.

To use the SMPTE Generator plug-in:

1. Create a new audio track.

2. Open the Track Inserts section in the Inspector area.

3. From the Plug-ins Selection drop-down menu, select the SMPTE Generator.

4. Expand the audio channel section in the Inspector area.

5. Assign the plug-in to a bus that doesn't contain any other audio signal. If you don't have an unused bus, see if you can use one side in a left/right setup, and then pan the plug-in on one side and whatever was assigned to that bus to the other side. For example, a bass on the left and the SMPTE Generator on the right.

6. Click the Edit button to access its panel (see Figure 14.1).

Figure 14.1
The SMPTE Generator panel

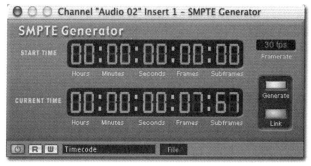

7. Make sure the Framerate field displays the same frame rate as your project. You can access your Project Setup dialog box by pressing the Shift+S keys to verify if this is the case. Otherwise, set the Framerate field to the appropriate setting.

8. Make the connections between the output to which the plug-in is assigned and the receiving device.

9. Click the Generate button to start sending timecode. This step allows you to verify if the signal is connected properly to the receiving device.

10. Adjust the level in either the audio channel containing the plug-in or on the

receiving device's end. This receiving device should not receive a distorted signal to lock properly.

11. After you've made these adjustments, click the Link button in the Plug-in Information panel.

12. Start the playback of your project to lock the SMPTE Generator, the project, and the receiving device together.

MIDI Clock

MIDI Clock is a tempo-based synchronization signal used to synchronize two or more MIDI devices together with a beats-per-minute (BPM) for guide track. As you can see, this is different than a timecode because it does not refer to a real-time address (hours: minutes: seconds: frames). In this case, it sends 24 evenly spaced MIDI Clocks per quarter note. So, at a speed of 60 BPM, it sends 1,440 MIDI Clocks per minute (one every 41.67 milliseconds), whereas at a speed of 120 BPM, it sends double that amount (one every 20.83 milliseconds). Because it is tempo-based, the MIDI Clock rate changes to follow the tempo of the master tempo source.

When a sender sends a MIDI Clock signal, it sends a MIDI Start message to tell its receiver to start playing a sequence at the speed or tempo set in the sender's sequence. When the sender sends a MIDI End message, it tells the receiver to stop playing a sequence. Up until this point, all the receiver can do is start and stop playing MIDI when it receives these messages. If you want to tell the receiver sequence where to start, the MIDI Clock has to send what is called a Song Position Pointer message telling the receiver the location of the sender's song position. It uses the MIDI data to count the position where the MIDI Start message is at in relation to the sender.

Using MIDI Clock should be reserved for use between MIDI devices only, not for audio. As soon as you add digital audio or video, you should avoid using MIDI Clock because it is not well-suited for these purposes. Although it keeps a good synchronization between similar MIDI devices, the audio requires much greater precision. Video, on the other hand, works with time-based events, which do not translate well in BPM.

MIDI Machine Control

Another type of MIDI-related synchronization is the MIDI Machine Control (MMC). The MMC protocol uses System Exclusive messages over a MIDI cable to remotely control hard disk recording systems and other machines used for recording or playback. Many MIDI-enabled devices support this protocol.

MMC allows you to send MIDI to a device, giving it commands such as play, stop, rewind, go to a specific location, punch-in, and punch-out on a specific track.

To make use of MMC in a setup in which you are using a multitrack tape recorder and a sequencer, you need to have a timecode (SMPTE) track sending timecode to a SMPTE/MTC converter. Then, you send the converted MTC to Cubase so that it can stay in sync with the multitrack recorder. Both devices are also connected through MIDI cables. It is the multitrack that controls Cubase's timing, not vice versa. Cubase, in return, can transmit MMC messages through its MIDI connection with the multitrack, which is equipped with a MIDI interface. These MMC messages tell the multitrack to rewind, fast forward, and so on. When you click

Play in Cubase, it tells the multitrack to go to the position at which playback in Cubase's project begins. When the multitrack reaches this position, it starts playing the tape back. After it starts playing, it then sends timecode to Cubase, to which it then syncs.

Digital Clock

The digital clock is another way to synchronize two or more devices together using the sampling frequency of the sender device as a reference. This type of synchronization is often used with MTC in a music application such as Cubase to lock both audio sound card and MIDI devices with video devices, for example. The sender device in this case is the sound card. This is by far the most precise synchronization mechanism discussed here. Because it uses the sampling frequency of your sound card, it is precise to $1/44,100^{th}$ of a second when you are using a 44.1 kHz sampling frequency (or 0.02 milliseconds). Compare this with the precision of SMPTE timecode (around 33 milliseconds at 30 fps) and MIDI Clock (41.67 milliseconds at 120 BPM), and you quickly realize that this synchronization is very accurate.

When you make a digital transfer between two digital devices, the digital or Word Clock of the sender device is sent to the receiver device, making sure that every bit of the digital audio from the sender device fits with the receiver device. Failure to do so results in errors and degradation in the digital audio signal. When a receiver device receives a Word Clock (a type of digital clock) from its sender, it replaces its own clock with the one provided by this sender.

A digital clock can be transmitted on one of these cables:

▶ **S/PDIF (Sony/Phillips Digital InterFace)**. This format is probably the most common way to connect two digital devices together. Although this type of connection transmits digital clock information, it is usually referred to by its name rather than Word Clock. S/PDIF connectors have RCA connectors at each end and carry digital audio information with embedded digital audio clock information. You can transmit mono or stereo audio information on a single S/PDIF connection.

▶ **AES/EBU (Audio Engineering Society/European Broadcast Union)**. This is another very common, yet not as popular type of digital connector used to transfer digital information from one device to another. AES/EBU uses an XLR connector at each end of the cable; like the S/PDIF format, it carries the digital audio clock embedded in its data stream. You can also transmit mono or stereo audio information on this type of connection. Because this type of connection uses XLR connectors, it is less susceptible to creating clicks and pops when you connect them, but because they are more expensive, you won't find them on low-cost equipment.

▶ **ADAT (Alesis Digital Audio Technology)**. This is a proprietary format developed by Alesis that carries up to eight separate digital audio signals and Word Clock information over a single-wire, fiber-optic cable. Most sound cards do not provide ADAT connectors on them, but if yours does, use it to send and receive digital clock information from and to an ADAT compatible device.

▶ **TDIF (Tascam Digital InterFace)**. This is a proprietary format develop by Tascam that also provides eight channels of digital audio in both directions, with up to

24-bit resolution. It also carries clocking signals that are used for synchronizing the transmission and reception of the audio; however, it does not contain Word Clock information.

▶ **Word Clock**. A digital clock is called Word Clock when it is sent over its own cable. Because Word Clock signals contain high frequencies, they are usually transmitted on 75-ohm coaxial cables for reliability. Usually, a coaxial BNC connector is used for Word Clock transfers.

To be able to transfer digital audio information in sync from one digital device to another, all devices have to support the sender's sampling rate. This is particularly important when using sampling frequencies other than 44.1 or 48 kHz, because those are pretty standard on most digital audio devices.

When synchronizing two digital audio devices together, the digital clock might not be the only synchronization clock needed. If you are working with another digital hard disk recorder, or multitrack analog tape recorder, you need to send transport controls to and from these devices along with the timing position generated by this digital clock. This is when you have to lock both the digital clock and timecode together. Avoid using MIDI Clock at all costs when synchronizing with digital audio. The next section discusses different possibilities and how to set up Cubase to act as a sender or a receiver in the situations described previously.

When doing digital transfers between a digital multitrack tape and Cubase, it is important that both the Word Clock (digital clock) information and the timecode information be correlated to ensure a no-loss transfer and that for every bit on one end, there's a corresponding bit on the other. This high-precision task can be performed through ASIO Position Protocol (APP).

APP uses the ASIO driver provided for your sound card and a compatible APP digital device, such as Alesis' ADAT. In this type of setup, the ADAT provides the master (sender) Word Clock and the timecode information to Cubase. The ASIO 2.0 compatible driver of your sound card simply follows this information and stays accurate to the last sample.

VST System Link

It seems that we never have enough power in one computer to do all that we want to do. Well, Steinberg understands this and developed a protocol called VST System Link, which allows you to connect two or more computers together using a digital audio connection as the link between these two computers. The VST System Link, after your computers are hooked up together, makes it possible to run two or more VST System Link compatible host applications in perfect digital audio sync with each other. It does this without any network cards, hubs, or other type of connection. In other words, if you have two computers, two compatible host applications, and a sound card with at least one digital input/output in each computer, you are ready to link!

After the computers are linked, you can activate the system link and use VSTi in one computer and control them using a keyboard hooked up to the second computer. You can also have audio tracks in two different projects on two different computers playing in complete sync. This means that you can split the tracks of your song into two projects, processing some tracks here, other tracks there, sharing the workload between two computers. If you don't want to split up your audio tracks, you can still run all your effects on one computer and monitor the result in the other. Using this system, you could run a Mac and a PC together, running, for example, Nuendo on one machine and Cubase SX on the other.

About System Link

VST System Link uses a single bit of the digital audio stream as a carrier for transport and synchronization information. It can also use other bits of the digital audio stream for MIDI information. Several computers can be linked in a daisy-chain configuration—each one passing on the accumulated information to the next via standard digital audio cables, with routing to the various systems controlled by a master (sender) software running on the first computer in the chain.

To run a VST System Link, you need the following items:

▶ Two or more computers

▶ A host application (such as Cubase SX, SL, Nuendo 1.6, or Cubase VST 5.2 System Link version) running on each computer

▶ A digital audio connection on the sound card of each computer to connect the VST System Link with other computers

▶ An ASIO 2.0 driver for the sound card on each computer

▶ At least one digital cable for each computer in your VST System Link network

Linking Computers

In its simplest form, you can connect two computers using a simple S/PDIF or AES/EBU digital connection, as shown in Figure 14.2. In this scenario, Computer A's digital out goes into Computer B's digital In and vice versa. If you don't have a digital mixer or even an analog mixer, you can simply send the analog output of Computer A to your monitoring system. Because the system link only uses one bit in your digital connection, you can still use the other 15 bits (19 or 23 depending on the digital word length available in your sound card) to transmit digital audio from Computer B to Computer A. Therefore, you would be mixing both the content of Computer A & B inside Computer A, sending the final mix to a pair of monitor inputs.

It is important, as in any digital linkup, that one of the two computers be the digital clock sender (master clock) and the other, the digital clock receiver (slaved clock).

Figure 14.2
Setting up a system link between two computers using S/PDIF or AES/EBU

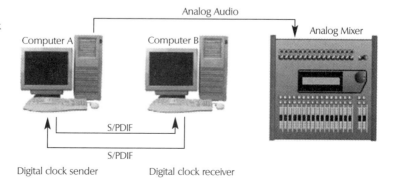

CHAPTER 14

In Figure 14.3, we've replaced the analog mixer with a digital one, allowing us to connect digitally to the mixer and use this mixer to forward any instruments you might want to record. As with the previous setup, Computer A is the digital clock sender and the two other devices are receivers. However, you could set the digital mixer as a digital clock sender and have the two computers receiving. It all depends on how your studio is set up. The figure displays an ADAT connection between each component in the linked network. This is probably the most convenient way of doing it, giving you eight digital channels that you can patch anywhere you want, but you could also do this with a S/PDIF or an AES/EBU connection.

This type of setup is pretty simple as well, but it also bears some limitations. Because the ADAT carries the audio information from A to B, you will be using Computer B to monitor or mix. Computer A, on the other hand, is receiving the digital mixer's outputs through its ADAT connection. You, therefore, have to configure your setup to properly monitor and record events from Computer B, or use Computer A as your main station, using the digital mixer's ADAT outputs to monitor Computer B.

Figure 14.3
Setting up a system link
between two computers
and a digital mixer
using any digital
connection

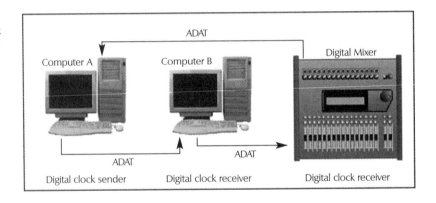

Figure 14.4's setup is similar to the one provided in the previous figure; however, in this case, an S/PDIF (this could be another format as well) feeds the digital input of the digital mixer, allowing you to monitor or control from Computer A, and then to the digital mixer to monitor the output in speakers. You could also draw an S/PDIF connection from the mixer's digital output to Computer A's digital input. As you can see, connecting hardware using System Link is quite easy. Now, let's look at how it all works inside Cubase.

Figure 14.4
Setting up a system link
between two computers
and a digital mixer
using two digital
connections

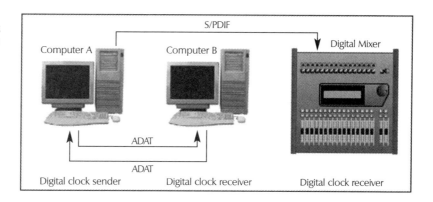

Latency Issues with System Link

As you saw earlier in this book, latency is the delay that happens between the processing stage and the monitoring stage—for example, the delay between the moment you press a note on your keyboard and the time it takes for a VSTi to play that note. With ASIO driver sound cards and Cubase SX, this can be kept to a minimum, hopefully below ten or twelve milliseconds. However, when linking computers together, the latency is the total amount of latency caused by both computers. So, if you have a ten millisecond latency on both, your total latency when linking computers is approximately twenty milliseconds. Note that latency does not affect the synchronization of events with the rest of your events because Cubase SX's technology compensates for this latency. Because the more latency you have, the more delay you hear between the action and the result, the harder it is for you to focus on the task at hand when recording events through a linked system with a high latency time.

You can generally adjust the latency time of a sound card by changing its DMA buffer size as mentioned earlier in this book. If you are not sure how to change these values, consult the driver documentation for your hardware device (sound card).

Setting Up System Link Inside Cubase

To configure your system link properly, you should start by setting up one computer, then the next, establishing a successful link. If this setup works, you can proceed with a third or fourth computer, adding one when you've established a working link.

All projects in all linked computers must be set at the same sampling frequency and should also be at the same tempo setting to work properly.

The following setup procedure assumes that you have properly connected the digital audio cables between the two computers, as illustrated in the previous section. It also assumes that you have at least two audio busses on one of the computers.

To set up two computers using the VST System Link:

1. On Computer 1, open the VST Input panel.

2. Activate all the inputs that you want to use to receive digital audio from Computer 2.

3. Now open the VST Output panel.

4. Activate all the bus outputs you want to use to send digital audio to Computer 2.

5. Go to Computer 2 and repeat Steps 1–4 on this computer. By doing this, you have essentially routed the outputs of Computer 1 to the inputs of Computer 2 and vice versa. We assume at this point that you are using Computer 1 to monitor what comes from Computer 2.

6. Back on Computer 1, create an audio track.

7. Enable the Monitor button in the audio channel's section of the Inspector area, or through the audio channel in the Track Mixer panel.

8. Select an audio input for this channel. This input should be used as follows: When you have events on Computer 2, you assign it to an audio output, for example, ADAT 3-4 outputs. On Computer 1, you set the inputs for this channel as ADAT 3-4 inputs, allowing you to monitor whatever is being sent from the output of Computer 2 in this channel of Computer 1.

At this point, you have established that whatever is assigned to an output in Computer 2 can be monitored through a corresponding channel in Computer 1, providing that you choose the corresponding input setting in this computer. But there's still no locking happening between the two computers, just monitoring. So, let's activate the system link.

To activate the VST System Link:

1. On Computer 1, select the Device Setup option from the Devices menu.

2. Select the VST System Link option in this dialog box and make sure that the Setup tab in the right portion of the window is active (see Figure 14.5).

Figure 14.5
The Device Setup VST
System Link options

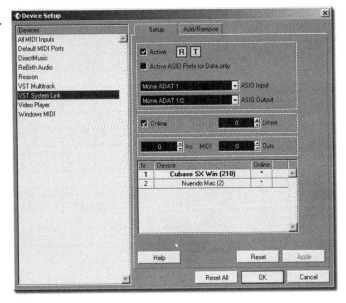

3. Next to the ASIO Input field, select the digital input from which you want to receive system link information.

4. Next to the ASIO Output field, select the digital output to which you want to send system link information.

5. Click the Active check box to activate the system link.

6. Repeat this operation on Computer 2.

7. After the setting is completed on Computer 2, click the Online check box to activate it.

8. Repeat this operation (enabling the Online check box) on Computer 1.

After you have completed this setup on the second computer, you should see the R (Receive) and T (Transmit) indicators next to the Active check box in the device setup start flashing to indicate that the computers are linked together and receiving or transmitting information when you begin playback on Computer 1. You should also see the name and number of the computer appear in the box found in the lower half of the Device Setup dialog box. In Figure 14.5, for example, Computer 1 is running Cubase SX on Windows while Computer 2 is running Nuendo on Macintosh.

Next to the computer name, you can see the Online column. When a computer is online, you can remote control its transport operations. For example, you can start Computer 2 from the Transport panel of Computer 1. However, if you want to set a computer offline so that it stays linked, but independent, deselect the Online option in the Device Setup dialog box.

You are now ready to put your VST System Link setup to the test.

Using System Link MIDI Ports

Besides the fact that system linking your computers together allows you to control transport functions from one computer to another and monitor the outputs of one computer on another, it also provides sixteen additional MIDI ports. As you probably know, a MIDI port can carry up to sixteen channels of MIDI. In other words, VST System Link provides you with an additional 256 MIDI channels. These MIDI ports can, however, only be used to control VSTi.

To use a system link MIDI port between two computers:

1. On Computer 1, create a MIDI track.

2. From the Track List area or the Track Setting section in the Inspector area, select the VST System Link MIDI output port of your choice.

3. Enable the Record Ready button for this MIDI track.

4. Open the VST Instruments panel and load an appropriate VSTi in an available slot.

5. On Computer 2, create a MIDI track.

6. Enable the MIDI Monitoring button for that track.

7. In the MIDI input port, select the VST System Link port number corresponding to the one you chose on Computer 1 (in Step 2).

8. In the MIDI output port, select the VSTi you have just activated.

As you might have noticed, Computer 1 is where the MIDI events are recorded if you were to click the Record button because the MIDI track has been record-enabled. On Computer 2, the MIDI track is only set to monitor whatever MIDI events are coming in and send those events to the appropriate MIDI output port (in this case, a VSTi). Note that in these steps, the audio for the VSTi from Computer 2 is not routed to Computer 1. We look at this in the following section.

You could also elect to proceed differently. For example, you could record on Computer 1 using a VSTi as your output or another external device, then after recording, simply assign the output of that track to the VST System Link and follow the same earlier steps. Another option is to play the events on your keyboard through Computer 1, and record on Computer 2 instead. In this case, you enable the Record Ready button for this track on Computer 2 rather than using the Monitor button. All this depends on how you want to proceed depending on the task and the resources at hand and where you want to place your events.

Monitoring Audio Using System Link

As you saw in the previous section, it is possible to link two computers through the system link MIDI ports. But as of yet, the audio, besides the connection we configured at the beginning of this discussion, is not very practical for effects or VSTi monitoring from one computer to the next.

This configuration assumes you have at least a pair of analog audio outputs and a digital output, such as an S/DIF on Computer 1 and a digital output on Computer 2 (as displayed in Figure 14.2). Let's also assume that what you want to monitor on Computer 1 is the audio output of a VSTi on Computer 2. From the logic established earlier in this chapter and through these steps, you should be able to understand how to set up the system link to monitor anything else, such as an audio track, audio send effect, or a group.

To monitor a pair of audio channels through VST System Link:

1. On Computer 2, open the VST Output panel.
2. Enable an output bus and assign an appropriate audio output. This should be an output that has already been connected to the other computer as described earlier.
3. Select the track you want to monitor on Computer 1.
4. In the Mixer panel, select the bus you have just enabled as your output for this track. This should send the audio content to Computer 1 through the system link.
5. On Computer 1, open the VST Input panel.
6. Make sure the input coming from Computer 2 is active.
7. Create an audio track.
8. In the Track Channels section of the Inspector area or in the Mixer panel, select the input you've assigned from Computer 2's output. For example, if you have selected Bus 3 on Computer 2 and have assigned Bus 3 to Outputs 3-4 (this could be your S/PDIF cable), then you should select the corresponding digital input 3-4.

9. Select an appropriate output for this channel as well. This should be something like Bus 1 if you only have one pair of analog outputs.

10. Enable the Monitor button on this channel.

Resolving Differences

Synchronizing Cubase implies that you are resolving the differences between different machines to follow a single sender clock, which guides other clocks and tells them where they should be at all times. The next section discusses how to resolve these differences and set your software and hardware preferences accordingly depending on the situation at hand.

Cubase SX/SL offers a solution for most synchronization situations. If you have an ASIO 2.0 compatible driver for your sound card and an ASIO 2.0 compatible external device, it allows you to have not only a sample accurate synchronization, but also provides a Positioning Protocol that calculates the relation between the Word Clock position and the timecode position to offer stable synchronicity. If your external hardware does not support ASIO 2.0, use MIDI Timecode options instead. You might want to consult your manufacturer's documentation in regards to ASIO 2.0 implementation to find out more about the possibilities it has to offer.

There are three different methods used by Cubase to synchronize to other devices: Resolving, Continuously Resynchronizing, and Referencing. These are not settings you can adjust in Cubase, but rather ways that Cubase uses to stay in sync.

▶ **Resolving**. Implies that all devices are synchronized to a single digital and timecode reference, resolving their clock to the sender's. This is the best synchronization method, but not always practical in a small home studio because it often requires an external module, called a House Sync, which connects all devices and locks them together using a very stable clock.

▶ **Continuous Resynchronization**. Implies that a timecode is sent to a digital audio device, which in turn, uses this timecode as a reference to make sure its digital clock is always in sync, thus continually resynchronizing itself to this timecode.

▶ **Referencing**. Implies that you create a SMPTE audio track by selecting the SMPTE Generator plug-in (as mentioned earlier in this chapter) whenever you don't have any timecode available but need to lock two devices together. This creates a timecode reference (sender), such as a timecode track found on an analog multitrack recorder. Generating such a file guarantees that the timing in this file coincides with the timing (clock) of your sound card because it is this sound card's clock that is being used to generate the file in the first place.

Internal and External References

First, you need to determine where your synchronizing reference is coming from. Because Cubase offers very stable synchronization, you might want to consider using this as your source, making it the sender for other devices. But in the real world, this is not always possible.

CHAPTER 14

Cubase can be either the receiver, sender, or both simultaneously: It can receive a sync signal from a sender sync device and send this sync signal to another receiver device, regenerating the sync information for a stable synchronization.

You need to keep two important factors in mind when working out synchronization between devices, especially when you connect multiple devices using digital connections, such as the ones mentioned earlier in this chapter:

▶ What device is responsible for the digital clock information? In other words, who will be sending its Word Clock information to others? If you don't have any digital connections in your studio, chances are your sound card is the sender. If this sound card is connected to any other device through a digital connection, you need to look at how it is connected and how it is set up. How devices are interconnected digitally influences how digital audio flows between these devices. (See Figure 14.6.)

▶ Where does the time-related (such as timecode and positioning) information come from? If you are working with an SMPTE video, multitrack tape recorder with a timecode on it, chances are, you need to slave (set as the receiver) Cubase to these devices. How devices are interconnected with a timecode reference influences who controls the transport and location functions.

Figure 14.6
Determining the source of the digital clock: In the top portion of Figure 14.6, the computer is master (sending) while the other device is slaved (receiving); in the lower portion, the computer is slaved to the other device

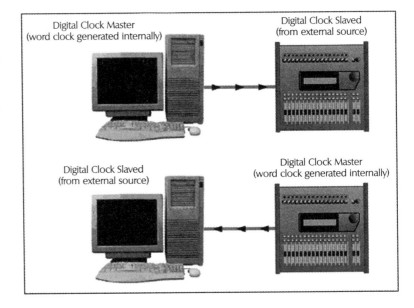

Digital Clock Master
(word clock generated internally)

Digital Clock Slaved
(from external source)

Digital Clock Slaved
(from external source)

Digital Clock Master
(word clock generated internally)

These are two synchronization issues that are often misunderstood, but essential in today's digital studio. So, let's first determine if you need to worry about digital synchronization, and then we'll look at timecode synchronization.

1. Does your sound card provide a digital connection of some sort (S/PDIF, ADAT, Word Clock, TDIF, or AES/EBU)?

    ▶ No, it doesn't: Then your computer's sound card is the digital clock reference (sender).

    ▶ Yes, it does provide a digital connection. Read the following question:

2. Is your sound card set to follow its internal Word Clock or is it set to follow an external Word Clock (or digital connection that carries Word Clock information)?

    ▶ My sound card's digital clock is set to internal: Then your sound card is the digital clock reference (sender). You should make sure other devices are set to follow (receive) this digital clock. This is done through your sound card's control panel. (Figure 14.7 shows an example of a sound card control panel; however, yours might differ depending on your sound card model, manufacturer, and driver version.)

    ▶ My sound card's digital clock is set to follow an external clock: Then your sound card is receiving an external digital clock and you should make sure that it is locked to this digital clock. This is done through your sound card's control panel.

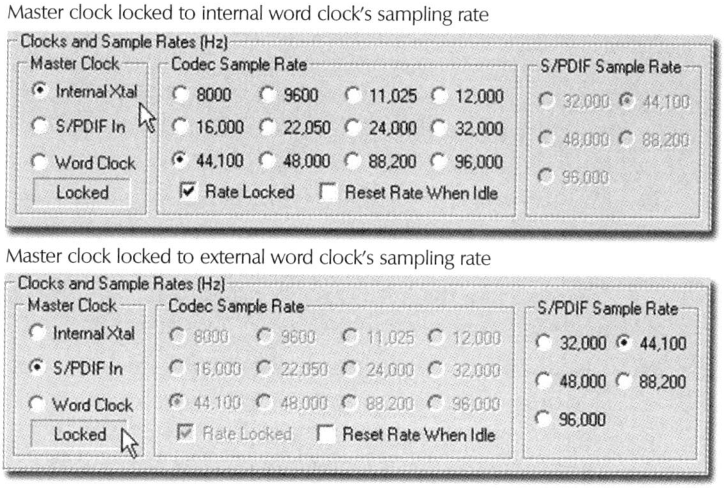

Figure 14.7
Setting up your sound card's Word Clock source in the sound card's control panel

Master clock locked to internal word clock's sampling rate

Master clock locked to external word clock's sampling rate

CHAPTER 14

After you've established that the proper digital connections are made and that the sender/receiver relation has been established, you can configure the second step in the synchronization setup: Who controls the timecode? Let's look at some potential setups.

Setting Up Synchronizations

Let's take a closer look at the Synchronization dialog box (see Figure 14.8).

Figure 14.8
The Synchronization
Setup dialog box

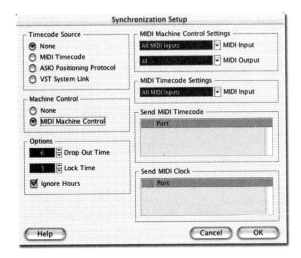

▶ **Timecode Source**. Allows you to select the source of your timecode. If Cubase is not receiving a timecode from any other devices or if Cubase IS the source of timecode, this option, by default, is set at None. Otherwise, you can select the appropriate timecode source. In the event that you are slaving Cubase's time to a MIDI Timecode, you need to select the MIDI input on which the MTC arrives.

▶ **Machine Control**. Lets you select whether Cubase receives and transmits MMC as described earlier. In the event that you have connected Cubase to a MMC-compatible device, you need to select both the MIDI input and output ports that communicate the MMC information to and from this device in the appropriate fields in the upper-right portion of this dialog box (see Figure 14.8).

▶ **Options fields**. Allow you to set both the Drop Out Time and Lock Time options. The drop out time is a frame value. When you are receiving timecode from a tape recorder, degradation of the timecode signal might occur, leaving the timecode unreadable for a number of frames. If this is the case, Cubase stops playing and then starts playing again when it can understand the timecode again. To avoid this problem, you can raise the amount of drop out time tolerated by Cubase before it stops playing. If your timecode is really bad, you might want to consider rerecording the timecode track rather than setting this option high because the shift in timecode between the estimated timecode (the one Cubase estimates it's at when the signal is dropped) and the real timecode (the one on the Sync reference) might create undesired effects. The Lock Time option represents the amount of frames Cubase needs to receive before it starts playing after it locks to that timecode. If you have many events to chase, such as program changes and mix automation parameters, you might want to set this to a higher value in order for all the data to load and play properly when Cubase starts playing. On the other hand, if you don't have that many events to chase, you can set this to a lower setting. Finally, the Ignore Hours check box allows you to ignore the hour value in the timecode. This has no effect on the position of the timecode itself unless you run projects that are longer than one hour. However, if you work on projects for which each section of a film starts with a different hour setting, ignoring the hour helps you in establishing an adequate offset time if needed.

▶ **Send MIDI Timecode and Send MIDI Clock**. Allow you to select the MIDI outputs Cubase uses to send these types of signals. If you have a drum machine that needs to receive a MIDI Clock, for example, you need to select the MIDI output connected to this drum machine.

To set up synchronization properties:

1. To open the Synchronization dialog box, Ctrl-click (Command-click on Mac) on the Sync button in the Transport panel or select Sync Setup from the Transport menu.

2. Select the appropriate timecode source for your project.

3. If you have selected MIDI Timecode as your timecode source, select the appropriate MIDI input port on which the MTC arrives.

4. If your project requires that you connect with a MIDI Machine Control compatible device, select this option, and set the appropriate MIDI output port to send and receive the MMC.

5. If you have other devices connected to your computer that require Cubase to retransmit synchronization signals to them, such as MTC or MIDI Clock, select the appropriate MIDI output ports.

6. You should leave the options (drop out time and lock time) in the Synchronization Setup dialog box at their default values. In the event that you need to change these values due to a bad timecode coming from a tape recorder or other source, you may access this dialog box and adjust the values until the timecode locks properly.

7. Close the Synchronization Setup dialog box.

8. Activate the Sync button on the Transport Panel. Cubase now waits for an incoming sync signal.

To achieve better results when synchronizing Cubase to MTC, it is recommended that the sync box converting LTC timecode to MTC also sends out Word Clock information as well. This provides a more stable synchronization for both MIDI and audio. This option requires that you have a sync box generating Word Clock information and that you set your sound card's Word Clock options to follow an incoming clock signal. Most SMPTE to MTC converters work fine until you start using audio in your project. If there is no audio clock information, the audio might shift during the project to adjust itself to a less accurate MTC signal.

When you configure Cubase to lock to an external timecode source, you might have to change the current start time setting. The start time setting found in the project preferences (Shift+S) tells Cubase the timecode reference of Bar 1, Beat 1—in other words, the time at the beginning of the project.

When working with video, for example, chances are the timecode does not start at 00:00:00:00. It is a common practice to start the timecode at a different hour for each reel of film. For example, a ninety-minute movie might be divided on nine reels and then transferred on the same videotape or separate videotapes. To make sure that cues on reel four are not mistaken for cues on reel seven, the timecode for reel four starts at four hours (04:00:00:00) and reel seven at seven hours (07:00:00:00). Furthermore, a lead-in time might be added before the reel to allow for video and audio calibration, setting the timecode to begin at least thirty seconds before the hour (in reel four, this is 03:59:30:00). If you want your song to begin at Bar 1, Beat 1, you need to offset the start time in Cubase to correspond to the timecode accordingly. In this example, you can set the start time for reel four to 04:00:00:00, which tells Cubase that Bar 1, Beat 1 (1.1.000) corresponds to this value.

The Display Offset field in project preferences then allows you to bring back the time displayed in the ruler to a 00:00:00:00 time. The fact that your song starts at the timecode address of 04:00:00:00, doesn't mean that you want to calculate the time starting at four hours. Changing the time in this field sets your start position (1.1.000) at something else than a time equivalent to 00:00:00:00 (see Figure 14.9).

Figure 14.9
Adjusting the Start and Display Offset settings to match incoming timecode

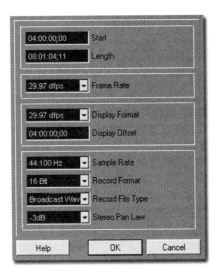

Getting Cubase to Sync With Others

Figure 14.10 displays a simple setup where a video player sends SMPTE information (most likely LTC in this case) to a MIDI interface. The MIDI interface (or patch bay) acts as a SMPTE to MTC converter, relaying the MTC to Cubase. In this setup, you should set the digital clock of your sound card to Internal and set the timecode source to MTC, making sure to select the MIDI input port on which the MTC arrives.

Figure 14.10
Simple synchronization
diagram

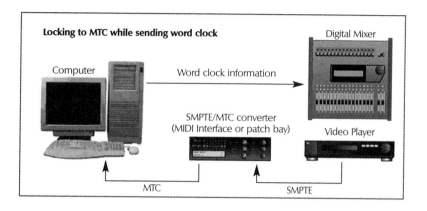

If, for some reason, the digital mixer or other digital device connected to your computer has to be the sender Word Clock, make sure your sound card follows the incoming clock by setting its digital clock source to External (this might be an S/PDIF, ADAT, AES/EBU, or Word Clock connection; see Figure 14.11). Consult your sound card's documentation to configure it appropriately.

In Figure 14.11, the setup is different in the sense that Cubase locks to an incoming MTC source; however, in this case, this MTC and the Word Clock information comes from a synchronizer. The synchronizer's role is to correlate both timecode and Word Clock together, making it the unique source feeding Cubase. This type of setup helps in keeping a simple, yet stable synchronization between devices. It also allows you to hook up other digital devices to the synchronizer in an effort to ensure that the source of the Word Clock information and MTC all come from one source. In this case, as in the previous example, Cubase's synchronization option should be set to follow an MTC source and your sound card should be set to follow an external digital clock (in effect, slaving to it).

Figure 14.11
Another simple
synchronization
diagram

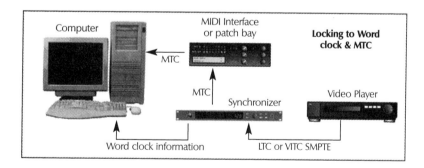

In Figure 14.12, things might look complicated, but you can break this down one item at a time. In fact, this type of setup displays different ways devices can be interconnected, transmitting and receiving various synchronization protocols at once.

Let's start with the drum machine. In this setup, Cubase is connected through its MIDI interface to a drum machine, sending a MIDI Clock synchronization signal to it. For the drum machine to lock with Cubase, you need to check the appropriate MIDI output port to send MIDI Clock in the

Synchronization Setup dialog box. You also need to set your drum machine to receive an incoming MIDI Clock; otherwise, it does not respond to this signal.

Below the drum machine is a multitrack tape recorder with a compatible MIDI Machine Control (MMC) interface. By connecting both the MIDI input and output to your computer's MIDI interface, you create the necessary MIDI bridge between Cubase and the tape recorder as described earlier in the MMC section. But for MMC to work, the tape recorder has to send out timecode information to the computer. This is done through the LTC (SMPTE) signal being sent to the synchronizer. The synchronizer converts the LTC into MTC, sending it to the computer. Note here that if all you have is a tape recorder and a computer, you don't need the synchronizer in between, but you still need a SMPTE to MTC converter. In either case, for the timecode source in Cubase to read the incoming MTC signal, the MMC option needs to be selected and the appropriate MIDI input and output ports receiving and transmitting the MMC information also need to be selected.

So, in this setup, Cubase's timecode source is external, yet it still generates a MIDI Clock to slave the drum machine to the project's location and tempo setting.

Figure 14.12
A more complex studio setup involving different types of simultaneous synchronization

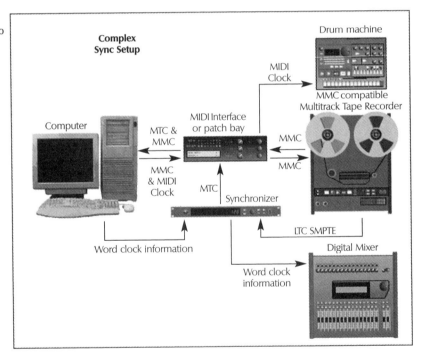

Now, let's try a little quiz to see if you understand these connections. In this setup:

1. Which device is responsible for the timecode information?
2. Which device is responsible for the transport commands?
3. Which device is responsible for the Word Clock information?
4. Which device is responsible for the MIDI clocking information that controls the drum machine?

Answers: In this setup, the timecode source is generated by the tape recorder. The transport commands are provided through MMC by Cubase (in other words, the computer). The Word Clock is provided by your sound card along with the MIDI Clock; although the fact that its location is controlled ultimately by the timecode, it is Cubase that generates the clock information passed on to the drum machine.

Linear Time and Musical Time

When working with video, you might want to place some sound effects, ambiances, or Foley where and when these events occur onscreen. These are timing sensitive events, not bar-and-beat sensitive events. Changing the tempo of a song might not only change where a song starts in relation to the video, but it also shifts all these time sensitive events with it as well. Changing the timebase of a track from musical to linear keeps events on this track from shifting in time when the tempo of the project changes. Furthermore, if you want to lock all events on this track from being edited or moved by mistake, you can lock the track.

Looking at Figure 14.13, you can see the same two audio events on the same two tracks. However, two things change in the project: the tempo setting and the way time is represented. The Audio 01 track is set as a linear timebase track, whereas the Audio 02 track is set as a musical timebase. 01 contains a sound effect and 02 a beat. In the top or first of four parts, you can see in the Transport panel that the tempo is set at 70 BPM and the display shows that the play line is at Bar 5, Beat 1. In the second part from the top, the only thing that changes is the time format displayed. In this case, the time is represented in seconds, showing that Bar 5, Beat 1 is now 13.714 seconds from the beginning. Both events are still aligned because the tempo hasn't changed.

In the third part from the top, things have changed. The events were not moved, but the Master track has been activated, bringing the tempo up to 120 BPM from its previous 70 BPM. As you can see, the Audio 01 track did not move in time and neither did the play line, but both are now at Bar 7, Beat 4, second sixteenth-note and some. That's because in the time needed to play five bars at 70 BPM, you can play more bars at 120 BPM. In comparing the seconds display found in the second part and the last one at the bottom, you can see that although the musical timebase track moved in time to stay at Bar 5 Beat 1, the linear timebase track moved in bars and beats, but remained at the same place in time.

Figure 14.13
Comparing linear
timebase events with
musical timebase events
at different tempo
settings

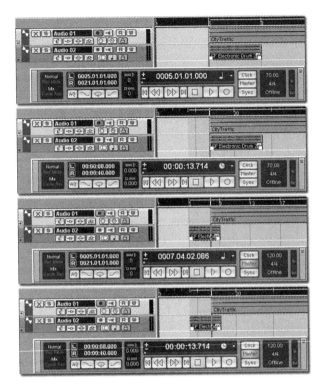

Working with Video Files

With the arrival of DV cameras on the market, more and more video enthusiasts are using their computers to edit their movies. Cubase allows you to take these video files and add sound to them to create original sound tracks or musical scores for them.

There are two basic methods of viewing a video inside Cubase: using your computer monitor to display the video, which implies your computer's CPU is processing the video codec in real time, or by using a special video card that connects to an external monitor. In the latter case, the video card handles the video codec and frees up the computer resources. This implies that you can get a better quality image and a bigger image all together while working on the sound.

The PC version of Cubase SX/SL supports three playback engines: Microsoft DirectShow and Video for Windows and Apple's QuickTime format. The Mac version supports the QuickTime format. In either platform, this implies that you can open AVI, QuickTime, or MPEG files in the following codecs: Cinepak, Indeo, DV, MPEG, or M-JPEG. To use the QuickTime playback method on a PC, you need to install QuickTime on your computer. If you haven't done so already and want to use the multipurpose method, a QuickTime installer is available on the Cubase SX/SL CD.

To set up for online video files in a Cubase project:

1. In the Devices menu, select the Device Setup option.

2. In the Device Setup dialog box, highlight the Video Player option to view the corresponding settings in the right side of the dialog box, as shown in Figure 14.14.

3. In the Playback Method drop-down menu, select the desired playback method.

4. Under Video Window, select the size of window you want to use. Note that the larger the Video window is, the more processing is required by your computer.

5. Click the Apply button, and then click OK.

Figure 14.14
The Video Player settings in the Device Setup dialog box

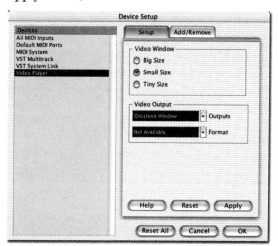

6. In the File menu, select Preferences.

7. Under Event Display, select Video. This page offers two options.

8. Click the Show Video Thumbnails to see a thumbnail preview of the video in the video track.

9. The video cache size represents the cache memory reserved to display thumbnails in the video track. If you are using a long video file or want to stretch the video track to see bigger frames, you need to increase the cache size for the thumbnails to display properly. Otherwise, leave this setting at the default value.

10. Click OK to close the window.

To import an online video file into a Cubase project:

1. Back in the File menu, select Import and then Video File.

2. Browse to the location of your file, select it, and then click Open. This adds the video file to the Media Pool.

3. Right-click (Control-click on a Mac) in the Track List area, and select Add Video Track from the context menu.

4. From this point, you can use one of two methods to add your video to the video track. First, you can right-click the video in the pool and select the Insert Into Project option in the context menu. Then, you can choose if you want to insert it at the current cursor position or at the video's original time. Second, you can drag the video, as you would for an audio event, in the video track at the desired location.

Note that when the Video window is active, you can right-click (Ctrl-click on Mac) on it to expand the size of the window to full screen.

15

Distributing Your Work

You have worked on your project long enough; now, it's time to mix everything down to two tracks. If you are new to this, make a CD and have your friends listen to what you have done. After you have collected enough comments to safely assume that everything you have done up until now is how you want it, you can start distributing the music you call your own. On the other hand, if you don't feel you need comments from others to know whether what you did sounds great, you can go straight from mixdown to mastering and then to distribution.

This chapter describes different possibilities involved in mixing down these arrangements into a stereo master mix. Let's take a look at the last steps after you have finished working on the arrangements. For now, just remember the following steps as you read how to do them later in the chapter.

In this chapter, you will:

▶ Create an audio version of your external MIDI instrument.

▶ Touch up your mix to include the newly converted MIDI tracks into audio tracks.

▶ After you are satisfied with the result of this mix, export a mixdown of this in a format that you can use to create a first draft CD.

▶ Listen to this CD in different environments, collect comments, and go back to your project to make changes.

▶ Generate a new audio mixdown of your material, this time using the highest quality rendering you can. Because the mastering process is a critical step, as you will see later in this chapter, using the best quality allows you to get the most out of your sound. If you choose to have someone else do the mastering for you, you can ask the mastering engineer which format and on which medium he/she wants to receive your material.

▶ If, on the other hand, you decide to tackle the mastering of your album yourself, export these files in a format compatible with your audio mastering tool. Again, compatibility is of the essence: If you export your files in a format your audio editing/mastering software does not support, it won't be of much help to you.

▶ After you are satisfied with the mastering of your album or songs, create a second draft CD and listen to it again in different environments. Just remember that an audio CD only supports the 44.1 kHz, 16-bit, stereo file in either WAVE or AIFF format.

CHAPTER 15

▶ At this point, if you need to change something in the mastering, you only need to make slight modifications; otherwise, you are ready to burn the copy zero of your CD. This should be done on a high-quality medium and at low speed to avoid introducing writing errors on this master copy. There are two acceptable media for master copies of your project: Compact Disc (CD) and Digital Audio Tape (DAT), which both contain decompressed versions of your audio in a format that is accepted in most mastering studios. It is not advisable to use a Mini Disk or files that are compressed in any shape or form for audio distribution on a medium such as a CD because these formats are lossy compression algorithms, which imply that you lose sound quality as a result of the compression. However, compressed formats are a must when it comes to Internet distribution.

▶ If you want to distribute your project commercially, you can look for pressing plants or distributors in your area. In the meantime, you can create your own Web site and add demo copies of your album in streaming format or even send potential record label A&R people invitations to visit your site and listen to your material.

Including your MIDI in the Mixdown

MIDI is a great way to lay down ideas and record music using synthesizers (external or sound card-based), samplers, and drum machines, among other things. However, distributing your work on a CD or through the Internet using MIDI is probably not the greatest solution. This is because, even with General MIDI standard, the sounds they produce are not necessarily what you had in mind and CDs just don't support MIDI. VST Instruments and Rewire instruments are also MIDI-based, so they also don't work well outside the VST environment. This is why you need to convert your MIDI events into audio events when you are satisfied that the tracks are what you want them to be. In the next couple of sections, you see how to do this. Note that if you are using sounds generated by a synthesizer, wave table, or any other sound-generating device found on your sound card or if you are using any software-based sampler that is not VSTi or Rewire compatible, you need to convert them into audio files to include them in your final audio mix.

Converting your MIDI Tracks

There are a few ways you can approach this task: the simple way, the multitrack way, and the sample-based way.

The simple way involves mixing all your MIDI events using the MIDI Track Mixer, and then recording a stereo mix of all MIDI events as a stereo audio file that you.then place on an audio track in Cubase.

The multitrack method involves recording each MIDI instrument as a separate audio file, mono or stereo depending on the instrument itself. Later, you can treat these instruments the same way as you do any other audio track in Cubase, using the track mixers to adjust the effects and mixing levels. In both these methods, the recording starts where the MIDI events start on a track, recording them as you record any instrument.

In the sample-based method, you proceed in the same way, but for space efficiency purposes, you record only the parts that are different, and then copy these parts on the tracks, as you would do for a drum. For example, if the bass line of a verse remains the same for the first eight bars, then changes for the second eight bars of each verse, you record the first eight bars, copy it across the track, and then record the second eight bars for the remainder of the verses. Which method you use is entirely up to you and involves the same procedure with different levels of manipulations.

To convert MIDI tracks playing external MIDI devices into audio tracks:

1.   Start by turning the MIDI metronome off, especially if the same device you are using to record generates this.

2.   Mute all your audio tracks and create an empty stereo (or mono) audio track. If you have a multi-input sound card AND a mixer with multiple output busses, you can record more than one track at a time if you are recording your MIDI tracks on separate audio tracks. Just make sure to read Step 4 carefully to avoid having feedback loops.

3.   Set up your MIDI tracks to play only the events (tracks) that send MIDI information to external events, muting all other tracks and unmuting the tracks you want to record. You can use the Solo button to quickly isolate a specific track for recording.

4.   Connect the outputs of your MIDI devices to the inputs of your sound card. If you have an external mixer, send the output of your mixer into the inputs of your sound card, making sure NOT to include the output of your sound card in the mix. This can be done in different ways depending on your mixer capabilities. For example, if you have busses, assign all your MIDI devices to the bus or busses you are sending to the stereo input(s) of your sound card, making sure that the output of that sound card is only sent to your monitoring system, not to those same busses. If your mixer does not have a busing system, mute the inputs of your mixer corresponding to the outputs of your sound card. This way you won't have a feedback loop. You may want to consult your sound card's manual to find out how to route the output of the soundcard back into the input internally using the sound card's mixer application if you are using the audio outputs as sound generators for your VSTi and Rewire instruments.

5.   Activate the inputs you want to use to record the MIDI events from (see Figure 15.1).

6.   In the audio track's Setting section in the Inspector area, choose a stereo or mono type for your recording. In Figure 15.2, this is set to mono.

7.   Select the input you've activated from the audio channel's input selection.

Figure 15.1
Activating an input in
the VST Input panel

8. Enable the Monitor button on the audio channel you are using to record the MIDI (see Figure 15.2).

9. Click Play to begin playback and adjust the input level of your audio channel. Remember that the audio channel's fader online controls the output level, not the input level. This means that you have to adjust the input level using an external mixer or control on the MIDI device itself.

Figure 15.2
Setting up your
recording through the
audio channel's
Inspector area

USING VST TRUETAPE

If you are using Cubase SX, you may also activate the VST TrueTape module to record in 32-bit mode if you want to add analog-like tape saturation into your signal.

10. After you are satisfied with the input levels, position your playback line at the beginning of the MIDI event(s) you want to record.

11. You can set the punch-in and punch-out to automatically punch in at the left and right locator positions on the Transport panel.

12. Start the recording of your MIDI events as audio events.

13. If you need to repeat the recording process, repeat Steps 2–12 before every recording and mute the previously recorded MIDI and audio tracks, creating new tracks for every recording.

14. If you choose to use the sample-based technique, you need to place the newly recorded events at their proper location on each track.

At this point, you can mute all your MIDI tracks and listen to your newly created audio tracks. Because there might be volume changes between the original MIDI tracks and the audio tracks, you will probably want to adjust their levels using the automation in the Track Mixer. You may also assign insert or send effects and adjust the EQ and dynamic processing for these tracks before moving on to the final mixdown of all these tracks.

About VSTi and Rewire Channels

As VSTi and Rewire channels exist as audio channels within the Cubase SX/SL Track Mixer, they will be included in the audio mixdown when the Audio Mixdown function is used. Just remember to unmute these tracks if you want to include them in the mixdown file, otherwise they will not be included in your exported audio file.

About Dithering

When you are recording material in Cubase, if your system allows it, you should be saving your audio data in 24-bit or even 32-bit resolution. This gives you the most dynamic range and the highest signal-to-noise ratio, which is the level of the noise with no signal applied expressed in dB below a maximum level. As you saw early on in this book, this ratio is around 146 dB in a 24-bit recording and 194 dB in a 32-bit recording. This suggests that when you record a sound using 32-bit resolution, your noise floor is at minus 194 dB. This is inaudible and negligible by any standards. Unfortunately, when you mix down to transfer to a 16-bit DAT recorder, or want to record it on a CD for compact disc players, you need to bring this precision down to 16-bit.

There are two methods used to accomplish this: truncating and dithering. Truncating simply cuts the lower part of the digital word that exceeds the 16-bit word length. Here's an example. If you have a sample that would be stored in 24-bit, it looks like this:

► 1110 0111 1100 0111 0011 1100

Now, if this sample were truncated to 16-bit, it looks like this:

▶ 1110 0111 1100 0111

What happened is that the last eight digits were cut off. These last eight digits are often reverb trails dying in the noise, or harmonics of instruments at low-level intensities. Cutting them off usually adds what is known as quantizing errors. This quantizing error sounds unnatural to human ears.

The solution is to add a special kind of random noise to the sound when you need to bring down the resolution. This random noise is dither noise. What it does in reality is change the last bit in a 16-bit word randomly, creating a noise at -98 dB, which is pretty low. But in reality, this noise is low enough to perceive sounds at -115 dB. Dithering is not needed when you are working in a 24-bit or 32-bit environment. So keep this for the end.

To set up dithering on your final mixdown:

1. Open the VST Master Effects panel (F7 on your keyboard).

2. Because dithering is and should be the last step in your mixdown process, it should only be added when you are preparing the final mixdown to a 16-bit sound file. Because of this, you should use the last VST Master Effect slot available (Number 5 in Cubase SL or Number 8 in Cubase SX). In this Master Effect section, select the UV22 (in Cubase SL) or UV22HR (in Cubase SX) found in the Other VST effect's submenu (see Figure 15.3).

3. Click the On button next to the master effect in order to activate the effect.

4. Click the Edit button to open the effect's interface, or in the VST Master Effects panel, click the left or right arrows to select the Normal Auto preset (see Figure 15.4). This will suit most of your dithering needs.

Figure 15.3
The UV22 dither processor above and its UV22HR counterpart (available in Cubase SX only) below

Figure 15.4
Using the VST Master
Effects panel to select
the presets in an effect

With this final option set, you are now ready to export your mix to an audio file.

Exporting your Final Mix

After you are satisfied with your mix and want to render a final mixdown, or simply render a selection, a track containing effects or a VSTi or Rewire track or tracks, you can use the Export Audio Mixdown function found in the File > Export > Audio Mixdown. This function does not export MIDI tracks, as mentioned earlier, but does export VSTi and Rewire channels, so the following steps assume that you have already converted your MIDI tracks into audio tracks.

To export your final mix as an audio file:

1. Mute the tracks you don't want to include in your audio mix and unmute those you want to include.

2. Position your left locator where you want to begin the audio mix and the right locator where you want to end the audio mixdown.

3. If you want to export the automation when rendering a mixdown, make sure all the appropriate Read Automation buttons are enabled.

SUBZERO!

It is important to make sure the master faders do not clip at any time during playback because this clipping causes distortion in your final mixdown. So, make sure that your levels stay below zero at all times.

4. Select Export > Audio Mixdown from the File menu. The Export Audio Mixdown In dialog box appears, as shown in Figure 15.5.

Figure 15.5
The Export Audio
Mixdown In dialog box

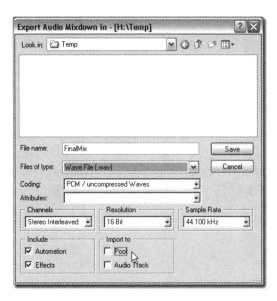

5. In the Export Audio Mixdown In dialog box, choose the proper folder in which to save the file. By default, this should be the same folder as your project file.

6. In the File name field, enter a name for the file you want to export.

7. Choose the Channels, Resolution, and Sample Rate you want to use for your exported file.

SPLITTING STEREO FILES

Note that the Stereo Split, found in the Channels area of the dialog box, creates a left and a right mono file rather than a single stereo interleaved file. This might be useful if you need to use this file in another audio application that does not support stereo interleave files, such as Pro Tools.

8. You can choose to include or ignore the automation and effects in your exported file. A check in the Automation or Effects check boxes indicates that this option will be included when rendering the file. If you have added dithering to your mix, make sure to check the Effects check box.

9. If you want to import this file into your Media Pool or add it as a new track in your project, check the appropriate options.

10. In the Include area of the dialog box, check the Automation and Effects options, if you have any automation that you would like to include along with VSTi and VST effects that might be part of your final mix.

11. Select the appropriate settings in the Files of type and Coding fields that you want to use for this file.

12. Click Save when done.

If you have checked the Import to Audio Track option, Cubase creates a new audio track and names it Mixdown. After the newly created track is in place, make sure to mute the source tracks for this new track (containing the audio mixdown). If you have chosen not to import the audio rendering of your mix back into your project, you can proceed with your work as usual, continuing whatever work needs to be done or save and close your project and start working on the mastering of your album, as is discussed later in this chapter.

File Format Options

You can export your final mix in two different lossless formats: WAV and AIFF. Both are standard formats and compatible with Mac and PC computers. You need to have your files in either of these formats to create an audio CD. But you need to leave the WAV format at its default "PCM/uncompressed Waves" format if you want to be able to import it back into your project.

The Internet and the Web have been quite helpful to musicians in allowing them to publish their material online and use it as an effective distribution medium and a way to promote their skills. This is one of the reasons why other Web-related exporting formats are now available and also considered standards in the industry. Among those, Cubase supports RealNetworks RealMedia format, Microsoft Windows Media format, MP3 format (from MPEG Layer 3), and Ogg Vorbis compression format. There are obviously a few other formats available, but they were not supported by Cubase at the time this book was written.

WHAT IS OGG VORBIS?

Ogg Vorbis is a new audio compression format that is roughly comparable to other formats used to store and play digital music, such as MP3 and other digital audio formats. It is different from these other formats because it is completely free, open, and unpatented.

Although not all artists realize it, MP3 is what is known as a "lossy" format. Thus, much of the sound data is removed when MP3 files are created. This results in a file with inferior sound quality to a CD. Vorbis is also a "lossy" format, but uses superior acoustic models to reduce the damage. Thus, music released in Vorbis sounds better than a comparably sized MP3 file.

Also, artists should be concerned about licensing terms for formats. If you decide to sell your music in MP3 format, you are responsible for paying Fraunhofer a percentage of each sale because you are using their patents. Vorbis is patent and license-free, so you never need to pay anyone in order to sell, give away, or stream your own music.

To find out more about this format, you can visit http://www.vorbis.com.

Note that at the time this book was written, the Ogg Vorbis codec was not well-implemented in Cubase, causing it to create unusable files. You may want to look for updates as this situation might be resolved by the time you read this.

Because these formats were developed with the Web in mind, they make it easy to stream or distribute content over a low-bandwidth system. As a result, a certain amount of data compression is applied to these file formats. The more you compress the files, the smaller they are and this is also directly related to sound quality: the smaller the file, the worse the sound quality gets. All these compression algorithms are lossy, meaning that they remove data from the original file when saving it into this new format and by doing so, they reduce sound quality as well.

It is important to understand at this point that there is a big difference between data compression, which is used to compress the size of a file, and dynamic compression, which is used to control the dynamics of the audio signal. The dynamic compression does not influence the size of the file. You will have a chance to experiment with this and will have to find a compromise that you need to be comfortable with in the end. Keeping this in mind, remember that there are more people using 56 Kb modems to download and listen to music than there are people with high-speed access. This fact is changing rapidly; however, until the time comes when everyone has high-speed access to the Internet, make sure your potential customers will not be discouraged by the size of your file.

The next two sections describe particularities related to RealMedia, Windows Media, and MP3 format conversion when exporting your files for Web distribution.

RealMedia and Windows Media

RealNetworks was one of the first companies to develop an algorithm to compress and deliver audio and video files over the Internet using a streaming technology. Today, RealNetworks is one of the leaders in this field and its RealMedia formats have become one of the most popular streaming standards for distribution of audio and video content over the World Wide Web. Not to be left out in the dark, Microsoft decided to offer its own type of streaming media technology, which is called Windows Media format.

The principle behind streaming technology is the same, no matter which format you use. The idea is to have a file, which is compressed to a user specification and then have this compressed file available to others over the Net. What makes streaming "streaming" is that this file is associated with a compatible player on your computer. When you click on the link to this file, it loads the player into memory. This player then starts playing the content as it arrives rather than waiting for it to be completely downloaded, thus reducing the waiting period before a user can listen to the content of this file.

For this to work properly, a go-between file is often created (see Figure 15.6). This is commonly known as a metafile. This metafile contains a simple piece of information: the location of the media file itself. Because a metafile is so small, it is downloaded quickly into your computer. After it is downloaded, the player loads into memory and reads the address, telling the server to start sending packets of data, which it stores into a buffer memory. When the buffer memory is filled up, it starts playing. The time it takes to fill up this buffer memory depends on the connection speed a user has, the connection speed of the server, the traffic over the Internet at that moment, and the size of the media file itself. For example, filling the buffer for a 100 Kb file is quicker than if the file is 100 Mb. But after this buffer is loaded, the file begins to play while your Internet connection stays active, continuing the transfer of the rest of the information for this file.

Figure 15.6
How information flows
as streaming media over
the Internet

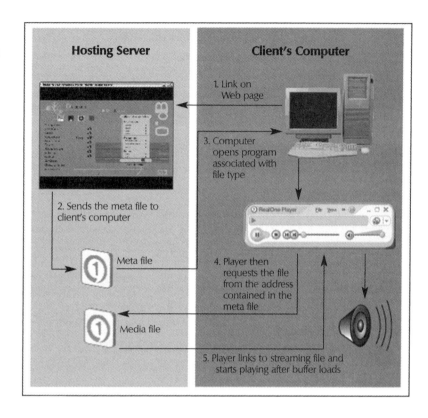

Now that you understand the basics about how streaming works, you'll understand how the settings in the Export Audio window under the RealNetworks (RealPlayer) format works and also what effect they have from the end user's point of view.

To export a file for RealPlayer or Windows Media Player compatibility:

1. Proceed in the same way as you would for any other type of file (and as described earlier in this chapter), up until you reach the format of the file you want to export. From there, you proceed as follows.

2. Next to the Files of type field, select RealAudio File G2 (.rm) as your file type or Windows Media Audio File (.wma).

3. Next to the Coding field (in RealAudio) or Attributes (in Windows Media), select the appropriate format for your content.

REALAUDIO SPECIFIC OPTIONS

Remember that the compression you apply here influences both the file size and the quality of the end result. If you are targeting a general public, then using a 34 kBit/s (Kilobits per second) format is more suitable. On the other hand, if you are targeting people who have high bandwidth-access, such as businesses or other users you know are using a faster connection, you can select a higher bit rate.

Make sure to select the bit rate and the appropriate type of codec compression: If you have music, you should use the Mono or Stereo Music presets. If you have mostly voice content with no music, use the Voice presets.

The RealNetworks codec treats those two types of audio information in a very different way, so making the right selection here is paramount. If your content contains both musical and vocal content, go for the music presets.

Choosing mono music over stereo music adds definition as it uses the additional space to allow a wider range of frequencies, whereas the stereo music is encoded in stereo and offers a stereo image with less high frequencies, as those are reduced to allow for the stereo information to fit in the same amount of bits per second.

Finally, below the Coding field, an information box tells you what this RealPlayer preset is most appropriate for, such as the example in Figure 15.7 in which the "56K Modem (34 kBit/s) Music (Stereo)" preset has been chosen.

Figure 15.7
The RealAudio options in the Export Audio Mixdown In dialog box

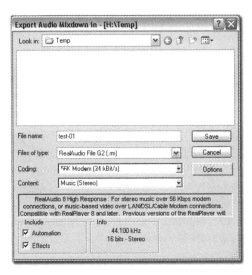

4. Click the Options button when all of your settings are complete in this window. This brings up either the RealAudio Options dialog box as shown in Figure 15.8 or the Windows Media Audio Options dialog box as shown in Figure 15.9.

Figure 15.8
The Real Audio Options
dialog box

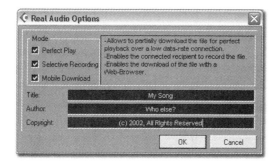

Figure 15.9
The Windows Media
Audio Options dialog
box

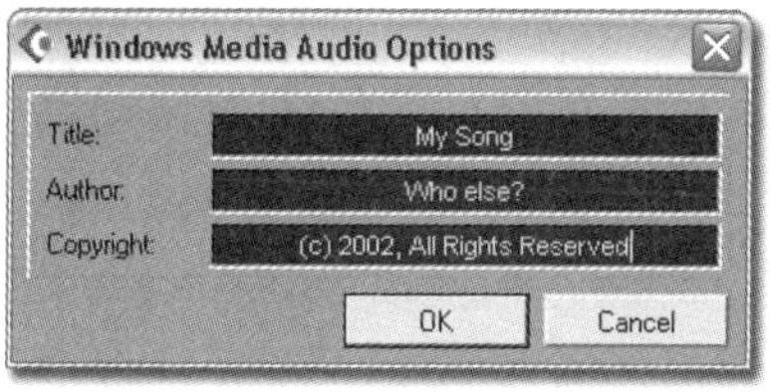

5. Enter the appropriate Title, Author, and Copyright information for your song. This information appears in the user's Player window when a file is being played.

6. If you are using the RealAudio format (this does not apply for Windows Media), check the appropriate Mode options. When you add a check to an option, a short description of what this feature does appears to the right of the option (see Figure 15.8).

7. Click OK.

8. Click the Save button to start the compression process. This can take several minutes if your song is long.

While the file is being rendered in the RealAudio format, a progression dialog box appears (see Figure 15.10), as with any other exporting feature. It is recommended that to avoid errors in the final document you do not use your computer to do other tasks while this process is completing.

Figure 15.10
The Export Audio
progression dialog box
allows you to monitor
the progression or abort
the process

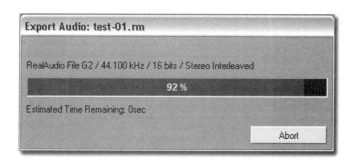

MP3

The MP3 files are similar to RealAudio (RA) or Windows Media (WMA) files in that they are meant to be sent over the Internet and then played on a computer. This format has literally changed the face of audio distribution, allowing for high-compression algorithms that reduce file sizes without compromising audio quality too much when using higher bit rates.

This said, Cubase SX allows you to save in MP3 format (available as an upgrade for Cubase SL users). As with RA and WMA, the smaller the files, the lower the quality. Compare this as an example: The compact disc standard of 44.1 kHz, 16-bit, Stereo in Wav format uses a bandwidth of 172.3 Kilobytes per second, whereas an MP3 file compressed at 320 kbps (the highest quality available with the MP3 codec from Steinberg) uses only 39 Kilobytes per second of bandwidth. This is because a one-minute file in WAV or AIFF CD compatible (44.1 kHz, 16-bit, Stereo) format uses 10.09 Megabytes of disc space, whereas the MP3 file at 320 kbps uses only 2.29 Megabytes, making it easier to transfer over the Internet. The MP3 standard relies heavily on algorithms that compress the information and then on the computer's processor to decompress this information as it plays back, as does any other file compression algorithm (ZIP, ARJ, Stuff It, and so on).

To export a file for MP3 compatibility:

1. As with RA and WMA, proceed with the export process as was demonstrated earlier in this chapter up until you reach the format of the file you want to export. Then proceed as follows:

2. Next to the Files of type field, select MPEG Layer 3 (.mp3) as your file type.

3. Next to the Attributes field, select the appropriate format for your content as shown in Figure 15.11.

Figure 15.11
Selecting the attributes for your MP3 files in the Export Audio Mixdown In dialog box

4. In the Quality field, select the Highest option, which takes more time to compress but yields better results.

5. Click the Options button when all of your settings are complete in this window.

6. The ID3 Tag Options dialog box appears. If you've entered information in the Broadcast Wave preferences, this information appears here automatically. Make the necessary changes and click OK.

7. Click the Save button to start generating the file.

About Mastering

Mastering is the art of subtlety and involves adjusting your final mixes so that they all sound coherent and cohesive when played one after the other. This means that the first mix you did two months ago when you started working on your album sounds as good as the one you created last night at 4:00 a.m. after consuming large amounts of caffeine.

When preparing an album, mastering is a must before pressing your master copy. The mastering process is used to reduce the aforementioned differences between various mixes by patching together every song in a one-to-two day span—listening to the songs in the order they will appear on your album and correcting the overall harmonic colors and dynamic range of your songs.

It is also a good idea to not master your album with the same listening reference as you have used for the recording and mixing process because your ears have probably grown accustomed to this sound and may no longer be as critical to some aspects or coloring of the music. Furthermore, if your monitoring system is adequate at best, you will probably benefit from a professional mastering facility rather than a home studio mixing environment, because the better ones provide the best all around listening and processing equipment to truly isolate problems in the consistency between your songs, not to mention a fresh pair of ears listening to your project. This can add a whole new untapped dimension to your project. This is especially true if you want to use this as a commercially distributed album. Finally, there will always be, no matter what the critics of pricey studios might say, a difference in quality between a home studio filled with inexpensive equipment with low-quality components and a quarter million dollar mastering facility in which every piece of equipment in the room is meant to optimize your sound.

If you don't have the financial resources or don't feel the need for a professional mastering because your project is for small and local distribution only, there are no recipes here and no settings that can apply to every situation, but rather pointers that should help you get the most out of a mastering session. If you are unsure as to how your mix sounds, try listening to music that you find is similar in style to what you have done and sounds like you want your music to sound. Then see if you can emulate these qualities. Another way of evaluating your mix is by listening to it in different environments, such as a car stereo, the room next door, or at a friend's place. Remember that the fresher your mind and ears are, the better it is for the mastering process. So, avoid starting a mastering session after a long day of work, or after mixing the last song on your album.

> ▶ Mastering is not where you mix your songs. If you are not satisfied with a mix, you should remix it rather than trying to fix it at the mastering stage.

> ▶ This might be very obvious to most people, but just in case: NEVER master an album using your headphones as a reference.

> ▶ When exporting your audio mixes in Cubase for the mastering process, use the highest quality available. If you have worked in 96 kHz, 32-bit stereo format and have a reliable system that can reproduce these specifications, go for it. You can always convert your final result after the mastering process to 44.1 kHz, 16-bit stereo format.

> ▶ Before you start your mastering session, sit down and listen to all the songs in order with your notepad and a pencil at hand. Take notes on inconsistencies between one song and another.

▶ Generally, there are two important things that you want to adjust in a mastering session, and this should be kept in mind throughout the entire mastering process of a single album: EQ and dynamics.

▶ When tweaking the EQ, you are not trying to reinvent the mix, just tweak it. Give the bass more definition, add presence to the vocals and crispness to the high-end, and most of all, make sure that all songs have the same equalization qualities.

▶ Dynamics give punch and life to a mix. Make sure all your tracks come into play at the same level—this doesn't mean they should all be loud or soft, but consistent with the intensity of the song. If a song is mellow, it can come in softer, but the soft intensity in one song has to be consistent in relation to the soft intensity of another song. As with EQ, consistency is the key.

▶ There are more and more software packages out there that do a pretty good job at EQing and compressing audio. Steinberg's Wavelab, Clean and Mastering Edition, and IK Multimedia's T-Racks are just a few tools you can use to help you get the most out of your home mastering session. You can either use the VST or DirectX effects (PC version only) in the Master Effects section or as with some of the previously mentioned software, use them as independent mastering tools.

Creating an Audio Compact Disc

Creating your CD is often one of the last things you do before having people outside of your studio environment listen to your music. After you create an audio mixdown of your MIDI and audio tracks as a premastering file (in whatever format you used to do so), master one or more tracks as discussed earlier, save your files and convert them into a compact disc compatible format, you are ready to create a compact disc.

Cubase does not offer any tools to actually burn (record) a CD. But Steinberg offers one solution through Wavelab. This is by no means the only tool available. If you purchased a CD recorder, it might have come with a CD recording application. One thing is certain: You need software capable of creating a CD-DA compatible disc (Compact Disc Digital Audio). This brings us to formats. When creating CDs, the two most common types of CDs are CD-ROM and CD-DA. CD-ROMs contain data suitable for your computer. CD-DA contains audio that is suitable for both your computer and CD player. There are two variations of this: the Enhanced CD and the Mixed Mode CD, which are available in some software and some CD recorders. The Enhanced CD is a multisession CD, containing a series of CD-DA compatible tracks in the first session, making it compatible with your home CD player, and a second session containing data, which is read by computers only. In Mixed Mode, it's the reverse: The data tracks are at the beginning and the audio tracks follow. This usually means that your CD player will not read it. This type of CD is used for multimedia content, such as games, or educational or multimedia sales presentations. In light of this, understand that you need to select the proper type of CD when creating a CD within the software application. There are a few rules to follow if you want your CD to play back in any CD player.

When recording a CD, there are three aspects that come into play: the format of the CD (CD-ROM, CD-DA, Enhanced CD, Mixed Mode, and so on), the session, and the disc. A session is an instance in which you decide to write something on a CD. For example, today you decide to record a wave file onto a CD. You write a session and to complete the process, you close the session for the disc to be understood by the CD-ROM drive. A disc is closed when you can't record anything else on it and opened when you can add other sessions to it. In our previous example, if you close the session but leave the disc open, you can record another session on it, making it a multisession disc, each time closing the session but leaving the disc opened for another recording. When you want to close the disc because the disc is full, you can do so after the last session you record, disabling it from being recorded anymore. This is called a multisession CD, which is common in CD-ROMs, Enhanced CDs, and Mixed Mode CDs, but this method of recording the CD is not compatible with audio CDs.

For an audio CD to play in a consumer CD player, you can only have one closed session and one closed disc in CD-DA format unless using the Enhanced CD format. When creating an audio CD, you may use two methods of writing the information onto disc: TAO short for Track-At-Once or DAO short for Disc-At-Once. You will probably want to consult your software and hardware documentation to see if these features are supported, but for now, understand the TAO records the audio CD one track at a time, leaving a two-second gap between each song that you added to the CD recording session. The DAO, on the other hand, does not record this two-second gap between each song you added to the CD recording session. (In Figure 15.12, you can see the Music CD creation window in the back, where the source files appear on top and the destination or audio CD files appear at the bottom. In front of this window is the Record CD Setup dialog box in which you can select whether you want to record the CD using TAO or DAO.)

Figure 15.12
Creating a Music CD in the Easy CD Creator application from Roxio (Adaptec)

With these basic principles in hand, you can create audio CDs in your own home using the audio CD creation software of your choice. It is also a good idea to create intermediate audio CDs to listen to your music on other sound systems and see if you are pleased with what you hear before you produce the final master. Most new domestic CD players accept an audio disk on rewritable media (CD-RW). Rewritable CDs are outside the specifications, but can be, if your player is compatible, a good way to create test mixes. But remember that for your CD to play, it has to be in audio CD format (CD-DA) and not in data CD format (CD-ROM).

Backing Up Your Work

Making backup copies of your work as you go is paramount. Not only does it prevent you from having to rerecord your material if you make mistakes and erase files, but it is also a good way to keep source material from being lost because of hard drive crashes. Another good reason to back up files as you are working with them is that you can always go back and change things later in an arrangement or create a new arrangement altogether using the source material rather than the master two-track recording. If these are not good enough reasons for you, consider this last piece of advice: When you are working on a project for someone else and charging studio time, I doubt that your client will be impressed by your work if you lose recordings!

There are many ways to do backups in Cubase and outside of Cubase:

> ▶ Create an Archive folder containing all the audio present in the Audio Pool of your project by using the Prepare Archive function in the Pool menu as shown in Figure 15.13. This prompts you to select a destination folder where a copy of all the audio files used in the pool are copied, making it easy to save this folder on a backup media, such as a CD-R (Compact Disc-Recordable), CD-RW (Compact Disc ReWritable), tape backup, or removable media drive. After you've saved the audio files, you can also copy the .CPR and video files as you might also need to include them in the backup.

Figure 15.13
Using the Prepare Archive function in the Pool menu to save all audio files in a single folder for backup

> ▶ Use your CD creation software to create a data disc that contains all the source material (audio, arrangements, song, preset, and setting files) used for this project, making sure to label your CD accordingly.
>
> ▶ Use a backup software or disk imaging software to create a backup image of your files.

Keeping in mind that computer crashes occur unfortunately quite often and that disc failures are not as infrequent as we would wish, making backup copies of your work makes sense—even after each working session. This way, you reduce the amount of time lost if ever something bad happens.

Reading the documentation provided with your CD burning software to understand how it works and how you can retrieve information from backup disks might prove useful, so take a little bit of time to familiarize yourself with these options.

Distributing Your Work on the Web

Distributing your work on portable media, such as tape cassettes, compact discs, or even vinyl, was at one point the only way of promoting your work and selling it. Today with the advances being made by software developers and the growing importance of the Internet in our lives, this new medium is becoming yet another way of distributing your work effectively and is also a low-cost solution to mass distribution of your work.

This section discusses how to integrate a RealAudio file and an MP3 file inside a Web document (HTML or HyperText Markup Language). If you don't feel comfortable with this or have no interest in knowing how to do this, please stop reading now.

Remember that we have discussed how RealAudio, Windows Media, and MP3 files use "go-between" files under the RealMedia and Windows Media header in this chapter. These "go-between" files are called metafiles. In the case of RealAudio, they have the RAM or RPM extension, and in the case of MP3 files, they have the M3U file extension. In both cases, their content is quite simple: It contains a link to the actual media found on your Web page's server. When a user clicks on a link to listen to your audio file from a Web page, this link points to the metafile. Because this metafile is small (containing only a path to the actual media file), it is transferred quickly and loads the associated player into the client's memory. This player then reads the path and starts downloading the file, filling up its buffer memory before it starts playing the content.

To do this, you need to prepare the following documents:

> ▶ The HTML page that will contain the link to your metafile
> ▶ The metafile containing the link to the streaming media file
> ▶ The actual streaming media file containing the audio

To create the actual HTML file, you can use any HTML editor or text editor, depending on the software you have on your computer. A link in an HTML document usually has three parts:

> ▶ The opening tag telling the browser that what follows is a link to another document. This tag tells the browser where to look for this file (its path). This reads something like this: <a href= "http://www.yourserver.com/yourfolder/yoursubfolder/yourmetafile.ram">, where "a href=" represents the HTML code for hyperlink references and what follows represents the complete path to the metafile in question. You would, of course, replace this path with the real location of your metafile's location.

▶ The text that appears in the Web page as being a link. This could be anything really and should immediately follow the opening tag.

▶ The closing tag telling the browser that what follows is not part of the link anymore. This always looks like this: </a>

Here is an example of a complete link as it would appear in an HTML document:

▶ <a href="http://www.yourserver.com/yourfolder/yoursubfolder/ yourmetafile.ram">Audio Demo</a>

To create the metafile, you can use an ASCII text editor and save the file with its appropriate extension. If you are creating a metafile for a RealAudio file, use the RAM extension and if you are creating a metafile for an MP3 file, use the M3U extension. In both cases, all you have to enter is the path to your actual streaming media content. Here are examples of these paths:

For a metafile containing a link to RealAudio streaming content, this file should be saved with the *.RAM extension and should contain the following type of link:

▶ http://www.yourserver.com/yourfolder/yoursubfolder/yourmediafile.rm

For a metafile containing a link to MP3 streaming content, this file should be saved with the *.M3U extension and should contain the following type of link:

▶ http://www.yourserver.com/yourfolder/yoursubfolder/yourmediafile.mp3

Now that you have created the HTML document pointing to the metafile, the metafile pointing to the media file, and the media file from the Export Audio option in Cubase, you need to upload these files to the appropriate location on your Web site server using an FTP (File Transfer Protocol) software or a Web browser if your Web site host allows it. After your files have been uploaded, test your link in the HTML file and move the original files from your local computer. This is only a precaution. You see, if you have made a mistake in creating your link on the HTML page, trying to load the page from the server might look like it's working. However, in reality, your browser is loading the file from your local computer, giving you the impression that everything works, when in fact the HTML link is not correct. Moving the files temporarily when testing your links gives you an error if it can't find the file either on the server or your local computer. On the other hand, if your link is correct, it plays the file after the player's buffer has been filled.

Remember that the time it takes to fill the player's buffer depends on the size of the streaming audio content and your Internet connection speed.

16

Score Editing

Creating a score with Cubase SX is a way of turning your MIDI sequence into a music sheet that can be read by other musicians. To accomplish this task, you take what you recorded into your MIDI sequencer and convert it into musical notation. Cubase SX provides powerful tools that help you produce professional-looking music sheets.

When you create and edit a song in Cubase, you create different tracks of MIDI events. Each one of those tracks can become a musical sheet. You can combine different tracks to create a more complex conductor score or create a lead sheet to give chord and rhythm indications to a group of studio musicians.

We do not cover everything there is to know about scoring in this chapter, because this could be the subject of an entire book. For a more in-depth look at the scoring capabilities of Cubase SX functions, you can read the online documentation provided with the software. We cover the basics and some of the more advanced techniques involved in scoring with Cubase. Finally, this chapter assumes that you know how to enter notes in a MIDI sequencer and focuses on laying out the information in a proper way.

Score editing functions are available in both SX and SL versions; however, the SL version does not support the Page mode display discussed in this chapter. In other words, whenever references are made to this mode, it applies only to Cubase SX users.

In this chapter, you will learn:

▶ About the score function and inherent differences with other editors in Cubase.

▶ How to prepare a project to get the best scoring results out of MIDI events.

▶ How the score function uses layers to place different types of symbols.

▶ What Layout settings are and why you should use them when preparing music sheets for musicians.

▶ How you can adjust Staff settings for each staff in your score.

▶ How to understand and work in different score modes.

▶ What you can do with the extended toolbar functions to change the appearance of notes on staves.

▶ How to use the Symbol Palette to insert additional markings in your score in order to make it easier for musicians to read.

▶ How to work with different types of text in a score.

▶ How to print and export a score to paper or graphic files.

About Score Editing

Scoring is an art form all to itself. To understand and make the best out of Cubase's scoring capabilities, it is useful to know music and music notation. What is important in score editing is that the result is legible to other musicians. It is simply a way to write down on a music sheet a standard set of notes and symbols, which is then read by musicians as they play their instruments. This is the whole purpose of creating a score. Sometimes, this might mean that you have to edit MIDI events in a way that makes the recording sound unnatural, because Cubase gives you tools to adapt what you played in a score but cannot interpret everything.

In many ways, the score approximates the basic MIDI information in a sequence (yes, only MIDI information can be translated into a score, not audio). A musician, in turn, interprets this score by playing the notes or symbols that appear on the music sheet and you can play back this performance as an audio or MIDI interpretation, depending on the instrument the musician plays. Obviously, if you already have the MIDI down, you don't really need to rerecord it. However, for interpretive reasons, this might be one of the useful applications for music scores. Because scores are approximations of the MIDI data, you might want to save a copy of your project as a playable file and another copy as a scoring file; the copy you use for scoring is well-quantized and straightforward. This helps you in creating a clean music sheet without having to change the way the original MIDI tracks were recorded.

You can score only MIDI events with the scoring tools. This is very important to understand. As a result, if you are recording a project that contains mostly audio content, you have to create additional MIDI tracks to create a score out of it. One thing to remember about MIDI recording is that the length and precision of your MIDI events greatly influences how the information is displayed in the score itself. You can tell Cubase how to interpret the information for an optimized layout; however, to avoid manipulating the events extensively, you should quantize everything before you start editing your score. Figure 16.1 shows a simple melodic line that was played without quantization.

On the top part, you can see how Cubase interpreted the information, creating a complex series of ties between the notes to reproduce what was played. On the lower part, you can see the same melodic line, but quantized and enharmonically corrected. This means that the "accidents," or notes that are outside the regular scale, have been adjusted to better reflect a correct way of scoring musical notes. This is possible because Cubase takes the MIDI events and compares them with the score settings to display the score layout. So, depending on your score settings and how you recorded your MIDI events, your result will vary.

Figure 16.1
You need to tell Cubase
how you want the MIDI
events to appear in the
score; here are before
(top) and after (bottom)
looks at a simple
melodic line taken from
the MIDI events

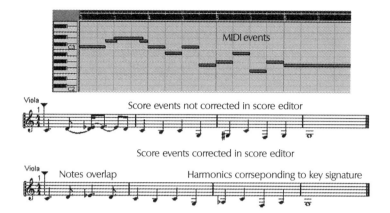

Score Editor Window

The Score Editor window, like the Key, Drum, List, and Audio editing windows, is available from the MIDI menu.

To launch the Score Editor:

▶ Select a MIDI part or track and press Ctrl+R (Command+R on Mac) on your keyboard or select Score Edit from the MIDI menu.

In the Score Editor, you have two basic display modes: Page mode and Edit mode.

You can switch from Page mode to Edit mode by selecting the option in the Score menu. This is a toggle option, meaning that if you are in Edit mode, the option displays Page mode to switch to that mode, and, inversely, if you are in Page mode, the option displays Edit mode. By default, Cubase opens the editor in Edit mode. The main difference between the two is that Page mode is like the Page Display mode on a word processor: It lets you see the page as it will appear once printed and includes the elements that are part of the page layout. Therefore, you can position your title, add printing elements, and so on. Both editing modes display similar toolbars, so let's look at the functions of these tools.

Figure 16.2
The Score Editor's
toolbars

Whenever you make a staff active by clicking in the area to the left of a staff, the content found in another opened editing window reflects the content of that activated staff. An active staff displays a thick border at the beginning of each staff line, and the Score Editor's title bar shows the name of the active staff. In Figure 16.3, the Cello staff is the active one.

Figure 16.3
The black line to the left of the staff clef indicates the active staff—in this case, the Cello; any other opened editing window also displays this staff

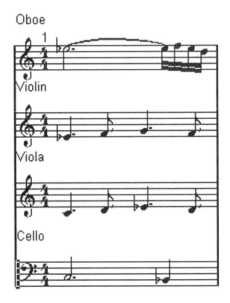

The toolbar is actually five separate rows:

▶ Toolbar. The first section below the Title bar, this represents most of the tools found in other editing windows.

▶ Info Line. The black row displays information on a selected event. When one event is selected, the information for this event is displayed in white. When more than one event is selected, the information appears in yellow. To reveal or hide this row, you can click the Info button found in the toolbar.

▶ Extended toolbar. This displays many of the tools you need to insert and edit notes, rests, and symbols in your score (see Figure 16.4). You will find more information regarding this toolbar later in this chapter.

Figure 16.4
The tools found on the Extended toolbar are displayed when the T button in the toolbar is pressed

▶ Filter bar. This displays a series of check boxes. Each check box is an invisible item that you can choose to see by checking the appropriate box. Filtered items do not appear on printed paper. To reveal or hide this row, press the F button in the toolbar (see Figure 16.5).

Figure 16.5
You can find additional buttons in this toolbar, such as the Info Line button, Extended Tools button, and the Filter button

▶ Ruler bar. Shown in points in Figure 16.2, and visible in Page mode, the Ruler bars allow you to align text elements from your score with a horizontal and vertical ruler, found on the top and left part of the editing window. You can change the units displayed in this Ruler bar by right-clicking in the Ruler. A context menu displays the available options. To hide the rulers, select the Off option from this context menu.

Score Preferences

The Score Preferences window offers different behavior options that can be set on or off. One of the options that you will find here makes your cursor change to the Arrow tool after a symbol has been inserted. This is useful when you don't insert the same symbol very often and want to position your symbol precisely after you've inserted it. Most of the options are self-explanatory and are well documented, but if you don't know what an option does, click the Help button at the bottom of the page to get context-sensitive help.

To change your score behavior preferences:

1. Select Preferences from the File menu.
2. Select the Scores option on the left side of the dialog box (see Figure 16.6).
3. To toggle an option, click the option to add a check mark in the State column.
4. Click Apply to accept your changes and then click OK to close the dialog box.

Figure 16.6
The Score Preferences
dialog box

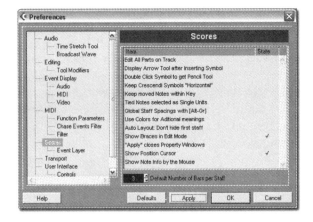

You will find most of the global preferences relating to the score in the Global Settings submenu found in the Score menu. These options offer a wide range of options you can set to make your score look and react the way you want.

Understanding Score Layers

When working on a score, you are placing and editing symbols on three different layers: the note layer, the layout layer, and the global layer.

The note layer represents MIDI events that you may open from a MIDI track. These MIDI events become note symbols on the note layer. On this same layer, you also find other note dependant information that is represented by symbols, such as tempo changes, dynamic indications, or special symbols that represent how notes should be interpreted graphically, such as a trill or an arpeggio. These symbols are all present as long as the note symbols associated with them are present. When you move a note or a bar containing a note, the associated symbols follow.

The layout layer represents elements that quite often define a group of instruments on a score and define how an instrument appears on a page. For example, a bracket across a brass section is considered as a layout item. You might decide that each brass part contains six staves per sheet by defining a layout called brass and then applying this same layout to all the instruments in that section. However, symbol elements that are in one layout do not appear in another layout, so when you want to have certain indications repeated on all the parts, use a symbol that is part of the global layer. Think of the layout layer as a preset setting for a group of instruments, where you can save the number of bars per staff, staves per page, and layout symbols for this particular layout.

The global layer represents symbols that are not associated with notes but give indications to the musician on how to play a part and are part of the greater picture (global) of the score. For example, a coda indication or a rehearsal marking is considered as layout symbols. To better understand the layout layer, let's look at an example. When preparing a big band arrangement, you need to create individual parts for each musician and a score for the conductor. Starting with the conductor's score, open all the tracks corresponding to the instruments in the arrangement, and then move notes, quantize note symbols so that they look good on paper, and add certain indications. Chances are, when you create the individual music sheets, you'll want to see the same indications on each sheet. Take, for example, rehearsal marks such as letters identifying different sections of a song. These indications are placed and saved in the layout layer.

Global Settings

These settings influence the properties of global symbols as described earlier as well as settings that relate to how Cubase handles specific representation of symbols, such as accidentals in the current score or text sets, which are style templates that you can assign to different types of text in your score.

Text Settings

The Text Settings in the Global Settings submenu offer two tabs of options: the global text and text attribute sets. The Global Text tab sets font attributes for different parts of your score, including bar numbers, track names, time signatures, and so on (see Figure 16.7). The Attribute Sets tab lets you create template text sets that you can use throughout your score.

Figure 16.7
The Text Settings dialog box

To create a text attribute set:

1. Select Global Settings > Text from the Score menu.
2. Click the Attribute Sets tab in the Text Settings dialog box.
3. In the Set field, type a name for your set. For example, if you want to create a set for lyrics, call your set "Lyrics." When you add lyrics, you can apply that set (similar to styles in Word for all you Word experts) to them without having to set your font, size, and attributes each time.
4. Change the font, its size, and its attributes (Bold, Italic, or Underline).
5. Select a frame type if you want to see a frame around your text.
6. Select a proper Melisma style setting. A melisma is a line that appears after a

CHAPTER 16

syllable when you are adding lyrics to indicate that the syllable is stretched over many notes. Figure 16.8 illustrates this. The melisma style represents the line itself, and the melisma end is how the line should end. In Figure 16.8, the melisma style is solid and the end is plain and the text's attribute is italic. You learn how to use melisma when looking at how to use text later in this chapter.

Figure 16.8
Example of a text set
using a melisma

7. Adjust the Positioning field to the left or right. This influences which side of the text is used to align this text with notes when the notes are moved around.

8. Adjust the Alignment field as appropriate (left, center, or right). This only makes a difference when you have more than one line of text. It is similar to a paragraph alignment setting, aligning the text to the left, to the center, or to the right.

9. Press the Store button to store this set.

10. Press Apply to accept your changes and then click OK.

The set you have just created is accessible in the Score > Text > Font Setting option or in the Text Settings dialog box found under Global Settings > Text as well.

Accidentals Settings

The Accidentals dialog box (shown in Figure 16.9) lets you determine how accidental notes should appear in your score. An accidental is an altered note that doesn't belong to the key signature. The rule for accidentals is that when one appears in a bar, each time the same note appears in this bar, it keeps the accident active until the next bar. If you want to add precision to this setting by repeating the accident each time the same note appears in the same bar, you can tell Cubase to repeat the accident. The right part of this page offers you a choice of most common tensions used and a sharp or flat setting for each one. The paramount rule is to go for clarity. Repeat an accidental in the same bar wherever there is a potential for confusion. Even though an accidental is cancelled by a bar line, a cautionary (bracketed) accidental in the next bar is often helpful.

For example, if you have a Cm with a flat ninths note, you can decide to show this as either a D flat or as a C minor chord with an augmented octave (C sharp). As a rule of thumb, keep flat tensions as flat notes and sharp tensions as sharp notes. Therefore, in our example, a musician would prefer reading a D flat rather than a C sharp.

Figure 16.9
The Accidentals dialog
box

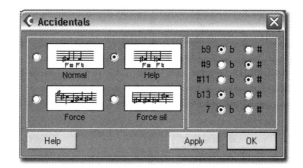

To set the accidentals preferences in a score:

1. Select Global Settings > Accidentals in the Scores menu.
2. Select the options you want to apply to your score. The dialog box is divided into two sections. On the left, you can choose how the accidental notes are handled and on the right, you can select how you want specific tensions in a chord to be represented.
3. Click Apply and then click OK.

Chord Settings

The Chord Settings in the Global Settings submenu offer two tabs of options: the chord types and chord font settings.

The Chord Types tab displays different ways of showing chord symbols. How to set up this page depends on how you prefer seeing chords displayed and from which scoring school you are. Different schools of thought exist on this subject, so the choice is up to you.

The Chord Font tab offers you three styles of music chords: English, with the A to G scale; French, with the Do to Si scale; and German, which is similar to the English style except that the B key letter is replaced by the H key letter and B flats become B.

You can select the font type and a font size for each part of the chord. Look at the sample in Figure 16.10 to see how the change affects the layout of the chord.

Figure 16.10
The Chord Settings
dialog box

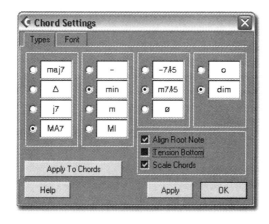

Other Global Settings

The Spacing option found in the Global Settings submenu is where you can tell Cubase how much space you want between elements on your score layout. You can set each element to a default value, or you can change it to customize the display of your score. To change a value, you select the field and enter the value manually.

The Notation Style option also found in the Global Settings offers three tabs of options: switches, beam and bars, and options. All of these options define how you want certain elements to be displayed in a score. For example, the Beams and Bars tab displays properties for bar numbering and layout in your score and beam properties, such as angles of beams when tied beams are slanted.

When working with chord intensive songs and creating guitar parts at the same time, you will find it useful to use the Guitar Library. This tool allows you to create and collect different guitar chord symbols alongside with their chord name (see Figure 16.11). In this dialog box, you can create new chords, remove them, and save them to a file

Figure 16.11
The Guitar Library
dialog box

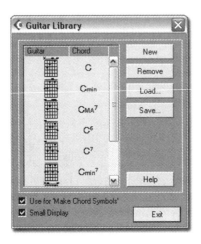

To create chords for your guitar library:

1. Select Global Settings > Guitar Library from the Scores menu.
2. Click the New button to create a new chord. A blank fretboard appears.
3. Double-click the fretboard to open the Guitar Symbol editor (see Figure 16.12). This dialog box is divided into two parts. On the left, you will find the fretboard. Clicking a fret adds a finger position on the fret. Clicking it again removes it. You can also click above the fretboard to add open string or an indication not to play this string (an X is inserted). Consecutive clicks change the symbol from one to the next. Clicking the top-left corner outside of the fretboard allows you to add position numbers. In the right section, you can enable the large symbol display or the horizontal symbol display by checking the Large or Horizontal check boxes. The Frets field allows you to change the number of frets displayed in the symbol, whereas the Capo fields allow you to create Capodaster symbols across the strings.

4. Create your chord by adding the appropriate finger symbols in the fretboard on the left.

5. When done, click OK. This chord creates a new guitar symbol in your library.

Figure 16.12
The Guitar Symbol
dialog box

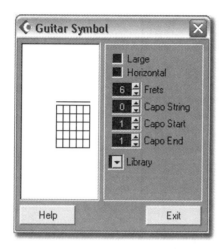

To add a guitar
symbol in your score:

1. Select Symbol Palettes > Others from the Scores menu.

2. Click the Guitar Chord symbol in the Tool palette.

3. Click in the score where you want to add a guitar symbol. The Guitar Symbol dialog box appears.

4. Either select a chord that you have created earlier from the Library drop-down menu, or create the chord as was described earlier. This dialog box differs slightly from the one you used when creating a guitar chord for the library because it has an Apply button rather than an Exit button.

5. Click the Apply button to insert the symbol in your score. You can also insert the notes associated with your chord by clicking the Insert Notes button.

6. Continue adding guitar chord symbols, and then close the dialog box when you are done.

You can easily save your guitar chord library for later use with another project by clicking the Save button in the Guitar Library dialog box. To load a previously saved library, simply click the Load button instead and browse your hard disk for the file. Finally, to remove a guitar chord from your library, simply select it and click the Remove button.

It is also possible to create drum parts using an existing drum map associated with a MIDI drum track through the Score Drum Map Settings dialog box (see Figure 16.13). This dialog box allows you to associate a drum instrument to a different pitch for the score layout and change the head of the note in this score to represent an instrument, making it easier for a drummer to read. You can also change the voice which is assigned to each drum instrument when working with polyphonic voice layouts.

Figure 16.13
The Score Drum Map
Settings dialog box

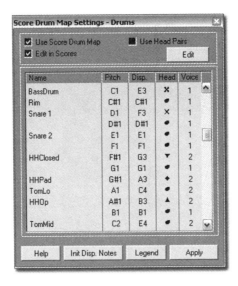

Here's a look at the options available in this dialog box:

▶ Use Score Drum Map check box. Allows you to associate the drum map used for the selected drum track and associate the name of each instrument in the drum map. When you click the Legend button, Cubase adds a note in the score for each instrument defined at the pitch used in the score to help the drummer understand how you've laid out the drum part.

▶ Edit in Scores check box. Enables you to make changes directly in the score's window, updating any changes you make there in this dialog box. For example, if you move the Bass Drum from an E3 to a D#3, the change appears here as well.

▶ Use Head Pairs check box. Allows you to associate a note length value to the symbol displayed in the score. When an instrument plays a note that is long (longer than a quarter note), the head in the left column is used. If the instrument plays a shorter note (shorter or equal to a quarter note), the head in the right column is used. Note that this option is not selected in Figure 16.13, so you only see one column of note heads. The Edit button allows you to edit the pairing of note heads.

▶ Drum map display. Is a series of rows in which each row represents an instrument and its properties. The columns show the instrument's name, the pitch associated with this instrument according to the drum map (which you can't change), the pitch displayed in the score, the note head associated with the instrument, and the voice assignment. The displayed note has no effect on the I-note, O-note setting for the drum map. The purpose of this option is to make it easy to lay out your drum part in a staff without having notes appearing far below a staff. Assigning instruments to voices allows you to later control the direction of the note stems using the polyphonic staff settings covered later in this chapter.

▶ Initial Display Notes button. Resets the displayed note value to the original pitch note value in the score.

▶ Legend button. Adds a series of notes at the current quantize value interval (also using the quantize length value setting for the note lengths). This serves as a guide to the drummer so that he/she can understand which note value is associated with the drum's instrument (see the bottom part of Figure 16.14).

Figure 16.14 shows a MIDI drum part opened in the Score Editor on top. Notice that the notes appear low on the treble clef staff. You can also see that the stems are all going in the same direction; accidents appear because some notes are associated with black note pitches and the spacing between each note is limited. All of this makes it very difficult for a drummer to understand what exactly needs to be played. On the lower half, the MIDI events have been formatted for the score layout of a drum part. A legend appears at the beginning, showing the drummer which note plays what. Also, the HiHat has been assigned to a second voice, allowing for stems to be sent up while the kick and snare have stems pointing down, making it easier for the drummer to interpret.

Figure 16.14
A before and after look at a MIDI drum part being edited in the Score Editor

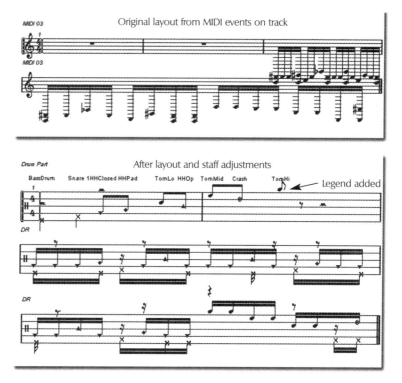

The last two options in the Global Settings submenu allow you to export all of your settings to a file for use in another project or in another studio and import setting files that you have previously saved.

Layout Settings

The Layout Settings submenu in the Scores menu allows you to manage layouts that are available in your project and switch from one layout to another. Usually, a layout is created when you open the Score Editor with a certain number of tracks, or a single track selected. For example, if you open the Score Editor after selecting all the brass tracks, piano, bass, and drum tracks, and start editing the layout for these tracks, a layout is created.

The Layout Settings dialog box (see Figure 16.15) lets you edit this layout. This dialog box is divided into two parts. On the left, you will find the tracks that are currently part of this layout. The first and second column are used to add braces or brackets.

To add braces or brackets in a layout:

1. From the Scores > Layout Settings, select the layout you want to edit from the available layouts in your project.

2. Once selected, go back to the Scores > Layout Settings and select the Setup option. The Layout Settings dialog box appears (shown in Figure 16.15).

3. Click and hold in the braces or brackets column next to the first track where you want to begin joining the braces or brackets. With your mouse button still depressed, drag it down over the tracks you want to join together.

4. Click OK when done.

Notice in Figure 16.15 that the braces span over all the tracks in this layout, whereas the brackets divide the four first tracks from the rhythm section.

Figure 16.15
The Layout Settings
dialog box

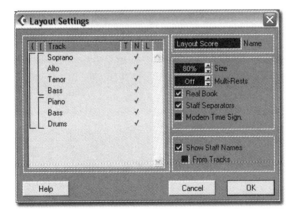

The T column allows you to display the time signature above the staff rather than inside the staff itself. Clicking in the track row in this column adds a check mark, indicating that this track will be displayed this way. The check in the N column determines if the track's name appears at the beginning of each track. Notice also that there is a check box in the lower-right corner of the other section of this window. The Show Staff Names option supersedes the N column in the sense that it determines if the names appear or not. Then you can add a check in the track's row to display a name for this track. You may also check the From Tracks option if you want Cubase to take the names from your tracks in the Project window.

The L column determines if the layout symbols that you have inserted are visible next to this track. In other words, you can decide if a rehearsal mark, for example, is repeated over each track in this layout. Looking at Figure 16.16, you can see in the top half that the L and N columns for the Piano part are checked. Consequently, the rehearsal mark and the name "Piano" appear above the piano staves. In the lower half, the N and L columns are not checked; therefore, the rehearsal mark and the name above the piano staves do not appear in the score's layout.

Figure 16.16
How the layout settings affect the appearance of the score

To rename a layout:

1. Select the layout you want to edit from the Layout Settings submenu in the Scores menu.

2. Then select Layout Settings > Setup from the Scores menu to open the Layout Settings dialog box.

3. In the upper-right corner, in the Name field, type the new name you want to give to your layout.

In the right portion of the Layout Settings dialog box, you will find the following items:

▶ **The layout's Name field**. This field changes the name of the current layout.

▶ **The Size option**. By default, a layout is set at 100% size. However, if you want to fit more tracks into one page, you might reduce the size until all the staves from the instruments in your orchestra fit in a single page. This can be very useful when creating an orchestral score.

▶ **The Multi-Rests option**. By default, this option is set to Off. However, if you want to display several complete bars of silence as a multi-rest symbol, showing the number of bars that the musician has to count instead, you can set the minimum number of bars you can have before the layout will tie the rests in a multi-rest symbol (see Figure 16.17).

Figure 16.17
Example of a multi-rest symbol; this tells the musician that he/she has to count thirteen bars of silence

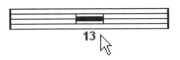

▶ **The Real Book check box**. When this option is selected, the clef for the instruments in this layout are displayed in the first staff only rather than at the beginning of each stave.

▶ **The Staff Separators check box**. When this option is selected, a special symbol appears between each stave to separate them from the preceding stave. This option is handy when you are working on a multi-instrument layout and your score displays more than one set of staves (called a system) per page.

▶ **The Modern Time Signature check box**. This option changes how the time signature appears in the score's layout. Figure 16.18 shows how the time signature is displayed when this option is not selected (above) and when it is selected (below).

Figure 16.18
The Modern Time Signature not selected above and selected below

The second option in the Layout Settings submenu found in the Scores menu allows you to manage the list of layouts available. Appropriately named Show List, this option brings up a dialog box displaying a list of existing layouts for your current project. You can use the Show List dialog box to:

▶ **Rename a layout**. By double-clicking the name of a layout and renaming it

▶ **Delete a layout**. By selecting it and clicking the Remove button

▶ **Import the layout symbols from another layout into the current loaded layout**. By selecting the layout containing the symbols you want to import and clicking the Form button

▶ **Switch to another layout**. By selecting a layout in the list and clicking the Show button

▶ **Remove layouts for which there no longer are track combinations**. By clicking the Clean Up button

Staff Settings

The Staff Settings menu offers various options related to how a selected staff is displayed and how MIDI events on this staff are handled throughout the score. In other words, what relates specifically to a staff's appearance can be controlled through the parameters available in the Staff Settings dialog box (see Figure 16.19).

These settings affect everything from the way a staff name is displayed, to the way beams are displayed, and also how many voices are available for polyphonic voice splitting. You can even set up a staff to handle guitar-specific tablatures.

Figure 16.19
The Staff Settings dialog box displaying the Main tab

To configure the staff settings:

1. In the Score window, select the staff you want to configure.

2. In the Score menu, select Staff Settings > Setup.

3. Make the necessary adjustments throughout the four tabs (Main, Options, Polyphonic, and Tablature), and then click Apply.

4. If you want to configure another track, simply select the other track. The Staff Settings dialog box updates its content to reflect the currently selected track.

After you are satisfied with the settings of a track and want to keep these settings for later use on another track, you may save these settings in a preset by clicking the Store button in the Staff Settings dialog box. You can also start with the existing presets by selecting it from the Presets drop-down menu.

For a full description of each item found in this dialog box, you may click the Help button. Cubase displays an online help file for each tab in the dialog box. Understanding each option saves you time and lots of headaches when addressing issues you are having with the staff's layout properties in your score.

Working Modes

There are two modes available in Cubase SX's Score Editor: Page mode and Edit mode. In Cubase SL, you will only have access to the Edit mode. You can do most functions in Edit mode, which is the standard mode for editing. As mentioned earlier, you can toggle between Page and Edit through the Score menu's first option. The advantage of working in Page mode is that you can see how your page is laid out and add layout graphics, text, and annotations. Figure 16.20 shows the Edit mode display, and Figure 16.21 shows the Page mode display with the title and copyright information properly displayed compared to the previous display.

Figure 16.20
The score's Edit mode display

Figure 16.21
The score's Page mode display

Extended Toolbar Functions

The main function of the score's Extended toolbar is to select the note value you want to add to a score. However, it holds many more little tools to help you lay out your page. You can show or hide this toolbar by using the T button in the toolbar of the Score Editor window.

Insert Buttons

For starters, the first button on the left is called the Voice Selector Insert button. If a track contains more than one voice, you can select in which voice within this polyphony you want to add your note. In Figure 16.22, you can see the active staff has two voices because next to the word Insert, you have two numbers: 1 and 2. These represent the number of voices currently available in this staff. Because the staff has two voices, you can select which voice you want to assign notes to by clicking on the number corresponding to the voice.

To add notes to a specific voice in a polyphonic staff:

1. Select the polyphonic staff for which you need to add notes.
2. Select the voice number in the Extended toolbar corresponding to the voice number to which you want to add notes. In Figure 16.22, because the first voice is active, notes you add are inserted in Voice 1.

If you see only one number next to the word Insert, this means that all your notes on this staff are assigned to one voice. Simply click on the number corresponding to the desired voice. To see more than one voice, set your staff to Polyphony mode in the Staff Settings dialog box found under the Score menu.

Figure 16.22
The voice selector in the
Extended toolbar
displays how many
voices are available in
the active staff

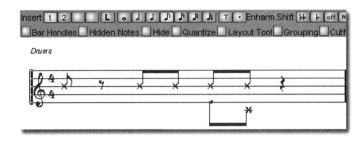

Next on the Extended toolbar, you find the L button. When activated, this Lock button prevents you from moving objects and notes from one staff to another. Most of the time, you will want to leave this off. However, if you need to transpose selected notes very high or very low, so that they appear below or above the current staff, enable it so Cubase does not think you want to move the notes to another staff.

Following the L button, you will find note values. These are used to select the note values you want to add to your score. When you select a note value, the quantize length value in the toolbar switches automatically to correspond to the value of the note you selected. For example, if you select a whole note, the quantize length displays "1/1 Note" value. When you switch to a quarter note, quantize length displays a "1/4 Note" value. Note, however, that the quantize grid setting remains the same.

Enharmonic Shift Buttons

The Enharmonic Shift buttons provide a way to change the enharmonic notes in your score. Enharmonic notes are different ways to represent the same pitch. For example, E flat or Eb could be represented by D sharp or D# or even F double-flat (Fbb). The Off button turns the enharmonic shift to off and the No button hides the accidentals. If you use many accidental notes, you might want to add additional markings. For example, if you have many voices on a staff and each one plays an accidental C sharp (C#), you can select subsequent C sharp notes in the bar and click the Question Mark button (?). This adds a helping accident. The notation rules don't require you to add this accident, but because you want to help the musicians who are reading the score, this provides them with additional information. Clicking the Parenthesis button [( )] adds this accidental in parenthesis.

Function Buttons

The I button, short for "Information," shows you information on a selected element in your score. What appears after you select the I button depends on what you select. For example, if you select a clef and click this button, the Clef window appears and allows you to change it. On the other hand, if you select a note and click this button, the Set Note Info dialog box appears, allowing you to modify different parameters for note representation.

By default, notes above the third line in the staff have stems going down, and notes below this same line have stems going up. The Flip Stems button allows you to manually flip the stems of selected notes in the other direction.

The Group button adds a beam across a series of selected notes. Figure 16.23 shows notes that were grouped together in the first bar.

To group a series of notes:

1. Select the notes in a staff you want to group together.

2. Then click the Group button on the Extended toolbar.

To ungroup notes:

1. Select the notes that are in a grouped beam.

2. Then click the Group button on the Extended toolbar.

Figure 16.23
The Group button
function

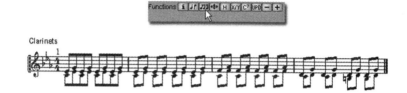

The Auto Layout button is a shortcut button for the Auto Layout function found in the Score menu. If you select an entire staff, it performs like the Move Bars. You can use this function to optimize the layout of bars on a staff.

The H, or "Hide" button, hides the selected elements from view. Use this function to hide elements from the score, such as rests or bar lines. This can be useful when you want to hide certain symbols from view while you are working on other aspects of your score layout. After you are done, you can unhide these symbols to view them again, or keep them hidden if you want your score to look this way.

To hide symbols using the Hide function in a score:

1. Select the symbols (bars, notes, rests, layout text, or anything else) you want to hide from view.

2. Click the Hide button in the Extended toolbar or select Staff Functions > Hide from the Scores menu.

Chances are, if you have decided to hide symbols rather than delete them, you will at some point want to see them again or at least see what has been previously hidden.

To reveal hidden symbols from your score:

1. Make the Filter bar visible by clicking the Filter (F) button in the score's toolbar.

2. Check the Hidden Notes option to reveal the hidden notes and the Hide filter option to reveal the other hidden symbols.

The Reveal function, however, does not remove the hide property from these hidden elements. As soon as you uncheck the Hidden Notes and Hide options, what is set as hidden returns to its hidden state. You can, however, remove this property from the hidden symbols. However, this is done differently for notes and other symbols.

To remove the hidden property associated with a symbol:

1. Make the Filter bar visible by clicking the Filter (F) button in the score's toolbar.

2. Check the Hidden Notes option to reveal the hidden notes and the Hide filter option to reveal the other hidden symbols.

3A. To remove the hidden note property for notes, select the hidden notes you want to unhide by dragging a box over these notes, double-click on one of them to bring the Set Note Info dialog box (or click the "I" button in the Extended toolbar), and uncheck the Hide Note option in this dialog box.

3B. To remove the hidden property from a symbol, select the hide symbol you want to remove and press Delete or Backspace on your keyboard.

As you can see in Figure 16.24, the top part shows the Hide filter as disabled. Therefore, the hidden symbols do not appear in the staff. The middle part of the figure shows the enabled state for the hidden symbols, revealing where hidden symbols are. You can then select them and remove them from your staff. In the bottom part, you can see that the meter and bar that was hidden previously now reappear on the staff as it was before you hid them from view.

Figure 16.24
The Hide function: With the Hide filter active, you can see the location of hidden symbols

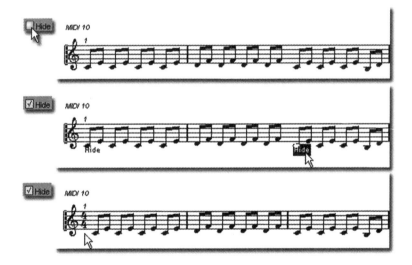

The X/Y Position button reveals the graphical position of your cursor in a horizontal (X/vertical; Y horizontal) display. When you click on a non-note event—the title, for example—you will see the Delta X (dX) and Y (dY) coordinates of the selected object changing as you move it around the screen. Use this to fine-tune the positioning of your graphic elements on the score. The X/Y Position window also allows you to toggle between the different ruler formats: inches, centimeters, points, and millimeters.

To change the format of the ruler:

▶ In the Position Info window, click the upper-left corner of the window where it says "Measure in…"

► Or, right-click (Ctrl-click on a Mac) in the ruler and select another measurement format.

► Or, click the menu arrow above the top of the horizontal scroll bar and select the appropriate measurement system you want to use.

In the last column (see Figure 16.25), you have the "To Prev Staff" and "To Next Staff" values. These values represent the space between the current selected staff and the previous and following staff in the score. Double-clicking either of these values allows you to type in a new spacing value.

Figure 16.25
The Position Info
window

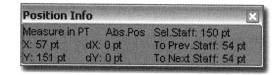

The C7 button is "Make Chords," which creates a chord out of the selected notes in your score. To make chords, you need to have a three-note polyphony to get accurate results from the Make Chords button. After your chords are created, they appear above the selected staff. You will find more information on chords in the following sections of this chapter.

After you have completed your editing, you may need to refresh your layout. If your layout is not refreshed properly, you can force an update by clicking on the UPD button or Update button. You can also do this through the Force Update option found in the Global Functions submenu in the Scores menu.

Symbol Palettes

In the Score menu, you will discover the Symbol Palettes option. In this option, you will find many palettes available to add graphical elements to your score. None of these symbols actually affects how the music is played back, but they are used to add interpretation indications for the musicians. There are ten palettes from which to choose, and they all work pretty much the same way.

To add a symbol from a symbol palette on your score:

1. Choose the appropriate symbol palette (the one that contains the type of symbol you want to use).

2. Click on a symbol, then click on the score where you want to add it. If the symbol needs more information, a dialog box appears to let you enter additional fields or text as required.

After you have a palette displayed, you can switch from one palette to another by right-clicking (Ctrl-clicking on Mac) anywhere in the button area of the symbol palette, as shown in Figure 16.26. This reveals the list of palettes from which you can choose. Selecting another palette replaces the displayed palette with the new one. Holding down the Ctrl key (Command key on a Mac) as you make your selection does not replace the existing palette, but rather opens a new, additional one.

Figure 16.26
Changing the displayed
symbol palette from the
context menu

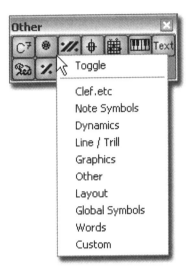

The last palette available is the Custom palette. This allows you to store symbols you use most often from other palettes.

To add symbols to the Custom palette:

1. Open the Custom palette.

2. Right-click (Ctrl click on a Mac) while holding down the Ctrl key (Command key on a Mac) in the symbol palette's area to open a new symbol palette window that contains the symbols you want to add to the Custom palette.

3. After the new palette opens, hold down the Alt key (Option key on a Mac) as you select that symbol.

4. Repeat this operation for every symbol you want to add to the Custom palette.

The first option on the Palette's context menu is the toggle option. Use this to switch from a vertical palette layout to a horizontal layout.

Some of the symbols in these palettes might be grayed out if you are in Edit mode. To activate these disabled symbols, switch to Page mode. That's because the symbols contained in the Layout and Global palette are only added to the layout and global layer respectively. In the Edit mode display, you can see these layers, but it is better to edit them in Page mode instead.

Working with Chords

You might have a harmony happening in your staff. You might also have a piano or guitar part with chords played as a harmonic rhythm track. In both cases, you can choose to add a chord symbol over the track by selecting the track and then clicking on the Make Chords button in the Extended toolbar, as discussed in the previous sections of this chapter. After your chords are created, chances are you will want to tweak them, because Cubase might not interpret them properly all the time.

Before you start creating chords, it is a good thing to set your chord display preferences in the Scores > Global Settings > Chord Symbols dialog box, as discussed earlier. What you set in this dialog box determines how the chords are displayed on the score and in the Chord Edit dialog box. For example, if you set the Major chord type to display MA7 rather than maj7 or simply j7, the MA7 appears in the Chords dialog box when you edit the chord. The chords you create after setting your preferences follow the rules you set here.

The next step is to actually create the chords using the Make Chords button on the Extended toolbar or by using the Chords button found in the symbol palette called Other (Scores > Symbol Palette > Other).

To create a chord from selected note symbols on your score:

1. Select the note symbols on the stave over which you want to create chord symbols. Note that you need at least three notes per chord selected in order for the automatic chord function to work.

2. Select the staff over which you want the chords to appear by using the up or down arrows.

3. Click the Make Chords button or select this option in the Scores > Staff functions submenu.

Sometimes, you might not have a complete chord structure but want to have one. Instead, you might simply have a melody and want to add some chord indication. In this case, you need to create your chords using the Edit Chord Symbol dialog box.

To create custom chords:

1. Select the Symbol Palettes > Other from the Score menu.

2. Click the Make Chords button (C7).

3. Then click over the staff to which you want to add a chord. The Edit Chord Symbol dialog box appears, as shown in Figure 16.27.

Figure 16.27
The Edit Chord Symbol
dialog box

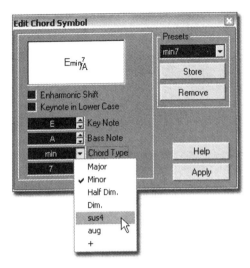

4. Enter the note that corresponds to the root of your chord. For example, if you played F, A, and D, this could be a D minor chord, with a root of D, or an F6 chord, with a root of F. Which chord it is depends on many things, so you have to know a bit about harmony to make that kind of decision.

5. Next, enter the chord type. This tells the player if the chord is a major, minor, diminished, half-diminished, augmented, or a sustained fourth degree chord. If you are not familiar with these terms, you might want to use automatic chord construction, found in the Score toolbar, instead. In the example in Step 4, the chord was a minor chord, so in this case, you would select minor.

6. Next, add the highest tension found in your chord. For example, if you have a minor seventh and a minor ninth, add the minor ninth tension, because it is understood in scoring theory that the minor ninth also contains a minor seventh (unless otherwise noted). On the other hand, if you have a tension on the fifth, such as a sharp fifth or flat fifth added to your flat ninth, you can type in the values manually. Figure 16.28 displays a D minor with a sharp fifth and a major seventh chord on the left. The center column displays different ways you can add the tension by clicking in the Tension field, and the right column displays the result depending on the way you typed in the tension. Note that the syntax used here is useful when you have complex tensions. Normally, you don't have to type anything if you have a simple tension.

7. The last field in your Edit Chord Symbol dialog box is for the bass note. If you want the bass to play a note different from the ones found in the chord, select that note in the pop-up menu. If your bass plays a note that is part of the chord structure but not the root, you usually don't have to write it in. However, in the example in Figure 16.28, if you want the bass to play an E, which is not part of the chord structure as it appears, you would add this in the bass note.

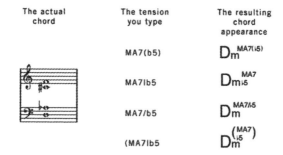

Figure 16.28
Adding text in the Tension field allows you to customize the tension's layout in the chord structure

8. If your chord needs to be an enharmonic chord, like D sharp instead of E flat, check the Enharmonic Shift check box.

9. If you want to keep this chord structure for later use in your score, click the Store button. This saves the structure in the library of your song file after you save this file. You will notice that the root of the structure does not appear in the library. This is because you might want to use the same structure with another key later on. To use it later on, just select the root note and then select the structure from the drop-down menu.

When creating chords using the Make Chords function, Cubase uses the Quantize value set in the Score window to determine the maximum number of chords it will add. If you don't want to have too many chords, reduce the Quantize value to represent a realistic number of chords per bar. There are no fixed number of chords in a bar, but usually, this should not be more than four chords per bar; in most cases, it is one to two chords per bar. The best way to create chord tracks is to play a MIDI track containing the chord structure played as simply as possible.

Cubase uses all the vertical notes in your layout to analyze and create these chords. If you have melodic lines or musical lines with many transitional notes, the software might interpret those notes as chords, giving you a superfluous amount of tensions and chords. So, when you create chords, select only the tracks that contain the basic harmonic structure of your song and set your Quantize value to the desired amount beforehand.

Cubase also assumes that chords are in their root positions. This means that if you play a first or second inversion of a chord—let's say a C chord played E-G-C or a second inversion G-C-E—it interprets this as a C chord on an E bass or a C chord on a G bass. To avoid this, simply hold the Ctrl key down as you click the Make Chords button in the Score toolbar. If you find that the chords produced automatically by Cubase do not match the correct harmonic structure of your song, you can double-click on a chord and change its structure in the Edit Chord Symbol dialog box. Again, Cubase only tries to interpret the chord, but because this is often a question of interpretation and context, some chords will be wrong and you will need to edit them.

CHAPTER 16

Adding Text

In a score, you usually want to add comments and indications as well as lyrics and song information. In Cubase, there are five types of text that you can add in a score:

▶ Normal text. This type of text can be used to enter comments or indications to the musician on how to play a particular passage. If you move a bar or staff, normal text moves with it as it is tied to these elements.

▶ Lyrics. This type of text is used to enter lyrics to a song. This type is specifically designed to allow you to add text under or over a staff, adjusting its position as you adjust the spacing of notes, bars, and staves. Lyrics are tied to the note position under or over which it is positioned. If you move the notes, the lyrics follow.

▶ Layout text. Think of this type of text as normal text you want to see for a group of instruments, rather than a single instance of this text somewhere. For example, if you are editing a brass quintet piece, you might add a comment in the conductor's part that appears at the top of the page when you print out this particular layout. When you open the trumpet part on its own, this comment does not appear because it is part of a different layout. The same applies for the four other individual parts that you create for this quintet.

▶ Global text. This type of text appears, unlike the layout text, on each individual layout or music sheet you create. Let's take the previous example of the brass quintet, adding a comment using the global text, you would find the text appearing on the conductor's score and on each individual part of the brass quintet. Global text is not tied to any notes, bars, or staves. This implies that if you move any of these elements around, the global text stays in place.

▶ Staff Name text. Staff text is linked to the staff setting and the layout setting. Usually, this represents the name of the track or of the instrument playing on that track in long and short format. For example, if you're laying out a violin staff in an orchestral score, the first staff could be named "Violin" and the following staves could be named "Vln." Staff name text usually appears at the beginning of each staff depending on your staff and layout settings.

If you want to add lyrics to a song, you should always use the Lyrics Symbol found in the Other symbol palette (Scores > Symbol Palettes > Other).

To add lyrics:

1. Start by selecting the staff under which you want to insert the lyrics.

2. Select Symbol Palettes > Other from the Score menu.

3. Click the Lyrics button in the palette. Your cursor changes to the Pencil tool.

4. Click under or over the note where you want to add the lyric and enter the first syllable for your word or enter a word.

5. Press the Tab key to move to the next note. If you have a word or a syllable that stretches over many notes, press the Tab key to move under or over the next note in order to add the next syllable or word.

6. Repeat until there are no more lyrics to add. When done, click outside of the box.

After you've completed inserting the lyrics, you can adjust the melisma lines to stretch a syllable or a word over a series of notes. A melisma, as discussed earlier in this chapter, is a line that carries through several notes.

To stretch a word or syllable across several notes:

1. Click the word or syllable you want to stretch using the Selection tool.

2. Drag the handle of the selected syllable to the right of where you want the melisma to end, as shown in Figure 16.29.

Figure 16.29
The selected word appears in reverse highlight and the handle appears as a square in the lower-right corner of the highlighted word or syllable

You can move lyrics up or down using the Selection tool, but you can't move lyrics to the left or right. You can also copy words or syllables by selecting them and keeping the Alt key (Option key on Mac) held down as you move the selection to a new area in your score. If you want to move all the lyrics you just entered at once, hold the Shift key down and double-click the first word or syllable in the lyrics. All elements from that set of lyrics are highlighted and ready to move.

Your lyrics might be crammed into a small space the first time you look at them on the score. To arrange the spacing so that the lyrics don't appear too squeezed, select Auto Layout > Move All Bars from the Score menu.

If you have created text attribute sets, you can select the lyrics, right-click (Ctrl-click on Mac) and select the desired set from the context menu. If there are no sets available, you need to create one before using this method.

Printing and Page Setup

The ultimate goal in using the Score functions is to print the result on a page so that musicians can read it. When you are in Page mode, you will see a gray border appearing around your page in Page mode display (shown previously in Figure 16.21). The default settings for your printer determines where this border appears.

To change the page size and margin settings:

1. From the File menu, select Page Setup. The default printer setup window appears.
2. Set the paper size and page orientation to the desired values.
3. Adjust the margin values for Top, Bottom, Left, and Right.
4. Click the Printer button at the bottom of the Page Setup dialog box.
5. Choose the printer you want to work with and click OK, or edit the printer's properties and then click OK twice.

It is also possible to export a score or a portion of the score to a graphic file for editing in a graphic editing or desktop publishing software.

To export a score to a graphic file:

1. Make sure you are in Page mode editing.
2. Select in the Scores menu, Global Functions > Select Range.
3. In the Score window, drag a box over the range you want to export to a graphic file. You can adjust the handles of the selected range using the Arrow tool if needed.
4. Select in the Scores menu, Global Functions > Export Score.
5. Adjust the Resolution field to get the desired resolution for your graphic file.
6. Select the desired file format for your graphic file.
7. Type in a name for your file and select an appropriate folder in which to save the file.
8. Click the Save button.

If you want to export an entire page of the score, only execute Steps 4–8 from the previous list. You need to repeat this operation for each score page in your layout.

Now You Try It

It's time to put the topics covered in this chapter into action—you can download a practice exercise at http://www.muskalipman.com.

Appendix A
The How To Do It Reference Guide

This appendix refers to every How To section in this book, offering you a quick guide to finding out how an operation can be done. Each How To section has been divided into a category and placed in a corresponding table in this appendix. There are ten tables (categories) in all. Here's a look at what you can find in each category:

▶ **Setup Operations**. This holds operations that relate to configuration procedures, setting up a project, or your environment inside a project.

▶ **Display Information**. This holds operations that explain how to display windows, panels, and certain dialog boxes within Cubase or zooming specific operations.

▶ **Project and Transport Specific Operations**. These operations relate to project tasks that are not related to audio or MIDI, such as Marker and Folder tracks and transport operations.

▶ **Non Object-Specific Operations**. These are editing procedures within a project that are not specifically related to MIDI or audio alone, such as quantizing functions and options that might be found in the Edit menu that don't relate to a specific type of object (event or part) in a project.

▶ **Recording Operations**. This holds operations that directly affect the recording process and the recording operations themselves.

▶ **Audio Editing Operations**: This holds all audio specific editing operations.

▶ **MIDI Editing Operations**. This holds all MIDI specific editing operations.

▶ **Mixing Operations**. This holds operations that directly affect the mixing process and the mixing operations themselves.

▶ **Automation Operations**. This holds operations that directly affect the automation process and the automation operations themselves.

▶ **Score Operations**. This holds operations that directly affect the score process and the score layout operations themselves.

Each header contains a table with columns corresponding to the following information:

▶ **How To column**. Represents the actual task, function, or option title as it appears in the book
▶ **Heading Title column**. Tells you in which section of the chapter this can be found
▶ **Chapter Number column**. Tells you in which chapter this can be found
▶ **Page Number column**. Tells you the page number on which you will find the corresponding How To steps

Table A.1
Setup operations

How To:	Heading Title	Chapter Number	Page Number
Activate a bus	VST Outputs	12	275
Activate the VST System Link	Setting Up System Link Inside Cubase	14	323
Add a bank to your device's setup	Managing a MIDI Device	5	105
Add a MIDI device	Adding a MIDI Device	5	103
Add a preset or a folder to your device's setup	Managing a MIDI Device	5	105
Add key commands	Key Commands Reference Guide	G	439
Add multiple presets to your device's setup	Managing a MIDI Device	5	105
Change the physical output assigned to a bus	VST Outputs	12	275
Configure the digital clock on your sound card	Recording Audio	9	193
Configure your DirectSound drivers	DirectX Drivers	2	21
Configure your metronome settings	Setting Up your Metronome	7	145
Create your own custom colors and associated color names	Project Editing Setup Buttons	4	76
Enable and configure a snap to grid setting	Setting Up a Quantize Grid	4	80

Table A.2
Displaying information

APPENDIX A

Show/hide Transport panel sections	Customizing your Transport Panel	4	91
View a track's MIDI input and output port setting	MIDI Port	1	11
View the Audio Part Editor window	Audio Part Editor	3	61
View the Beat Calculator window	Beat Calculator Window	3	55
View the Devices panel	The Devices Panel	3	46
View the Drum Editor window	Drum Editor	3	58
View the Drum Map Setup dialog box	Drum Map Setup Dialog Box	3	59
View the Key Editor window	Key Editor	3	57
View the List Editor window	List Editor	3	59
View the Marker window	Marker Window	3	54
View the Media Pool window	Media Pool Window	3	61
View the Metronome Setup dialog box	Metronome Setup Dialog Box	3	45
View the MIDI Device Manager panel	MIDI Device Manager	3	47
View the Plug-in Information panel	Plug-in Information Panel	3	48
View the Project Setup dialog box	Project Setup Dialog Box	3	56
View the Browse Project window	Browse Project Window	3	55
View the Quantize Setup panel	Quantize Setup Panel	3	57
View the Sample Editor window	Sample Editor	3	63
View the Score Editor window	Score Editor	3	60
View the Spectrum Analyzer dialog box	Spectrum Analyzer	3	64
View the Synchronization Setup dialog box	Synchronization Setup Dialog Box	3	45
View the Tempo Track window	Tempo Track	3	54
View the Track Mixer window	Track Mixer Window	3	47
View the Transport panel	Transport Panel	3	45

View the TrueTape Input Effect panel	TrueTape Input Effect Panel	3	49
View the Video Display window	Video Display Window	3	53
View the VST Inputs panel	VST Inputs Panel	3	49
View the VST Instruments panel	VST Instrument Panel	3	50
View the VST Master Effects panel	VST Master Effects Panel	3	50
View the VST Master Setup dialog box	VST Master Setup Dialog Box	3	51
View the VST Outputs window	VST Outputs Window	3	51
View the VST Performance panel	VST Performance Panel	3	52
View the VST Send Effects panel	VST Send Effects Panel	3	52
Zoom into your work using the appropriate tool	Using the Overview Panel	7	154

Table A.3
Project and Transport specific operations

How To:	Heading Title	Chapter Number	Page Number
Add a tempo change	About the Tempo Track	5	109
Add a time signature change	About the Tempo Track	5	109
Add commands to a macro	Macros	D	427
Add cycle markers in a project	Adding Markers	4	82
Add Markers in a project	Adding Markers	4	82
Assign a color to parts and events	Project Editing Setup Buttons	4	76
Change the order of a track in the Track List Area	The Track List	5	97
Change your Cycle mode on the Transport panel	Record Mode	4	86
Change your cycle recording mode preferences	Recording Audio in Cycle Mode	9	197
Change your locator's position in the Transport panel	Locators	4	87
Create a macro	Macros	D	427

Create a Marker track	Working with Markers	4	81
Create a new project	Creating a New Project	4	68
Create a template project	Creating Templates	D	426
Create a window layout	Window Layout	D	425
Find missing files in the pool	Dealing with Missing Files	11	241
Import a Cubase VST song, arrangement, or part	About Cubase Documents Imports	7	161
Import an online video file into a Cubase project	Working with Video Files	14	336
Move the left and right locators to the position of a cycle marker	Navigating Using Markers	4	83
Move tracks into a folder track	Folder Track	6	136
Move your play cursor to the position of a Marker	Navigating Using Markers	4	83
Organize your window layouts	Window Layout	D	425
Position your play line at the locator's position	Locators	4	87
Rename a track using the Inspector area	Folder Track	6	136
Set up for online video files in a Cubase project	Working with Video Files	14	336
Use a macro in a project	Macros	D	427
Use Rewire	Sharing Resources with Rewire	12	267
Zoom into the location of a cycle marker	Navigating Using Markers	4	83

Table A.4
Non object-specific editing operations

How To:	Heading Title	Chapter Number	Page Number
Add a track to your project	Adding Tracks	6	114
Apply a groove map to events	Creating and Using Groove Maps	11	256
Apply a quantize method to selected events	Applying Quantize	7	152

Apply an automatic quantize during the editing process	Applying Quantize	7	152
Apply an envelope process to a selected object	Envelopes	10	225
Change the order of overlapping audio parts	Audio Track	6	125
Change the time format displayed in a project using the Transport panel	Main Transport	4	89
Choose which event you want to hear when editing a track	Recording Audio in Cycle Mode	9	197
Convert a shared copy into a real copy in the Project window	Audio Part Editor	11	256
Convert one audio object type into another	Converting Audio Objects	10	220
Duplicate objects using the Object Selection or Range Selection tool	Duplicate	9	205
Erase tempo or time signature changes	About the Tempo Track	5	109
Fill an area with selected objects using the Fill Loop option	Fill Loop	9	207
Freeze quantized events	Applying Quantize	7	152
Move a Marker	Editing Markers	4	84
Move a tempo change or time signature change	About the Tempo Track	5	109
Move the position of a cycle marker	Editing Markers	4	84
Mute one or several events	Muting Events	8	176
Remove a Marker (or cycle marker)	Editing Markers	4	84
Remove a quantize setting from the preset list	Setting Up your Quantize	7	150
Rename a Marker (or cycle marker)	Editing Markers	4	84
Repeat selected objects or range over time	Repeat	9	206
Resize objects (events or parts)	Normal Sizing	9	207

APPENDIX A

Resize objects while moving its contents	Sizing Moves Contents	9	208
Resize the start or end position of a cycle marker	Editing Markers	4	84
Save a quantize setting to a preset	Setting Up your Quantize	7	150
Select events	Editing MIDI Events	8	175
Set up quantize parameters	Setting Up your Quantize	7	150
Shift events inside an object	Shifting Events Inside Object	9	210
Split a range of selected objects	Splitting	9	203
Split objects at the cursor's location	Splitting	9	203
Split objects at the locator's position	Splitting	9	203
Stretch the content of an object while resizing it	Sizing Applies Time Stretch	9	209
Undo a quantize on selected events	Applying Quantize	7	152
Unmute muted events	Muting Events	8	176
Use the crop events to a desired range	Splitting	9	203

Table A.5
Recording operations

How To:	Heading Title	Chapter Number	Page Number
Apply an automatic quantize during the recording process	Applying Quantize	7	152
Change your Record mode on the Transport panel	Record Mode	4	86
Filter MIDI events during recording or playback	MIDI Filtering	7	143
Record a single track of audio in Cubase	Recording Audio	9	193
Record MIDI events on one or multiple tracks	1Recording MIDI	7	146

Record MIDI in Step Recording mode	Using Step Recording	8	182
Set up automatic punch in and out with pre- and post-rolls	Pre- and Post-Roll	4	88
Use TrueTape effect in a recording	Using TrueTape	9	196

Table A.6
Audio editing operations

How To:	Heading Title	Chapter Number	Page Number
Add a plug-in effect to a selected object	Using VST and DirectX Plug-Ins	10	232
Add a Region to a project from the Sample Editor	Working with Regions	11	248
Add silence in an audio event	Basic Editing Functions	11	248
Apply a fade over selected objects in a range	Working with Fade Envelopes	10	221
Apply a Gain Change process to a selected object	Gain Process	10	226
Apply a Noise Gate process to a selected object	Noise Gate Process	10	227
Apply a Normalize process to a selected object	Normalize Process	10	228
Apply a Phase Reverse process to a selected object	Phase Reverse Process	10	228
Apply a Pitch Shift process to a selected object	Pitch Shifting Process	10	229
Apply a Stereo Flip process to a selected object	Stereo Flip Process	10	231
Apply a Time Stretch process to a selected object	Time Stretch Process	10	231
Apply an Offline process to an object from the Pool window	Offline Processes in the Pool	11	246
Bounce audio objects to a new file	Bounce Selection	10	220
Change the default crossfade (fade) settings	Working with Fade Envelopes	10	221

APPENDIX A

Change the fade curve type of an audio object	Working with Fade Envelopes	10	221
Close gaps between slices in a part	Creating and Using Audio Slices	11	255
Convert hitpoints into a groove map	Creating and Using Groove Maps	11	256
Create a folder in the pool	Understanding the Information	11	238
Create a new Region	Working with Regions	11	248
Create an audio part from existing events in the Project window	Audio Part Editor	11	256
Create an empty audio part in the Project window	Audio Part Editor	11	256
Create audio slices	Creating and Using Audio Slices	11	255
Create hitpoints	Creating Hitpoints	11	252
Create Regions using the Detect Silence function	Detect Silence	10	218
Disable audio tracks	Disabling Audio Tracks	9	211
Edit the snap point's position	About the Snap Point	11	250
Edit the start and end of an event in the Sample Editor	Sample Editor Areas	11	246
Export or import a pool	Archiving and Exporting a Pool	11	244
Find a selected object in the pool	Finding your Objects	10	223
Hear the content of an event in the Audio Part Editor	Audio Part Editor Areas	11	257
Import an audio track or tracks from an audio CD	About Audio CD Track Imports	7	162
Import audio files	About Audio File Imports	7	164
Import media files into the pool	The Pool Areas	11	236
Insert a hitpoint manually	Editing Hitpoints	11	254
Insert an object at its origin time or cursor location in the project	Understanding the Information	11	238
Merge the content of the clipboard with a selected object	Merge Clipboard Process	10	226
Minimize file sizes in your project	Optimizing the Pool	11	243

Table A.7
MIDI editing operations

Table A.8
Mixing operations

How To:	Heading Title	Chapter Number	Page Number
Add a master effect to the master fader	VST Master Effects	12	274
Add a MIDI insert effect	MIDI Track Inserts	6	122
Adjust an EQ band from the audio track equalizer section	Audio Track Equalizer	6	131
Adjust the EQ settings for an audio channel	Channel EQ	12	279
Assign a dynamic plug-in to an audio channel	Using Dynamics	12	281
Assign a MIDI track send	MIDI Track Sends	6	123
Assign a send effect to an audio track	Audio Track Sends	6	133
Bypass all the tracks sent to the same effect	Audio Track Sends	6	133
Bypass one or all MIDI inserts from playback	MIDI Track Inserts	6	122
Bypass/activate the signal sent to all send effects in a track	Audio Track Sends	6	133
Bypass/activate the signal sent to one send effect in a track	Audio Track Sends	6	133
Change the automation parameter displayed in a subtrack	The Track List	5	97
Convert MIDI tracks playing external MIDI devices into audio tracks	Converting your MIDI Tracks	15	340
Create a channel mixer view set	Common Panel	12	262
Edit the patch configuration of a master effect in surround mixes	Using Effects in Surround Mode	E	433
Export a file for MP3 compatibility	MP3	15	352
Export a file for RealPlayer or Windows Media Player compatibility	Real Audio and Windows Media	15	348

Table A.9
Automation operations

Table A.10
Score operations

APPENDIX A

Appendix B
Using MIDI Effects

MIDI effects allow you to control how MIDI is played and can also be used creatively depending on the MIDI effect you apply to a MIDI track. When used as an insert, MIDI events pass through the MIDI effect, which transforms the events played at the MIDI output port of the track in which it's inserted. When used as a send effect, MIDI events still pass through the MIDI effect, but you can also send the output of the MIDI effect to another MIDI output port and/or MIDI channel. This gives you a great tool to create new MIDI events that can add interesting effects to your original content.

All the steps in the following sections describing how to use an effect assume that you have already assigned the effect to a MIDI track's insert or send effect and have configured the MIDI output appropriately (if using a send effect).

These effects have been grouped into two categories: the event creation effects and the event modifying effects.

Saving Your Presets

As with many other windows, panels, and dialog boxes in Cubase, you can save settings made to MIDI effects as a preset for later use. You will find a Presets menu (see Figure B.1) whenever it is possible to save a pattern or setting. When you save a preset, you can later retrieve it and use it on another track or in another project.

To save a MIDI effect preset:

1. Click the Save button next to the Presets menu (it's the button representing the folded page with a plus sign inside).
2. A Preset Name dialog box appears. Enter a name for your preset and click OK.

To remove a saved preset, select it, and click the Remove button next to the Save button (the button with a minus sign inside).

Figure B.1
Managing your MIDI effects presets using the preset functions in each MIDI effect

Event Creation Effects

These effects generate MIDI events when passing a track through them. This implies that new MIDI messages are produced as a result of these effects.

Arpache 5

The Arpache 5 is an arpeggio and note pattern generator (see Figure B.2). There are three main areas in this effect that allow you to control how the effect generates its arpeggios. The Playmode area with its six buttons determines the direction of the arpeggiated notes. An arrow pointing up means that the notes generated move upwards along the chord or note you play and an arrow pointing down means that the notes move downwards. The question mark generates a random direction based on the note or notes you played. The Order button activates the Play Order section. This allows you to create a specific order in which notes are played in your arpeggio. If you look at the last staff in Figure B.3, you will notice that the Play Order used was 1-2-1. Because the chord played was C-E-G, the lowest note is considered as Note 1 and the highest as Note 3. In this case, the arpeggio plays a 1-2-1 pattern before going up one level, then it repeats this pattern, creating a more complex arpeggio.

The Quantize field determines the distance between each note in the arpeggio. In this case (Figure B.2 and B.3), this is set to sixteenth notes. The Length field determines the length for each note as well. The Semi-Range determines the range in semitones covered by the arpeggio. This defines how high or how low the arpeggio will go from the lowest note played. In this example, the range is set to 24 semitones, or two octaves.

Because the Arpache can be played in real time or assigned to a track, you can decide if you want to include the chords or notes you play to trigger the effect using the Thru button. When this button is active, you hear the chords as you play them. When this button is deactivated, you only hear the notes generated by the Arpache, unless of course you already have notes recorded on a track. In this case, you can set the MIDI output port for this track to Not Connected. This allows you to hear the events generated by the events recorded on the track without hearing these actual events. In our Figure B.3 example, this would prevent us from hearing the original C chord while we hear the resulting arpeggio.

Figure B.2
The Arpache 5 MIDI
effect panel

Figure B.3
Different results generated by the different Playmode settings; the name above each staff indicates which play mode was used when generating these events

Autopan

The Autopan allows you to generate Control Change messages over a period of time. Its best use, however, is to create an autopan effect, creating pan values that change over time. In the example provided in Figure B.4, you can see that a square wave has been selected. The different wave buttons allow you to choose how the events are created. The frequency of each wave, or its period, is determined by the Period field. In this example, it is set to quarter notes. This means that the pattern of the wave repeats every quarter note. The Density field determines how often a value is added. Again, in this example, the density is set to sixteenth notes. As you can see, there is a value added every sixteenth-note in the controller lane of the Key Editor. The Controller field allows you to choose which Control Change message is added to the MIDI track. In other words, this example uses the AutoPan with the Pan Control Change message, but you can use any other Control Change message if you want. The Min and Max fields allow you to set a minimum and maximum value for generated Control Change messages. Because this example uses a square wave, each value that is added is either 0 or 127. But if you were to use a sine or random wave, for example, you could have intermediate values as well.

You should also know that when you want to use a smoother transition between pan value changes, you will achieve a better result with a higher density value. However, the shorter both your period and density are, the more MIDI events you generate, and this might cause your MIDI port to choke if it is overwhelmed by such MIDI events.

The two last waveforms on the right can be used with the AmpMod field, which controls the amplitude modulation variations of the controller messages. This works much like a low-frequency oscillator, adding a variable waveform into the equation, thus creating a more complex change in the waveform appearance of the generated messages.

Figure B.4
The Autopan MIDI effect panel over the MIDI result (in the Key Editor) provided by this effect

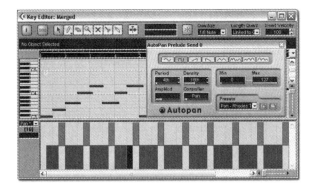

Chorder

The Chorder effect allows you to generate chords when you play a single note. It offers three basic modes: Normal, Octave, and Global.

In Normal mode, you can assign a chord to each note of your keyboard, up to 128 different chords. You create chords using the upper keyboard, clicking on notes you want to include in your chord and you define the key that triggers this chord by selecting it on the lower keyboard. In Figure B.5, playing the C3 note generates the chord found in the upper keyboard.

The Octave mode is similar; however, you can have up to twelve chords, or one per semitone in an octave. This means that no matter which C key you press, it plays the same chord at the corresponding octave.

In Global mode, the entire keyboard plays the same chord, so the Trigger Note keyboard shown in Figure B.5 is not visible. The chord plays the corresponding chord at the pitch determined by the key you play.

In all three modes, you can also assign zones. Zones allow you to create different chords for the same note and are triggered in one of two ways: either by velocity or by note combination.

When chords are triggered by velocity, the velocity scale is divided equally among the number of zone splits you create. For example, if you have two zones, playing a note at a velocity range of 0 to 63 plays one chord (the one you assigned to Zone 1), and playing a note with a velocity between 64 and 127 plays the second zone chord (the one assigned to Zone 2). If you use notes to determine which zone is played, you can only play one chord, or one note at a time. The lowest note you play determines the pitch of the chord, and the second simultaneous note you play determines which other note is played. The interval between the two determines which zone is played. For example, if you play the notes G3 and G#3, the interval is one semitone; therefore, the chord played is the one assigned to this zone. If you play G3 and A3, the interval is two semi-tones; so, the Zone 2 chord plays, and so on, for a maximum of eight different chords for eight different zones.

Figure B.5
The Chorder MIDI effect
panel in Normal mode

Figure B.6 displays an example of chords changing depending on the method used. The upper staff shows the notes played to trigger the different zones when notes are used to switch between zones. As you can see, the interval between the two notes in this staff is a semitone. This tells the Chorder you want to hear the chord assigned to that zone. In the third bar, the pitch is now different, but the relation between the two notes in the first staff is the same, so the Zone 1 chord is played starting on the lower note's pitch. The second staff from the top shows the notes played to trigger the different zones (each note is played at a different velocity). The lower two staves show the chords generated, which are a C Major 9th chord, C Major 7#11 chord, and a C 13 added.

Figure B.6
Using different chords
associated with different
zones to create
harmonic structures in
the Chorder MIDI effect

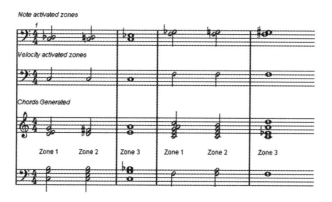

Because the three modes are similar, we take a look at how to create chords and zones in the Octave mode. Remember that in Normal mode, you can have up to 128 different chords. The note that plays them does not affect the pitch, but serves as a trigger. In Octave mode, the same applies, with the exception that you hear a different octave depending on the octave you play the trigger note in, and in Global mode, the played pitch determines the chord's pitch. The example in Figure B.6 was generated by using the Global mode using three separate zones.

To create chords in the Chorder MIDI effect:

1. Select the desired mode. The following steps assume you selected Octave mode.
2. In the trigger keyboard, click the note you want to use to trigger the chord. The note becomes red.
3. In the Chord Setup keyboard, click the notes you want to include in the chord. Clicking the note turns it blue, meaning it will be part of the chord. Clicking it again removes it from the chord.
4. Play that note on your keyboard controller to hear the result.
5. Repeat Steps 2–4 for each additional chord you want to create in your octave.

To use zones in the Chorder MIDI effect:

1. Click the up or down arrow in the Use field to add the desired number of zones for each note. You can have up to eight zones.
2. Select the first trigger note on the Trigger Note keyboard (only available in Normal or Octave modes).
3. Select the desired zone number button to make the chord for that zone.
4. Add notes to the Chord Setup keyboard by clicking on the notes you want to add to the chord.
5. Select the next zone number button to add a new chord to the same trigger note, but different zone.
6. Repeat Steps 2–4 for all the zones.
7. Select another trigger note from the Trigger Note keyboard and repeat Steps 3–6 for as many trigger notes as you want (this is also determined by the mode you have selected).
8. Select the Velocity Zone Split button (second button to the right in the Zone Setup area) or the Note Zone Split button (third button to the right in the Zone Setup area).

Density

The Density MIDI effect panel (see Figure B.7) creates random notes to simulate a denser MIDI track or mute notes to simulate a sparser track. Which one it does depends on the percentage you assign to the slider bar in the control panel. When a value of 100 is displayed, this means 100% density and no changes are made to the MIDI events. A larger value causes the effect to generate progressively more random notes and smaller values cause it to start muting progressively more and more notes. You can use this to create MIDI effects using a MIDI loop that varies through time, for example.

Figure B.7
The Density MIDI effect
panel

MIDIEcho

The MIDIEcho (see Figure B.8) is similar to an audio delay but creates MIDI events to simulate
this echo rather than changing the actual sound coming from the MIDI instrument. It does this
through a number of parameters that you can adjust to get the desired echo effect and also offers
the possibility to change the pitch of echoed notes. Here's a look at these parameters:

▶ Quantize. Determines how close the echo is to a quantize value. The values can
be adjusted using the slider bar or the up and down arrows on the right side of
the field. When using the slider bar, each value corresponds to 1/480 tick of a
quarter note.

▶ Length and Length Decay. Determines the length value of each note. It can be
adjusted the same way as the Quantize parameter. As for the Length Decay, this
determines if each repeated note is the same length or not.

▶ Repeat. Determines how many echoes are generated from the input note. You
can have up to twelve repeated notes.

▶ Echo-Quantize. Determines the time between the input note and its first echo.

▶ Velocity Decay. Allows you to increase or decrease the velocity of repeated
events by a certain velocity amount. You can set this parameter to values
between plus or minus 36.

▶ Pitch Decay. Allows you to change the pitch of each repeating echo by the
amount of semitone you assign to this parameter, where each value corresponds
to a semitone. So, a value of seven makes each echo repeat a perfect fifth above
the preceding echo. You can use this to create arpeggios by adding or subtracting
notes to repeated notes.

▶ Echo Decay. Allows you to increase or decrease a value corresponding to the
time added or removed between each echoed event. If you set this to a positive
value, echoes repeat with more and more time being added between each
repetition, or with less and less time if you set this parameter's value to a
negative number.

You can start with presets and change the parameters to find the desired effect.

Figure B.8
The MIDIEcho MIDI
effect panel

Step Designer

The Step Designer MIDI effect is a step sequencer that allows you to create up to 100 patterns using up to 32 steps per pattern. Each step is defined by the quantize setting in the Step Designer's panel. The Step Designer does not use or need incoming MIDI events. You create these patterns inside the interface itself. Let's take a look at the pattern creation process inside the Step Designer. Each number in the following steps correspond to the numbers in Figure B.9.

To create patterns in the Step Designer MIDI effect:

1. Select the Pattern number from the Pattern field.

   You can copy a pattern from one to another by clicking Copy, selecting the next pattern, and then clicking Paste. The Random button creates a random pattern and the Reset button resets all steps.

2. Adjust the length in steps, quantize value, and swing value for the steps inside the grid below.

   For example, a Length of 16 means that there are 16 steps in the sequence. A Quantize of 16 means that each step is a sixteenth note. You can add a Swing amount to create a shuffle or swing feel to your pattern.

3. Select the range you want to see.

   There is an octave range displayed on the left. Clicking and dragging this bar allows you to move the range up or down. This does not affect steps placed inside the grid, but only affects the events that you see. Events that are in the grid, but outside of view are displayed as red events with their note number and they are in the upper row when found above the current view or in the lower row when below the current view.

4. If you want to shift an entire octave up or down, use the Shift Octave buttons. This, unlike dragging the range described in Step 3, affects the notes found in the grid on the right.

5. Add the events in the grid. The steps falling on beats are displayed in black numbers below the grid and the steps falling between beats are displayed in a cyan (or turquoise) color. To add a step on the second beat at D1, align your cursor at the crossroad of the appropriate column and row and click inside the grid. Clicking again on an inserted note removes it. You can also drag your mouse across the grid to add several events.

6. If you want to tie two or more notes together, click the Tie button corresponding to the step or steps following the first step number where you want the tie to begin. For example, in Figure B.9, if you want to tie the second step to the first, you would click in the tie line on the Tie button number 2.

7. You can adjust different control change parameters. To choose which controller is displayed below the step grid, click the Controller drop-down menu and select the controller of choice. The default controllers displayed are Velocity, Gate (which allows you to shorten the notes), Harmonics, and Brightness (how the last two controllers change the sound depends on the instrument playing back the steps found in the Step Designer). If you want to adjust other controllers not found in this list, click the Setup button and choose the

appropriate controllers from the dialog box.

8. Adjust the selected controller corresponding to each previous step by dragging the vertical bar up or down to get the desired effect.

9. If you want to shift all the steps one step forward or backward in time, use the Shift Time buttons. This can create interesting variations to a beat or rhythmic pattern.

10. If you want to reverse all the steps in your grid (the last step becomes the first and vice versa), click the Reverse button. This option can also be used to create interesting beats or rhythmic variations.

11. When you are satisfied with the patterns that you have created, you can save them as a preset. Each preset can hold up to 100 patterns. So before you save a preset, you can choose another pattern, and edit it by repeating the previous steps. When all the patterns have been created, you can proceed to saving them in a preset.

Figure B.9
The Step Designer MIDI
effect panel

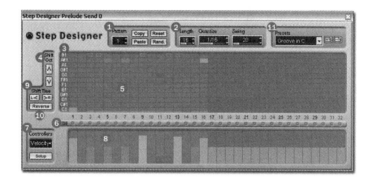

After your patterns are created, you can automate the changes by recording MIDI events using note events on the MIDI track. The notes you record as MIDI events in the part are not played back by your VSTi or other external MIDI device. Pattern 1 corresponds to C1 on your keyboard, subsequent patterns follow on C#1, and so on. In other words, recording a MIDI note playing on C1 at bar 1.1.000 then a C#1 on bar 5.1.000 causes the Step Designer to play the Pattern 1 from Bar 1 to Bar 5, and then change to Pattern 2 from Bar 5 until you enter the next MIDI note corresponding to a new pattern.

To automate the pattern changes in a MIDI track using the Step Designer MIDI effect:

1. Create your patterns in the Step Designer as previously described.

2. In the Event Display area, position the left and right locators so that they cover the range of bars where you want to create automation events for the Step Designer.

3. Double-click the MIDI track to create a new part that corresponds to the length found between the left and right locators.

4. Double-click this part to open its associated editor (Key or Drum).

5. Set up your quantize grid appropriately and activate it.

6. Select the Draw tool from the toolbar.

7. Enter notes at the location in the part corresponding to desired pattern change locations. Remember, C1 is Pattern 1, C#1 is Pattern 2, and so on.

Event Modifying Effects

MIDI effects in this category do not create any new MIDI events, but modify them in some way.

Compress

The Compress MIDI effect (shown in Figure B.10) allows you to compress or expand the velocity values of events on a MIDI track by adding or reducing the Note On velocity of these events. The Compress effect has three controls: the Threshold level, the Ratio, and the Gain control. The Threshold level determines the velocity value needed to trigger the compress effect. The Ratio can act as an expander or a compressor depending on the value set in this field. A one to one ratio means there is no change in the velocity values. A ratio greater than one to one compresses the velocity values by that proportion and a ratio that is less than one to one expands the velocity value by that same ratio. For example, if you have a ratio of 2:1, for every two values passing the threshold, only one is added to the final velocity. So if you have a threshold of 80 and play a velocity of 100 with a ratio of 2:1, the end velocity result is 90. On the other hand, if you have a ratio of 1:2, playing a note with a velocity of 90 using the same threshold causes the velocity to move up to 100.

The Gain control determines a value that is added or removed to the velocity of MIDI events passing through this effect.

Unlike the previous MIDI effects described in this appendix, this effect does not generate new MIDI events, it simply modifies the events going through it.

To use the Compress MIDI effect:

1. Adjust the Threshold value to the desired velocity value. Velocities below this threshold are not affected.

2. Adjust the ratio appropriately to expand or compress the velocity of events passing through the effect.

3. Adjust the Gain level to add or remove velocity values to all the events in this MIDI track.

Figure B.10
The Compress MIDI
effect panel

Control

The Control MIDI effect allows you to control up to eight MIDI control change parameters. As you can see in Figure B.11, the left column is used to set the value for a controller that is defined in the right column. You can select any available controller from the drop-down menu in this (right) column. You can use this to automate different control change parameters using MIDI automation as described in Chapter 13.

Figure B.11
The Control MIDI effect
panel

MicroTuner

This effect allows you to simulate different types of tuning. It does so by giving you control over fine tuning between each semitone in a chromatic scale, and then applies these tuning modifications over the range of the keyboard. The best way to use this is to use one of the many available presets. Changing the tuning for one MIDI instrument playing strings, for example, might help make the overall sound a bit richer if this instrument is doubled by another string pad that is not microtuned.

The Micro Tuner panel (shown in Figure B.12) features twelve sliders, one for each semitone. Each one can be adjusted separately. You can also select the Convert method, which adjusts the microtuning method depending if this is applied to a VSTi or external MIDI device using SysEx to alter the tuning of the device in question.

Figure B.12
The Micro Tuner MIDI
effect panel

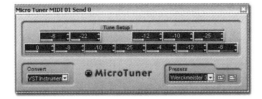

Note to Control Change Converter

This MIDI effect (see Figure B.13) allows you to convert a MIDI note number into a value that
you can assign to a MIDI Control Change message. For example, you can create a MIDI track,
play notes, then assign this MIDI effect to affect the pan. Whenever a note is played high in the
keyboard range, the pan goes on one side and when a note is played low, the pan goes on the
other side. All you need to do is select which MIDI Control Change message you want to use
with the converted note number values.

Figure B.13
The Note2CC MIDI
effect panel

Quantizer

The Quantizer (shown in Figure B.14) offers the same effect as the main over quantize functions
that were described in Chapter 7. In this case, you can assign to a track and change the quantize
values dynamically using automation. It offers the same parameters as the quantize setup;
however, it does add a delay parameter that lets you assign a delay in milliseconds that can be
added to each quantized note.

Figure B.14
The Quantizer MIDI
effect panel

Track Control

The Track Control allows you to control additional parameters provided by GS and XG compatible
MIDI devices. Roland GS and Yamaha XG MIDI devices extend on the General MIDI (GM) standard
by offering more sounds and better control over them. The Track Control effect provides a ready-
made interface to control these devices when using such a device as your MIDI track output. If you
don't have a GS or XG compatible device, this effect does not serve any purpose.

The panel itself (see Figure B.15) offers different controls of specific parameters displayed below the control. You can choose from the top drop-down menu which type of controls you want to see, depending on the GS or XG instrument you want to control.

Figure B.15
The Track Control MIDI
effect panel

Track Effects

The Track Effects (see Figure B.16)offers essentially the same parameters as the Track Parameters section, with one addition: the Scale Transpose module. In other words, you can use this if you need to add random values to MIDI events and the two random generators in the Track Parameter are already used for something else, or when you want to use the Scale Transpose module.

Figure B.16
The Track FX panel

This module allows you to set a scale and assign a mode to your track, converting any recorded or played notes to notes found in the transpose scale and mode. If you take a look at Figure B.17, you will notice that a C major scale was recorded in the first staff. Using the Track Effect MIDI effect with the Scale Transpose set to an Oriental mode preset from the drop-down menu with a scale based on C, the notes in the original major scale are transformed to fit this new mode (lower staff in Figure B.17). In other words, you can quickly change the colors of harmonic and melodic content using this feature in the Track Effects. Here's an example: If you use the default C scale and play in this scale as well, you can change the mode so that a C major scale becomes a C minor or C pentatonic scale instead. You can also change the scale itself to any other note in a twelve-tone scale and all other notes will be changed appropriately.

Figure B.17
Using the Track Effects
effect to modify the
scale mode of melodic
or harmonic content

Transformer

The Transformer MIDI effect offers a way to change the content of MIDI events going in using the same tools and menus described in the Logical Editor, which is described in the following appendix. The main difference is that the transformer acts as a MIDI effect assigned to a track, modifying events in real time, whereas the Logical Editor edits selected events as a process applied to MIDI events, changing these MIDI events rather than transforming them as they are being played. Please refer to Appendix C for more details.

Appendix C
Logical Editing

Logical editing is another way of editing MIDI data. Using this method, you create specific parameters for Cubase to look for and then decide to change them, delete them, or move them. This is for the MIDI-savvy user, because you need to know how MIDI messages work to fully understand how logical editing works.

The Logical Editor affect events differently, depending on the location from which you launch it, but it always performs the tasks in the same way. For example, if you are in the Project window and have not selected any MIDI parts, it performs edits on all the parts for the selected tracks. On the other hand, if you have a part selected, it looks for and edits only events in that part. Finally, if you are in MIDI Editor, the Logical Editor performs its modifications on the events selected in this part or all events if none are selected.

You may use already created logical edit presets included with Cubase, or you may create your own and save them. Logical edits are stored as separate files on your hard disk and are common to any project.

Let's take a look at an example to begin describing how this interface works. You may refer to Figure C.1 to see what the following example is describing.

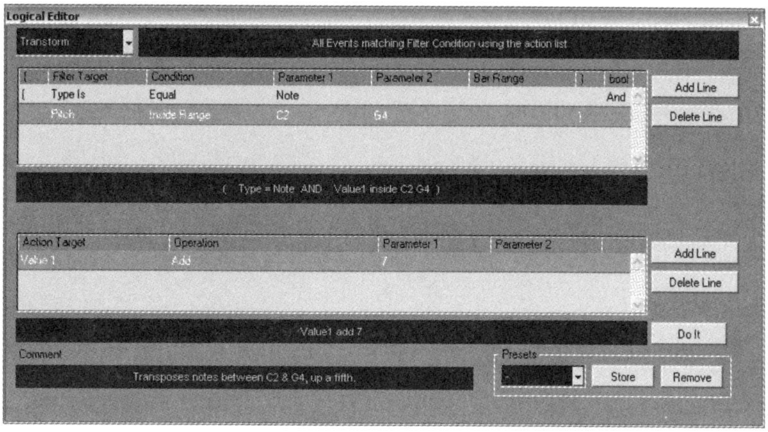

Figure C.1
The Logical Editor used to transpose notes between C2 and G4 up a fifth

Suppose you want to transpose notes that are between C2 and G4, up a perfect fifth. You can start by defining a function. Functions are what you want to do with the events you edit logically. In this case, you want to transform notes. So, in the upper-left corner of the interface, you select Transform from the drop-down menu (functions in this list are described later in this appendix).

Then, you can ask: What do I want to transform? In this case, once again, you want to transform notes. In Logical Editor terms, this is the target. To correctly target what you want to transform, you have to define it using a filter, which tells Cubase what to look for, a condition that needs to be met, and parameters within the filter that should be applied. In our example, the target for your filter is a type that is equal to notes. That's why you see "Type is" under the Filter Target, "Equal" under the Condition, and "Note" under the Parameter column.

Now, do you want to transform all notes? In our example, we only want to transform the notes between C2 and G4. This is a second "target" you want to apply to the Logical Editor, so you add a second line using the Add Line button. If, at the end of the first line, you have a Boolean expression with the word "And," this tells Cubase to look for the target set in the first line AND the second line. Events must then match both targeted conditions for the logical editing to occur. We then apply a filter to our second target, saying we want notes, but the pitch is important in our editing. So, Cubase filters certain pitch values. Because we want only pitch values between C2 and G4, the condition that needs to be met is set to "Inside Range." By selecting this type of condition, you can enter a note value in the Parameter 1 and Parameter 2 columns. These parameters correspond to the Pitch Inside Range values, which in this case is C2 and G4.

At this point, we've told Cubase to target a type of event that is equal to notes and the pitch value must be inside the C2 and G4 range. From this point forward, you tell Cubase what to do with these targeted events. This part occurs in the lower portion of the window.

Changing the pitch of these notes corresponds to the value 1 in the MIDI message because the pitch is the first value passed by the Note On message. You can, therefore, select this as the target for your action in the Action Target column. Now, what you want to do is transpose these notes up a perfect fifth. In other words, you want to add seven to each value passed on. This refers to MIDI note numbers. For example, a C2 note is equal the MIDI note number 48. If you add 7 to this value, you get the note value 55, which is G3—a perfect fifth above C2. The operation you want to apply in our example is "Add" and the Parameter 1 value is 7.

All that you need to do from this point is click the Do It button to apply this logical edit to the selected events or parts. What the Logical Editor affects depends on the location from which you launched the editor and if any events were selected. The Logical Editor allows you to edit a selected track, a selected part, or a selected range of events in a part, depending on the point at which you launch the Logical Editor.

Remember that using the Logical Editor allows you to modify events in a way that normally takes much more time if done manually in one of the editors. The previous example is just one of many ways you can quickly and effectively transform MIDI events, not to mention the creative aspects of the Logical Editor. For example, creating a textured melody using a copy of the MIDI events, transposed a third above but using a velocity level set at 25 percent of the original version, simply adds color to this melody without having it stand out. The following sections allow you to get an understanding of these principles, and you can decide how you want to apply them.

Logical Editor Parameters

Let's take a closer look at the parameters found in the Logical Editor. The following paragraph contains the logic established by the Logical Editor. If you don't understand what this means right away, don't panic, just read on as each of these terms is described in the following sections. By the end of this appendix, you'll probably get it.

A function is applied to a target. This target is defined by meeting certain conditions, which serve as a filter mechanism to achieve this desired target. After a target is identified, you can apply an action to a parameter through an operation.

About Functions

The function determines what you want to do inside the Logical Editor. When selecting certain functions, you need to define an action in the bottom half of the editor, whereas other functions only need to have a target, for example, the Delete function. The functions available in the upper-left corner of the Logical Editor include:

▶ Delete. Deletes the targeted notes that pass through the filters.

▶ Transform. Transforms the targeted events that pass through the filters. The transformation is set by the values set in the Action section (or processing stage found in the lower half of the window). This doesn't add any new events; it just changes the existing ones.

▶ Insert. Adds the targeted events that pass through the filters. The transformation is set by the values set in the Action section. This adds new events to the part(s).

▶ Insert Exclusive. Adds the targeted events that pass through the filters, while deleting the events that do not pass through the filter.

▶ Copy. If you launch the Logical Editor from the Project window, it copies the events that pass through the filters out of the part or parts and then creates a new part or parts with the extracted events only. You cannot use this function if you are not launching the Logical Editor from the Project window.

▶ Extract. If you launch the Logical Editor from the Project window, it cuts the events that pass through the filters out of the part or parts and then creates a new part or parts with the extracted events only. You cannot use this function if you are not launching the Logical Editor from the Project window.

▶ Select. If you launch the Logical Editor from the MIDI Editors, it simply selects the events that pass through the filters for future processing directly in the editor, after you have exited the Logical Editor. You cannot use this function if you are not launching the Logical Editor from the Editor windows.

The best way to understand all of this is to look at some of the presets. Load them and look at how they change the values in different parts of the window. Because the preset names are pretty descriptive, you'll get a good sense of what's happening.

About Filter Target

This field tells the Logical Editor what to look for.

▶ Position. Requires you to enter a position in the Parameter 1 (and Parameter 2 field if you choose a range in the Condition column). For example, you might want to select notes between Bar 3 and Bar 4.

▶ Length. Requires you to enter a length value in the Parameter 1 (and Parameter 2 field if you choose a range in the Condition column). For example, you might want to select only quarter notes.

▶ Value 1, 2, and 3. Usually added as a second line in the targeted filter area because the value they represent depends on their type. For example, if you add a first line that reads, Type is Equal to Note, then on the second line, Value 1 automatically represents the pitch. If you select Value 2 instead, this automatically represents the velocity of the note, and Value 3 represents the Note Off velocity. In other words, the type selected determines what the value represents.

▶ Channel. Allows you to specify a specific channel for your transformation. You enter the channel number in the Parameter field. If you set the condition to a range, you then add this range to both Parameter fields. For example, to select all events between Channel 4 and 7, the line should read as follows: Channel Inside Range 4 and 7.

▶ Type (from the Filter Target column). Lets you choose what type of MIDI message you want to target. Parameter 1 offers you the following choices: note, polyphonic pressure, control change, program change, aftertouch, and pitch bend messages.

▶ Property. Allows you to choose events for which a specific property is either set or not set. These properties include the following options: an event can be muted, selected, or locked. For example, you can target all events that are not muted in a part by entering the following information: Property is not set to muted.

About Conditions

As you have just seen in the Filter Targets, the condition column varies depending on the targeted events. For example, choosing the Type target offers different conditions than if you select the Property target. Generally speaking, the conditions are similar to mathematical conditions.

As a practical example, suppose you want to find events that are not between Bars 5 and 9 of a project. You would choose the Filter Target Position, with a condition that reads Outside Range. You would then proceed to the Parameter fields and enter 0005.01.01.000 in Parameter 1 and 0009.01.01.000 in Parameter 2. You could even specify a range within a bar using the Inside or Outside Bar Range condition. In this case, a bar range display appears, allowing you to drag a range within a bar to determine this range. The values corresponding to this range are added to the Parameter 1 and 2 columns.

About Boolean Expressions

The Boolean expression column is used when more than one line is present in the target area for the Logical Editor. If you want Cubase to include events targeted in one line AND the other, use the And Boolean. If you are trying to achieve one or the other, select the Or Boolean.

Figure C.2 displays an example of Boolean expressions in use. In this case, notes with a velocity ranging from 0 to 64 "or" 100 to 127 will be targeted. Notice the Boolean expression between the first and second line is And. This tells Cubase that you are looking for Note events, but wait, there's more, you also want it to look for notes with specific velocity values.

You will also notice the braces at the beginning of line two and at the end of line three. These allow you to set boundaries, as in a mathematical formula. For example, $2 + 3 \times 4$ is not the same as $2 + (3 \times 4)$. If you were to have these braces, defining that the velocity needed is one of the conditions; the other condition is the length. In the same way here, we want to find notes that have a velocity of 0 to 64 or 100 to 127, then we could add a fourth line stating that the length has to equal 1.000. The end of the third line would have the And Boolean expression.

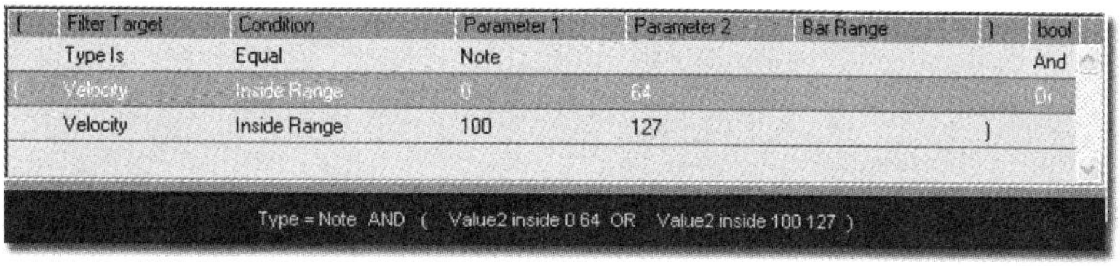

Figure C.2
Example of a setting
using a Boolean value

Specifying an Action

After you've determined what the target is, you can specify the type of action you want the Logical Editor to apply to those targeted events. This is done in the second (lower part of the window) section of the Logical Editor.

The Action Target column holds the same options as the Filter Target. That's because you can apply an action to the same types of events that you can target. However, it doesn't mean that if you targeted the note events with a certain velocity, that you will necessarily apply an action to the velocity of those events. You could change the position of those events, for example. How the action is applied is determined by the Operation column. As with the Condition column in the previous section, the Operation column holds different options depending on the Action Target column's selection.

If we take the target specified in Figure C.2, for example, we could select notes with a specific velocity, and apply the actions specified in Figure C.3. As we can see, the Position of the notes is changed by adding 200 ticks to these notes. Further more, their length is modified by setting a random length value between 600 ticks and 1000 ticks (there are 480 ticks in each quarter note).

Figure C.3
An example of actions
taken on targeted events

Appendix D
Optimizing Through Customizing

This appendix discusses ways that you can customize settings and create reusable documents to suit your working preferences.

Window Layouts

If you find yourself constantly opening the same sets of windows every time you create a new project or open an existing one, you should create custom window layouts. Window layouts are saved separately and are common to all projects inside Cubase. Window layouts allow you to save the current position and state of windows inside your project. You can create several layouts and recall them through a set of default key commands. By doing so, you can create a layout for your editing tasks, another one for your audio record tasks, and another layout for your mixing tasks.

To create a window layout:

1. Open the windows you want to display on your desktop. For example, if you always place your Send Effects and VST Instruments panel on the bottom of your desktop, place these windows there.

2. After you are satisfied with the window layout, select Window Layouts > New from the Window menu, or press the default key command Ctrl+0 (from the numeric keypad) or Command+0 if you are on Mac.

3. Name your layout appropriately.

4. Repeat these steps to create an additional window layout.

To organize your window layouts:

1. Select Window Layouts > Organize from the Window menu or press the default key command W.

2. Click the Remove button if you want to remove a layout from the list. Click the New button if you want to save the current layout or Activate if you want Cubase to display the selected layout in the Window Layouts panel.

Creating Templates

When we work, we often start with basic settings. For example, if you have a favorite VSTi that you load for drums, a favorite window layout, or a number of tracks that you always name the same way, you might consider creating a template. Templates are Cubase project documents that are saved in a Templates folder found inside your Cubase program folder. Saving a project as a template before you start recording events into it allows you to save all these settings, including preferences, output and input settings, and all of the previously mentioned settings. To use a template, you simply select Create New Project from the File menu. This displays the New Project dialog box (see Figure D.1). The options available in the New Project dialog box are the template files found in the Template folder.

Figure D.1
Templates appear in the New Project dialog box when you create a new project

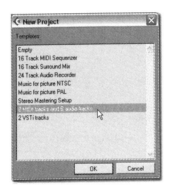

To create a template:

1. Organize your project as you normally do. For example, create the tracks you normally use, activate the outputs/inputs, assign send effects, and so on.

2. When you are satisfied that this is a worthy template, select the Save As Template from the File menu.

3. Enter a name for your template. The name you enter in this dialog box is the name that will appear in the New Project dialog box as shown in Figure D.1. This is also the name given to the file.

Because templates are just like regular files, you can rename or delete the files from your hard disk to rename or remove a file from the template list. It also implies that you can save events within a template file.

Another way you can customize your environment at startup is by saving your default preferences as the Default.cpr file in the Cubase program folder. To edit the default file, simply open it, make the desired changes, and save it.

Macros

Using Cubase macros is a way to save a number of tasks that you perform regularly one after the other. For example, you can quickly create four audio tracks, a Marker track, select a window layout, and a select a zoom level. Performing these tasks can take many steps, or one single step when programmed as a macro command.

To create a macro:

1. From the File menu, select the Key Commands option.
2. In the Key Commands dialog box, click the Show Macro button. This reveals the Macro section at the bottom of the dialog box, as displayed in Figure D.2.
3. Click the New Macro button. This adds a new macro in the Macros area.
4. Double-click the new macro's name and type in a new name for the macro.

Figure D.2
Creating Macro commands in the Key Commands dialog box

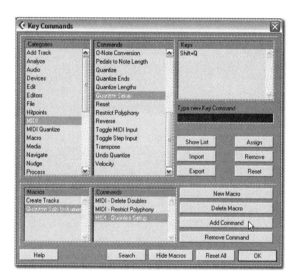

Now your new macro is created, but it won't do anything. Let's add commands to it.

To add commands to a macro:

1. In the Key Commands dialog box, click on the category of command you want in the Categories area.
2. This displays the related commands for this category in the Commands area. Select the command you want to add to your macro.
3. Click the Add Command button in the Macro section. This adds the selected command in the Commands area of the Macro section.
4. Repeat these steps for each command you want to add to your macro.
5. When you've completed adding commands to your macro, click OK to close this dialog box.

To use a macro in a project:

1. From the Edit menu, select the Macro option at the bottom of the menu. The applicable macro commands appear in the submenu of the Macro option (see Figure D.3).

2. Select the macro command you want to apply to start the list of commands it holds.

Figure D.3
Selecting a macro
command

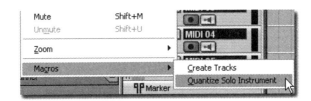

Appendix E
About Surround Sound Mixing

Cubase SX offers the possibility to mix in several surround modes as well as in stereo mode. Mixing in surround, however, requires a multiple output sound card to monitor the signal sent to these additional outputs. It also requires an external monitoring system that supports surround sound. The advantage of mixing in surround is that beyond the left/right field available in stereo mixes, you can literally place your sound anywhere in space around the listener using various surround configurations.

When using surround setups in Cubase, the master output displays a number of monitoring levels to reflect the signal being sent to each channel in your surround spectrum. You will also find at the bottom of each channel a new set of options allowing you to route the signal to a specific channel in the surround configuration or to switch the pan control to a special surround pan control (see Figure E.1).

Figure E.1
An audio channel using
surround pan control

VST Master Setup

The VST Master Setup dialog box allows you to change the master output configuration setting. When you change the settings, the master channel in the Channel Mixer window adapts itself to reflect the selection you have made in the VST Master Setup dialog box.

You can choose from the regular stereo default master setup to one of six other surround sound output configurations. You can change the Label or Name entry in their respective columns inside the VST Master Setup dialog box (see Figure E.2), but the outputs and speaker position, as well as the number of outputs used for any specific surround setup, can't be changed.

To distribute your signal appropriately in a surround configuration, you have to enable more than one stereo output from the VST Outputs panel, otherwise all channels are sent out to the same outputs, which defeats the purpose of mixing in surround in the first place.

Figure E.2
The VST Master Setup
dialog box

To set up your master channel in surround mode:

1. Open the VST Outputs panel.

2. Activate the appropriate number of outputs needed for your surround mix. Typically, you need to have four to six outputs depending on the Surround preset you will use.

3. Select VST Master Setup from the Devices menu.

4. Select the appropriate preset for your surround mix setup.

5. Click OK to apply.

The Mixer's Surround Options

After you have set up your master channel outputs for surround sound mixing, you can assign the SurroundPan output to the desired channels. This allows you to control the position of the channel's audio content within a surround field. You can automate a surround pan just like regular pan automation.

You can also choose to send a channel only to a specific output if you want. The additional outputs are displayed according to your VST master setup configuration in the output selection field below each channel.

Surround Pan Control

When the SurroundPan control is selected as an output for a channel, you can access the SurroundPan Control panel by double-clicking on the SurroundPan display in a channel (this is the circle pan control shown in Figure E.1). Double-clicking in this control area brings up the Panner settings panel (see Figure E.3). This panel offers a graphic display showing the position of speakers depending on the Master Setup panel. You can disable a speaker by holding down the Alt key (Option key on a Mac) while you click on it. As a result, no audio is sent to this speaker. In the same display, you will find either one or two control handles depending on the mix mode set (see the following list). The control handles allow you to place the source of the sound appropriately in the surround sound mixing field. Lines emerge from the speakers indicating the level being sent to each output. In the example provided in Figure E.3, you can see the single control placed in the upper-left portion of the display. Consequently, the front right speaker's level is set to minus infinity, the center speaker to -6.7, and the left speaker to -5.0, while the left surround and right surround output levels are set to -7.4 and -27. These are the levels required to position your sound in the current configuration. Consequently, the level of this channel is distributed to each output using these levels. The only speaker that is not represented in this display is the low frequency subbass speaker, which has its own control in the lower part of the Panner.

You can move the source of a signal by dragging the control handle where you want in this display. If the source is stereo and if you are not using the Mono Mix mode (found in the lower part of the Panner), you will find two control handles labeled L and R. When positioning a stereo sound within the surround panner, you will always move the right control handle (labeled R). The direction the left control handle takes depends on the surround mixer mode set. You have four basic mix modes to choose from:

> **Mono Mix**. When used on a stereo source, both sources are mixed into a mono channel and you control where this channel is positioned in the surround field. (See Figure E.3.)

> **Y-Mirror**. This causes stereo sources to become mirrored vertically. When you move the right control handle's position to the left or right, the left field moves in the opposite direction. When you move this control to the front or back, the left control moves in the same direction. In other words, the position of the right control is reflected vertically.

> **X-Mirror**. This causes stereo sources to become mirrored horizontally. When you move the right control handle's position to the left or right, the left field moves in the same direction. When you move this control to the front or back, the left control moves in the opposite direction. In other words, the position of the right control is reflected horizontally.

> **X/Y-Mirror**. This causes stereo sources to become mirrored both vertically and horizontally. In other words, the left control always move in the opposite direction of the right control.

Figure E.3
The Panner settings panel in Mono Mix mode

The Center Level slider allows you to determine the percentage assigned to the center speaker. When this slider is set to zero percent, the signal that would be positioned in the center speaker is shadowed by the left and right speakers instead, creating a virtual center speaker without using this source. By default, this value is set to 100 percent.

The following three rings are called diverge control fields and they determine the attenuation curves used when positioning sound sources, for X-axis front (the first ring to the left), X-axis back (the center ring), and Y-axis (the ring on the right). By default, these values are set at zero percent. Raising these values changes the shape of the dotted line square representation inside the graphic display and causes the signal to start appearing in other speakers even when you place the source on a single speaker. This is because you change the attenuation curve and set the room to react unnaturally, attenuating the sound coming from one source more than the sound coming from another source. As a result, the speakers generate a different level to compensate for this attenuation.

The last control is used by the subbass (LFE) speaker. You can decide the level being sent from this source in the subbass channel.

You can automate the SurroundPan plug-in as you would any channel automation (described in Chapter 13).

Using Effects in Surround Mode

As you might have anticipated, using effects in surround mode might become an issue because most effects are designed to work on two channels rather than four, five, or six channels. Cubase offers a special signal path diagram, which is accessible in the VST Master Effects panel. Double-clicking the display as shown in Figure E.4 opens the Patch Editor panel for the master effect in question.

Figure E.4
The signal path diagram in the VST Master Effects panel allows you to edit and view how the effect is routed in the surround configuration

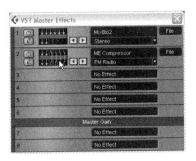

The Patch Editor displays three sections: the In section, the effect itself, and the Out section. The In section represents the channels going in the effect from the surround outputs. In Figure E.5, these are the six current surround channels as configured in the VST Master Setup dialog box. In the center, you find the effect itself. At the bottom of Figure E.5 in the Out section are the outputs of the effect and how they are routed to the outputs of the surround mix. Then, you can see the connector lines. These lines allow you to connect different channels to the inputs available on the effect and connect the outputs of the effect to the VST outputs, adding the effect on these channels. In Figure E.5, you can see that the output channels L and R are the only ones being sent to the ME Compressor plug-in assigned to the Master Effects section. The remaining channels bypass the effect completely. This means that only the Left and Right channels are compressed by this effect. Using the connector lines, you can change which channels are processed by the plug-in. Because you can only process two channels at a time with most plug-ins currently available with Cubase, you can add multiple instances of a specific effect in the VST Master Effects setup and assign each instance to a different set of outputs if desired.

Figure E.5
The Patch Editor panel

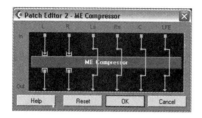

To edit the patch configuration of a master effect in surround mixes:

1. Open the VST Master Effects panel.

2. Assign the desired effect to one of the master effect's space.

3. Double-click the patch diagram as shown in Figure E.4.

4. In the Patch Editor, drag one of the In connectors from the desired input to the effect. For example, in Figure E.5, you could drag the R channel connector to the Rs channel to connect the right surround channel to the input of the effect.

5. Drag the output of the effect connector to the desired output channel. Again in Figure E.5, you could connect the R output connector to the Rs output to have one of the effect's output sent to the right surround channel output (look at Figure E.6 for an example of this).

6. Click OK when done.

Figure E.6
In this example, the left and right surround channels are processed by the effect

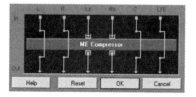

Figure E.7 shows an example of a different application to this patch configuration. As you can see, the left and right output channels are sent to the Reverb A effect, but the output of the effect is not sent to the left and right channels, but the left surround and right surround channels instead. The left and right channels are in fact sent to both the effect's input and output channel, whereas the surround channels will not receive any signal from the master outputs Ls and Rs channels. As a consequence, what you hear is a wet reverb version of the left and right channel sent out in the left and right surround channels.

Figure E.7
Another example of the
Patch Editor connector
configuration

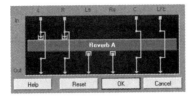

You can also use an alternative method to route a signal to a different set of outputs in a
surround mix. In the VST Send Effects panel, each effect can be routed to any available output
bus. For example, effect Sends 1 and 2 can both have reverbs with effect Send 2 being routed to
Bus 2 or 3. This way, mixer channels can be routed to stereo plug-ins in any bus by simply
activating the appropriate aux sends in the mixer. This method might prove to be more flexible
than using the master effects as numerous channels can access differing amounts of the effects
individually.

Exporting a Surround Mix

After you have completed your surround mix, you can export it as you would normally export a
final stereo mix. The only difference with surround mix is that you can choose an additional
number of output file formats in the Export Audiomix dialog box, as shown in Figure E.8. This
generates either six mono audio files or three stereo audio files that can later be edited by a
special software or hardware to convert them in an appropriate surround sound encoding format
such as DTS.

Figure E.8
Exporting audio files for
a surround sound mix

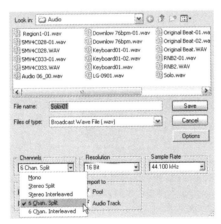

Appendix F
Cubase Resources on The Web

This appendix gives you some of the best-known resources for information on the World Wide Web. These links have been separated into two sections for your convenience: "Finding Help" and "Plug-In Resources and VST Instruments."

Finding Help

Cubase is pretty well-documented and now that you have a book that simplifies the most common functions and operations, you might still want to find out about a specific issue that you might be dealing with for a while. These resources offer some relief and insight by sharing their knowledge base with you. They can also provide updates on available upgrades, fixes and patches, and the most valuable of all—discussion forums where thousands of users like you join to discuss many topics.

If you want to subscribe to a Cubase newsgroup, you should look for alt.steinberg.cubase. There is also a number of online mailing lists for Cubase users. To subscribe to the main mailing list of Cubase users, send an e-mail to cubase@yahoogroups.com. You should also look for upgrades directly on Steinberg's FTP site at the following address: ftp.steinberg.net.

Cubase.net

If you are looking for news, interviews, tips and tricks, or even a group forum discussing Cubase and other Steinberg products, Cubase.net is the place to go. This site provides the information you can't find on Steinberg's site, but has close ties with that company. You can also subscribe online to Club Cubase, a support group for registered Cubase users, at this site.

http://www.cubase.net/

Steinberg's Information Center

This is ground zero for Cubase users. Steinberg provides additional tutorials, information on newly released software, plug-ins, and VST Instruments. It is also a good place to look for special events, such as trade shows or master classes.

http://www.steinberg.net/

K-v-R VST

This site is dedicated to VST Instrument resources, such as up-to-the-minute news, resources, beta testing results of software applications, ASIO and latency issues related to sound cards, VST Instrument patches, and much more. This is a very nice and well-thought-out site. A must if you want to get quick information.

http://www.kvr-vst.com/

Plug-In Resources and VST Instruments

Cubase as a stand-alone software is quite nice, but adding VST or DirectX compatible plug-ins or VST Instruments transforms it into an unusually versatile creative instrument. In this section, you will find some of the manufacturers that develop third-party software that can be integrated into Cubase. For a complete list of all VST plug-ins and Instrument manufacturers, you can visit Steinberg's site (www.steinberg.net). Once there, select the Professional section in the portal page. Once in the main Professional section, select World of VST under the Share menu on the right of the page. Once inside the World of VST, click on the VST Instrument Details link to access all the information available on VSTi.

Antares

Antares develops high-end audio plug-ins. The Autotune and Microphone Modeler software allow you to shape your input by adding a virtual model of a high-quality microphone response curve, then with Autotune, correct any pitch problems you might have had when recording the session. These two tools combined will transform an OK performance into a pretty good one.

http://www.antares-systems.com

Arboretum

This is another top-notch plug-in maker. Arboretum has developed tools that will transform your sound in many different ways. Countless recording artists, including Nine Inch Nails, White Zombie, and Public Enemy, have used its Hyperprism plug-in series. The effect the plug-ins produce is as amazing as the names for these plug-ins: HyperVerb, New Granulator, Hyperphaser, Formant Pitch Shifter, Harmonic Exciter, Bass Maximizer, and so on.

http://www.arboretum.com

Native Instruments

You can't talk about VST Instruments without talking about Native Instruments. This company has created some of the best "virtual synthesizers" musicians have seen on the market. The legendary B3 organ has been perfectly reproduced (sometimes surpassing the original) by their B4 software version, for example.

http://www.native-instruments.net/

Propellerhead

This company seems to have worked closely with Steinberg throughout the years because some of their applications work very well in conjunction with Steinberg's Cubase products. This is the case for Reason, which can be controlled from Cubase and adds a rackful of instruments to your Cubase production system.

http://www.propellerheads.se

Prosoniq

Have you ever wondered what an Orange Vocoder was? To find out, you can head out to Prosoniq's Web site. Again, this company has turned out some very cool VST-compatible plug-ins. With Orange Vocoder, Prosoniq offers you an all-digital simulation of a realistic analog vocoder effect that is fully customizable and comes with an 8-voice virtual analog synthesizer unit, Freeform EQ, and Filterbank Reverb, all in one plug-in.

http://www.prosoniq.com

Spectral Design

This company develops software that is distributed by Steinberg. So, it's safe to say that they integrate very well in Steinberg's suite of software. The deNoiser, deClicker, Clean, and Freefilter applications are probably their best-known products. The deNoiser plug-in works especially well with constant noises in your recording, such as hums and tape hiss.

http://www.spectral-design.com

TC Works

TC Works have been at the forefront of the high-end plug-in industry with their TC Native Bundle. All tools are heavily performance optimized, so they really work in your multitrack environment without bringing the computer to its knees. The intuitive user interfaces make these plug-ins invaluable tools you'll be able to use instantly. They also produce a very nice VST Instrument called Mercury-1, which nicely emulates old analog monophonic synthesis.

http://www.tcworks.de/home/content/en/Welcome/render_top

Waves

Waves has been developing plug-ins originally for Pro Tools as TDM software. With the arrival of VST and the potential power this format provided, they proceeded in developing their VST version of their popular plug-in packages. The Native Power Pack is the package that started it all for Native users. This package includes a De-Esser and a special two-tap version of SuperTap rounds out the essential collection for everyday music and production work. They also provide support for 88.2/96 kHz for many native components. A one-stop shop for all your professional processing needs.

http://www.waves.com

Appendix G
Key Commands Reference Guide

Working effectively on a project begins with understanding how the tool you are using works and what you can do with it. After you know what to do, how to do it using the menus, toolbars, and buttons onscreen, the next step to working effectively is learning the keyboard shortcut associated with the tasks you perform on a regular basis. This helps you increase your productivity simply because it usually takes less time to press a key or combination of keys on your keyboard than to find the same option in a submenu somewhere in your software. The following list contains key commands that will serve you time and time again.

Because you can modify key commands associated with your installation, you might find it easier to replace some of these default key commands with other keystrokes, or add some of your own shortcuts. For example, you can add a key command to undo a quantize on selected events rather than selecting this option in the Advanced Quantize submenu found in the MIDI menu.

To add key commands:

1. Select Key Commands from the File menu. The Key Commands dialog box appears as shown in Figure G.1.

2. Select an appropriate Category in the Key Commands dialog box.

3. Then select a command in the Commands pane.

4. Click in the Type New Key Command field and type the key or key combination you want to assign to the selected command.

5. Click the Assign button.

APPENDIX G

Figure G.1
The Key Commands
dialog box

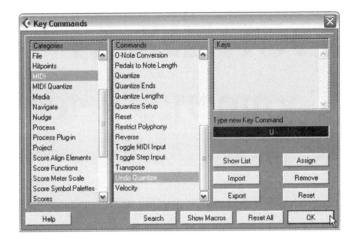

To remove key commands:

1. In the Key Commands dialog box, select the appropriate category and command.
2. Then select the key associated with that command in the Keys pane.
3. Click the Remove button.

In the same dialog box, you can also click the Show List button to view the current active key command list associated with Cubase. If you want to reset all your key commands to their default values, click the Reset button.

You can also import or export key commands from or to a file on your computer using the Import or Export buttons. This allows you, for example, to save your custom key commands, save them to a disk, and bring them with you when working in another studio.

If a key command already exists for the selected function, it should appear in the Keys pane when you select the command. If you want to change this key command to another, use the remove key command procedure described previously, and then assign a new key command using the add key command procedure (described previously as well).

Devices

Table G.1
Device key commands

Commands	PC Keys	Mac Keys
Mixer	F3	F3
Video	F8	F8
VST Inputs	F5	F5
VST Master Effects	F7	F7
VST Outputs	F4	F4
VST Send Effects	F6	F6

Editing

Table G.2
Editing key commands

Commands	PC Keys	Mac Keys
Adjust Fades to Range	A	A
Copy	Ctrl+C	Command+C
Crossfade	X	X
Cut	Ctrl+X	Command+X
Cut Time	Ctrl+Shift+X	Command+Shift+X
Delete	Del, Backspace	Del, Backspace
Delete Time	Shift+Back	Shift+Back
Duplicate	Ctrl+D	Command+D
Insert Silence	Ctrl+Shift+E	Command+Shift+E
Left Selection Side to Cursor	E	E
Lock	Ctrl+Shift+K	Command+Shift+L
Move to Cursor	Ctrl+L	Command+L
Mute	M	M
Mute Events	Shift+M	Shift+M

Open Default Editor	Ctrl+E	Command+E
Open Score Editor	Ctrl+R	Command+R
Open/Close Editor	Enter	Return
Paste	Ctrl+V	Command+V
Paste at Origin	Alt+V	Option+V
Paste Time	Ctrl+Shift+V	Command+Shift+V
Quantize	Q	Q
Record Enable	R	R
Redo	Ctrl+Shift+Z	Command+Shift+Z
Repeat	Ctrl+K	Command+K
Right Selection Side to Cursor	D	D
Select All	Ctrl+A	Command+A
Select Non (Deselect)	Ctrl+Shift+A	Command+Shift+A
Solo	S	S
Split at Cursor	Alt+X	Option+X
Split Range	Shift+X	Shift+X
Toggle Auto-Scroll On/Off	F	F
Toggle Show/Hide Infoview	Ctrl+I	Command+I
Toggle Show/Hide Inspector	I	I
Toggle Show/Hide Overview	Alt+O	Option+O
Toggle Snap On/Off	J	J
Undo	Ctrl+Z	Command+Z
Unlock	Ctrl+Shift+U	Command+Shift+U
Unmute Events	Shift+U	Shift+U

File

Table G.3
File menu key commands

Commands	PC Keys	Mac Keys
Close Document	Ctrl+W	Command+W
Create New Document	Ctrl+N	Command+N
Open Existing Document	Ctrl+O	Command+O
Quit	Ctrl+Q	Command+Q
Save	Ctrl+S	Command+S
Save As	Ctrl+Shift+S	Command+Shift+S
Save New Version	Ctrl+Alt+S	Command+Option+S

Project Menu

Table G.4
Project menu key commands

Commands	PC Keys	Mac Keys
Open Browser	Ctrl+B	Command+B
Open Markers	Ctrl+M	Command+M
Open Master Track	Ctrl+T	Command+T
Open Pool	Ctrl+P	Command+P
Open Project Setup	Shift+S	Shift+S

Tools

Table G.5
Tools key commands

Commands	PC Keys	Mac Keys
Delete tool	5	5
Draw tool	8	8
Drumstick tool	0	0

APPENDIX G

Glue Tube tool	4	4
Mute tool	7	7
Next tool	F10	F10
Play tool	9	9
Previous tool	F9	F9
Range Selection tool	2	2
Object Selection tool	1	1
Split tool	3	3
Zoom tool	6	6

Transport

Table G.6
Transport key commands

Commands	PC Keys	Mac Keys
Fast Forward	NumPad +	NumPad +
Input Left Locator	Shift+L	Shift+L
Input Right Locator	Shift+R	Shift+R
Insert Marker	Insert	Insert
Locate Next Event	N	N
Locate Next Marker	Shift+N	Shift+N
Locate Previous Event	B	B
Locate Previous Marker	Shift+B	Shift+B
Locators to Selection	L	L
Loop Selection	Shift+G	Shift+G
Nudge Down	Ctrl+NumPad -	Command+NumPad -
Nudge Up	Ctrl+NumPad +	Command+NumPad +
Play Selection Range	Alt+Space bar	Option+Space bar
Record	NumPad *	NumPad *
Return to Zero	NumPad .	NumPad .
Rewind	NumPad -	NumPad -

Set Left Locator	Ctrl+NumPad 1	Command+NumPad 1
Set Markers 3 to 9	Ctrl+NumPad 3 to 9	Command+NumPad 3 to 9
Set Right Locator	Ctrl+NumPad 2	Command+NumPad 2
Show/Hide Transport Panel	F2	F2
Start	Enter, Space bar	Return, Space bar
Stop	NumPad 0, Space bar	NumPad 0, Space bar
To Left Locator	NumPad 1	NumPad 1
To Markers 3 to 9	NumPad 3 to 9	NumPad 3 to 9
To Right Locator	NumPad 2	NumPad 2
Toggle Auto Punch In On/Off	I	I
Toggle Auto Punch Out On/Off	O	O
Toggle Cycle On/Off	NumPad /	NumPad /
Toggle Metronome On/Off	C	C
Toggle Sync Online On/Off	T	T

Window Layout

Table G.7
Window layout key commands

Commands	PC Keys	Mac Keys
Create New Window Layout	Ctrl+NumPad 0	Command+NumPad 0
Organize Window Layout	W	W
Recall Layout 1 to 9	Alt+NumPad 1 to 9	Option+NumPad 1 to 9
Recapture Window Layout	Alt+NumPad 0	Option+NumPad 0

APPENDIX G

Zoom

Table G.8
Zoom key commands

Commands	PC Keys	Mac Keys
Zoom Full	Shift+F	Shift+F
Zoom In	H	H
Zoom In Tracks	Alt+DownArrow	Option+DownArrow
Zoom Out	G	G
Zoom to Event	Shift+E	Shift+E
Zoom to Selection	Alt+S	Option+S

Index

Note: Italicized page numbers refer to "Note", "Tip" and "Caution" boxes and to illustrations.

INDEX

Electronic Musician

Mail in the attached card today to receive your

3 free issues

of **Electronic Musician**!

Courtesy of **Muska & Lipman** and **Electronic Musician**.